The Collapse of the American
Management Mystique

The Collapse of the American Management Mystique

ROBERT R. LOCKE

OXFORD UNIVERSITY PRESS

1996

Oxford University Press, Walton Street, Oxford OX2 6DP
Oxford New York
Athens Auckland Bangkok Bombay
Calcutta Cape Town Dar es Salaam Delhi
Florence Hong Kong Istanbul Karachi
Kuala Lumpur Madras Madrid Melbourne
Mexico City Nairobi Paris Singapore
Taipei Tokyo Toronto
and associated companies in
Berlin Ibadan

Oxford is a trade mark of Oxford University Press

Published in the United States
by Oxford University Press Inc., New York

British Library Cataloguing in Publication Data
Data available

Library of Congress Cataloging in Publication Data
Locke, Robert R., 1932–
The collapse of the American management mystique/by Robert R. Locke.
Includes bibliographical references and index.
1. Management—United States—History. 2. Comparative management.
I. Title.
HD70.U5L63 1996 95–50917
658'.00973—dc20
ISBN 0–19–877406–0

1 3 5 7 9 10 8 6 4 2

Typeset by J&L Composition Ltd, Filey, North Yorkshire

Printed in Great Britain
on acid-free paper by
Bookcraft (Bath) Ltd., Midsomer Norton, Avon.

To Vera, without whom . . . , nothing

There are two different ways of writing history: one is to persuade men to virtue and the other is to compel men to truth. . . . Perhaps they are not irreconcilable.

Robert Graves, *I Claudius*

ACKNOWLEDGMENTS

NOBODY writes a book without incurring obligations. It is my pleasure as well as duty to acknowledge them here. Like most people who are not Japanologists, my awareness of Japanese management dates from the collapse of the American management mystique. I am deeply grateful to Professor Tsunehiko Yui, of Meiji University, for facilitating my belated introduction to Japan. In particular I want to thank him and his colleagues, Professors Reiko Okayama, Etsuo Abe, and Ryoichi Iwauchi, for the exquisite hospitality shown during the fellowship I spent, at their behest, in the summer of 1990 at Meiji University. I must thank Professor Yui, too, for visits arranged at the Tokyo Plant of KAO Soap Co., 29 May 1990, and to Toyota Motor Company in Toyota-shi where we visited three plants (1 June 1990). Company staffs during these visits were kind and helpful. To John and Hiroko Charles I am indebted for the opportunity to experience Japanese negotiating style first-hand. They were extremely considerate for including me on the 'British' team that worked out a scholarship agreement between the International Student House, London, and the municipality of Toyota City. I am also indebted to Mayor Kato of Toyota City and his staff for their indulgence. I wish, too, to express my gratitude to Professors Nobuo Kawabe, of Waseda University, and the organizing committee of the Fuji Conference for arranging a second visit to Japan in January 1992. Although brief, the intense interaction with my Japanese colleagues over three weeks added much to my Japanese education. Among those who were especially helpful during the Fuji conference were Professors Takeshi Yuzawa, Akira Kudo, and Keiichiro Nakagawa.

In Germany I have been at home for some years. Nonetheless, research for this book would have suffered serious complications without the help of old friends and new acquaintances. Among the old friends are Professor Dr. Eduard Gaugler of Mannheim University and Professor Dr. Hartmut Wächter of Trier University. Both have helped me so many times in the past that I hesitated to call on them

Acknowledgments

once more. But I did and they responded with their usual generosity. Among the new acquaintances, I must count Dr. Axel Schumacher of the Koblenz School of Corporate Management. I owe Dr. Schumacher, Professor Gaugler, and Professor Wächter special thanks for arranging meetings with the following experts: Dr. Thomas Breisig (Trier), Professor Arnd Huchzermeier (Koblenz), Dr. Dieter Kirchner (of Gesamt-Metall, in Cologne), Professors Manfred Perlitz and Alfred Kieser (Mannheim), and Dr. Wolfgang Ollmann (of McKinsey and Company, Hamburg). I warmly thank all for their time and insight.

Elsewhere in Europe I have also accrued debts. I owe thanks to Professor Roland Calori, of the Lyons Business School, for his time and counsel and especially for introducing me to M. Dominique Turcq, of McKinsey and Company (Brussels), one of the leading French experts on Japanese management. I am grateful, too, to M. Turcq for his hospitality in Brussels, for copies of his publications, and for his wisdom. In the United Kingdom Professors Peter Lawrence of Loughborough University and Geoffrey Jones of the University of Reading have given the project much encouragement. And two academic accountants, Professor Mohamed Ezzamel of UMIST and Dr. Keith Hoskin of the Warwick Business School, have in conversation and in their written works helped me through the accounting intricacies of the quality revolution. My editor, David Musson, has not only encouraged me but has sent publications and references to publications to me along the way. Two Swedes must also be singled out for special thanks, Professor Gunnar Eliasson of Lund University and Professor Lars Engwall of Uppsala University.

In the United States, the debt extends across the country. It reaches to Robert Hall, of the Associations of Manufacturing Excellent in Wheeling, Illinois, who, aside from passing on information about AME and the Quality Revolution, introduced me to Professor Dr. Horst Wildemann of the Munich Technical University, a leading advocate of the quality revolution in the German Federal Republic, to Professor H. Thomas Johnson, Portland State University, whose observations inform the book in many places, and to Professor Kosaku Yoshida, of California State University, Dominguez Hills, a Deming disciple. I give my thanks to all.

In Hawaii, Professor Shirley Daniel, of the University of Hawaii Business School, fed me articles on Japanese accounting techniques, and the staff at Hamilton Library a steady steam of books and articles from our excellent Asian holdings. My colleague George Akita kept an eye open for suitable materials in Japan, collected them, and sent them along. Two graduate students have also helped on Japanese educational issues. Mr. Larry Holmes, in Political Science, shared first-hand knowledge of the Japanese secondary school system with me; and my graduate student, Joseph Adams, who worked for two years in elementary education in Japan before coming to the University of Hawaii at Manoa, informed me about Japanese education K through 9. Indeed, the sustained dialogue about Japanese education and management that Joe and I have carried on over the past two years has been invaluable in the preparation of the book.

Finally, the debt to those who worked through the manuscript and to family: James Kraft, labor historian, read the manuscript, suggesting improvements in content and style. Rainer Buschmann proofread the German chapter, Julia Nakano-Holmes and James Fujita the Japanese sections. Robert Fahs read the entire text, offering very helpful comments. The comments of Mark Braly of Davis, California, improved the focus and presentation of the work. Vanessa Locke arranged the interviews with Professor Kosaku Yoshida and Mr. Hugh Leonard in California. Swavek Bejmo prepared the tables. My thanks to them all.

These are the people who readily come to mind. I am grateful to them and to others that a faltering memory might have made me overlook. I alone, of course, am responsible for the book.

R.L.

Honolulu, Hawaii
July 1995

CONTENTS

Contents

TABLES

Introduction

THIS introduction presents the work in two ways: first, it identifies the subject matter, and secondly, it explains why the subject has been neglected.

Management is an American term and an American creation. Although American management has always hankered for universality, it is nothing more than a cultural peculiarity. It has never played the role in economic success that managers believed, and its irrational persistence in America threatens this nation's role in the new world economy, the American standard of living, and even domestic stability. This is the thesis of the book.

In order to manage the argument, some points have to be established at the outset. First, I am not interested in management in a technical sense. Peter D. Anthony observes that managers deal with narrow functions, like how to set up an accounting system, model a supply chain, or figure out the technical component of manufacturing. But they also deal with functions of a governmental nature, those, as John Child puts it, that promote 'action through other people'.[1] In this book the technical dimension of management is subordinated to the governmental. The emphasis does not restrict management to generalists because, as Peter Anthony explains, 'from the wide . . . direction of affairs at the board level to specific, narrow, and specialized responsibility [in the smallest sub-unit]' action through other people takes place.[2]

To those familiar with American management, the definition 'action through other people' might seem to limit the subject to what Americans call Human Resource Management. HRM, however, expresses the American managerial outlook since it is just another tool in the manager's satchel. Rather, I am interested in the Gestalt of management. I want to explore each society's view of how action is achieved through other people and how economic necessity and historical inheritance shaped these views at various historical moments, including our own. I seek to establish how perceived economic success engendered mystiques about a society's management, or, in the American case, how perceived failure destroyed a management mystique, and the grounds for it, that earlier perceived success had spawned. In short, I am not interested in investigating America's management problem or problems but in coming to grips with the problem called American management.

In order to do so, I have to approach the subject from an international as well as an American perspective, for, if management is a peculiar cultural expression, it exists in different forms in different countries. Nonetheless, the various manifestations of management need not be exhaustively examined. I am concerned only with those varieties that have acquired notoriety and validity because they have challenged American management's universalist claims. I have accordingly limited the international perspective primarily to Germany and Japan. Both countries have posed the most significant and successful alternatives to the American management model. Indeed, I argue that the relative success of German- and Japanese-run business and industry contributed much to the collapse of the American management mystique.

I have had to be careful to depart from customary American thinking about management. American management and management science reflects traditional American ownership forms and methods of control. These in turn affect how American management sets corporate goals and carries out 'action through other people'. But German and Japanese firms, even within a dynamic capitalist system, work with slightly different ownership forms and control methods; they have set appreciably different corporate goals and have acted through other people differently from the Americans. Views about how managerial action is conceived and achieved are comparatively more varied and complicated internationally, therefore, than those elaborated within the confines of traditional American management theory and practice. Moreover, it is just possible that learning about these non-American views might make Americans manage better. At least knowledge of them helps us to understand how American management has become a dysfunctional cultural peculiarity.

Another point: Throughout most of this study both the form and goals of American management have been subsumed under the rubric 'managerialism'. As used here, this expression is juxtaposed with the term 'management', much like the historian Alfred Vagts over fifty years ago juxtaposed the terms 'militarism' and the 'military way'.[3] The military way means setting a military goal and developing the most efficient organizational means to see to its accomplishment. That is what 'management' as applied to commercial and industrial organizations—to firms—also means. 'Militarism', on the other hand, has a much different connotation. As Vagts wrote, it

> presents a vast array of customs, interests, prestige, actions and thought associated with armies and wars and yet transcending true military purposes. Indeed, militarism is so constituted that it may hamper and defeat the purposes of the military way. Its influence is unlimited in scope. It may permeate all society and become dominant over all industry and arts. . . . Militarism displays the qualities of caste and cult, authority and belief.[4]

Managerialism has the traits of militarism. It represents 'a vast array of customs, interests, prestige, actions, and thought' associated with but nonetheless transcending the needs for the efficient running of commercial and industrial organizations; its influence is almost 'unlimited' in scope, extending into almost every kind of organization in America, profit and nonprofit, commercial and educational, governmental and military. Managerialism as it grew up in America came to exhibit 'the qualities of caste and cult, authority and belief'. And it will be argued throughout this book that American management and the mystique it generated developed into a system that 'defeated and hamper[ed] the purposes' of management itself, that is, denied organizations the means needed to formulate and effectively reach goals.

This book, in effect, asks readers to reorient fundamentally their thought about American management. Americans have trouble believing that their views on the subject are incorrect. When they hear that Germans and Japanese operate under different managerial assumptions, Americans expect reality to prove American managerial ideas right and the foreigners wrong. Accordingly, if Americans hear that Japanese firms currently rue the day that they foreswore lay-offs as a way to deal with downturns, they are reassured. Lay-offs, the standard

American managerial policy, is proved correct. This study challenges the reader to take another look at what has happened in management since the Second World War. If we start with the premise that American managerialism must be held accountable when American business and industry suffer through comparatively hard times, and add to it the assumption that different management systems in Germany and Japan must have merit because they have generally managed the economy and society of these nations well, we can at least approach the managerial question with an open mind. This study asks the reader, then, to suspend belief in the canons of American managerialism, step back and critically reevaluate the American managerial experience, and do so with the yardstick provided by successful foreign alternatives.

One final point: Charles de Gaulle, who could cut to the heart of a matter, said that all his life he had a certain conception of France: France could not be France without glory. All my life, I have had a certain idea about America: America could not be America without a people of plenty residing within its borders. The generation that won World War II and their siblings breathed this idea in the air. And they linked American plenty with American management. The rise of the American management mystique and its demise is judged here in these terms.

People have tried constantly to measure empirically the efficacy of American management, but they have talked precious little about a specifically American management mystique and even less about its collapse. One reason for the relative silence could be that the American management mystique has not collapsed, and that the notion of a collapse is a mere shibboleth. Since the subject will be more thoroughly investigated in the text, suffice it to say at this juncture that the evidence of a collapse is everywhere. Of course, awareness does vary by place, time, and circumstance. Roland Calori of the Lyons Business School notes, for example, that French businessmen, for whom the Americans had been management teachers, perceived with surprise a crisis in management confidence in America, and that among French groups the average French businessman still scarcely recognizes any American managerial deficiencies. But he goes on to say that those in larger international firms have been quite conscious of America's managerial decline, and that management consultants and experts in

France have been fully aware for some time that the American management mystique has disappeared.[5] Because Europeans have fixed their managerial eyes mainly on America, consciousness of the collapse elsewhere in Europe has generally followed this French pattern. It stemmed initially as much from Europe's reaction to American alarm about Japanese management as from European reaction to Japan proper.

Hence, doubts about America's managerial prowess arose earlier and more intensely in America than in Europe. From the 1979 NBC White Paper, 'If Japan Can, Why Can't We', through the 1980 Special Issue of *Business Week*, 'The Reindustrializion of America'; in the countless articles about Japanese management, propagated throughout the 1980s in specialized journals like *Quality Progress*, academic ones like *The Harvard Business Review*, or popular ones like *Fortune*; through the foundation and development of Deming Societies in every region of the country, the creation of The Association for Manufacturing Excellence, and similar reform-minded organizations, this critique of America's managerial abilities gained force. It is important to stress the unprecedented character of the doubts. Plenty of people criticized management during the depression era. But that critique had amounted to a general attack on capitalism. For the first time, beginning in the late 1970s, American management found itself singled out for its shortcomings in terms of efficiency among capitalist forms of management. Even those who sought to confirm excellence in American management, like Thomas J. Peters and Robert H. Waterman, really underscored the collapse; for affirmation was necessary only because of the sagging confidence, and the yardstick used to measure excellence in their best-selling work extended to the managerial achievements of foreign, mainly Japanese, firms.[6]

If this be true, then, why have knowledgeable scholars generally failed to foresee the collapse; why, when it came, have they tended to avoid the idea of a specifically American collapse and the consequence it has had for the American polity; why, after initial alarm on the part of some, has the concern rather quickly dissipated and things returned to 'normal'; why, in short, has the rise and fall of the American management mystique not been subjected to extended scrutiny? Three reasons for the neglect seem pertinent, each of which reflects the scholarly posture of a particular constituency. They are (i) the anational approach of management scientists to their subjects, (ii) the problems historians of a successful nation have in facing up to the fact of their nation's subsequent decline, and (iii) the limitation that the habit of excluding labor studies from management studies places on the experts' evaluation of American managerial performance.

The first reason has to do with management scientists and the nature of the management studies they have developed. American management and American business school academics have seldom used national adjectives when describing management. In America's management heyday, people thought that management everywhere would conform to best practice which, needless to say, for unconsciously egocentric Westerners, existed primarily in America but was not expressly American. This convergentist attitude prompted American managers, as Shirley Daniel and June Y. Aono observed, to engage in 'universalistic modes of thinking, where information is interpreted in context of general principles, using logical and scientific methods . . . '.[7] Business school academics grounded the functional parts of business studies (accounting, marketing, finance, etc.) and management studies proper, for example decision science and strategic thinking, in the social sciences.

Because it strives to be authoritative, there is a certain conceit and pretentiousness in all scholarship. But the conceit of the social sciences, in which management studies found a home, has been reinforced by the shakiness of its methodological foundation. Social science procedures cannot withstand, as Peter Anthony explained,

> the most elementary tests of the validity of scientific method. This is not an idle accusation. It has been argued by a number of authoritative analysts of scientific method that scientific propositions are advanced as the result of a hypothetical-deductive method in which the resultant theories, although they can never be proved, continue to stand while the scientist rigorously looks for evidence to *overthrow* them. The scientist's theories stand for as long as he fails to upset them. This is the opposite of the way in which most behavioral scientists go about their work; they advance theories which they have 'proved' as the result of a singularly hasty search for evidence that will *support* them. If there are methodological problems concerning the validity of behavioral science theory these problems are multiplied by the time unreliable theories have been vulgarized by consultants and then simplified by teachers in

order to transmit them to managers, whose knowledge of basic behavioral science theories may be nil.[8]

In the twentieth century mutterings of doubt about the epistemological foundation of science never stopped the natural scientists from proceeding with their work on grounds of practicality. But the practicality of the social sciences has been questioned. The questioning extends to the most 'scientific' of the social sciences, economics, and the marginal utility principles upon which it rests. Paul Krugman asked the right question: 'even if the key to export-oriented success [is] simply that free markets work', does that mean any country 'that liberalized its markets' could expect industrial success? The answer Krugman gave was no. He observed that Chile under Pinochet radically opened its economy to foreign trade, so that its share of GNP in 1985 more than doubled what it had been in 1965.[9] Chile followed the same export-oriented free trade policies as Taiwan and Singapore, but in contrast to these Asian countries, Chile's exports surged in agriculture rather than manufactures. After the adoption of free trade policies Chile's industrial exports in the mid-1980s still 'only accounted for about 7 per cent of total exports'. Chile's free trade policies certainly did not pose the threat to domestic American manufacturing that Singapore's did. So, Krugman concludes, 'at the very least we should not base our expectations on the assumption that very rapid growth [in manufacturing] can be automatically summoned with the invocation of free market principles'.

Then upon what assumptions should our expectations be based? Krugman believed that Singapore President Lee Kwan Yew answered this question when he was himself asked about the secret of Singapore's success; instead of praising his own policies, he cited the 'inner dynamism of East Asian man', or, to use Krugman's 'less elegant terminology, [Lee Kwan Yew] asserted both that Singapore had "It" and that other (non-Chinese) countries probably did not [have "It"]'.[10] There is no need to try to fathom the mysterious meanings of this East Asian man or, for that matter, to define the exact nature of Krugman's 'It'. These statements simply indicate why confidence in American economics declined. The 'science' this American-centered social science practiced was not sufficiently scientific to predict results.[11]

Such practical problems, as opposed to epistemological ones, have forced management studies in recent times to examine historical specificities. One of these specificities, which has drawn attention because of the enormity of the Japanese economic achievement, has been management in Japan. Books about the subject abound. Still, Western students of management, driven by the prestige of science, of which they yearn to remain a part, have not been comfortable describing national historical events. Consequently, ideas or methods emphasized in Japan were soon either traced directly to the influence of Western thinkers on Japan, principally American (for example, W. Edwards Deming, Joseph Juran, and Armand V. Feigenbaum), or attributed, with scant mention of Japanese usage, to sources in Western Management literature. The comments of Professor Manfred Perlitz, in a recent article, illustrate this process. 'In 1983,' he observed from his European perspective, 'U.S. enterprises were still regarded as exemplary. Today, Japanese management techniques . . . have become the role model.' But he goes on to say that '[n]early every Japanese management technique has a Western counterpart which anticipated its basic idea much earlier'.[12]

It was an easy step, which management scientists and consultants have consistently made, to fold the critique of American management that merged from studying Japan into the body of Western-created management studies, thereby downplaying the non-American origins of the management critique and its primarily American target. References to 'Japanese' management have tended to disappear in management literature in favor of general discussions about 'management' strategies and techniques. This has even been true of postmodernist studies that have attacked American management. The postmodernist references are to French philosophers mainly—Michel Foucault, Jacques Derrida, Jean Baudrillard—and the management problems are universalized.[13]

Such a view of events is bad history. The critique of American management methods did not evolve naturally through scientific debate out of a body of management knowledge; management scientists have discovered the precedents *ex post facto* when scurrying to the literature in a hunt for 'scientific' justifications for events (in the rise of Japan) that because of the inadequacies of their science generally had not been foreseen. This search may have salved the conscience of distraught American management experts, caught by surprise, but the translation of events into management science led them to ignore or at least partially forget the national historical source of organizational behavior. Scholars, managers, and journalists wrote continually about management shortcomings but they did not write much about the shortcoming of American managerialism as a historically rooted dysfunctional system. Besides, like American professional public school administrators, most American management scientists were not going to bite the hand that fed them. They were not about to consider themselves and the institutions that created them as the source of the management problem. Accordingly, no thesis about the collapse of an explicitly American management mystique has emerged in the management literature.

Historians are a second group that has ignored the collapse of the American management mystique. They have more than any other group made people keenly aware of the *rise* of an American management mystique. Diplomatic and economic historians writing about America's post-1945 political and economic hegemony have actively explored the expansion of American corporate business in considerable detail. Curiously, however, they have neither talked much about a subsequent collapse of American management's reputation, nor, when discussing that reputation, noted factors present at its creation that could have contributed to its eventual collapse. Even American business historians working under the influence of Alfred D. Chandler, Jr.—indisputably the great historian of American corporate management—have said little about decline or collapse.[14] Why?

For historians dealing with short-term causation silence is reasonable: since they handle events concluded in the past, comments pertaining to today's problems could not be expected. The observation applies to much that has been written about goods and capital exports from America to Europe during the Marshall Plan. Even if this aid promoted Europe's take-off into postwar recovery, as admirers of the Marshall Plan claim (and their opponents deny), its effectiveness was limited to the immediate postwar era.[15] Knowledge, in short, about goods shipped to, and capital invested in, Europe, *circa*-1948–52, might be interesting to the historian studying the period, but it tells us little about the origins of subsequent American industrial decline.

But knowledge of the past is not *ipso facto* inapplicable to the

9

present or knowledge about what is going on in the present useless to informing our understanding of the past. Obviously historians must be careful not to distort the past by reading current concerns into their interpretation of it, but they also must not falsify the past by ignoring current problems, for an analysis of the period of American ascendancy after World War II is different when it is done with the idea in mind of a continuing ascendancy than when it is done with the idea of subsequent trouble and decline.

Marshall Planners and other postwar reformers believed that Europe needed to acquire organizational and managerial know-how from triumphant America if recovery and sustained growth were to occur. The literature, therefore, describes scores of American-sponsored voyages of discovery, sending Europeans and Japanese to America to learn the secrets of American organizational and managerial strength, bringing American experts to foreign countries to propagate American know-how. This work affirms that in the post-1945 free world, recovery and sustained growth resulted from the triumph abroad of the American organizational and managerial way.[16] There is, indeed, a certain aura of understandable self-congratulatory smugness, rife especially in the writings of surviving American Marshall Plan participants, policy-makers, and historians about the postwar superiority of this American managerial way and how the economic resurrection of Europe and the rest of the free world depended on their managerial Americanization. There is hardly a whisper in the historiography about the subsequent tarnishing of the American management ideal, even in works written well after the Japan shock.

This is true, it might be added, of that most perceptive historian Charles S. Maier, whose work, while deftly analyzing the importance of American managerial influence in twentieth-century Europe, also skillfully describes the limits of that influence.[17] He points out, for instance, that the ideology of capitalist managerialism was 'peculiarly American . . . . Europeans remained more reserved: in Britain businessmen did not possess the cultural hegemony . . . , in France the state still claimed a major share of technocratic leadership, even in West Germany, where the American model might be received most congenially, the existence of a Social Democratic Party provided some counterweight'.[18] But he seemed sufficiently seduced by the American management mystique himself to have let the thought perish that

Europe's rejection of American productivity-enhancing formats could have been inspired by better productivity alternatives. He simply affirmed that, despite differences from America ' . . . in all these countries, engaging in the discourse of productivity meant accepting a good deal of American managerial ideals'.[19]

The same confidence in American managerialism colors the work of the Chandlerian school of business history. Optimism was *de rigeur* when Chandler's first books and articles appeared; they were written before any sign of decline.[20] Their initial popularity with economists and management specialists, as well as with historians, is, perhaps, thereby explained. They were not histories as much as commentaries on how contemporary managerial capitalism came into being. Chandler and his students at the Harvard Business School assumed that this American managerial capitalism set the pattern of convergence worldwide.[21] Even with the publication of Chandler's Pulitzer Prize-winning *The Visible Hand* in 1977, when some people had some doubts about American managerialism, the mainstream tide of optimism swept on.[22] However, by the time Harvard University Press published Chandler's most recent book, *Scale and Scope*, in 1990, optimism had finally turned to apprehension, and why not, since the collapse of the American management mystique had occurred almost a decade before.[23]

Unlike his previous works, *Scale and Scope* has the stamp of a bygone era. Seemingly troubled by the signs of American decline, Chandler closes the book (p. 621–8) with the interrogative subtitle: 'A New Era of Managerial Capitalism?' He could have added, in answer to the question, yes, and that coming era would not necessarily be American. There is no indication in the body of the book, however, that anything about America's managerialism could be wrong, or how, in short, six hundred pages of success led to that interrogative subtitle in the final chapter. It is as if Professor Chandler, indeed American business historians generally, had remained until very recently unaware of the problems of American managerialism and how they might be inherent in its very growth.

Why have historians been so impervious to the evidence of the collapse of the American management mystique and the need to explain it historically? It is hard to say, but Professor Kosaku Yoshida, a student and disciple of W. Edwards Deming, suggests one explanation that can serve as the second reason for Americans' neglecting the subject.

In 1970 Yoshida left an industrial accounting position in Japan for graduate study at New York University, where he discovered to his delight that Dr. Deming taught statistics. Considering Deming's fame in Japan, Yoshida was surprised to find few students in the class. I asked him why Americans neglected Deming for almost thirty years after he had achieved cult status in Japan. Yoshida answered that it would simply have been impossible for Americans in 1971 to have paid much attention to him.

It was too early for Americans to think the 'unthinkable', that something was wrong with American management. After all, just sixteen years before Yoshida showed up in New York, Winston Churchill, looking out at Fortress Europe, had proclaimed the invincibility of the 'American clear-cut, logical, large-scale, mass production style of thought' which he correctly saw preparing the powerful Normandy landings.[24] And just two years before Yoshida arrived in New York, the English-language edition of Jean-Jacques Servan-Schreiber's *The American Challenge* trumpeted the glories of American managerial capitalism to eager ears and nodding heads on both sides of the Atlantic and the Pacific. From World War II, through European postwar reconstruction and the Cold War, proponents of capitalism just celebrate America's management virtues.

When trade news turned bad, Presidents and politicians repeatedly told the American people well into the 1980s that the problem arose from the absence of a level playing field: nobody seems to be willing to add that problems might persist if the playing field were level. There is, again understandably, an American reluctance to consider carefully the actual state of affairs and how it came about. And this reluctance is not just an attitude; it is embedded in the very structure of how we go about analyzing our recent past. Perhaps, to ask Americans, especially educated ones who are completely enmeshed in American managerialism and benefit from its conventions, to have doubts about it, is asking too much.

The third and last reason why Americans have not taken much interest in the collapse of the American management mystique has to do with the peculiar organization of this country's labor studies. Actually many labor scholars and historians have been quite sensitive to the managerial defects of American capitalism. Their analysis, moreover, stays abreast of recent trends in historiography. Howell John Harris's book on the *Right to Manage*, for example, reflects postmodernist ideas about the role of language in the construction of reality. In the book, he emphasizes the rhetoric of American capitalism, and how its language conventions became the instrument which formulated the consciousness of the nation during American management's victorious political campaign in the late 1940s to defeat trade unions and reassert its right to manage.[25] The book's premise clearly expresses the postmodernist tenet that 'it is not consciousness that produces politics but politics that produces consciousness'.[26] The work of labor scholars and historians is a valuable source for the analysis of managerialism; it is drawn upon frequently in this book.[27]

Nonetheless, professors of management and business historians have ignored the analysis of labor scholars about as much as American management has ignored labor unions. In sum, the marginalization of labor studies, their separation from the study of management, results from a categorization of study that the very triumph of managerialism has imposed. Labor has simply become management's problem, one which disallows the disturbing possibility of management being labor's problem as well. By divorcing labor from management studies, the sort of scholarly dialogue necessary to develop a thesis about the collapse of the American management mystique could not easily take place.

The inability of labor scholars to make their voices heard also stems from events occurring within academia that have deflected people's attention from labor problems. Since the 1960s academics have been reconsidering so-called 'metanarratives'. The history of the 'working class', of 'labor', or of 'management' is a 'metanarrative'. People have objected to them because they are allegedly not real subjects, only constructs of the observer's mind, fictions, not lived experiences. In one sense, this book, too, objects to metanarratives. It asks readers to believe in the complexity and diversity of the managerial experience. But it also asks them to accept the metanarrative of managerialism as far as America is concerned, to accept as fact the commonality of the management experience for all working Americans, regardless of diverse racial, ethnic, and/or gender experiences. The postmodernist attack on metanarratives has stopped people from contemplating this common American work and managerial experience. Indeed the recent focus on particular, subjective narratives, by diverting people into writing *petite histoire* (about blacks, women, homosexuals, or ethnic minorities) keeps them from coming to grips with the problem of managerialism in America.

Despite exceptions like Howell John Harris's work, the postmodernist invasion of the American mind has generally had a deleterious effect on labor studies. Postmodernism identifies itself negatively, in terms, that is, of the thing it attacks, Modernism. For the postmodernist, modernists are naive people who still believe in the 'Enlightenment project': in human dignity (hence the modernist's concern about the exploitation of working people), in human reason, science, democracy, and human progress. Postmodernists take this modernism apart and along with it the labor metanarrative. By denying the validity of binary realities (black vs white, men vs women) the postmodernists have also attacked the metanarrators currently preaching in black and women studies programs throughout American academia. But labor studies, which the new binary metanarratives have tended to displace, have not won back ground within a postmodernist agenda, because postmodernism denies the validity of the old labor metanarratives as well.

Pushed to epistemological extremes, postmodernism ends in Jean Baudrillard's contention 'that nothing exists outside the endless circulation of ungrounded arbitrary signs', which leaves labor scholars with no external referents (like work experience) to support the concepts they use.[28] By denying, as Christofer Norris observes, 'that there are real and present facts of experience—inequality, deprivation, urban squalor, unemployment, massive and increasing differentials of wealth and power', by questioning 'the experience oriented analysis of conventional history', the postmodernist presumption has destroyed the base of labor studies.[29] In the new postmodernist environment the core experiences of work, upon which labor scholars traditionally have focused and upon which a general critique of managerialism must be based, has evaporated.

These are the reasons why I believe the subject of this book has been neglected. It begins with a chapter on 'The American Management Mystique' which establishes the thesis. The second chapter, 'German Obstinacy', deals with early German dissent in certain managerial matters and how this dissent, over the years, created a very different managerial system in that country. Chapter 3 covers the Japanese managerial challenge and Chapter 4 describes the collapse of the American management mystique. The work ends with a chapter entitled 'Quo Vadis', 'Whither Goest Thou', an attempt to evaluate American managerialism today, with suggestions, based on the book's historical exposition, for reform.

Chapter One

The American Management Mystique

THE American management mystique emerged from and is identified with the management system that grew up inside American business and manufacturing during the past century. This management system appeared in three interrelated places: (1) the shop floor (in factories), (2) the corporation, and (3) the university; all three are examined here. The second half of the chapter deals with the propagation of American management ethics, methods, and techniques since World War II. For propagators and propagandized alike, success was achieved less because of measurable or measured appreciations of American management's effect on praxis than because of the mystique engendered by an economically powerful, militarily victorious America. It was the historical situation not the management system that counted most.

Shop Floor and Factory

Evaluating the American contribution to shop-floor management, Joseph A. Litterer wrote that about 1900

[t]he skill and knowledge of Europeans . . . was the equal and sometimes the superior of that of Americans. The difference was in how this technical knowledge and skill was used. The European manufacturer used it to make a product. The American manufacturer used it to make a process for making a product. A high class machinist in Europe could be found setting up a semiautomatic machine for less skilled labor to operate and to make this product, or he might be engaged in making the semiautomatic

machines with which to make a product. The literature of the time
frequently mentioned that American machine tools were superior to the
European. This, however, should be understood to reflect not a difference
in abilities as much as a difference in the thinking of European and
American management. One appreciated the importance of, and understood how to obtain, the advantage from machinery; the other did not.[1]

The American system of manufacturing that Litterer writes about was
long in the making. It started in the armories of New England in the
early nineteenth century, then spread throughout sister industries,
employing standards and gauges to achieve interchangeability of parts
and components. The going was slow; it took the Springfield Armory
twenty years to establish interchangeability of parts, and Singer Sewing
Machine, founded in 1851, thirty years. But a respectable level of
standardization with less skilled labor had been achieved by the Civil
War.[2]

From the 1870s, American factories introduced continuous-process
machinery on the floor to increase the volume of production through-
put. Ford's assembly line epitomized this mass production technique:
'a simple car (model T) affordable by the common man, designed with
a minimum of parts, precisely engineered so that they would be
absolutely interchangeable'.[3] The basic design once in production,
Ford's engineers adjusted layouts and equipment until they hit upon
the idea of the assembly line. Ford had this assembly line in full
operation by 1913, but the most famous examples of mass production
layouts took shape at his River Rouge plant, built in the 1920s, and the
Willow Run factory that assembled B-24 Liberator bombers during the
Second World War.

Professor H. Thomas Johnson observed that 'the system Ford
created [at the River Rouge] boggles the mind. . . . Ships and rail
cars delivered steady streams of iron ore, coal, and limestone continuously to blast furnaces from which iron went directly to a casting
foundry where engine blocks and other parts were made in a continuous flow'.[4] 'Our product cycle', Henry Ford calculated in 1926, 'is
about eighty-one hours from the mine to the finished machines in the
freight car, or three days and nine hours . . . '.[5] At Willow Run a mile-
long assembly line, equipped with 1,600 machine tools and 7,500 jigs
and fixtures, constructed, when in full operation, a Liberator bomber

every sixty-three minutes around the clock. Hence the wartime slogan: 'It's being Done at Willow Run'.[6]

Standardized, high-volume process production required a different sort of management than previous manufacturing systems. When the firm reached a sufficient size during the industrial revolution, family owners could no longer directly supervise work; nor could they rely on the apprenticeship–master craftsman system of training and supervision, for apprentices were tied to the masters and not to the owners. Where this occurred, as in British shipbuilding, the owners lost control over the labor force.[7] Most firms relied, therefore, on inside contracting, with the hiring and supervision of the labor force contracted out. The system worked reasonably well, for mid-nineteenth-century contractors were prosperous entrepreneurs who engaged skilled people to do vital shop floor production work. But the system also encouraged 'scams' that resulted, as Frederick Winslow Taylor described it, in 'a jungle of restrictive practices, ca' canny, hanging-out, or soldiering', none of which induced efficient production in standardized American process manufacturing.[8]

The invention of administrative theory and its injection into workplace practice solved the problem. The system introduced the formalized management that Taylor and his disciples called scientific. But there was nothing particularly scientific about it, if one thinks in terms of the methodologies of natural science. Taylor purported to substitute, in his words, 'obedience to fact and law, for obedience to personal authority'. The search for fact and law perfectly suited the temperament of the production engineers who were principally responsible for devising this 'scientific management'. They introduced the first techniques, 'work study', towards the turn of the century. Two books published in 1911, one by Taylor and the other by Frank Gilbreth, divided this work-study method into two complementary parts: method study, 'the systematic recording and critical examination of existing and proposed ways of doing work as a means of developing and applying easier and more effective methods and reducing costs', and secondly, work measurement—'the application of techniques designed to establish the time for a qualified worker to carry out a specified job at a defined level of performance'.[9] The 'whole foundation of the apparatus of job analysis, the micro division of tasks, production planning, and control, and functional organization' rests on this analysis by experts.[10]

Incentive wage schemes also replaced the contract-labor system. Rather than contract piece rates with foremen, management pretended to share savings on overall unit costs with workers. In 1889, Henry Towne reported to the American Society of Mechanical Engineers about the first incentive pay system set up at the Yale and Towne Lock Company. Taylor himself worked hard on such systems, establishing the standards, experimenting with machine tooling, feeds, and speeds, to turn the 'black art' of unsubstantiated personal know-how into systems of objective standards. Since incentive pay schemes required accurate cost calculation, Taylor also pioneered standard cost accounting to replace 'historical costs', and devised budgeting techniques. Employers extended and modified his ideas for use in factories of all kinds, producing the line and staff hierarchies that persist today. As workers lost control over the conception and execution of work a considerable de-skilling occurred, the consequence of the shift from a factory in which the skilled worker made the product to one in which the production engineer and his staff designed the production system and the semiautomatic machines that low-skilled operators used to make the product.[11] The big winners were Taylorist engineers who planned the work process which the workers merely ran. Since the engineers analyzed and then divided and subdivided skills within the workforce, Taylorism brought the separation of thought (management) from doing (labor) into the workshop, and with it a 'science' based on a moral claim: managers, because they are experts, exercise legitimate authority over those who work.

The Corporation

Taylorism enabled American industry to produce good-quality, if relatively unsophisticated, products at low prices. It also called into being the corporate restructuring of American firms that has been described so thoroughly in the works of Alfred D. Chandler, Jr. and the Chandlerians. These historians, especially in their earlier publications, depicted this restructuring in evolutionary convergentist terms.

For example, Alfred Chandler and Fritz Redlich in their 1961 article 'Recent Developments in American Business Administration and their Conceptualization', pinpointed a threefold structural development: from the 'single product, single function' firm, typical of American industry before the Civil War, through the 'single product, multi-function' firm of the late nineteenth century, to the 'multi-product, multi-functional firm' characteristic of international twentieth-century multidivisional firms.[12]

The authors argued that each organizational type required a unique form of business administration. A single-product, single-function enterprise, like the railroads, functioned at two levels. It needed general managers of the operating units concerned with the 'mechanics of day-to-day responsibilities', and a central office that made decisions we would call 'entrepreneurial'. The 'single product, multi-function' firm, which had integrated backward and forward, had to create more administration to handle the elaborate marketing and raw material procurement functions. The 'multi-product, multi-functional' firm, unable to organize the purchasing, manufacturing, and marketing of multiple products within the old administrative structure, had to set up divisional organizations, with each division possessed of a full set of functional departments—manufacturing, sales, finance, purchasing, engineering—headquarters being charged with strategic decision-making. Although organizational forms coexist within advanced economies, the Chandlerians really advocated a stage theory of managerial history, which culminated in the twentieth century when international corporate giants spawned the divisionalized form of administration.

These organizational concepts were not new. At the end of the eighteenth century, the French military developed multidivisional organization and control (MD forms), under which divisions and army corps handled tactical events, headquarters and staff strategy, and overall planning. This management structure permitted the French to march and fight large, multifunctional armies much more effectively than their opponents, with their functionally organized centrally managed administrative systems.[13] Whether twentieth-century American corporate businessmen learned anything about MD structures from the military is not clear, but army staff planners certainly understood them at the end of the nineteenth century.

Chandler and Redlich claim, however, that business forms unfolded situationally, that is, that technological demands mainly called them into being. Hence, particular manufacturing, such as cotton mills, leather factories, etc. never developed MD managerial structures or moved to them much later than industries based on other technologies. As stage theory, the work of these business historians assumed that the giant multiproduct, multifunctional firm would dominate the business world, and with it the MD form corporate governance. Although the economist Oliver Williamson assessed corporate structures with analytical tools quite different from those of historians, he agreed. He hypothesized that 'the multidivisional structure more nearly approximates neoclassical profit maximization than does the functional structure for the large, complex firm'.[14]

The managerial needs induced by corporate reform differed quite distinctly from those of Taylorism. Because top managers concentrated on the dynamics of money rather than product management, they required staffs that could deal with corporate finance and marketing. They required managerial accountants who could oversee money flows through the various corporate divisions because this information was much more vital to decision-making in a multifaceted strategic setting. Moreover, emphasis on Return-On-Investment (ROI) at headquarters required financial reporting from the engineers below, accounting information that, if it satisfied the money men upstairs, did not serve the needs of the technocratic-minded shop floor. They needed physical measurements more than monetary ones. And so we entered the era when comptroller, financial experts, and accountants dominated the firm. While in the workshop skilled workers had lost control to the system's managers of Taylorism, in the big corporation the owner-stockholder lost control to the professional money managers at the top. Since engineers' influence waned outside the factory proper, the money managers at corporate headquarters set the new managerial tone.

Accordingly, management style changed. Since under Taylorism the 'rhetoric of bureaucratic control conflates management as a moral order with management as a technical-scientific order' technical-scientific exigencies imposed a form of management wherein engineers and workers alike submitted to 'fact and law' of an impersonal nature.[15] Perhaps the customarily unchallenged and unexamined acceptance of authority by the workshop managerial hierarchy and by 'those inhabitants of industrial organizations who possess no authority, the manual employees', could be attributed to this technically disciplined environment.[16] But such a view of management ignored human psychology. The Hawthorne studies at Western Electric drove this point home: worker motivation and organizational behavior turned out to be anything but techno-rational.[17] Although the Hawthorne experiments implied much for workshop management, they implied more for a nontechnical middle management ensconcing itself in the new multidivisional corporate structures, for they were not subject to the work discipline of the technical production process. Hence, the growth of corporate management added a human relations dimension to American managerialism.

Management's goal remained increased productivity.[18] But, inasmuch as management wished to awaken the enthusiastic cooperation of employees, the methods of attainment had to be quite different from Taylorist fact and law, command and obey procedures. This meant, if management were to be effective, it had to acquire human relations skills as well as technical and professional qualifications. Managers had to learn how to recognize the psychological needs of their workers, how to construct psychological tests, how to manage by integration and self-control, how to profile subordinates, how to understand individual aspirations. They found themselves delving into depth psychology in order to help people overcome inhibitions, neutralize defenses, free blockages, and stimulate insights and feedback. Managers got involved in group psychology, embracing such social orthopedics as role-playing, brainstorming, creativity stimulation, and T-group activities in order to modify behavior by teaching people to know themselves in relationship to others, thereby fostering the emotional and 'moral well-being' essential to group cohesion.

The human relations movement tried to substitute 'democratic leadership' for the 'authoritarian leadership' of Taylorism. This switch required 'nothing less than a "conversion", for unless each individual sincerely desire[d] to change his behavior both as an individual and as a member of the group, this program could accomplish nothing'.[19] Accumulating adherents during the era of the 'New Deal', the human relations movement, although it hardly supplanted Taylorism, eventually transformed the style, if not the substance, of American corporate management. Its advocates recognized that the social-psychological climate of an enterprise is as much a factor in productivity as technical capability.[20]

Education

Higher education is the third component of American management. Americans like to think of theirs as a quintessential democratic country, but in fact America is elitist as much as it is democratic, especially with regard to its systems of higher education. The American elite is a meritocracy based on individual talent; it is broad-based, including government, military, business, and industry leaders in its ranks. All, moreover, share common values that are deeply rooted in the nation, and among them is an instrumental view of education, that knowledge can be applied to problem-solving in a variety of situations. This view has led to a great appreciation of intelligence and knowledge in the elite and much knowledge crossover between managers in various occupations and professions. Nothing illustrates this better than the interaction between business and the military. Ivan Prashker observed, for example, that General

> Westmoreland had an advanced management course at the Harvard Business School in 1954, fitting in so seamlessly among the business executives who were his classmates that one of them later said, 'He might have been a vice-president of a corporation.' Throughout his career, Westmoreland indicated a passion for efficiency and a fondness for percentages. This meant he and McNamara, who'd not only once taught at Harvard but also emphasized charts and statistics when he was president of Ford, had many of the same instincts and spoke the same language.[21]

Lest one think that this is a recent phenomenon, it is well to remember how far back the West Point–business knowledge crossover extends. American business historians are familiar with it. Professor Alfred D. Chandler, Jr. notes that 'The United States Military Academy provided the best training in civil engineering in this country until the 1860s', which led not surprisingly to the employment of its graduates in the building of America's railroads.[22] The influence, moreover, was managerial as well as technical. West Pointers, working for industry, used systems learned at the Point to improve workshop discipline and cost accountability. They were directly involved in working out the 'power-knowledge configurations' that brought about the reorganization of factory management and the development of corporate managerialism in this century.[23]

It is best not to exaggerate this education–management connection c.1900; most managers were shop- or office-floor-trained, not college educated. Nonetheless, the nineteenth-century precedent bore fruit. It bore fruit in the business community itself, which, as the names of so many business schools attest, generously financed business education, and in taxpayer-supported educational institutions that did the same. By 1939 ten percent of all undergraduates at American colleges and universities studied business; by 1949 the figure had climbed to seventeen percent. But the really decisive breakthrough came with the introduction of the scientific paradigm into management education.

At first, considering that Americans had always admired business acumen and that scientific knowledge, in the state it had reached c.1900, was of no apparent use to management, the influence flowed from business to non-business activities. Again, the business–military connection provides the obvious example. The Americans had so poorly managed the conversion of industry from civilian to military production in the First World War that Congress, in the National Defense Act of 1920, planned for an economic mobilization that would avoid recurrent misfortunes. The various services (Quartermaster Corps, Ordnance, Air Corps, Corps of Engineers, etc.), were composed of military men, officer technicians, but, as Charles de Gaulle so perceptively pointed out in 1934,

> and this is the originality of the American organization, each one of [the service corps] is assisted by a permanent study committee formed from the business world which directly aids it (the service corps) in its work. . . . The Americans have taken steps to assure that both sides have the right personnel.[24]

Business education for serving officers counted among these steps. An Army Industrial College was, de Gaulle continued, 'established to give the military in the technical services the desired training. Some of them have even been sent to take courses at the Harvard School of Business Administration.'

Science's capacity to assist management also augmented considerably after the Nazi seizure of power, when European intellectuals emigrated to the United States, many finding homes in American universities. To a large extent immigrants dominated the commission that the Chicago businessman Alfred Cowles founded in 1932, which made important contributions to the development of econometrics. Jacob Marschak and Tjalling Koopmans, who directed the commission, were, respectively, Russian and Dutch; Abraham Wald, the gifted statistician who had a strong influence on the commission's work, was Rumanian by birth and partly by education (he was also educated in Vienna). Oskar Morgenstern was Austrian and John von Neumann, who developed game theory (von Neumann also contributed to the development of computers and worked with the Cowles Commission on mathematical statistics), was Hungarian. Like the scientists who made the atomic bomb, among whom, incidentally, von Neumann counted, those formulating managerially useful science literally brought intellectual distinction and practical prowess to America from abroad. The same was true of the small group of German refugees, led by Kurt Lewin, who contributed much to the creation of a 'science of human relations' in the United States.[25]

The Second World War dramatically intensified intercourse between science and management. Initially, the Americans learned from British scientists and engineers who, at Air Ministry Research, Bawdsey, began work in 1936 on 'the operational use of radar'. The experts realized that they 'needed unbiased scientific assessment of the efficacy of radar', and 'how to implement the systems in service'.[26] The success of British wartime operational research (OR) is legendary; more important for this story, the British passed on much of what they learned to the Americans when they entered the war. Indeed, with their superior material resources, with the strength gained from private management know-how used in war, and with a distinguished group of scientists present and assembling, the Americans surged ahead.[27] Examples of science gone to war are legion: the economists Stacy May and Robert Nathan applying statistical analysis to war production programs; F. L. Hitchcock elaborating transportation theory to deal efficiently with the complicated problems of moving vast amounts of men and material; Kurt Lewin working on human relations at his new Research Center for Group Dynamics. They covered the wide spectrum of 'hard' and 'soft' management subjects.

The Cold War, so soon after the Second World War, perpetuated this scientific trend. The management teams put together after Pearl Harbor for the duration had to be reconstituted, to operate on a permanent basis in order to maximize the input–output ratios for the new immensely complicated and expensive weapons systems. Postwar defense-based science generated significant management applications, among them linear programming, which George B. Dantzig and his associates at the Rand Corporation developed for the Air Force in 1947. The Cold War also stimulated computer use. The first big commercially built computer, UNIVAC 1, did not reach an industrial user, the General Electric Company, until 1954. Before that date (except for a UNIVAC 1 delivered to the Bureau of the Census in 1952), computers worked only on military problems and atomic research. By 1955, however, 'an avalanche of preparation by almost all firms had been made for the adoption of such equipment', heralding the widespread use thereafter of computers in private business and industry.[28]

The 'scientization' of management automatically required its institutionalization where science takes place. This did not necessarily mean in universities, for much science application, like the work of the Rand Corporation, occurs in 'think tanks' and government research institutes. But in America, with its utilitarian educational traditions, university involvement in management research would become commonplace during the Cold War. The Case Institute of Technology in Cleveland started the first operation research (OR) department. It did so at the urging of industry (financial support from the Chesapeake and Ohio Railroad Co.) and in response to the Air Force requests (funding research on airplane design). This institute organized a national conference (November 1951) on operations research in business and industry to which 150 people came from all over the country. Several leading American universities also established OR programs (Carnegie Tech, U.C.L.A., Ohio State University, University of Chicago, Johns Hopkins, Cornell University, University of Pennsylvania, etc.). Of these, Ohio State University and Case were engaged actively in industrial consultancy by the mid-1950s. Private consultancy firms worked with universities (Booz, Allen, and Hamilton alone had fifty-two offices which counseled clients on operations research). And the American Management Association, in frequent symposiums, included academics in its educational efforts.[29] By the mid-1950s the teaching staffs in leading American universities also propagated group psychology methods: at the Advance Management Training seminars (Harvard), the Executive Roundtable, New York University, the executive Institute, Northwestern University, the Executive Conference on Coordination and Policy (University of Pennsylvania), and the Management Problems for Executives seminars in the University of Pittsburgh.

The impressive results, achieved and promised, brought the impregnation of management education systems with mathematics and science, as well as their expansion, originally into departments of industrial administration within engineering schools, where the knowledge of mathematics and statistics preexisted; and then, in the late 1950s and 1960s, into business schools proper. In order to accommodate scientific method, business schools radically upgraded admission standards in mathematics and introduced mathematical models and statistics into behavioral science, traditional functional management (marketing, finance, etc.), general management, and decision science courses.

The number of undergraduates studying management grew constantly after mid-century, from an already impressive plateau in 1949–50. Already in that year 617 institutions of higher education offered courses in business and commerce primarily at the undergraduate level, with 370,000 students, nearly double the numbers in engineering, and 72,187 business baccalaureates graduating. By 1968–69 the number of business baccalaureates had increased to 93,356, thirteen percent of all baccalaureate degrees conferred.[30] But graduate business schools constituted the real educational innovation. After they adopted tough requirements, the era of the MBA began: 4,814 in 1960, 23,400 in 1970, 49,000 in 1980, 70,000 in 1990, with some 200,000 plus studying for the degree today.

Thus in post World War II America, higher education fused with shop floor and corporate management. The fusion clearly served management in H(Hierarchical)-model organizations, for the linear programming, cybernetic feedback, statistical analysis, and electronic data processing taught in the academic business school proved useful for a management in the H-model firm, where a 'high degree of formalization, standardization, and centralization' reigned, where 'good top-down decision making abilities, good problem solving, analytical skills, and a capacity to devise good externally imposed evaluation systems' prevailed.[31] In addition, the social orthopedic techniques presented in human relations courses proved useful to fledgling managers, trying to enhance productivity by improving the social-psychological climate of firms.

But university education aimed at more than teaching techniques. It sought to professionalize management, management by a properly credentialed, highly paid elite of experts. A medical analogy to this new professionalism would not be inappropriate. Doctors study medicine, managers business administration; doctors open consultancies to help sick people, managers consultancies to help sick firms. Medical schools do research to improve medical science, business schools do research to establish the theoretical basis of the science of business administration or one of its subdisciplines, and to develop the tool kit necessary to minister to business firms. Although the medical profession offers in one sense a false analogy, because the MBA, unlike the MD, has never been a legal or nonlegal requirement for professional activity, the correlation is very strong between the rise of American managerialism and the American graduate business school, with its MBA pretensions.

Americans, therefore, invented management and with it the American way of doing business. Gilbert Burck's article in *Fortune*, a veritable paean to American know-how, expressed it admirably: 'The American way of doing business in an expanding market is the natural way of doing business', in which American management is the key, 'flexible, unfettered by tradition, creative, expansion-minded, democratic in its relations with employees as well as customer'.[32] Or, to use Heinz Hartmann's words, 'managerialism' constitutes in the American mind a 'fourth production factor', a 'strategic variable for the development of the firm'.[33] And with all this management, the intensity of supervision grew. 'Between 1948 and 1966', David M. Gordon reports, '. . . the ratio of supervisory to nonsupervisory employees in the private business sector increased by nearly 75 percent—from roughly thirteen supervisory employees per hundred nonsupervisory employees to more than twenty-two'.[34]

The 1945 version of 'managerialism', however, contained two additional elements, big labor and big government. Both entered the American managerial equation during the New Deal and the Second World War to become very important factors in the immediate postwar years. Not much can be said about either here, since they are vast subjects in themselves, but a few words are appropriate to explain how they fit into the creation of the American management mystique.

The American government's relationship with American business is historically complex. A Robert Reich story identifies one constant in this relationship. In 1950 the National Association of Manufacturers (NAM) distributed free to hundreds of thousands of workers 'a comic book' which stated that the American Revolution had been caused by 'government planners' in London.[35] Most American businessmen agreed and agree with NAM's view of government: the less of it the better. The ideological justification for the view can easily be traced to men of the seventeenth and eighteenth centuries—specifically to John Locke and Adam Smith. Locke's political philosophy made the individual's access to life, liberty, and property natural rights, limiting government's role to that of referee (the use of governmental authority to guarantee the preservation of life, liberty, and property). In the 'forest of firms' of a premodern small-store, workshop economy this philosophy of government was not particularly undemocratic.

Smith added an economic and a moral corollary to Locke: to assure consumer satisfaction, the market mechanism which is best served by a competitive capitalist private property manufacturing and commercial system should operate without government interference. Those meddlesome eighteenth-century London bureaucrats got what they deserved when the colonies revolted. This article of faith is professed loudly and clearly by a great business-fueled propaganda machine, in which the NAM holds a prominent place, whenever American governments adopt liberal agendas of interference.

Nonetheless, there is a minor thread of business–government cooperation and even interpenetration that runs through the fabric of American history. Cooperation has been there almost from the Republic's beginning. Manufacturers have relied on tariffs to protect them from foreign competition; in fact, America became the mightiest manufacturing nation in the world behind high tariff walls. Business, too, has relied extensively on the government as an information service. The Bureau of Labor, the Department of Commerce, the Census Bureau, and a host of other government agencies have for decades collected and fed statistics to businessmen and consumers about multiple facets of national life. Ironically, as any business historian working in French and German sources knows, America had a much more complete state information system about business-related subjects, and much earlier, than either France or Germany, despite their long and strong bureaucratic traditions.

Business and government also gradually intertwined through people exchange. Business hostility to the New Deal and New Dealers to big business is well known. But the Second World War introduced businessmen into government service and changed the climate of opinion. The transformation can be followed through the career moves of people involved in the business-dominated Committee for Economic Development (CED), which organized first in 1942. One-third of the 150 people who served as CED trustees during the first fifteen years of its operation eventually held Federal government positions, elective or appointive. Paul Hoffman, President of Studebaker, and William Benton, Chairman of Encylopaedia Britannica, CED founders, Philip Reed of General Electric, William Batt of SKF, David Zellerbach of Crown Zellerbach, and William C. Foster of Pressed and Welded Steel Products are examples. By 1944 CED participation in 'long-range planning' involved over 40,000 businessmen operating through 2,000+ community-level planning groups. These CED businessmen, who had come to terms with the New Deal, were 'enormously influenced by the scope of industrial planning and growth during the war'.[36] The businessmen's invasion of government continued with the Cold War. By 1948 over forty percent of the people in the 'higher echelons of the executive branch had business, finance, or law backgrounds'.[37]

If management went to Washington, Washington reacted with open arms, for the attitude of anti-business New Dealers also changed. 'The wartime mobilization of the United States', Donald Duncan Gordon stresses, 'was probably the ultimate achievement of that Western industrial civilization which reached its zenith in the mid-twentieth century. . . . It was planning, industrial production, and above all new technology that mattered. Technology meant efficiency and efficiency always won.'[38]

And technological efficiency also meant the triumph of corporate management within the American economy and inside the American psyche after the war. Large-scale mass production necessitated the mass consumption of washers and dryers, refrigerators, electrical kitchen appliances, cars, and track housing that the returning GIs so enthusiastically purchased in the great postwar buying binge. Five hundred major corporations produced half of the nation's industrial output, employed twelve percent of the nation's nonfarm workers, and dominated the economy. And they had no real foreign competition, for as late as 1960 'only four percent of the cars, slightly more than four percent of steel, under six percent of the television sets, radios, and other consumer electronic products, and three percent of machine tools [consumed in America] were built outside the United States'.[39]

The gap between rich and poor closed.[40] After the war the success of the country's core corporations and the well-being of individual citizens seemed inextricably bound. This environment converted the sharpest critics of business to pro-business stands. David Lilienthal, a New Deal Planner, in a 1953 book, *Big Business: A New Era*, echoed the sentiments of the American people, the vast majority of whom, in a 1953 public opinion poll, approved of big business.[41] Under these circumstances the business of America was indeed business, including the function of government itself, which, through the entry of businessmen into its ranks, with their much-admired managerial capacities, became a preserve of business managerial outlooks.

Corporate management's capture of government determined the place that labor unions would play in postwar American management and government. Just as most American businessmen objected to government interference in their affairs, so did they dislike, even more, the presence of labor unions on business premises. They followed and still follow NAM's party line in favor of a 'union free' work environment. Before 1934 the government and the courts had cooperated fully with business leaders to keep the unions at bay, but the great depression shattered big business confidence and introduced, through the New Deal, some government neutrality in areas of business–labor relations. For the first time 'enlightened' big business executives learned to live with, and at times to appreciate, the value of labor unions. A few even learned to accept employee–management interpenetration. The most durable example of this was the Scanlon plan, a worker participation scheme, named after labor leader Joseph Scanlon, that was implemented at fifty insolvent steel companies in 1938. The plan's fundamentals were: (1) bonuses to workers for reduction in labor costs, and (2) the use of joint labor–management committees to gather and implement suggestions for production improvement.[42] When the war came, the initiative seemed to bear fruit. The War Production board asked in 1942 that joint committees be voluntarily organized in defense plants. Within three months of this request over 800 plants, with approximately two million employees, had established labor–management committees; by July 1945, the number of plants reporting active joint-production committees had expanded to 3,200.

But this joint labor–employer management initiative proved a false dawn. Seldom in their sweetest liberal dreams did American big business executives seek to end adversarial relations with workers. Nor did their New Deal Democrat 'pro-union' opponents expect this adversarial relationship to disappear. Only the Democrat reformers sought to level the playing-field in the labor–management contest. Labor's resultant Magna Carta, the Wagner Act (1935), simply forced the employers to stop interfering with their workers' effort to organize, to bargain collectively with their employers, and, if need be, to strike. The law established the National Labor Relations Board (NLRB), which refereed union certification elections and arbitrated, according to codified grievances procedures, violations of collective bargaining agreements that had been freely concluded by both sides. The conservative counter-offensive that produced the Republican-dominated Congress of the immediate postwar years and the Taft–Hartley Act (1947) even negated many of these modest labor gains. The law outlawed closed shops and secondary boycotts and gave the President the power to enjoin strikes threatening national health and safety. It authorized him, should he think it prudent, to require a ninety-day cooling-off period before a strike could be declared. The act was, in the words of CIO president John L. Lewis, a 'slave-labor' law.

Nonetheless, labor's victories had not been a sham. Collective bargaining agreements hammered out in tough labor–management negotiations allowed unions a serious voice in the definition of job content, pay, and work process. And the NLRB administrative machinery permitted aggrieved workers to correct an employer's violation of these agreements, although the lengthy appeals process and the fact that employers did not have to correct grievances until the NLRB decided the case led to frustrating delays. On the other hand, pattern agreements, which set the pay and working conditions for entire industrial segments, pleased the union leadership very much. Well might the head of the American Federation of Labor, George Meany, have reasoned in 1951, 'Where you have a well-established industry and a well-established union, you are going to get to the point where a strike doesn't make sense.'[43] And well might Walter Reuther, the head of the United Auto Workers, after reaching agreement in 1950 with General Motors, have echoed this sentiment. This five-year contract called for an annual wage increase, pegged on anticipated productivity gains, that was cushioned against inflation by a cost-of-living bonus. For American labor this accord was truly historic.

In the postwar years, then, big labor played a considerable role, for not only did collective bargaining provide better wages and working conditions, it brought company retirement schemes, medical plans, and other social benefits. By the late 1940s the experts spoke increasingly of 'harmonious, pluralistic industrial relations' carried out through 'elaborate collective bargaining' in an 'enlightened' capitalism.[44] Between 1948 and 1953 the Inter-University Labor Relations Program sponsored the publication of a significant academic literature on industrial relations. These monographs, written by industrial labor relations people soon to be renowned (Clark Kerr, Frederick Harbison, John Dunlop, Charles Meyer, and others) emphasized that 'the extension of democracy in industry through collective bargaining' permitted the 'two sides of industry . . . to mould good or bad relations'.[45] Despite the admonition 'good or bad relations', the tone set in these writings was decidedly upbeat. For 'enlightened' academics, businessmen, and labor leaders collective bargaining promised to solve the social question, increase labor peace, and elevate productivity.

Nonetheless, this much-touted industrial democracy did not extend to management. If the academics recognized that labor was a stakeholder in the firm, it was not a shareholder. Since shareholders, as owners, appointed management, labor's claim on management was legally mute. It was also functionally mute because the modern corporation, under American management, strove 'to prevent unions from interfering with its essential prerogatives'.[46] 'American management', *Business Week* wrote in 1975, 'felt no need or great desire to give workers a large share in decision-making.'[47] But this statement is too meek. The fact is that corporate management fought hard and tenaciously to maintain its 'Right to Manage'.[48] Not that, except during the Second World War, unions seriously challenged this 'right'. U.S. unions considered themselves to be a countervailing power to management, one whose effectiveness depends on maintaining a clear distinction between management and labor. Talk of good will notwithstanding, the system was based on labor's self-exclusion from management and mutual distrust. Even the old labor warrior George Meany recognized divergent jurisdictions when he acknowledged that issues like production standards, location of plant, investment policy, new product development, new plant construction, reinvestment of profits, and the raising of new equity capital were not subject to collective bargaining or union interference. They were very important to the firm but they were not the workers' business.[49]

Thus, despite talk of industrial democracy, American management and American labor ended up living in two cultures. The difference began with management and labor's physical location in separate venues. Not considered part of the firm, union headquarters and hall had to be located outside the plant. As the management ideal extended throughout American organizational life, the same separation happened in unexpected places. Faculty unionization in universities, for instance, has produced the incongruity of faculty representatives being forced to headquarter off campus, with the administration, management in this case, constituting the firm (university). Professors have become employees. Because of this mutual isolation union and management cultures became quite distinct in terms of mannerisms of speech, of gastronomy, in respect even to the way gangsterism and organized crime is expressed in each culture, and in regard to how labor and management relate to government and higher education.[50]

The American business school can be used to illustrate the point about higher education: it is management's academic home, a place that scarcely concerns itself with labor, except as a problem with which management has to deal. The human resource management

35

techniques that flourished there and in the firm itself constituted, as much as any Taylorist stopwatch, instruments for managerial mastery and workforce manipulation.[51] As for government, the interpenetration between businessmen, business educators, and bureaucrats reached the point, to use words appropriated from George Orwell's *Animal Farm*, where it was 'impossible to say which was which'. Whereas businessmen and management educators moved with ease in government precincts, labor leaders protruded out of this environment like hammered thumbs. Tributes to workers in Labor Day speeches aside, American management took credit at mid-century for the plenty that the highly effective mass production economy offered American consumers. Management claimed that it, the 'fourth productive factor', thought, planned, acted—achieved this plenty in factory, corporate board room, government agency, and in the War Department. Since the results were there to see, Americans believed!

The Internationalization of American Management

World System analysis, which is itself largely an expression of American social science culture, has provided a convenient dynamic with which to explain the internationalization of American management.[52] The dynamic consists of the interaction between a hegemonic center, in this case America, and a client-state periphery. The Center from its position of global authority, assuming 'guidance' responsibilities, transfers its 'social theoretic' and 'ideological convictions' to the periphery states which in turn remodel their institutions on the Center. Like metal filings on a surface, these client states oriented themselves to a giant magnet, America, when it turned itself on. World systems theory, which is especially vulnerable to postmodernist attack, sounds rather dated now. But if theoretically questionable, it is useful to historians, because it offers insight into what happened in the free world after the Second World War.

The antecedents of postwar management were not entirely American. Scientific precedent reached back in Europe to well before 1945.

In France engineer-economists carried out pioneering work in managerial economics in the nineteenth century.[53] One man in particular, Jules Dupuit, worked on marginal cost pricing in the 1840s, a work of a practical nature, for he sought solutions to transportation problems encountered on the job. Educated as a scientist, he formulated solutions in mathematical-economic terms.[54] Although cut off from their foreign colleagues, French *ingénieurs-économistes* continued to think about economics during the occupation. Maurice Allais's book *A la recherche d'une discipline économique* (1943) offered a complete explanation of Pareto's theory of the optimum (under the nomenclature, theory of social return) which relied particularly on marginal cost analysis.[55] The existence of these engineer-economists facilitated the postwar transfer to France of mathematically rigorous techniques like linear programming as well as the indigenous development of French scientific management concepts.

As noted, other Europeans contributed significantly to American scientific management when they emigrated to America. But they took as much, if not more, than they gave. Jean Monnet, for example, the father of postwar French planning, acknowledged his debt to Americans, incurred in Washington, D.C. between 1943 and 1954. He 'earnestly cultivated contacts in higher political, military, legal, banking, academic, and business circles in the United States. . . . The success of American war production impressed the French mission who [observed] . . . wartime mobilization techniques'.[56] Monnet's story typifies that of scores of distinguished mathematicians and scientists who joined with native Americans to apply science to war-generated management problems.

Abroad, during the war, the American managerial influence reached into the United Kingdom first.[57] Alistair Mant claimed that 'Dependence on the U.S.A. was massive, to the point where it is hardly an exaggeration to suggest that the leadership function in the collective mind of British industry was vested in America. This process, begun during the war, was carried on through the import of "T.W.I." (Training Within Industry for Supervisors) based on group discussion methods.'[58] The invasion of Europe quickly awakened management consciousness in liberated countries. There is much truth in the statement of F. J. Gosselink, who studied Marshall Plan aid in the Netherlands: 'I am convinced that this so-called "mental revolution" [management] could generally not have taken place amongst the leading institutions and the population in the Netherlands, because it had already been realized before the Marshall Plan had come into being.'[59] The massive evidence of American know-how the Dutch witnessed during the liberation sparked their subsequent enthusiasm.

Nonetheless, most people date America's pervasive managerial involvement in Europe from the Marshall Plan. In other words, Gosselink's 'mental revolution' had been more psychological than methodological. Although exhausted, deprived Europeans in 1945 had been deeply impressed by the organizational ability and material plenty of the invading Americans, they had no precise idea about the managerial method and thought that produced them or what lay behind their attainment. The transfer of specific knowledge about American management and its sources really got underway after 1948.[60]

The Foreign Assistance Act of that year established the Economic Cooperation Agency (ECA) to administer a European recovery program. The legislation set up special missions in the major countries to administer the aid. During the next four years Americans made available thirteen billion dollars to the sixteen Western European countries that agreed to sign bilateral accords with the U.S.A. The signers committed themselves to four major aims: a strong production effort, expansion of foreign trade, the maintenance of financial stability, and the development of European economic cooperation.[61]

On the American side the same managerial–business elite that had devoted their talents to winning the war now spread American management know-how abroad through the Marshall Plan agency. The co-founder of the Council for Economic Development, Paul Hoffman, former president of Studebaker, took over the top Marshall Plan job. As head of the Economic Cooperation Agency (ECA), he administered the European Recovery Program (ERP).[62] W. Averell Harriman, Maurice Moore (of *Time* magazine), Thomas McKittrick of Chase National Bank, and William G. Foster, the Pressed and Welded Steel executive who became Hoffman's assistant deputy chairman (Harriman was the deputy chairman), joined that Washington staff. Overseas, in the U.K., Sir Stafford Cripps, Chancellor of the Exchequer, and Paul Hoffman set up an Anglo-American Council on Productivity (AACP) to tackle the management problem. General

Electric's Philip Reed headed this AACP, while William Batt, of SKF, took over the mission to London, and David Zellerbach, of Crown Zellerbach, the mission to Rome.

The American Marshall Plan administration, then, externalized the American management *Gestalt*. Andrew Carew notes that it was in all major respects a business organization run by businessmen. Of course, since, in Hoffman's phrase, the contest pitted 'the American assembly line' against the 'Communist Party line', the Marshall Planners had to win the hearts and minds of European peoples. They had to woo the workers away from socialism. Moreover, they had to be careful not to alienate America's many allies, the non-Communist European socialist Left. Despite the unavoidable necessity to assuage Leftist sensibilities, capitalists, not workers, drove the Marshall Plan. Marshall Plan ideology—productivity—came from American management as did its leaders: almost none of the heads of mission to European countries was an American labor executive. American labor leaders only got involved on the secondary level.

But they were involved. The American Federation of Labor, which had embraced 'business unionism', actively battled Communist influence in European labor unions. Somewhat later (1951) the Congress of Industrial Organizations (CIO) set up a European Office in Paris, from which it carried on the same anti-Communist fight. This emphasis on 'non-political unionism' perfectly expressed American traditions of management–labor relations. But American labor did not necessarily swallow Marshall Plan rhetoric. Victor Reuther, CIO representative in Europe, commented that General Clay in Germany used the Marshall Plan to 'force the energies and hopes of the European peoples into the mould of American enterprise'.[63] European trade unionists on mission to America discovered that reports about worker–manager harmony idealized American capitalism and were a great exaggeration. A British Trades Union Congress delegation 'found little evidence among American unions of any positive commitment to scientific management. The predominant attitude to this development among the leading unions ranged from outright hostility to passive but reluctant acceptance.'[64]

Labor representatives on the Marshall Plan staff, however, seemingly ignored, perhaps deliberately, these negative union assessments. One principal Marshall Plan advisor, Clinton Golden, through 'selective borrowing from a number of exceptional experiments and isolated cases', rhapsodized about a whole new system of industrial relations in the making in America, based on labor–management cooperation.[65] The propaganda projected abroad mirrored the propaganda in America itself about management's productive achievements and the benefits the nation enjoyed because of them. Assuming that the essence of industrial society is best expressed in the 'managed', 'open', and 'affluent' capitalism of America, these Marshall Planners proclaimed that Europe's prosperity depended on how quickly and well Europeans followed the example of the transatlantic colossus. American Marshall Planners believed, therefore, that in Europe the same sharp distinction should be made, as in America, between unions and management, the former being allotted the scarcely creditable right to 'trim the edge off managerial decisions'.[66] Americans, in an effort to fulfill management-set productivity goals, would try in Europe to restrict severely the area of human relations where union involvement would be permitted; or, to use cynical trade unionist language, 'to make human relations gimmicks', a substitute for 'constructive labor–management relations'.[67]

If the Marshall Planners stressed productivity and if they insisted that aid recipients establish productivity boards to oversee improvements, they seemed beyond that to have had no very clear idea about how to achieve these productivity goals. As Michael J. Hogan observed,

> The ECA targeted only a modest amount of funds for the technical-assistance programs, including the so-called productivity teams, in fiscal year 1949–50, and only a 'negligible portion' of the commodities it shipped to Europe consisted of the capital goods that would 'increase the productivity of the European farm or factory'.[68]

Three years after the war, Americans had still not mounted a systematic international transfer of this famous American managerial know-how. Although the Cold War evoked America's 'sense of responsibility' and enhanced the threatened client states' receptivity to American ideas, during the four-year aid program, the Marshall Planners allotted just thirty-six million of the thirteen billion dollars to 'technical assistance', the budget category that covered the transfer of managerial knowledge and know-how. This expenditure, moreover, occurred late in the program; by 1949 not 'a single industrial engineer [had been] employed by the ECA in Europe'.[69]

Why so much delay? The answer is not that the Americans and pro-American Europeans really did not care about productivity. They did, but it took longer than people realized for the managerial transformation perceived necessary actually to take place. The delay happened, for one reason, because American managerial capitalism was not prepared early on to carry through the task. It was evolving rapidly in the immediate postwar period—in the development of its capacities (science-based systems like linear programming), its hardware (computers), and its institutions (the research-based graduate schools of business administration). They could only be mobilized when sufficiently developed themselves. Delay occurred, too, because the Europeans had to prepare for the transformation.[70] For these reasons talk about Marshall Plan influence on European management needs to be extended to years beyond those actually covered by the Plan.

The ECA, which administered the European Recovery Program, the Marshall Plan agency, ended before its original four-year manadate expired. It was replaced in 1951 by the Mutual Security Agency, charged with the mission of European rearmament, not European recovery. The Mutual Security Agency found itself in 1954 turned into the Foreign Operations Agency, which became the International Co-Operation Agency in 1955, before in 1961 being transformed into the Agency for International Development. Each agency had a management development program; each but the last spent monies drawn from the original Marshall Plan counterpart funds. Indeed, the Marshall Plan successor agencies spent most of the money on the transfer of management know-how that had been accumulated under the Marshall Plan for that purpose.

The task, however, had not been left entirely to these government agencies. Paul Hoffman moved to the Ford Foundation in 1950, taking many Marshall Planners with him. At the Foundation they proselytized management, sponsoring its development in Europe originally and then outside Europe, globally. During the 1960s American corporations invested heavily in Europe, on the same scale, it might be added, as Japanese corporations did in America during the 1980s. The corporate invasion of Europe directly transferred American management to the old continent. And American management consultancies like Booz, Allen and Hamilton, The Boston Consulting Group, and McKinsey and Company expanded abroad, bringing American management philosophy and method with them. A long process, lasting roughly from 1945 to 1970, the propagation of American management in Europe and throughout the world went through multifaceted phases.

In the start-up first phase, the technical assistant program tried to bring business, industrial, and professional practitioners together from both sides of the Atlantic. 'The American expert', Theodore White wrote from Paris, 'has become as much a stock character in the outer world as was the British traveller of the nineteenth century or the Roman centurion 2,000 years ago'.[71] If the era of the travelling American management expert had arrived, so had that of the travelling European. Almost all monies in the technical assistant program financed trips for dollar-starved Europeans. The Anglo-American Council on Productivity, 'one of the largest experiments in adult education ever undertaken', sent 138 teams of managers, workers, and specialists, 900 people in all, on visits to America between August 1948 and June 1952.[72] And these teams 'returned full of glowing and uncritical admiration of the American management education scene.'[73] During the peak year 1950–51, the AACP's visiting teams produced a report a week, with over 600,000 copies sold in total. Later, the economist Graham Hutton, in a burst of hyperbole, referred to these reports as a 'set of documents the likes of which, on such a scale and of such practical value, has never been seen in the history of international and cultural borrowing'.[74]

The teams from Continental countries started for America somewhat later, and at first on a more limited scale. But by 1951 their numbers began to approach the British. Germany, for example, spent $1.3 millon dollars (compared with the million pound budget of the AACP) mostly to finance trips; France by 1952 had sent 200 teams across the Atlantic (2,600 Frenchmen in all) and distributed their reports to management, government, and labor groups at home. In Holland, around 170 study-trips to the United States took place, with about 1,100 people involved, while Americans in the Netherlands carried out eighteen projects within the framework of the Technical Assistant program.[75] The velocity of correspondence between Europe and America matched that of people exchange. By 1951, 2,000 people worked in the ECA's Paris headquarters; Paris secretaries and typists sent four million words of reports to Washington monthly and received two million words back.[76]

Travel contacts facilitated forthwith the spread of American management techniques. Luc Boltanski observed that the diffusion of American industrial psycho-sociology to France, particularly the 'techniques de groupe', stemmed directly from the *mission psychotechnique* which the Marshall Plan-inspired French Productivity Association sent to the U.S.A. in 1952.[77] Among these travelers, aside from the head of mission Paul Fraisse, could be counted Jean Bonnaire (*chef du service psychotechnique de la Regie Renault*), Jean Marie Faverge (attached to Ministry of Labor, Centre d'études et de recherches psychotechniques), and Suzanne Pacaud, head of the Laboratory for Psychotechnique in the French National Railroad (SNCF) and research assistant at the CNRS (French Science Foundation). Strategically located, with impeccable scientific credentials and easy access to praxis, this mission ably transferred the knowledge acquired in America to France. Moreover, they prepared the way for other French travelers to visit the United States in order to look at the American techniques. Boltanski observes that the people up to 1958 who contributed to the development of 'techniques de groupe' in enterprises, and who promoted strong ties between university research and the firm, had been deeply impressed ('vivement frappé tous les visiteurs aux Etats-Unis') by the close collaboration between universities and industry that they had witnessed in America during Marshall Plan visits.[78]

While the transatlantic shuttle of experts continued, NATO, preoccupied with the rearmament of Europe, initiated a new phase in the transfer of American management know-how. In the United States the demand for increasingly complex weapons and complicated military operations systems spurred the Rand Corporation and other defense-related agencies to apply scientific method to military managerial problems.[79] If the American forward deployment strategy were to succeed, allies in Europe and elsewhere needed to learn how to manage these complex systems. Consequently, military officers and Department of Defense civilians specializing in operations research not only organized well-attended conferences in the United States but propagated operations research techniques among allied military circles in OR conferences abroad. These were not just meetings of military OR people. Rather military OR people, both American and European, participated in the many international meetings sponsored by OR societies when OR came to Europe during the 1950s. Sometimes American associations—for example, The Operations Research Society and The Institute of Management Studies—met in a European city; sometimes the International Association of Operations Research Societies held meetings in Europe. Well publicized in the periodicals, the meetings were fully attended by Americans and Europeans, military and civilian, from NATO member states. The American military also indirectly promoted management science through support given to American computer firms. IBM, the obvious example, an important defense contractor, taught the new computer-based techniques—game theory, linear programming, queue theory, search theory, information theory—assiduously to both the military and the civilian side of the managerial fence.

While these networks of contacts thickened, the third transfer phase of American management know-how arrived in the guise of management education. In a sense everything had been education. Education had been the purpose of the technical assistance program, with its transatlantic shuttle of experts. But Americans and their foreign partners keenly sensed that Europeans as well as allies in other regions of the world needed to be profoundly reeducated in management. Michael A. Bernstein points out that European-educated Marxists dominated Japanese economic thought right after the war.[80] Since this could not be permitted to continue, during the 1950s and 1960s American government officials and advisors worked hard to spread American ideas about economics. Eisenhower's economic advisor Raymond Saulnier began after 1958 to share the annual *Economic Report of the President* with the Bureau of the Economic Planning Agency of Japan. As Director of the National Bureau of Economic Research, Arthur Burns exchanged researchers with Japan's Economic Research Institute.[81] Fulbright and Social Science Research Council grants financed economic study-trips to Japan and the United States.

In Europe, formal educational efforts had already taken place. In 1956 the EPA sent fifty-six European university teachers to America to learn management subjects at American universities. The EPA also sponsored summer school courses for European lecturers in economics, social science, and engineering to improve their knowledge of management. By 1958 it had run 340 courses in 'management techniques' for 15,000 participants, one study mission to America, fifteen courses in America for European teachers, and seven international conferences about management—all of which included material on social science, which Europeans rarely covered in their education.[82]

Under former High Commissioner for Germany John J. McCloy, who succeeded Hoffman, the Ford Foundation, still well staffed with former Marshall Planners, contributed much to these educational labors. Following Dean Acheson's advice to fund projects 'related to the overseas promotion of American managerial values and know-how', it espoused adult education and, especially, the management education of trade unionists. The Ford Foundation created an Adult Education Fund with a budget of $5.4 million and a steering committee that included Philip Reed, American co-chairman of the AACP, and labor's Marshall Plan spokesman, Clinton Golden. One early project, which was co-sponsored by the Adult Education Fund and the American Management Association, presented management's view of how industrial relations should be taught.[83]

Yet, pro-American management zealots would be satisfied with nothing less than a fundamental remodeling of European higher education along American lines. The reform began with the introduction of specific American scientific management techniques into European higher education. Lawrence Stein, a future Nobel Laureate, developed macroeconomic modeling at Cambridge in the 1950s; Professor Harry Johnson, of the University of Chicago, restructured the economics curriculum at the London School of Economics in the 1960s. But American graduate schools of business administration clearly provided the high-profile reform model, not only in France and the United Kingdom, but also in other Western European nations.

In Great Britain some influential British businessmen attended senior executive courses at the Harvard Business School. They had first-hand exposure to American academic business education. In 1963 a group of industrialists, during a series of luncheons with leading members of the House of Commons, established the Foundation for Management Education, which collected funds for the promotion of management teaching in universities. The group wanted to create an independent Harvard-like business school in London.[84] In the meantime, the National Economic Development Council, which had been created in 1961 to foment planning among and between people in government, industry, and trade unions, reported in April 1963 that there was a 'need' for at least one very high-level new school or institute, somewhat on the lines of the Harvard Business School, or the School of Industrial Management at the Massachusetts Institute of Technology. A committee representing all these groups, headed by Lord Franks, gathered to formulate a concrete set of recommendations. Franks's job was simplified because the Robbins committee had just proposed a general reform of British higher education. It recommended that 'two major post-graduate [business] schools . . . be built up in addition to other developments already probable in universities and other institutions'.[85]

The American business school example not only inspired the creation of two new British business schools in London and Manchester but deeply influenced their educational structures. 'London', Richard Whitley, Alan Thomas, and Jane Marceau wrote,

> was particularly keen to acknowledge its debt to the United States. The full title of the School, for example, the London Graduate School of Business Studies, was a borrowing from Harvard practice, and its literature spoke of 'Programmes' (Senior Executive Program, London Executive Program, Master's Program, etc.) an 'Alumni Association', and 'electives'. Manchester stuck to the more parsimonious 'Manchester Business School', and was more inclined to talk of 'courses', a 'Manchester Business School Association', and 'course options'. Even so, in 1968 it drew particular attention to the number of staff who were training in the major American schools, such opportunities being particularly welcome 'in view of the fully established and highly advanced state of graduate business education in the United States today'.[86]

Europe's first and most successful business school INSEAD started in France at Fontainebleau in 1957. But this private, very European school is not part of the French system of higher education. That bifurcated system had taken shape in the nineteenth century. The *grandes écoles* of engineering and commerce formed one branch; the university faculties, in which commercial subjects were not taught, the other. When France emerged from the Second World War, no American-style management education took place in either branch, not even the *grandes écoles* of commerce. Reformers transformed the

Ecole des Hautes Etudes Commerciales (HEC), one of the more significant commercial schools, into a business school *à l'américain* beginning in 1957. In this year the undergraduate curriculum dropped the old commercial and science courses that had been its previous mainstay. Students in the first year now devoted their time to general studies and to an introduction to management, in the second year to more advanced management studies and an analysis of the nature of the firm, and in the third to a special management project that was often done with a firm. The year 1968 brought computer programming (by 1980 thirty terminals were available to students). The innovators also reformed teaching methods. 'In fact', Marc Meuleau, HEC's historian, remarked,

> the reform of 1957 amounted to the adoption of American management education . . . . The school took up most of the methods it had discovered in the 1950s and the inauguration of its new installations at Jouy-en-Josas (1963) was done in the presence of the American ambassador. The organization of studies at Columbia University in 1956—40% lectures, 20% case studies, 20% discussions after lectures, 20% seminars where students make reports that are criticized by their classmates—could be found at the school c. 1965–67. It also agreed to accept engineers seeking management education, a common practice in the United States.[87]

The other *grandes écoles* of commerce, particularly the most prestigious rivals of HEC—the Ecole Supérieure des Sciences Economiques et Commerciales (ESSEC) and the Ecole Supérieure de Commerce de Paris (ESCP)—introduced similar American-style reforms.[88] The lesser schools adapted more slowly, but they could not escape the fallout from the American-induced management education revolution.

In the French university sector, the first steps in management, as opposed to 'economics', education came as early as 1955 when Gaston Berger founded Enterprise Management Institutes, the Instituts d'Administration des Entreprises (IAE). The IAE offered a two year MBA-type diploma (the Certificat d'Aptitude d'Administration des Entreprises, CAAE).[89] In the 1960s, and especially after 1968, management studies invaded the undergraduate curricula in all French universities but especially in Paris IX (Dauphine), which specialized in the business and economic sciences. Paris IX rapidly became the chief place for graduate research studies in management.

Still, since French higher education, as late as 1969, lacked the wherewithal to train professors in management, reforms could not be pushed vigorously. To solve this problem, French businessmen, industrialists, bureaucrats, and educators combined to set up the National Management Education Foundation (FNEGE).[90] To educate the educators, FNEGE decided to send graduate students in management to America for training. The French foundation worked out special programs with business schools at Northwestern, the University of Texas (Austin), and Sherbrooke (Canada). Usually a student spent some time on study programs and meetings before leaving France, then about thirty percent of the travelers entered three-year doctoral programs in the United States and Canada while the others took either one-year individual courses or a one-year course tailored by the host school especially for the French. In the years 1969–72, 210 French academics underwent this American management education.[91]

Events in the United Kingdom and France, then, amply illustrate how Americans influenced European management educational reform at every level. Similar events happened in other European countries. The Belgians, to give an example, turned to the Americans for help. In fact, the Belgian Inter-university College for Doctoral Studies in Management (CIM) probably mounted the most direct European appeal to American business school expertise, greater even than that of FNEGE.[92] Organized by the *Fondation-Industrie-Université*, under Gaston Deurinck, itself a product of Belgian–American cooperation stemming from the Marshall Plan, between 1970 and 1980 CIM sent Belgians to earn doctorates in management in the United States. Over half of them became professors of management in Belgium. It was a relatively natural consequence, therefore, for the Belgian professors at Leuven University to offer an MBA course which, to nobody's surprise, was based almost entirely on American management literature and which was taught in English.[93]

Such persistent educational efforts paid off. A few figures illustrate the progress. In the mid-1960s very few people studied management in academic institutions in Europe. Moreover, those who did went primarily to post-experience graduate institutions. By the mid-1980s the number of undergraduate students majoring in economics or management at European institutions of higher education averaged eleven percent of total student numbers, ranging from a low of 10.5

percent of students in the Federal Republic of Germany to a high of 13.98 per cent in the United Kingdom.[94] These figures are not as high as American (about twenty percent), but they are nonetheless impressive. The great European effort to promote management education had produced significant results quickly. Not only did the new discipline massively infiltrate the sacred confines of undergraduate education, but academic post-experience business education also flourished.

Thus, the Americanization of international management occurred in three overlapping phases: (1) The Marshall Plan phase, epitomized by the traveling experts of the late 1940s and very early 1950s; (2) the NATO phase, a Cold-War intensified military-backed transfer of American managerial know-how during the 1950s and 1960s; and (3) the education phase, when Europeans, under American auspices, renovated their institutions of higher education in order to make management studies an integral part of the system. During these years American firms, expanding abroad, directly projected their skills and people onto the international scene. And private American organizations like the Ford Foundation lent support. But there is a fourth factor that cannot be overlooked in this conversion process: the management press. America had a developed business press at war's end. The creation of an equivalent managerial journalism was not a phase in the Americanization process, but a process that accompanied the internalization of American managerialism through its various phases of development.

Business and industrial journalism had existed for a long time in Europe, most of it devoted to an industry (*Stahl und Eisen*), or a trade or professional association (*Zeitschrift Vereine deutsche Ingenieure*). A specifically business press also predated the war (*Wirtschaftswoche*, for instance, was founded in 1926), and a financial press served individual investors (*Les Echos*). But none of the periodicals spoke for 'management'. Indeed, with 'management' being a peculiarly American notion, non-Americans, when they encountered the term, had to search for a suitable word in the lexicon of their own languages and often ended up just using the American one (*le management* or *der Manager*). American management required, as Luc Boltanski affirmed, 'the formulation of a new ideology and a new representation of social space'.[95] This new ideology, management as a 'fourth productive factor', could not be based on the traditional *grand* or *petit patronat* of the small

49

property holder, if for no other reason than that they were not concerned with productivity. Productivity, the gospel Americans convincingly preached, presupposes the existence of a new middle class of managerial functionaries to fill the leadership space—trained in modern management methods, dedicated to the cult of work, competence, and efficiency.[96] The business press which evolved very rapidly after the war created the ideology of this new management middle class.

It began when the old press started to support the new managerialism from America—weeklies like *Der Spiegel* (1947) and *Die Zeit* (1946) in Germany and *L'Express* (1953) in France, and daily newspapers like the *Frankfurter Allgemeine Zeitung* (1949).[97] By the late 1950s a new economic press appeared, through the transformation of older business periodicals (*Wirtschaftswoche*) or the creation of new ones (*Direction, Economie contemporaine, La France industrielle, Entreprise*) which specifically publicized 'le management moderne'.[98] This press broadcast the ideology of the new 'managerial' class and in effect helped itself to create the class. Then, as the class took shape towards the mid-1960s, another group of periodicals appeared to serve it directly (*L'Expansion* in 1967, consciously patterned on America's *Fortune*; *Manager Magazin*, in 1971, whose German clientele is obvious) or to serve special groups within it (*The Business Graduate*, organ of the MBAs issuing from the new business schools of the United Kingdom). This pro-American press functioned as a crucial information pipeline, publicizing courses, describing techniques and methods, supporting governmental managerial programs, advocating management educational reform in academic institutions, pushing the management idea within management itself, and finally, after twenty-five years of work, developing within its own ranks special periodicals for managers that confirmed the success of the American-initiated management movement.

The Mystique

But this book talks of a 'mystique'. For Americans and their allies in foreign lands, the issue had not been one of 'mystiques'. For them the adoption of the American managerial way had straightway produced the material recovery of postwar Europe and Asia, fostered the subsequent sustained prosperity of the free world, and eventually defeated Communism. Michael J. Hogan presents the thesis distinctly:

the keys to a neo-capitalism in Western Europe [were] similar to the one that . . . led to a new era of economic growth and social stability in the United States. Through American aid, and particularly through the use of counterpart funds, Marshall Planners tried to underwrite industrial modernization projects, promote Keynesian strategies of aggregate economic management, overhaul antiquated systems of public administration, and encourage progressive tax policies, low-cost housing programs, and other measures of economic and social reform. Through production centers and productivity teams, they sought to build an alliance of labor, business, and professional leaders behind these reforms. And through the technical-assistance program, of which the productivity campaign was a part, they hoped to transform distributive battles into the search for a shared abundance and political problems into technical ones that were solvable, they said, by adopting American engineering, production, and marketing techniques and American methods of labor-management teamwork.[99]

Hogan, who is so convinced of his thesis that he entitled his concluding chapter 'America Made the European Way', underwrites the macro-micromanagement Americanization theme.

Indeed, this historian's account scarcely, except in judicious tone and documentation, differs from the partisan sentiments of the most pro-American postwar managerial activist. Octave Gélinier, one of the more ardent disciples of the new creed, had already mined Hogan's vein:

Today we can see things more clearly. To begin with, the economic and political system of traditional Europe has proved to be bankrupt. That strange amalgam of medieval concepts and modern technologies was able to hold the spotlight for three centuries . . . , but its collapse . . . is final . . . . The American model, imperfect though it may be, offers industrial civilization its unifying principle. . . . The Protestant ethic, reborn as the science of management, has renewed its strength. It is no longer taught in catechism classes but in business schools. To spread the faith throughout the world, missionaries have been replaced by 'productivity institutes'. Every year, leaders from all over the world come to the United States on pilgrimages (called 'productivity missions') to see and hear the latest revelations. The Protestant ethic, as management science, is today sweeping the entire world.[100]

And similar statements can easily be dredged up for Japan: 'the U.S. as teacher . . . ultimately informed the creation of the Japanese economic miracle'.[101]

This new managerial class believed and believes that the creatures of their management reforms brought about the world's postwar economic successes. Philip Nind, in a history of the *Foundation for Management Education*, an agency he so skillfully headed for years, noted that Professor Kenneth Andrews drew a direct connection between performance and management reform. After investigating Harvard's advanced management programs, Andrews concluded that 'post-experience university programs had valuable effects in changing behavior, increasing effectiveness and improving management skills'.[102] Peter Forrester in 'A Study of the Practical Use of the MBA', prepared in 1984 for the British Institute of Management, figured that 'nearly all MBA's five years after their course found it to have been highly effective and were using in their work a significant part of the knowledge and skills they had learnt'.[103] Since a business school MBA epitomized American 'managerialism', what satisfaction its advocates must have had to discover the salutary effects that this utilitarian education had!

There was, however, plenty of evidence to the contrary. In 1971, the Owen survey of large U.K. manufacturing firms concluded that the MBA's usefulness in management was doubtful. Executives and business journalists, moreover, said the same thing. Ivan Fallon's comments in *The Sunday Times* (21 April 1991) are pertinent: 'John Major's thought on the value of a university education', he wrote:

> finds echoes around the business world—or rather the entrepreneurial world. Jimmy Goldsmith, with never an O-level to his name, feels so strongly about business schools that he would probably disinherit one of his children if they went there. If you run your eye down *The Sunday Times* list of the rich, all the top self-made men left school early.

American business schools are criticized for teaching 'pseudo-skills when [students] might be getting on-the-job experience of acquiring genuine skills'.[104] Their professors are chastised for 'building elegant, abstract models', and their graduates condemned as 'critters with lop-sided brains, icy hearts, and shrunken souls'.[105]

Even the cherished Marshall-Plan-savior thesis has not been sacro-sanct. The clear-sighted historian Alan Milward has pretty much laid to rest any idea that American Marshall Plan aid saved Europe economically. The moderate historian Richard F. Kuisel observed at a Marshall Plan retrospective: 'In the end Europeans found their own way forward, their own route to prosperity and international competi-tiveness, without imitating America.'[106] Meanwhile, Professor Leslie Hannah and his group in the Centre for Economic Performance, London School of Economics, have, using econometric evidence, quite dispelled the idea that American management forms, on their adoption, increased a firm's or an economy's efficiency.[107]

Researchers should not head for the archives to ferret out the information that would resolve these conflicts of opinion. More studies are not needed because, to invoke Peter D. Anthony's com-ment once more, social science methods are quite incapable of solving the issues at hand.[108] Indeed, it is ironic to report that the very 'scientific' research methods that management scientists proselytized cannot prove the usefulness to economic process, of their very adop-tion, in business schools and praxis. Therefore, we are left with the fact of postwar economic recovery, growth, and prosperity and solid evidence of the spread of American managerialism, but with no sure way to establish a causal link between them.

But if no triumph of American management can be proved, certainly a triumph of the American management 'mystique' can. Webster defines a mystique as follows: 'A complex of transcendental or semi-mystical beliefs and attitudes directed towards or developing around an object (as a person, institution, idea, or pursuit) and enhancing the value or significance of the object by enduing it with esoteric truth or meaning.'[109] 'Semimystical attitudes developing around' American management as an 'institution, idea, or pursuit', 'enhancing' the value of managerialism by 'enduing it with the esoteric truth or meaning' as the source of plenty and prosperity in modern society—this was certainly characteristic of the behavior and speech of those plying American managerialism after the Second World War. For this gen-eration managerialism was never held to be mean-spirited. It did not just provide stockholders with greater profits; it promised the average man a society free from want through 'managed' productivity. The rhetoric was used as a weapon against the collectivist enemy. It was the American answer to the phoney promises of Communism.

It was an answer, however, limited in time and space; indeed over time the limitation grew in space. Until 1970 the prestige of American management was geographically quite great. Japanese experts at that time believed, too, that their corporate future required them to adopt American management principles and methods.[110] But, since it is a fair assumption that the managers in the most successful economy are considered best, the American management mystique faded in the late 1970s and 1980s along with the reputation of American manufacturing. Even in their heyday, however, American management ideas and institutions did not necessarily take hold. They remained and remain deeply enrooted in America's economic culture, but in Germany and Japan their arrival had been problematic, despite initial enthusiasm.

Chapter Two

German Obstinacy

HISTORICAL moments do not move in some mechanical, clock-like way. There are times when nothing much seems to happen, although the seedbeds of change might be surreptitiously in preparation. There are other times when a rush of change comes followed by recession. In the history of German management three periods are significant after the Second World War. The first happened immediately postwar (1946–52) in the battle over co-determination and participation in management, a battle, although occasioned by the unprecedented nature of Germany's collapse, that had deep roots in Germany's past. The second occurred with the reaffirmation within German business and industry of traditional German ideas about leadership—the rejection, that is, of American managerialism. This reaffirmation coincided with the German economic recovery and prosperity of the 1950s and early 1960s. The third period of significance arrived when the Social Democratic Party (SPD) gained partial access to power in the coalition governments of the late 1960s and 1970s.[1] It brought legislative reforms and a labor-union-backed democratization of German economic and social life that greatly affected German organizational behavior. All three periods combined led to a German alternative to the American management way.

The Battle over Co-Determination

Two German traditions must be considered in order to understand the German postwar battle over co-determination: (1) German attitudes toward the state, and (2) the nature of the German trade union movement. Usually the two are discussed separately in German history but they are coupled here because the character of the German labor movement is informed by German attitudes toward the state.

In the Anglo-American world, political theorists have made the state mostly an oppressor, in the sense that government almost by nature arbitrarily infringes on an individual's right to life, liberty, and property. The distrust of government, moreover, extends from the political sphere into the economic: a nation's growth should be left largely to market forces which, through competition, allocate resources efficiently, thereby promoting consumer interest and accommodating, through the diffusion of political and economic power, the entry rights of all into the economy. This Anglo-American view of competition is a democratic doctrine. There is, as Eleanor Hadley points out, room for an Adam Smith in the eighteenth century because there was a John Locke in the seventeenth.[2]

The German attitude towards the state is very different from the Anglo-American. Hegel in his *Philosophy of Right* makes the critical distinction between civil society and the State. This viewpoint is important because it is intrinsic to what Leonard Krieger called the 'German idea of freedom'.[3] That idea emerges from a very mundane observation, that civil society is composed of many individuals with contrary interests and passions, beset with numerous factions and parties. Civil society, because of the self-seeking nature of its components, is incapable on its own of organizing a satisfactory human community. Since the stronger self-interest within civil society will deny justice to the weak, to achieve a satisfactory human society the existence and the action of a supra-body, the State, is required. It is easy to see why Americans and Englishmen, with their deep distrust of government, reject this German idea, especially with the recent example of state terror in mind. But the German idea of freedom raises two pertinent points.

1. Since civil society is made up of self-interest groups, from the general interest perspective of the State each group's self-interest is legitimate. This is so because, if it cannot be identified with the general interest, a legitimate self-interest nonetheless does constitute a valid special view within civil society. The State, properly constituted, can, therefore, be an instrument through which oppressed groups within civil society can attain freedom. Nineteenth-century German history

offers numerous instances where enlightened civil servants (*Beamte*) advanced particular interests in order to promote the general interest, when these particular interests, because of other competing stronger interests, could never have won out in the selfish rough and tumble of civil society. This happened, for example, when the state ended serfdom against the opposition of a powerful landed aristocracy.

2. German businessmen, industrialists, and workers have had much less faith than the British or Americans in the efficacy of market mechanisms. On the contrary, German businessmen have sought not only the protection of cartels but have done so expecting the State's cooperation, support, and approval. The State has willingly granted all three, but it has also not hesitated to interfere with the market in order to protect the 'legitimate' interest of the working classes. Bismarck's social insurance program of the late nineteenth century (health and accident insurance, old-age pensions, and unemployment compensation) is the most famous example of state intervention, but there were others, including the Law for the Protection of Labor (*Arbeiterschutzgesetz*) of 1891, which is of special interest here because it raises the issue of co-determination.[4]

Co-determination has to do with employee participation in the governance of the firm. It can also mean employee participation in extra-firm economic committees and councils. Ardent advocates of co-determination within the German trade union and socialist movements aimed to implement its fuller form. They intended to establish co-determination at all levels of economic governance within the nation. Inasmuch as the broader movement failed, the subject covered here is worker participation at the company level.

Ideas about worker participation had been around for decades in many advanced industrial countries. In Germany their modern career began in the 1830s when, with profit-sharing concepts bruited about, the necessity for workers to gain access to management seemed obvious. 'Professor socialists' in the *Verein für Sozialpolitik* embraced the idea during the third quarter of the nineteenth century.[5] It gained respectability. Emperor William II, in a reformist mood, incorporated the concept into a speech in 1890, asking for the creation of worker-representative bodies within factories that would defend employee interests in negotiations with employers. The resultant Law for the

Protection of Labor, which Friedrich Lange sponsored in the Reich-stag, granted workers joint consultation rights (*Mitberatungsrecht*) on social matters. This was not co-determination (*Mitbestimmung*) but the law authorized the organization of plant committees in all factories covered by the Industrial Code of 1869, if they had more than twenty employees. And it required management to issue and abide by shop regulations spelling out relations with workers.[6]

Two points are of interest in this account: (1) co-determination is deeply rooted in German history, and (2) the State, in the German tradition, has been implicated in the story for a long time. The German State did not relentlessly advocate co-determination; its position on the subject shifted according to who controlled the State (just what Americans would suspect). But with Germans looking to the State to guarantee particular rights, it was inevitable perhaps that the civil conflict between labor and management over co-determination turn into a constitutional crisis involving the State.

This constitutional crisis erupted fully at the end of the First World War. During the war employer willingness to concede co-determination rights to workers increased in proportion to the growing weakness of the Imperial regime, its need for workers' support for the war effort, and the employers' fear of the red specter. By the end of 1916, the military dictatorship running Imperial Germany felt that permanent plant committees had to be created in order to reward the workers for their sacrifices. Employers refused to cooperate. As the regime began to collapse the employers' associations themselves leaned, with increasing desperation, towards granting workers a greater voice in management. Perhaps, owners reasoned, concessions could stave off a socialist takeover. By the revolutionary month of November 1918, employers, fearing Bolshevism, capitulated almost entirely. Unions and the employers' associations signed collective agreements which gave employees rights of co-determination with management in social policy and the right to be consulted in personnel and economic decision-making.

Agreements between powerful corporate bodies in civil society, like an employer association and a trade union federation, carried much weight. But because to the German mind private agreements lack sufficient authority, co-determination quickly assumed political importance. Already in December 1918 a socialist-dominated provisional government decreed that the trade union federation and employer association agreement would become legally applicable throughout the Reich. The following July a socialist–liberal–progressive majority in the Constituent Assembly wrote co-determination into the Weimar Constitution: Article 165 called for 'the equal participation of blue- and white-collar workers (*Arbeiter* and *Angestellten*) in the regulation of wages and working conditions as well as in the entire economic development of production forces'.[7] A conservative victory in the ensuing elections, however, permitted the Reichstag to reduce workers, rights in the actual legislation (4 February 1920). This reneged on promises just written into the Constitution.[8] The Reichstag, however, did pass a Works Constitution Act (*Betriebsrätegesetz*) that set up works councils in firms with twenty or more employees. It also provided for the election of a shop steward in those firms with five to twenty employees. Although the law spoke of employee participation in social, personnel, and economic decision-making, the extent of works councils jurisdiction varied.[9] In personnel matters works councils were limited to consultation and in economic circumstances to 'cooperating' with management in the implementation of new work methods and wage rates. Only in social matters did the law give works councils serious co-determination rights.

This outcome hardly settled the issue. Labor unions pressed for full worker participation. In the twelfth congress of German unions (Breslau, 1925), Rudolf Hilferding called for a hierarchic system of economic councils based on co-determination in which unions would formally participate. The congress established a commission to investigate the subject, with an eye to the formulation of an action program. The commission produced a book by Fritz Naphtali, one of the best union theoreticians during the Weimar Republic, which crystallized trade union thought on co-determination—*Wirtschaftsdemokratie— Ihr Wesen, Weg und Ziel* (Economic Democracy—Its Essence, Way, and Goal).[10]

Employers for their part fought a bitter battle with the unions against worker participation in management. Wherever feasible, they withdrew tactical concessions induced earlier during the period of threatened economic collapse and social chaos. In typical German fashion, moreover, they sought state help. The role employer groups played in Hitler's rise to power cannot be covered here. One thing needs to be said, however: the crushing of German socialism and free trade unionism did not displease employers fearful of co-determination, for the Nazis dissolved the works councils and applied the authoritarian principle (*Führerprinzip*) in the management of firms just as they did in the management of the National Socialist State. Total Nazi victory in the constitutional conflict, therefore, brought total defeat of co-determination in the economy.

Postwar Encounters with American Managerialism

Germans, when they crawled from the rubble, left the concentration camps, returned from exile, the Eastern front, or from prisoner-of-war camps, carried the burden of history with them. Otto Brenner, one of the postwar labor reformers, remembered that 'the union leaders during the recovery period', at whose head stood Hans Böckler, first president of the German Federation of Unions (Deutscher Gewerkschaftsbund, DGB), 'had lived through the fall of the Weimar Republic and had at the time participated in discussions about the concept of economic democracy'. The postwar leaders formed a living bridge, with their knowledge and experience, between the trade union ideas of the 1920s and the social programs that the united trade union movement advocated after the collapse of Nazi Germany. Obviously, they had scores to settle, not only with the Nazis but with the business and industrial leadership that had supported them. They wanted to exclude both from power. But their programs also drew on the past. Ludwig Rosenberg, another postwar activist, remembered that 'many reflections, numerous proposals, and not a few of [their] impulses . . . found their origins in Naphtali's book. The postwar claim for economic democracy . . . [was]—as Naphtali and his friend formulated it . . .— as much an old as a contemporary goal.'[11]

In 1945 German trade unionists, like British, and much more than American, believed that capitalism was in its death throes. DGB leader Hans Böckler proclaimed its end in March 1946, which he avowed should cause rejoicing, since the capitalists could never again betray the workers as they had done in 1920–21.[12] Similar views, afoot in the German Social Democratic Party, prompted delegates at the Party's first postwar rally in May 1946 to make the building of socialism their principal national task. German capitalists and their political representatives obviously disagreed, but their previous closeness to the now defunct Third Reich made their views suspect. Hence, the socialization of basic industries appeared inevitable.

Why the predicted demise of capitalism did not happen need not detain us here. The German Economic Miracle obviously contributed most to the acceptance within West Germany of the privately owned social-market economy. If the West Germans eventually sided with the Americans on the private ownership issue, they parted company from each other on the subject of co-determination. The free trade unions took up co-determination where they had left off in 1933: it was part of their heritage. They were joined by advocates of private property in Germany who believed, after the war, that something had to be done to give workers a voice in management. The Christian churches and the Christian trade unions also went on record for co-determination; so did the Christian Democratic Union, Konrad Adenauer's party, in its Ahlener party day program which, with Adenauer's approval, spoke out in its favor.[13]

Between 1947 and 1950 eight of the newly constituted states (*Länder*) in West Germany passed works constitution legislation which went far beyond that of Weimar. The legislation gave employee-elected works councils co-decision rights on social matters; in personnel 'they were granted rights of participation which ranged from joint-consultation to the right of veto'; and, in the all-important economic area, they were granted rights of co-decision in basic matters that vitally affected the future of an enterprise, such as 'expansion, consolidation, and shutdown, and joint-consultation in such matters as the purchase and sale of equipment, changes in production methods, determination of accounting procedures and sales policies'.[14] The laws also stipulated that works councils elect one to two members of supervisory boards. Hence the legislation restored and expanded empowerments claimed during Weimar, so that for the first time economic decisions became part of the works councils' purview.

What of the Marshall Planners and other advocates of American managerialism? Their views mattered very much, for in 1945 if most Germans were keen about creating some sort of co-determination, it was largely beside the point. A totally defeated nation, Germany's fate depended on the occupiers. Without their approval Germans could do nothing. And, Soviets aside, the Americans were the major partners in the occupation. This American influence increased with the creation of the bizone (1947), which amalgamated the American with the British occupation zone, wherein the bulk of West German heavy industry lay. Americans, with their faith in managerialism, and Germans, with their statist traditions and belief in co-determination, were bound to clash.

German historians tend to simplify the U.S. reaction to co-determination, arguing for the most part that Americans opposed it as champions of free enterprise and Cold War anticommunists. Actually, the American response was more complex. In 1946, before the Cold War really set it, the U.S. State Department, under Secretary James Byrnes, did not oppose co-determination. After all, America's closest ally, Great Britain, was doing worse, rushing headlong into socialism. When the British foreign secretary, Ernest Bevin, following Labour's nationalization of major industries, announced (23 October 1946) that the United Kingdom favored nationalizing German industries, too, Byrnes answered (17 December 1946) that the U.S.A. had no objections to the British plans. People in America also recognized that what might be ill-advised for their country could, considering German history, fit German conditions. George Meany articulated the subtlety of this position. He noted: 'For the American Federation of Labor I can say flatly that collective bargaining is not a means of seeking a voice in management, we do not want so-called co-determination.'[15] But he added that, although not for America, 'co-determination in Germany has some logic as a means of maintaining economic democracy'. Americans thought that the penchant of German industrialists to rely on the State for political and economic protection (e.g. the fascist's oppression of trade unions, the state's support of cartel-building) had to be curbed. To do this could mean supporting policies that clashed with American principles. Consequently Americans agreed at Potsdam that big business collaborators would lose control over their firms.

To some extent, too, different American and German conceptions about the state's relationship with civil society provoked misunder-

standings over co-determination. Germans want, Gloria Müller specified in her history of the subject, 'a legal foundation for practical
activity'.[16] But Englishmen and Americans do not, at least not in the
sense that they want everything spelled out. When the allied control
commission issued Law 22, 10 April 1946, regulating works councils,
it reflected Anglo-American thinking: the law was brief (thirteen short
articles) and it did not even make the organization of works councils
obligatory. Workers and managers were free in a firm, through collective bargaining, to set up, without interference from the state, whatever arrangements they wanted, including no works council at all—to
Americans a perfectly sensible idea. To the Germans this simply meant
that the British and American law stopped the formation of works
councils. A serious law would have made them obligatory and have
regulated their operation in considerable detail. This dispute, therefore, expressed different ideas of freedom.

Still, American views about German co-determination should not be
misrepresented. Co-determination clearly confronted American managerialism head-on. Everybody knows, since James Burnham's *The
Managerial Revolution* (1941), that those who own the firm have
been separated from those who run it. But the despoliation of the
stockholders that resulted, to the benefit of the new managerial elite,
had strict limits. Managers, who remained dependent juridically upon
stockholders for their jobs, had to see to it that company stock values
and paid-out dividends remained high, otherwise a stockholders'
revolt could throw the rascals out.

But neither juridically nor in the popular American imagination did
a firm belong to its employees. The laws on collective bargaining
simply required management to recognize and bargain in good faith
with the union, should its employees in free elections choose to have
one. The workers and the union they selected to represent them were
'outsiders'. This automatically meant that the employees' interests
could never be synonymous with the firm's.

Moreover, the separation of employees from the firm, although
typical of large British and American private corporations, was not
limited to them. *The Economist* noted in 1950 that nationalized
industries did not belong to their workers either, but to the nation.
Since the government, representing the nation, selected the management, ultimately the management of nationalized enterprises

63

answered to the government and not to their workers. The dominant view in America and Britain in both private and nationalized firms had always been that employee control over management would lead to company inefficiency, if not ruin because the workers would put their interests first and that these interests would be incompatible, in the long run if not the short, with those of the firm's owners, whether private capitalists or national citizenry.

Americans, then, disliked co-determination and, as the Cold War brought more conservatives to power, this dislike deepened. When George Marshall replaced James Byrnes as Secretary of State, Ernest Bevin also solicited his support for British plans to nationalize German industry. Marshall answered that he would leave the matter to the military administration on the scene, a response tantamount to refusal because that military administration, from General Lucius Clay down, represented very conservative American circles. Not only did it fight communists, but the military administration excluded anti-communist trade unionists and socialists from consideration when recruiting personnel for the reconstituted German administration. The policy resulted in a German civil service with a conservative economic bent.

The American military authorities, moreover, opposed German co-determination.[17] Initially, General Clay could not control events in the Ruhr, where British military authorities approved the co-determination deal struck between German trade unions and management in the steel industry. When the German state governments in the American zone wrote co-determination provisions into their constitutions, Clay first rejected them, then reluctantly accepted the constitutions with economic co-determination stricken from the texts. Clay's veto provoked a protest storm throughout the zone.[18] He justified the veto on constitutional grounds, stating that decisions about co-determination should not be made by individual state governments; this important subject required the approval of the German people living in a sovereign German national state. Since General Robertson, the British military governor and a former executive with Dunlop Tire Co., concurred, the British also blocked economic co-determination legislation in their zone. Germans distrusted Clay's constitutional arguments, viewing them as a rearguard action, to delay co-determination until, with the recovery of capitalism, it could be defeated or at least tamed.

Clay's obstructionism, therefore, postponed a showdown until the creation of the German Federal Republic. That showdown, which resulted in the Co-Determination Law for the Iron and Steel Industry (1951) and the Works Constitution Act a year later, vindicated Clay's delaying tactics, if indeed that had been his intent, for proponents of co-determination did not achieve as much in 1951 as they most certainly would have three or four years earlier. It is true that the 1951 law granted parity (50% elected by employees, 50% by stockholders) in the selection of supervisory boards. The law also provided that employee-elected members of a company's supervisory board choose a Labor Director, to join the commercial and technical directors on the firm's managing board (*Vorstand*). Inasmuch as managing boards make decisions collectively, this Labor Director had real authority in running a company. And since employee-elected supervisors selected him, the law considerably increased employee powers of co-determination. But the 1951 law only applied to coal and steel firms.

Advocates of co-determination failed when they tried to extend the provisions of the 1951 law to all business firms. The 1952 Works Constitution Act authorized employees to elect just a third of the members of their supervisory boards, thereby leaving the stockholders in command. The 1952 law also ignored the provision of the 1951 law that gave employee-elected supervisors the exclusive right to choose the Managing Board's Labor Director. The entire stockholder-dominated supervisory board would elect him. Finally, the 1952 Act, if it did permit co-determination on social issues, restricted the jurisdictions of works councils to consultation in personnel and economic matters.

Cold War politics tempered American reaction to the 1951 law on co-determination. John J. McCloy, the American High Commissioner, assumed a hands-off attitude; he even precipitated German action, and hence forced adoption, by pressuring Adenauer to address the co-determination issue in order to fulfill Clay's promise to act when a sovereign German state existed. This state, the German Federal Republic, came into existence in 1949. Still, McCloy was not neutral about the legislation. Although recognizing Germany's right to decide the issue for itself, he told German trade unionists not to be surprised when Americans refused to invest in companies co-managed by workers, a not too subtle pressure against adoption.[19]

Private American business representatives, however, did not have to engage in diplomatic niceties. They openly criticized co-determination. Getting wind of the German project, the National Association of Manufacturers sent a delegation to Europe led by Eldridge Haines to lobby against the bill. Gordon Michler, head of the German Committee in the American National Foreign Trade Council, joined the transatlantic trekkers to speak against co-determination. And in America a representative of the National Association of Manufacturers wrote an open letter to the German Council in New York, published in the *New York Times*, warning that Americans would not invest in German industry if the co-determination law passed.

Occasionally the protests proclaimed that co-determination was, to use the words of a *New York Times* editorial, a 'new socialism in the relations between capitalism and labor'.[20] But usually they employed softer language, pointing out that co-determination robbed stockholders of their right of control. The argument was somewhat disingenuous, inasmuch as the stockholders had already lost these rights to professional managers, but it was nonetheless true that co-determination would challenge the control of an exclusively stockholder-elected management.

The Americans proclaimed that worker involvement in management would also bring inefficiency. One commentator, Gilbert Burck, stated in *Fortune* after the bill passed: '[German] labor managed to hang what may turn out to be a millstone on the necks of management, consumers, and itself. When management and labor go to bed together, it is usually the consumer who gets raped.'[21] Co-determination, he continued elsewhere, 'was the worst possible approach to making the economy more dynamic' because it would lead to 'crippled national productivity, a retarded standard of living, and cartels'.[22] Burck even appealed to American labor leaders for support. He quoted two on German co-determination, one saying it was 'the worse approach to trade unionism I ever saw'. The other, after meeting a labor-elected member of a supervisory board, who in his opinion had taken on management airs, exclaimed: 'How can a guy like that represent labor!' This is an interesting case of reverse snobbery, because the American criticized the German for not having the rough manners of the workers and for being almost indistinguishable from the other executives on the supervisory board.

The reports about American labor's rejection of co-determination were partially true. Robert Bowie, one of the Marshall Plan people, observed retrospectively that American labor opposed co-determination and urged German labor to assume a proper union attitude: to represent workers through collective bargaining in opposition to, not in partnership with, management.[23] Werner Link, on the other hand, asserts that American labor generally supported co-determination.[24] If this be true, it was clearly not out of any deep conviction, for co-determination concepts had few adherents in American labor.

Thus for Marshall Planners German labor–management relations evolved in an unwanted direction. Indeed, the German co-determination laws mainly expressed German prewar historical, not American postwar managerial, dynamics. Americans fought hard to put their ideas into effect, sometimes with great success, since forces opposing co-determination quickly strengthened with economic recovery. But the Americans never entirely succeeded. By 1951, a difference had set in between the way postwar American and German employees would intermesh and interact with the management of each nation's firms.

German Leadership Traditions

Although major participants in modern industrialization, Germans held views about leadership and social interaction within business and industry which were different from those expressed in American managerialism. Whereas modern U. S. industry around 1900 assumed the high volume, mass production form that Americans made famous, these were not the only industrial forms through which industry progressed in the twentieth century. Comparative studies stress that German industry mostly shunned mass production until well after the Second World War, concentrating instead on 'low volume, high value added, specialized niche' manufacturing.[25] Nonelectrical machinery manufacturers (Humboldt, MAN, Demag, Borsig) produced top-line heavy machinery often to custom order; the electrical manufacturers (Siemens, AEG) competed most successfully in the manufacture of complex, made-to-order systems, for example, power plants, industrial .

equipment; the world-renowned chemical firms (Bayer, BASF, and Hoechst) dominated international markets in dyestuffs and pharmaceuticals, not bulk chemicals; and big steel prospered through the sale of finished and semi-finished, rather than primary, steel products.[26] Although scholars cite instances of German industry's involvement in high volume, low value-added, standardized production, it was, as Dornseifer and Kocka emphasize, in 'relatively low volume, high value-added [industrial] segments [that] German firms proved to be most competitive'.[27]

The skills this type of industrialization demanded differed from those in the mass-production factory. Whereas, as the Litterer quote underscored in the last chapter, in mass-production facilities skilled American engineers designed and installed machinery and supervised work processes, at the turn of the century engineers and skilled craftsmen still made the products in the low-volume, niche-production German industries. German business and industry, therefore, put great weight on *Fachkompetenz* (expertise), on everybody right up the line knowing his or her craft and technical job thoroughly. Indeed, those at the top got there by working their way, through *Fachkompetenz*, up the ranks—everybody started at the bottom. Those at the top could talk shop with individual skilled craftsman on the floor, or to the salesman, who, also *fachkompetent*, was technically and linguistically able to understand and supply customers' needs, even to anticipate them. Success depended on quality products, delivered on time, and after-sales- delivery service, that is, *Fachkompetenz*, not low prices.

Success also depended on maintaining high knowledge and skill levels in the work force. German firms at the turn of the century were famous for their apprenticeship training programs, inherited from a pre-industrial era, that kept skills at high levels. But skills alone no longer sufficed. Modern manufacturing, of the type in which the Germans excelled, required the blending of skill with science (*Wissenschaft*)—what the Germans call *Technik*. By 1900 Germany had a number of first-rate technical institutes (*technische Hochschulen*) in which a research-fostered engineering flourished.[28] In these institutions professors and doctoral students worked closely with industry in the identification and completion of research projects; professors required student engineers (candidates for the degree *Dipl.-Ing.*) to work in praxis (*Praktikum*) to learn how to combine knowledge with shop-floor skills.

There was, moreover, a sub-university sector of higher education sandwiched between apprenticeship training and study at technical institutes. These were the technical *Fachschulen* which bestowed the title *graduierte Ingenieur*. Entry to the technical *Fachschulen* required that the candidate complete an apprenticeship program. Even then, the subsequent study period in the *Fachschule* included, besides classroom and laboratory work, practical work on a job. German industry prized these *graduierte Ingenieure* because their theoretical training did not outweigh their practical skills. *Graduierte Ingenieure*, consequently, could be found at every level in the managerial hierarchy of German industry.[29] The German industrial work hierarchy, therefore, integrated technical management, through mutually supporting *Fachkompetenz*, from skilled worker, *Meister*, *graduierte Ingenieur*, *Dipl.-Ing.*, up to *Dr.-Ing.*, into a well-functioning highly qualified manufacturing whole.

Leadership capacity in this environment, especially in family businesses, resided less in physical or bureaucratic than moral authority. And this moral authority depended on *Fachkompetenz* in the leader, plus years of experience working closely with the men. This had been the case in America, too, before a codified management know-how, written up too frequently in a cookbook-recipe fashion and published in management manuals, took its place. Germans eyed this American sort of managerialism with suspicion. Dornseifer and Kocka instanced how German industrialists reacted to the American managerial type: 'It seems [in German firms] that the elaboration of formal control systems was not only constrained by structural conditions but to some extent also slowed down by the often dominant technically trained executives and middle managers.' For example, 'the leading executives of IG Farben . . . had a strong distaste for corporate management based on "statistics" and "bookkeeping," just as they [did] for demands put forth by non-technical executives to create a corporate office along the lines of American corporations such as Dupont in order to centralize control. ' "What", Carl Duisberg of Bayer asked, "are these men at the corporate office supposed to do all day long? And how in case of important decisions should they get the urgently needed contact with manufacturing and sales?" '[30]

German leadership views, it must be stressed, were as generalized in German organizations as American managerial concepts were in American organizational life at mid-twentieth century. Considering the popularity of total war in the first half of this century, this meant that German views manifested themselves in the army, just like, as Charles de Gaulle pointed out, managerialism infiltrated American military organization, except that the German and American ways stood in sharp contrast to each other. Since the Americans won the war, it is worth dwelling on the differences, to show not only how broadly generalized German leadership beliefs were in their society but why Germans, despite losing the war, could be convinced of their superiority.

The German army between the wars (1918–39) had no military academy like West Point to groom officers for predetermined fast-track elite military careers.[31] All officer aspirants in the German army applied for officer training in a regiment. To advance to candidacy, the applicant had to have an *Abitur* (qualification for university entry) and to have passed a physical and psychological test. Once accepted, the officer-aspirant underwent six months of basic training in the regular training unit of his regiment, followed by one-year regular training in a battalion. He experienced practically a complete training cycle as an enlisted man during which he 'was given a thorough insight into the varied functions of a unit, and [studied] the reaction to all orders and disciplinary matters by the troops'. During basic training, group instruction of the officer-aspirant was undertaken at organizational levels not duplicated in the U.S. army.

This happened, for example, when teaching the use of small arms and machine guns. In the American army instructors took trainees to a firing range for approximately two weeks of formal training, shooting exclusively at targets. The course, which centered wholly on weapons training, was separated from the rest of the training program. The soldier learned to master weapons but in a target-shooting mode. In the German army, while soldiers learned to fire weapons individually, too, the exercise was integrated into the regular training schedule. The soldiers would, for example, spend a day firing rifles at targets and the next day either firing machine guns or perhaps firing their rifles in concert with machine-gun crews. The following day might include a hike and tactical problems, combined with use of weapons. In this way

German training sought at all times to implant the concept of team-work into the soldiers and to coordinate men with equipment.

All entering the German army underwent this training. Conse-quently, officer candidates learned weaponry as members of a func-tioning, integrated regular army unit in company with their enlisted counterparts, thus reinforcing both the practical and the psychological character of their group preparation.[32] They learned soldiering on the job. During all this time the command granted no special favors to officer candidates. They did all service routines, including fatigue duties. This preparation enabled the officers subsequently to under-stand the mentality of the enlisted man, and to be able to judge from their own experience how a leader's actions affected men. Each officer candidate did two years of active service with the troops. Even during the war, with officers in short supply, no officer candidate could receive a commission unless he had fought in combat as an enlisted officer-aspirant for two months in order to learn the practical art of warfare and to know the men. Success depended on the officers in the candidate's regiment, who would know his skill and character best, for without their unanimous approval the commission would be denied.

Because of this training the skill of the German officer and soldier at the operational level was unsurpassed:

> Here the German combined extreme hardihood and their noted cohesion with a mastery of the *practical* arts of warfare, that resulted in an overall battle sense that transcended that of their enemies. The principal *practical* aspects of war needed to conduct successful combat can be summarized as follows: 1) sense of direction; 2) terrain appreciation, i.e., cover and concealment; and 3) accuracy of fire.[33]

German officers and soldiers excelled at night fighting, because a good sense of orientation and a knowledge of terrain permitted them to set up accurate fire. While it is best to avoid pejorative comparisons in these matters (American officers were especially capable in manage-ment of supply train and logistics) wartime accounts describing the nitty-gritty of combat frequently compared the confusion of the American field commanders to the sure sense of purpose of the Germans. American

> units lacked continuous contact, and consequently were not able to mutually support each other or make an accurate assessment of the

strength of the attacking force. Automatic weapons were not emplaced to afford fields of fire, nor were the individual riflemen dug in for effective resistance, and there was no provision made to designate targets for the artillery. When attacked they were subject to defeat in detail and the panic that comes from lack of knowledge of the situation.[34]

Fachkompetenz acquired through job-rotation and on-the-job training generated the leadership skills of German officers in combat situations. This training contrasted sharply with that at West Point or that received at the ninety-day officer-candidate installations Americans set up during the war.

German officers had learned to be soldiers before receiving their commissions. American officers had not. As late as the war in Vietnam, officer training at West Point had very little to do with the soldiers' trade. Norman Fretwell, who was First Captain in the Class of 1966, noted after his Vietnam experience:

> The army at West Point was the epitome of what the army was supposed to be. But I found [that] we were so naive about what [the army] really entailed. We'd learned a few drills at West Point and we knew how to march pretty well. But we didn't know anything . . . There was a toy-element to West Point; it's as if we were being trained to be generals, not soldiers.[35]

The German army was not so much the 'school of the nation' as the place where the officer-candidate received schooling typical in the nation. It is certainly the German approach to leadership training in industry, the tradition that the returning German soldiers encountered when they set about rebuilding business and industry after the war. And it was the leadership tradition that confronted victorious American managerialism immediately after the war.

During the Marshall Plan years German leaders, like other Europeans, streamed across the Atlantic to the American management Mecca, as experts from the Mecca came to West Germany (FGR). Professor Link catalogued the technical visits (see Table 2.1). These figures refer only to the Marshall Plan technical aid program. Non-Marshall Plan sponsored visits to the United States occurred as well. For instance, in 1949, 642 Germans in leading positions (politics, trade unions, agriculture, and other fields) traveled to America in order to study work methods in their particular specialties. In 1950, 2,426

Table 2.1. Technical programs (number of participants), FRG–USA

	Germans to USA	Americans to FRG
1949	–	2
1950	80	30
1951	109	21
1952	321	44
1953	357	17
1954	373	15
1955	305	6
1956	194	25
Combined totals	1,899	

Source: Werner Link, 'Building Coalitions: Non-governmental German–American Linkages,' in Charles S. Maier (ed.), *The Marshall Plan and Germany: West German Development within the Framework of the European Recovery Program* (New York, 1991), 312

Germans took part in study and training visits to the U.S.A., in 1952, 2,559. Link notes that the American trips made 'a deep impression [on Germans] after long years of international isolation'.[36]

Although they admired German order and efficiency, managerially confident American visitors accused German leaders of making no more effort to understand the workers than German trade unions did to understand management. After a research study-trip to Germany, one co-sponsored by U.S. and Western German governments in the mid-1950s, Thomas H. Carroll of the Ford Foundation and Thomas L. Norton of New York University recommended that a new national institute for executive development be established in Berlin. The institute would help by teaching American human relation techniques, to repair the 'enormous [defects] in human relations in German firms, some of the biggest of which do not even have personnel departments'.[37]

American disapproval of German management persisted for decades. Even in the early 1970s the American consultancy, Booz, Allen, and Hamilton, in an investigation the West German government commissioned, evaluated German management quite negatively.[38] Its well-publicized report severely censored German management for, among other things, an excessive technical outlook, a lack of strategic thinking and planning, and a failure to employ modern management methods like MBO (Management by Objective) or Investment Portfolio Diversification. Inasmuch as these were American management techniques, the Booz, Allen, and Hamilton consultants merely measured German management against an American benchmark and found it wanting.

Since the American consultancy firm issued this negative report in 1973, it is obvious what the German managerial response had been to the proselytizing American management expert immediately post-war. After initial enthusiasm, German ardor for American managerialism cooled. This statement does not apply to American management techniques and methods. Computerized mathematical model-building, concern for group dynamics, much of which Americans pioneered and developed, continued to draw German attention. Their popularity in Germany can easily be discerned by inspecting the instruction manuals of the most significant post-experience management educational association in Germany (the *Wuppertaler Kreis*).[39] These manuals show continuing American influence right into the mid-1970s.

Nonetheless, Germans failed to develop two essential attributes of American managerialism. One was the partnership that American management established with academic business schools, the other the management idea itself.

Management Education without Business Schools

The management education issue in Germany differed somewhat from that in engineering education. German engineering faculties in technical *Hochschulen* have worked closely with industry for decades.[40] In nontechnical business studies, however, the connection between higher education and business praxis has always been tenuous. The disparity makes sense. If technically oriented German managers could easily perceive the usefulness of science to engineering, its usefulness to commerce was much less obvious. But professorial attitudes also kept academic business studies and business praxis apart.

German universities at the turn of the century had attained great prestige because of their dedication to *Wissenschaft*, the value-free pursuit of 'scientific' truth through systematic research. The footnote, the article, the Ph.D. thesis, the *Habilitationsschrift*, the original contribution to knowledge, were an integral part of this world. If business studies (*Betriebswirtschaftslehre, BWL*) were to gain status and respectability in the university, it had to become a *Wissenschaft*. Consequently, the commerce institutes (*Handelshochschulen*) that emerged in Germany about the same time that Americans created their first business schools faced a hard choice: either to serve business praxis or honor the canons of *Wissenschaft*. Arguments raged for years among the fledgling business economists about the choice, and *Wissenschaft* won.

It won not so much because the academic business economists denied the need to serve business praxis but because they decided to satisfy its *Wissenschaft* requirement first in order to gain acceptance in the university community. To become a professor of *BWL* in 1950 the student had to have an *Abitur* (earned after thirteen years of schooling), followed by four to five years of study for a first degree (*Dipl.-Kaufm.*). Then the graduate student had to complete two more degrees, a doctorate and a *Habilitationsschrift*. The *Habilitationsschrift*, not the doctorate, enabled him to become a professor. Since this rigorous and lengthy study program eliminated the possibility of prolonged work experience, the academically highly qualified person landed in a professor's chair without having had any real contact with active management. Then, the necessity for the young professor to publish the academically respectable books essential to a career kept prolonged contacts with firms to a minimum. Or, if he did establish contacts, their purpose had to be to advance *Wissenschaft*, not to solve practical business problems.

German businessmen visiting America after the war learned much about the American business school, enough certainly to know that it differed considerably in its interaction with business from German faculties of business economics. After attending a Harvard Senior Executive course, Dr. Ludwig Vaubel noted in his widely read description of the experience (*Unternehmer gehen zur Schule*, Entrepreneurs go to School):

> The conditions in the Harvard Business School are particularly favorable because an excellent teaching staff assembled a rich case material over decades that is at the disposal of the business school. . . . But this can

succeed only if the material serves practical business needs . . . , a task which the *Hochschule* tradition in Germany . . . does not fulfill.[41]

So the German businessman had either to change German academia along American lines, or to do something else.

Efforts to change ran into serious opposition within an academic community that refused to let *Wissenschaft* be superseded by practicality. The following exchange (1965) between businessman Hans Dichgans and a group (twenty) of university business economists, whom he criticized, reveals the tenor of academic resistance. Dichgans had complained in public that German business economics was not willing to be judged on how well it accommodated business. 'Everything must above all serve an abstract idea of higher science. Our young professors have less and less contact with praxis.'[42] He recommended that more professors work for extended periods in business and industry and that their best students prepare for business rather than academic careers. Students 'should learn enough in a three-year course to qualify for a beginning position in the economy, from which they could then improve their knowledge through post-experience education.' The reforms Dichgans suggested to the German professors at this meeting would have seemed quite acceptable and desirable to people in American business schools.

The professors were not insensitive to the call for more contacts between business and industry, but they could not imagine accomplishing it in the manner Dichgans outlined. To the idea that professors acquire practical experience Professor Wolfgang Kilger, of Saarbrücken University, replied that 'for both academics and practicing managers the crucial years in a career occurred between ages thirty and forty. . . . As a young professor he . . . had to devote efforts to academic science, so there was not much time to work in business.' Professors also objected to Dichgans's suggestion that the *Habilitationsschrift* be eliminated as a requirement for a professorship in order to attract more men from business into academia.[43] One observed that a man who had worked for years as an accountant was ill-suited to teach academic accounting. Another pointed out that 'business does not understand reality, which is getting more complicated every day'. ' . . . *Praktiker* need the professors and their science because of its abstractions', or, as another professor explained, precisely because most scientists are interested in generalities, not, like the *Praktiker*, in particulars.

This dialogue of the deaf impeded American-style business educational reform. There was one partial success. In 1968 the Universitäts Seminar der Wirtschaft (USW), which moved into Schloss Grache in 1976, began operations. The USW was not strictly speaking a U.S.-type business school. It was only a 'neutral' ground established between university and praxis, an institution of continuing education to which companies posted active managers to take short courses and to which university faculties posted their professors—on temporary duty assignment—to teach these courses, along with a teaching faculty also drawn from government and business. No permanent teaching and research corps existed at USW, and there was no course equivalent of the two-year American MBA. The MBA taught-course never caught on in postwar German management education.

For management education, therefore, the Germans had to do that 'something else'. And this meant following their own educational traditions. The German business economist Karl-Heinz Ackermann remarked that educationally Germans distinguish between making people *berufsfähig* (job able) and *berufsfertig* (job ready). They also distinguish between imparting *Wissen* (knowledge) and *Können* (skill). Making people *berufsfähig* is what academic faculties of business economics do, that is, they make people able to do a job by teaching them how to analyze, to plan, and to think in specialized fields of knowledge like finance, marketing, accounting, and insurance. Such capacities are what Germans have in mind when they speak of a 'scientific' education; it provides a *Denkschulung* (schooling of the mind). They never pretend, therefore, that this university *Denkschulung* actually trains people to manage. It only helps them to become capable of managing. People in praxis, too, often accept this educational distinction, even Hans Dichgans. 'It is not readiness to work (*Berufsfertigkeit*) that business and industry expect to find in the graduate', he said, 'but the capacity (*Fähigkeit*) during special training in praxis quickly to make himself occupationally ready (*berufsfertig*).'[44] According to this view, to concentrate on *Denkschulung* is, from the viewpoint of praxis, not a bad thing, because it creates people who can quickly absorb what the firm wishes them to learn on the job.

If business and industry were prepared to let academia provide the *Denkschulung* for unexperienced undergraduates, they were ready and willing themselves to arrange post-experience management education. Most of it occurred on the job, but large firms sometimes added management training to their usually large palette of technical and commercial apprenticeship programs. Siemens, Lufthansa, and others operate their own renowned in-house training schools. The firms themselves, joined by business, industrial, trade, or professional groups, sponsored management education in other venues. In 1955 the first Baden-Baden Managers Conference (*Unternehmer-Gespräch*) gathered groups of senior managers for relatively unstructured discussions among themselves about management. The same year the German Association for the Advancement of Continuing Management Education—the Wuppertaler Kreis—came into existence; seven important trade and professional organizations joined this association, including the *RKW*, *REFA*, and *VDI*, none of which had academic credentials, and all of which had been involved in post-experience education for years.[45]

People in these associations studied American management literature; based on it, they organized a series of short courses (three to five days) for active managers at various installations all over the Federal Republic. German professors participated individually in this post-experience education, lecturing part-time in some field of expertise. Most of the instructors, however, came from the ranks of active managers. German business and industrial managers kept a tight rein on continuing education, outside the firm as well as within. German post-experience management education, unlike its American counterpart, really excluded academia.

Leadership without Management

Postwar Americans sought to make management the 'fourth' factor of production by cultivating the dogma of management in both the firm and society. German entrepreneurs, however, fostered job competence and individual responsibility in their underlings, less through codified forms of management knowledge than intuition and *Kniff* (knowing the ropes). While Americans stressed managerial functions, adding ever new layers to the management team, German entrepreneurs let it be known, by making personnel, sales, advertising, and public relations staff, rather than line positions, that people in them were not 'key players' in the organization. When a technical director, member of the managing board of a firm with 8,500 employees, interviewed every new job applicant personally, he made a statement about leadership style. He, not the Personnel Department, handled personnel. Success did not depend on sales techniques and ballyhoo, but on building a quality product and delivering it on time: success depended on *Fachkompetenz* and personal leadership. Leaders established personal ties with the led.

In short, while in the early 1950s German business and industrial leaders had been impressed with American management techniques, they eventually rejected American managerialism ('God save us from the professional managers', Hartmann reports one commenting).[46] Within management Germans singled out Human Resource Management as a tool of impersonal manipulation.[47] 'What do the Americans have in their human and public relations?' asked a German business leader rhetorically. 'They have precisely no relations. Workers and entrepreneurs only work for dollars. By contrast, here we can move our people at a fast pace (*Husarenritte*). Here we have real contact between superior and subordinate. This might seem a bit patriarchal at times. But our people want to know those at the top personally.'[48] Considering the workers' intense struggle for co-determination, this entrepreneur romanticized employer–employee relations. But his view constituted no less a rejection of American thinking. Hartmann observed that '[American Human Relations Management] had become the fashionable import in the early 1950s, . . . [after which] this bull market turned bearish, so that today one sees this program only as a typical and scarcely exportable product of American economic culture'.[49] American human relations techniques developed in America, Hartmann concluded, 'are no longer spoken of [in Germany] today (1963)'.[50]

The Emergence of the German
Management Alternative

Although postwar German management accepted co-determination and spurned American managerialism, the German managerial alternative did not immediately take shape. Even if legally empowered to participate in some management decision-making, the ability of employee representatives to do so depended on their skill and knowledgeability. Unless the employee representatives sitting on supervisory boards, works councils, economic committees, or at the head of trade union groups understood the legal and technical dimensions of managerial issues, they could not hope to serve effectively the interests of their constituents and the firm. Authority to be meaningful required the education and training of those legally empowered. The third historical moment in the creation of the German managerial alternative came, therefore, when the education and training of employee representatives began to take place seriously. This happened during the Social Democratic ascendancy of the late 1960s and early 1970s.

SPD political power, if limited by the FDP partnership, is important because the legislation the coalition passed spurred management change. The Works Constitution Act of 1972, for example, although leaving stockholders in control of management on 'economic' issues, did broaden and regularize works council governance rights in social and health matters. More importantly, that Act also forced employers to allow works councilors, members of economic councils, and supervisory board members to take extramural courses designed to help employee representatives master the technically complicated issues with which co-determination compelled them to deal.[51]

The co-determination law of 1976, even though it too preserved stockholder supremacy on supervisory boards, increased the number of employee-elected representatives from one-third to one-half of the board membership (steel and coal firms were still regulated by the 1951 act).[52] Staunch defenders of co-determination did not like the law for two reasons: (1) the stockholders controlled the tie-breaking vote in cases of a deadlock between employee and stockholder representatives on supervisory boards; (2) the employee representative on a supervisory board could not appoint the Labor Director to a Managing Board (*Vorstand*). The law, in short, still did not give employee representatives on supervisory boards equal power with stockholder representatives. Advocates of co-determination wanted the 'parity' that the 1951 law provided for employee and stockholder representatives in the steel and coal industry. If German supporters of co-determination were unhappy with the 1976 legislation, so were the Americans, but for opposite reasons. American management reacted hostilely to the measure because it went too far. The American Chamber of Commerce in Frankfurt-am-Main reported general dissatisfaction with the proposed legislation in German branches of American-based firms. Henry Ford II, while visiting Ford's German Works, pointedly rejected this interference with management's right to manage.[53] Nonetheless, German trade unions, social democrats, and liberals, drawing upon their own traditions, ignored these American protests and enacted the law.

Coincidentally, the crisis in higher education that erupted in the student protest movement of the late 1960s hastened educational reform. The German universities during the period of postwar economic growth had remained essentially unreformed places following the *Wissenschaft* tradition in research and teaching. The German trade unions in league with the Social Democratic Party set out to increase student numbers in higher education and to make German *Hochschulen* socially responsive institutions, that is, to make them institutions that served community needs as well as ones that sought 'scientific truth'.[54]

Because in the German Federal Republic education is constitutionally under the jurisdiction of the individual states, SPD-governed ones, in which trade unions usually flourished, led the reform quest. In higher education reformers concentrated on creating *Gesamthochschulen*, megauniversities. They brought old and prestigious German universities into a university amalgamate that included new universities, either created from scratch or from the old sub-university educational sector, by turning *pädagogische Hochschulen* into universities or elevating technical and commercial *Fachschulen* into *Fachhochschulen*.[55] After the transformation, graduates from the former sub-university sector received *Hochschule* degrees. For example, the *graduierter Ingenieur* now became a *Dipl.-Ing.*, the same title that engineering graduates from universities received, although the designation FH was appended (*Dipl.-Ing. FH*) to retain a pejorative distinction. The law also permitted instructors in the 'new' *Fachhochschulen* to call themselves 'professors'.

Consequent to reform, the number of people attending *Hochschulen* increased rapidly, both in absolute numbers and as a percentage of the population. Among the 914,000 students in West German *Hochschulen* in 1977 (18.4% of the age cohort), 150,000 attended *Fachhochschulen*. They were students who, before the *Fachschulen* acquired *Hochschule* status, would not have been counted as university-level students. Their presence among *Hochschule* students inflates the amount of actual growth. Still, figuring that in 1963 only 150,000 (7.6% of the age cohort) studied in West German *Hochschulen*, the reforms had wrought considerable change, change that continued into the 1980s and beyond.

This educational reform made little immediate difference to working-class children. Sylvia Verdier points out that in 1975 only 7–8 percent of the students in *Hochschulen* came from working-class families.[56] The increased numbers of 'university' degree holders among the workers could also be attributed to nomenclature sleight of hand, as, for instance, when turning *Fachschulen* into *Fachhochschulen* gave students from the working classes 'university' degrees.

But the educational expansion had an unexpected effect that favored employees involved in co-determination: because it proved impossible to absorb so many new *Hochschule* graduates into traditional leadership positions, they had to take regular jobs in office and factory. Consequently, the general educational level of the workforce rose as *Hochschule* graduates entered positions that heretofore no 'educated' person would have held. Verdier observed that most *Hochschule* graduates got white-collar jobs (*Angestellten*) and that among them most were locked into middle-range white-collar positions: only three percent of *Hochschule* graduates rose to 'leading positions' as defined by the Works Constitution Act. Hence, *Hochschule* graduates increasingly could be found on the employee, as opposed to the managerial, side of the fence, as graduates moved into works councils and economics committees.[57]

If an educational upgrading of the working population marked this period of change, so did a change in people's views about what could be expected from the work process. During the 1950s West German workers were happy just to be fully employed. Although in industry most of them still worked in high-skill, low-volume industrial production, more of them than ever before took jobs in American inspired and pioneered mass-production industries, in which Taylorist work processes reigned. In these factories the managerial control system resembled a pyramid: at the top a manager, often making decisions alone, and other top managers responsible for different departments; below in each department more functionally determined subdepartments, led by a single person; authority moving from top down and responsibility from the bottom up. The process through which the motivation of the workforce took place followed the same one-way street top down, with only a small amount of counter-movement from the employees, upwards through skilled workers, foremen, *Meister* towards the top. There was not much room for worker input into job design and work process or for worker initiative, or worker participation of any sort in the system.

As younger workers became better educated and German firms engaged fewer foreign workers, 'the pressure grew stronger in the direction of [creating] more discriminating (*anspruchsvoller*) work . . . as well as work that was not too taxing and unhealthy'.[58] Demand for change would not have gotten far without employees' voices reaching some sympathetic ears. They did, in SPD-led governments, state and federal, in trade unions, works councils, and even within employer ranks. For the employers realized by the late 1960s that Taylorist work methods had reached their productivity limits in assembly-line work, indeed, as Gerhard Leminsky phrased it, 'in all forms of work that were closely tied to time-cadences, especially in short series production, in production which required high quality, and in production that needed frequent model changes'.[59] Something had to be done.

Granted that Taylorism had seen its day, conflicting interest nonetheless came into play when seeking alternatives. The employers had to make sure that changes in the work process, if they benefited the workers, did not reduce productivity levels from those attained under the Taylorist regime; the workers had to be assured that any change in work process operated to their advantage, that is, were not just speed-ups, another form of Taylorism. But 'deconstructing' Taylorism also entailed a multitude of managerial problems that went beyond conflict of interest: technical, organizational, personnel, and pedagogical questions, questions of work layout, of people management—all problems of great complexity which had to be solved if the assembly lines could be abandoned in favor of cooperative work in groups.

In the early 1970s, the Federal government, inspired by some work process reforms in Scandinavia (primarily at Volvo), sponsored a work-study program under the nomenclature 'Humanization of Work' (Humanisierung der Arbeit, HdA). It was housed primarily in the Federal Ministry of Research and Technology, the BMFT.[60] To bring employers, trade unions and works councils, scientists and technologists, and bureaucrats together, the BMFT financed pilot projects in firms and well-known research institutes to promote productivity through the 'humanization' of work process. The German trade unions held back somewhat suspiciously until 1974, when they decided to join the program. Gerhard Leminsky, who was involved, underlined the complexities. For employers the humanization of work program entailed changing production processes which had to be coordinated between a firm's headquarters, department management, staff and production departments, and between technicians, personnel planners, and the works councils. Ministerial bureaucrats suffered because of conflicting jurisdictions: the Ministry of Labor, having never done much research of a technical and scientific nature, had to be left out of the project, and the Ministry of Research and Technology, with little experience with labor but much in technical and scientific research, had to take over.

The scientists, leaving their ivory-tower research institutes for the firm, found themselves applying 'scientific standards' and recommending changes that, although scientifically sound, violated factory rules that were embedded in works constitution acts or written up in collective agreements that had been concluded between trade unions and employers. Many hapless and helpless scientists discovered that employers or work councils interpreted what seemed to scientists to be value-free data in a totally partisan fashion. The 'objective' facts had been dragged into the conflict between management and labor.[61]

Indeed, as the scientists attempted to use 'science' in this work-humanizing process, four problem sources distinctly emerged:

1. Scientists did not, in their education and research, take the social dimension into consideration.

2. The scientists, working within the norms and standards of their disciplines, did not speak the same language as trade unionists or works councilors, working with the tension-filled employee–employer realities of organizations.

3. The 'Taylorization' of science, its division into disciplines that do not correspond to the problem areas encountered in praxis, hindered effective work. The solution of real problems required information drawn from many disciplines.

4. Scientists, because of their lack of contact with working people, set mistaken goals for themselves and pursued them with methods that were ill-suited to solving people-related work process problems. In short, this Humanization of Work program generated within it almost all the problem fields that post-Taylorist work reorganization presented to employers, bureaucrats, and scientists.

As for employees, they faced two big difficulties when dealing with scientists, bureaucrats, and employers. One was a legal problem. In the 1970s both trade unions and works councils defended employee interests. They were, however, legally separate bodies, with separate jurisdictions. The German trade unions were industrial unions, that is they were organized on an industry-wide basis, so that all people in an industry joined one union. This stopped jurisdictional fights of the sort so frequently encountered in America and Great Britain. There were sixteen major industrial unions in West Germany after the war, which, although independent, were federated in one central organization, the DGB. Unions mainly negotiated wage agreements, concluded through collective bargaining between unions and employers' federations, at the regional level.[62] Before reaching regional settlements there are lots of informal discussions between the DGB, the employer federation (BDA), the government, and the State Bank (Bundesbank) because the regional agreements set the broad percentage increase that most sectors of the economy follow within one or two percentage points. The wages of workers in nonunion as well as union firms are tied to the settlement. This prevents the great wage gaps from opening up between union and nonunion workers that happens regularly in the United States. Although the union–employer wage settlements are very important, none of this activity regulates the work process in office and plant. They are legally co-determined not between unions and management but between the works councils and management.

Therefore, since trade unions had no legal authority within the firm, their ability directly to participate in managerial decision-making about work process depended on the influence they could gain in works councils. Although union influence predominated in works councils where militant unions members were elected, in this two-tier system of workers' representation, the works councils had the legal jurisdiction, through works constitution acts, to deal with management in the operations of the firm.

The rights and prerogatives that the legislation gave works councils varied. Where the issue was the protection of employee health and safety, the law empowered works councils to co-determine policy and program with management or it gave works councils veto power over employer decisions: measures to prevent work-accident and job-related illness, to eliminate hazardous materials from the work place, and so forth. To establish health and safety norms, the works councils needed scientific knowledge drawn from ergonomics, work psychology, work pedagogy, hygiene, and organizational psychology. To carry out their mandate under the law, works councils had to develop the requisite expertise or call in consultants (*Referenten, Sachverständiger*). It was the same body of knowledge that Human Resource managers used in the United States, only the works councils approached it from the employees' perspective.

Works councils also co-determined pay rates (piece rates and bonuses) not covered in the trade union–employer agreements. They set the hours (but not the number of hours) of the work day. But generally in matters concerning the running of the firm, works councils had no veto rights or even rights of co-determination. Management had by law to inform the works councils about plans to rationalize work methods or change organizational structures. But the management process under the law made works councils reactive rather than proactive organs. The law required that management-proposed business, technical, and organizational changes or management plans to implement new performance and behavior surveillance methods not violate human rights (works councils could 'soften' or attenuate the abuses if they did). Works council approval was necessary, too, for the implementation of apprenticeship and training programs, an important right since the adoption of new technologies and/or the installation of work processes often required training.

Hans Rehhan described how the reactive mode of behavior limited the role of works councils in the management process. He choose an investment planning case to illustrate his point. Investment planning seldom

> develops in a straight line. First the goal is described in general terms. But then precise planning usually calls for the cooperative work of many functional areas: sales people, business economists, finance planners, production engineers, environmental and safety engineers. Each representative of a specialty brings a particular point of view to the planning process. . . . The result is a complicated series of compromises.[63]

It is a series, moreover, in which the viewpoint of the works council, whose mission is to make sure the process creates responsible and legal forms of human work (*menschengerechte Arbeitsgestaltung*), is excluded until late in the game. Then, after all the technical, economic, and organizational compromises have been made, 'all the representatives that arrived at these hard fought compromises unite against the representatives of [the works council]'. The best procedure obviously would be to include works council viewpoints in the investment planning process from the beginning—a solution, however, requiring management to accept the works councils' jurisdiction in the management process and the works council to command a level of skills permitting it to work usefully with the various experts throughout every stage of the planning process. Neither condition prevailed in 1970, but subsequently much progress has been made in the development of both.

If legal restrictions limited works-council jurisdiction, a lack of capacity restricted its ability to exploit the opportunities the law presented. Knowledge about health and hygiene had always been important to employee representatives. They did their best work on these issues. Ignorance about work processes had hardly mattered under Taylorist discipline. After consulting with works councilors and dutifully listening to the councilors' suggestions, management would implement whatever work processes and new technologies it pleased. But the collapse of Taylorism brought the introduction of group work, job enrichment schemes, and the like. The works councils and unions had to be knowledgeable, if they were to participate in the work planning and decision-making of the new regime. That was the point Leminsky made when analyzing the involvement of scientists in the Humanization of Work program.

Without this knowledge the employee representatives were clearly disadvantaged. 'On one side of the negotiation table', the IG Metall trade unionist Hans Preiss observed, 'sits the employer with hundreds of semesters of university studies, on the other, works councilors and youth representatives to defend the interest of employees with only quick, cram courses under their belts.'[64] Since paragraphs ninety and ninety-one of the Works Constitutions Act specified that changes in the regulation of work conditions must be based on 'solid knowledge of the sciences of work' (*gesicherte arbeitswissenschaftliche Erkenntnisse*), ignorant employee representatives were not equal partners in work process reforms. Or, as another trade union spokesmen commented,

> If we ask our colleagues in the Education Center why thousands each year ask for seminar places, despite long waiting lists and increased conflict with employers about release time, the answer comes from the daily life of works councilors, shop stewards, and youth representatives. Here, in the life of the firm, where conflict is unavoidable, they find themselves saddled with tasks for which they are insufficiently prepared. If works council business were reduced uniquely to knowledge of laws and regulations, more than thirty texts would have to be mastered. Considering that on the other [employer's] side most people have several semesters' professional study and special training, then the knowledge gap at the outset between the different interest-representatives is clear.[65]

During this reform period unions, works councils, government, and schools worked hard to close this 'capability' gap.

The dual nature of employee representation complicated the task. The fact that all employees within a firm voted for the works councils and only trade union members elected union leaders meant that they did not have the same constituencies. Indeed, employers usually favored works councils to trade unions because the former's constituency was the firm. Works councilors were not outsiders. If trade unions wanted to exercise influence within the works councils they had to win the support of that firm's employees, and this meant that they had to pay close attention to issues that were important to people in the firm, many of whom were not union members. West German unions won employees over in works council elections, for as Lowell Turner remarked, 'over eighty percent of all works councilors are union members, and the overwhelming majority of these are members of one of the sixteen industrial unions of the DGB'.[66]

Thus a combination of forces spurred efforts to educate employees and their representatives. Probably the most important was the opportunity for education itself, established through the proviso in the 1972 Works Constitution Act that guaranteed employee representatives release time from work for continuing education. To protect union interests and what was perceived to be the interest of the employees, unions believed that the training of works councilors should not just be done in *Hochschulen*. Indeed, Kurt Johannson, a union activist from an active union (IG Metall) stated that *Hochschulen* should not even try to play a 'neutral' role in the continuing education of works councilors: 'This "neutrality" can only serve the interest of the employer and unions must resist this idea energetically.'[67] Accordingly, the DGB, which already had a *Bundeschule* operating in Springe, got involved, through this school, in educating the teachers who would teach the works councilors, primarily in union establishments, about co-determination matters.

The most important of the union-run establishments was undoubtedly IG Metall's Education Center at Sprockhövel. During the first four years after it opened in 1971, Sprockhövel welcomed 25,000 visitors, most probably from trade unions, both German and foreign, but also experts and scientists 'in big numbers' (*in starker Masse*). Indeed Sprockhövel quickly gained recognition, even in the 'employer' press, as a 'model Adult education school'.[68] In 1971 26,080 seminar participants (works councilors, youth representatives, shop stewards) came to Sprockhövel to attend the forty-four types of seminars (2,000 works councilors and youth representatives the first two years took seminars just on labor's legal rights under co-determination).[69] By 1977, according to an IG Metall poll, almost twice as many people

(43,000) sought seminar places at Sprockhövel as the installation could accommodate (25,000).[70]

Still, as Ute Cabarusm, Jürgen Jöns, and Gerd Syben affirmed, 'those in unions . . . could only establish the concept of the Humanization of Work and use and expand the possibilities of co-determination if workers had the scientific-technical intelligence necessary to work for these concepts'.[71] Since the unions could not provide this technical-scientific instruction exclusively in their own educational programs, they turned increasingly to *Hochschulen* for help. The traditional universities, with their emphasis on value-free research and teaching, eschewed trade-union advances. Conservative politicians and employers' associations supported their 'independence'. For this reason, and because the unions were themselves careful to choose the right partners, the effort to broaden the educational horizons of works councilors and other employee representatives generally took place in new universities operating in industrial districts that were especially sensitive to union and SPD pressure, or in *Hochschulen* raised from sub-university status in SPD-run states.

This frequently meant that the unions concluded education agreements with institutions with which they had long-standing relations. This happened at the Hochschule für Wirtschaft und Politik (HWP) in Hamburg. This school, which changed its name several times, from the Academie für Gemeinschaft, through the Academie für Wirtschaft und Politik, to become, in 1970, the Hochschule für Wirtschaft und Politik, had been established with union support in 1945. An 'autonomous scientific institution', the HWP had recruited working-class youths from almost all occupations. Many of these young people, who had done apprenticeship, did not have an *Abitur*, the secondary school leaving certificate usually required for university study. So HWP allowed students to enter through examination. In the mid-1970s one-sixth of HWP's 900 students were Hans-Böckler-Stiftung grantees (a trade union-supported scholarship foundation); most of the faculty at HWP were members of a DGB-affiliated teacher's union; and the names of many HWP graduates could be found on 'the list of prominent trade union people'. It was safe and easy for trade unions to enter into adult education agreements with HWP.

Elsewhere, in Oldenburg (Lower Saxony) the DGB in the early 1960s had participated in a series of weekend seminars arranged through the Pädagogische Hochschule. When the Pädagogische Hochschule in the era of reform turned into Oldenburg University, unions comfortably concluded cooperative educational agreements with the new university just as they had done with the former Pädagogische Hochschule. Ditto for the Ruhr University at Bochum, which had also been a Pädagogische Hochschule, the Fachhochschule at Dortmund, the Fachhochschule and Pädagogische Hochschule in Saarbrücken, the Freie-Universität in Berlin, and, although an older and greatly admired institution, the Berlin Technical University (Charlottenburg).

These agreements and others provided for adult education. The Departments of Psychology and Sociology in Berlin's Freie Universität started seminars of a week's duration on 'Psychology for Working Unions' for works councilors, personnel councilors, shop stewards, members of supervisory boards, and youth representatives. Participants learned 'Trainer feedback, role-playing,' and negotiating and discussion-leading techniques. The courses were 'very highly prized'.[72] The Technical University in Berlin and IG Metall developed a lecture series on 'Rationalization: Danger and Necessity', and organized adult seminars on how decision theory and electronic data affect employees. And, just to stay in Berlin, the Hochschule für Wirtschaft in 1976 introduced seminars on labor laws that works councilors attended.

In Oldenburg, a joint committee of union representatives and professors organized seminars for works councilors. Held twice yearly, the seminars used educational materials taken from IG Chemie, the chemical industry's union, specifically from its training program for works councilors. The same planning committee instituted a program to evaluate the 'learning effectiveness' of the IG Chemie's training programs. In 1972 IG Metall worked out a cooperative course for works councilors with the Ruhr University that was taught partly in university facilities in Bochum and partly in the union's Education Center at Sprockhövel. Adi Ostertag and Lothar Zimmermann from Sprockhövel gave seminars in the university's social science department on 'unions and co-determination' that hundreds of students attended over a nine-semester period.

In Dortmund (1970) at the Fachhochschule the architecture department attempted to 'integrate knowledge from the "sciences of work"' (*arbeitswissenschaftliche Erkenntnisse*) into the educational program of architects; and the Pädagogische Hochschule organized seminars composed for works councilors, youth representatives, and professors that dealt with 'training in unions'; in 1973 the Fachhochschule in Saarbrücken, in cooperation with the Chamber of Labor (Arbeitskammer) of the Saarland, developed a course on ergonomics for the department of engineering, and the Pedagogical *Hochschule* created a didactic model for adult education. This cooperation between unions and *Hochschulen*, more examples of which could easily be cited, clearly shows the scope and intent of the trade unions' adult education activity. Although limited geographically mostly to SPD-run states and within them to non-university *Hochschulen* and universities of modest reputation, it amounted to a significant educational effort to raise the 'scientific' knowledge quotient and the general educational culture of union representatives and works councilors.

Unions and universities did not take up the educational mission alone. The works constitution acts admonished employers and employees to work together in good faith in order to promote common interests. Honoring the spirit of the legislation, employers set out to teach their management about co-determination. Furthermore, inasmuch as employers rejected the idea that works councils represented the unions, the management side also felt obliged to instruct the employee representatives about co-determination. So during this era of reform, management, professional groups, and employer associations began to sponsor courses on co-determination for employee representatives. Sometimes management conducted a short course in the firm, but usually it sent employees to outside courses given in post-experience management education establishments. The Wuppertaler Kreis's 1977 Manual on Management Post-Experience Education lists courses for Germany. A content analysis of the manual's offerings is somewhat tedious reading but important because it shows how hard management education people worked in the 1970s to give life to the laws on co-determination.

The manual describes the teaching activities of thirty-two institutions that belonged to the Wuppertaler Kreis that year (1977). Among them ranked West Germany's most famous post-experience educators, some like RKW and REFA dating back to the interwar period, others like the University Economic Seminar (USW) of more recent origins.[73]

The thirty-two institutions provided post-experience education in courses of short duration to hundreds of thousands of *Praktikern* each year; their accumulated students over the years amounted to millions. All these educational associations—but especially the Baden-Baden Conference (*Gespräch*) and USW—offered management courses to top management; all gave special management courses to beginning managers. But their educational offerings reached groups lower down the managerial ladder than American management courses do. Here are some examples.

The German Chemical Industry Management Education Association (ACHI), aside from its seminars for top and middle management, offered a one-week course on management, a *Meistertreffen*, and a *Seminar für Meister und Betriebsassistenten* for foremen-level crafts-men.[74] The Educational Foundation of the Bavarian Economy (BBW) ran, besides its seminars for top managers, management seminars for secretaries, foremen, and *Meister*; the Educational Foundation of the North Rhine-Westphalian Economy (BWHF) gave management courses to *Meister* as well as to upper management; the Educational Foundation for the Palatinate (BWRP), aside from middle management and upper management seminars, offered management seminars of three days' duration each to *Meister*, foremen, and secretaries; the Technische Akademie Esslingen (TAE), again in addition to regular middle management and upper management courses, offered a two-day course on 'Leadership for Foremen and *Meister*' taught by a professor from a *Fachhochschule*. And so forth, for this list of courses only samples the management education possibilities these establishments presented to people from the top, down to the lowest levels in the management chain.

These courses covered a wide range of management issues, including co-determination. For example: The USW ten-week management course devoted part of the ninth week to teaching staff and line managers with personnel responsibilities about co-determination. This seminar's stated goal was: 'analyze the leadership tasks arising from the works councils' right to co-determination and cooperation (*Mitwirkungsrecht*). The special seminar on labor law and the Works Constitution Act (*Betriebsverfassungsgesetz*) at the Technische Akademie Wuppertal detailed the rights of works councils; at the Schleswig-Holstein Society for Education and Advancement (STFG) there was a

Meister seminar on 'Labor Law' and a 'specific management seminar' on 'labor law fundamentals for management'. The Management Akademie München (MAM) held three-day seminars on co-determination while the Management Institute for Continuing Education (IMA) in its two-week management seminars devoted part of the second week to 'Co-determination, Entrepreneurial Performance, and Co-worker Responsibility'.[75] A final example of this burgeoning management interest in co-determination: Wuppertaler Kreis member BWRP offered a seminar to managers specially charged to work with employee representatives that examined 'the co-determination of works councils in personnel, social, and economic matters'. It also held seminars for *Meister* (of two and a half days) on 'learning to work realistically with works councils'.

The institutions in the Wuppertaler Kreis, in their zeal to educate management about co-determination, did not forget to enlighten the workers' representatives, too. Indeed, it was as if, in organizing these courses and seminars, institutions that had traditionally been identified with management had come to recognize that works councils had become part of management. The following are examples of courses for employee representatives in the 1977 *Handbuch*.

The BBW presented two five-day seminars: one for works councilors, another for works councilors who were members of supervisory boards. The following subjects were covered in one seminar's sessions:

1. The enterprise and firm as field of operation for works councils; the firm's constitution; selected problems in business praxis; introduction to labor law; cooperative work in the firm.

2. The enterprise in competition; works councils and business accounting; current questions in labor law; the organization of the activities of works councils; selected aspects of labor and social medicine.

3. The organization of the economy; works councils and the personnel field in the firm. Peculiarities of certain groups in the firm; selected questions in labor law; the social order in the German Federal Republic.

4. The organization of the firm; performance evaluation and the science of evaluation; workers and management relations in the firm;

negotiation procedures of works councils; work safety as the province of works councils.

The Federal Association of Young Entrepreneurs (BJU) offered a one-week course entitled 'works council seminars, type A, B, and C' whose purpose was 'to support the works councils in carrying out their tasks defined in the Works Constitution Act and to provide information about the environment that especially influences events in the firms'.[76] The material covered included (1) group dynamics: cooperation and group behavior/motivation and leadership/command and request, and (2) decision-making in groups, expertise covered: the essential rules of labor law/protection from dismissal, work order, maternity leave, child labor law. Other subjects handled were: youth representative committees, apprenticeship and training, cooperation and co-determination for employees; elementary economics, the employment market, the economy and society; origins, goals, tactics, and strategies of nuisance groups, the reaction to them of works councils.

Another member of the Wuppertaler Kreis, the German Society for Personnel Management (DGFP) began offering twenty-seven one-week 'works council seminars' in 1972, wherein they taught the works councilors about labor law and certain special knowledge about the selection and improvement of personnel, in order for works councilors to learn to appreciate fully the concepts and measures developed in human resource management.[77] DGFP offered additional seminars in specific functional areas of concern to works councils, for example for works councilors on committees dealing with pay questions, for works councilors on personnel committees, for young adult representatives on works councils, for works councilors sitting on the economic committees (*Wirtschaftsausschusses*).

Backed by legislative authority, the works councils had to organize themselves effectively into specialized work groups in various jurisdictions if they were to come to grips with their problems. The members of the Wuppertaler Kreis, both in their seminars and courses for managers (down the line through *Meister* and foremen) and for employee representatives, effectively fomented cooperation among all parties involved in the new co-determination management regime.

During the 1970s this post-experience educational effort turned the shotgun wedding, forced on employees and employers by the earlier passage of co-determination laws and works constitution acts, into living relationships. Love there may not have been between the partners, but there was respect. Or, as Mario Helfert and Gundrun Trautwein-Kalms observed about the Humanization of Work program (*HdA*), 'the fights over poor working conditions did not become easier because of the *HdA* but because of it the unions' discussions of the issues became much more thorough and began much earlier than they would have done before. This made the unions' input better, both in terms of quality and perhaps of outcome.'[78] Successful efforts to raise the general educational level of the working population and to inform the trade union representatives and works councilors about the complexities of their tasks made co-determination possible.

By the late 1970s, then, a German alternative to American management had appeared. It drew strength from two major sources: from customary German ideas about leadership and from co-determination. American management gurus and their European disciples misread these German management developments.[79] They thought German leadership lacked, as Peter Lawrence states it, 'planning and control, analysis, especially quantitative analysis, and marketing and business strategy, together with all the systems and techniques that support them'.[80] Since the Americans identified good management with these capacities, and good management education with an educational institution's ability to impart them, those who succumbed to the American management mystique traced German managerial incapacities to educational roots.

It is rather astonishing to observe the extent to which American managerialism has gained a hold on people's minds, for this hold has stopped them from appreciating the German managerial alternative. This failed perception has persisted to the present and not just in America. It exists particularly in those European circles that have embraced American views about management education. Nothing better illustrates this educational myopia than a survey undertaken a few years ago by the European International Business Association.[81] The survey sought to establish the state of international business education (IBE) in Europe. The results ranked the United Kingdom at the top of major European countries in IBE; fifty-seven of fifty-eight U.K. institutions responding to the questionnaire offered international business courses, contrasting with twenty-one out of the thirty-six respondents in West Germany. The disparity between the U.K. and Germany increased when surveyors' questions distinguished between international business programs as opposed simply to courses (see Table 2.2). And this disparity remained when levels of international business education in West Germany and the U.K. were compared (see Table 2.3).

Table 2.2. International business programs (1989)

Country	In operation	Planned
U.K.	27	18
West Germany	3	6

Source: Reijo Luostariner and Tuija Pulkkinen, *International Business Education in European Universities in 1990* (Helsinki, 1990), 54.

Table 2.3. Levels of offerings in business programs (1989)

Country	Undergraduate	Graduate	MBA	Doctorate
U.K.	50	15	19	3
W. Germany	0	21	3	0

Source: Luostariner and Pulkkinen, *International Business Education*, 64

There is no special reason to limit comparisons to two countries, except to save space. In fact, if the survey's data for all European countries were included, the U.K. would place at the top in international business education and West Germany somewhere near the bottom. Of major European nations, West Germany had the poorest record in academic international business education.

From the American managerial perspective this survey's inescapable but not stated conclusion would be: inferior German international business education equals inferior knowledge in German management of international business, if not for today, certainly for the future. But there is an incongruity here. Studies of German managers show them among the most skilled in international business. One survey, which is based on interviews with 800 marketing and purchasing agents in five European countries, established German managerial excellence quite clearly. In this survey each interviewee replied to questions about his or her marketing and purchasing experience with people in firms outside his or her country (i.e. in the other four). Non-British respondents rated British firms poor in meeting delivery deadlines, which requires close cooperation between production and marketing, and in offering new technology to their customers, which requires close cooperation between research and marketing. In fact, the British were at or near the bottom and the Germans almost at or near the top (second only to the Swedes) in every category judged. The investigators explained:

> The marketing staff in German companies have an exceptionally high reputation, not only for their technical competence but also for their commercial ability. In technical matters, the German suppliers are found to be innovative and at the forefront of development. They stress technical excellence and high quality, rather than emphasizing price. . . . They keep buyers informed of developments and follow up on product application in customer firms. Their export experience has given them a very sound knowledge of how foreign firms operate. They are outstanding in speed and punctuality of deliveries.[82]

Obviously, Germans educated their managers well for international business. What the poor standing of Germans in Luostarinen's survey really shows, then, is simply that Germans did not copy American international management educational forms after the war and that the British did. And the study also shows the prejudices of the surveyors in favor of American approaches to education.

The issue that really needs explaining, therefore, is how the German management functioned so well without American-style management education. Professor Arnd Huchzermeier, who has lectured at the University of Chicago Business School and the Koblenz School of Corporate Management and who received his education in both countries, offers some convincing reasons for German management success.[83] He notes that professors at good American business schools (he cites Stanford, MIT, Chicago, and a few others) work on real business problems, translating them into formal systems that businesses use to add value to their production-distribution chains.[84] American professors activate the transfer of problem-solving techniques because American business schools are places where business comes to learn how to carry on operations, thus making the American management school, and the 'science' it creates, a part of actual management process. Hence in top American business schools, tenure and promotion decisions (the value professors have for the school) depend on the professors' ability (through consulting and counseling) to add value to the activities of business and industrial clients. Business school professors get high salaries for the same reasons that American corporate management is well paid: they create added value.

Huchzermeier observes that German faculties of business economics do not possess the concentrated knowledge and skill of American business schools (German BWL is particularly weak in mathematics). Consequently, their professors are usually incapable of translating business problems into formal systems, applicable in praxis—not, at least, nearly as capable as professors in the premier American business schools. No doubt this incapacity explains the near contempt that is sometimes encountered in American business professors when they speak of German faculties of business economics.[85] But the contempt is misplaced because, as Huchzermeier affirms, solving problems in praxis is not their intent. To have contempt for people not doing what they have no intention of doing is contempt misapplied. Here the traditional German distinction between being *berufsfähig* (having capacity) and being *berufsfertig* (being ready for work) applies: routinely, German academics in BWL develop the science (*Wissenschaft*) involved in schooling the mind (*Denkschulung*); they are not concerned with solving actual business problems.

But Professor Huchzermeier also affirms that within German academia plenty of people have the requisite skills and knowledge needed to translate actual business problems into formal usable systems. These people are not, however, concentrated in faculties of business economics as much as dispersed throughout the university in various departments and institutes. When brought together from their scattered university venues, the scientists form teams that are quite as capable as professors in American business schools of solving business problems. Many of them in fact do just that every day. The difference between the Americans and the Germans in this respect is in knowledge management. The firm, more than academia, is the activating agent that puts together the requisite skills and knowledge in Germany. And Huchzermeier claims that the German way of concentrating and exploiting academic knowledge is very effective, more effective perhaps than the American because the firm can more easily identify the managerial difficulty, assemble the problem-solving team, and effect a solution than a business school. The firm is closer to and more intimately involved with the problem.

Huchzermeier's comments, therefore, illustrate the general point made throughout this chapter: the locus of German management is in the firm, not in the management profession itself, and the instrumentality Americans attach to it, the business school. The leadership locus also explains why German management attributes differ from American. Because of the specificity of the firm's leadership environment, German executives disregard, in Peter Lawrence's terms, 'the general processes of communication, decision-making, coordination, and control', the sort of managerialism taught in American business schools, for the specialism of their actual work.[86] To acquire the managerial attributes that Germans prize, they follow a different education path. They focus on subject based pre-experience education (law, business economics, and above all engineering) and do research projects at university. Graduate students do research degrees; doctorates, which most top German corporate executives hold, are not earned through course work like an MBA but by intensive work on a substantive issue in a field of knowledge, written up as a thesis. Managers undergo post-experience management training in short courses that delve into specific topics instead of general management subjects. Germans are underrepresented at famous international management educational institutes like INSEAD, IMEDE, and the Harvard Business School. Germans want to learn useful functional leadership skills for the job rather than the generic skills of a management professional.

Co-determination is the second source that shaped the German management alternative. Huge numbers of Americans do not vote because they believe the democratic process has nothing to do with their lives. In one important sense this is true; the workplace where they spend so many hours each day is not touched by democracy because American managerialism deprives employees of any effective say in things that really matter to them, the planning and control of their work. The German workplace is not democratic either, in the sense that employees make managerial decisions democratically. But long years of struggle, and especially the peculiarly favorable constellation of political and social forces immediately after the war, produced co-determination rights that in turn have promoted effective employee participation in the governance of firms.

German conservatives were not, thereby, routed; they managed to restrict employees' co-determination rights primarily to the noneconomic spheres of the firm's activity, to decisions about health, working conditions, and training. But as Taylorism receded, these noneconomic rights, especially in process work requiring employee input and imagination, have acquired very significant management implications. Consider how, after Taylorism, the following 'noneconomic' rights actually impede management's right to economic control:

- works council rights in hiring, firing, training, and retraining;
- works council jurisdictions in work reassignments occasioned by reorganization and technological change;
- the legal requirement that management negotiate 'social plans', providing compensation for displaced workers, that works councils monitor work performance and working conditions that because of job design are not 'suitably' human;
- and the legal requirement that the firm's business affairs be fully disclosed to economic councils.

These rights, even in areas where management's right to decide is indisputable, give works councils a real voice in work reorganization issues. Management might legally be able to decide alone about the implementation of a new technology or production process, but at some point in the implementation works council rights of co-determination, as for example in workforce retraining, will come into play. It turns out to be easier for management to bring German works councils into the management process than, by arousing their animosity, to let them act as the spoilers that their legal rights would permit.

Besides, works councils have not been prone to act as spoilers. The managerial environment in which, over time, the works councilors have come to move promotes cooperation with management. This cooperative mode expresses itself in the adoption of a common language. As educational reforms took effect, German union leaders and works councilors as well as management started using words like *Wissenschaft* (science), *wissenschaftliche* (scientific), or *arbeitswissenschaftliche Lehre* when they spoke. These terms would rarely crop up in an American labor-management context and they are difficult to translate.

Arbeitswissenschaftliche Lehre is a case in point. A direct translation would be 'labor-science discipline', implying that work and the work process could be treated as a science. Americans might think that work process could be analyzed scientifically in a technical sense, but they usually do not think the workers' interests could be trusted to such a discipline. Frederick Winslow Taylor tried to create a 'scientific management' but American workers smelled a rat. German unions and works councils also believe that the *arbeitswissenschaftliche Lehre* developed by employers and university scientists ignored their dimension. The issue is not just about conflicts of interest. It goes to the heart of the social science problem. If employees (or employers) thought that the social sciences were sufficiently robust to solve work-related problems in a discipline-determined objective way, they might accept scientific conclusions. But the epistemological and methodological weaknesses of the social sciences have inspired distrust if not outright contempt towards their conclusions. Rather than eliminate the whole social science enterprise, the German experience suggests that vested interests be incorporated into the science. When this happens the science becomes useful as an instrument for enlightening the self-interest of people.

Once the co-determination laws included employees in the process of developing this 'scientific work discipline', they tended to accept the legitimacy of studying work process scientifically. And they began to use the terms that were appropriate to this sort of study. The respect for knowledge, which the vocabulary reveals, explains why the works councilors and the trade unionists worked so hard in the 1970s to educate themselves and why management, by sponsoring continuing education, worked so hard, too, to help them. If they wanted to participate effectively, they had to speak the language of the firm: that language was *Fachkompetenz*.

Co-determination in German management, then, became less an expression of democracy than a recognition of the fact that capacities are firm-contextual, and that everybody has a role to play based on functions. Peter Lawrence notes 'the marked lack of deference between people at different hierarchial levels [in German firms.] . . . Case studies [show] staff variously criticizing their superiors (and each other) for breaking rules, dereliction of duty, getting things wrong, expressing silly ideas, not taking precautions, not looking ahead, and not spending enough on the plant and equipment.[87] Elsewhere he notes how *Technik*, 'the engineering knowledge and craft skills that goes into making things and producing three-dimensional artifact', permeates the work atmosphere of German manufacturing firms.[88] The point is that employee representatives on works councils and on supervisory boards accept this commonality, expressed in such terms as *arbeitswissenschaftliche Lehre* and *Technik*.

Professor Alfred Kieser, of the Mannheim Business Faculty, tells a story that indicates how well German co-determinationists have succeeded in building a work community within the firm.[89] In it he compares Germans with marginalized American workers and their unions. At a restaurant in Rome, Kieser was disturbed by a raucous party in a nearby room, rough fellows of the drunken girly-bottom-pinching variety. Inquiring about them, he was informed that it was a delegation from the American Federation of Labor. Kieser when telling the story sought less to disparage the Americans than to emphasize how in a room of German managers and works councilors it would be impossible today to tell one group from the other; they wear the same clothes, carry the same briefcases, speak the same language, and in many cases they have the same education.

Professor Horst Wildemann, who has worked hard implementing new work processes in German industry, echoes these sentiments but in a different way. He observes that the IG Metall-led works councils not only cooperate with management but in many instances are ahead of management in the introduction of new work organization and technological change.[90] Only people schooled to the right levels, with necessary legal jurisdiction, could do these things. For, if they do not have the requisite knowledge themselves, they know where and how to get it. This fusion of co-determination and traditional German management, with both accepting the managerial attributes of specialization, *Fachkompetenz*, and performance, emerged full-blown in the 1980s. It constitutes the German alternative to American managerialism in the governance of firms.

Chapter Three

Japanese Self-Absorption

S o far the contention has been that German management evolved differently from American managerialism, despite the great influence of the Americans in postwar Europe. But this difference does not mean that some iron law of cultural determinism was at work. Nobody lives in the past, and, consequently, as Andrew Gordon affirms, 'the political and social system [is] continually reformulated or renegotiated' within the parameters of each generation's life experience.[1] If a particular management-institutional configuration cannot produce effectively in the economic arena (or for that matter in the social), it must adapt, malfunction, or die—economic and social realities in this regard discipline cultural contingency.

On the other hand, no generation has *carte blanche* when carrying through its 'renegotiations'. Social constructionists argue that people, engaging in a continuous search for meaning, create rules for action which in turn continuously influence the nature of future action. Action, therefore, provides its own constraints and is dependent on them. These rules, structures, or constraints are called institutions. 'Institutionalization occurs', Peter L. Berger and Thomas Luckmann state,

> whenever there is a reciprocal typification of habitualized actions. . . . [Institutions] cannot be created instantaneously. [They] always have a history, of which they are the product. It is impossible to understand an institution adequately without an understanding of the historical process in which it was produced.[2]

Cultural rules, therefore, do not just 'influence' people's behavior, they define the meaning and identity of individuals and the pattern of appropriate economic, political, and cultural activity engaged in by those individuals. They similarly state the purposes and legitimacy of organizations, professions, interest groups, and states, while delineating activity appropriate to these entities. Institutions objectify cultural rules giving collective meaning and value to particular entities and activities, integrating them into larger schemes. Institutionalized values appeared in the German case, for example, legalism and reliance on the state shaped the way that Germans reorganized their management after the Second World War, even though specific manifestations from the past (the military-bureaucratic institutions) had been discredited and discarded. Historically institutionized cultural rules did not just 'influence' German behavior after the war; they defined the pattern of appropriate activity engaged in during the 'renegotiation'. The same logic pertains to Japan. The generations that experienced postwar occupation and reconstruction (1945–60) and the era of high growth-industrialization and globalization (1960–85) 'renegotiated' Japanese management within the constraints of that nation's shared values. The rise of a Japanese management mystique and the collapse of the American one was, therefore, contingent on how these shared values guided postwar political, social, and economic events.

Before 1945

During the nineteenth century and most of this, Westerners mistakenly believed that individualism was a necessary prerequisite for the modernization of society. Egocentrism forms the core of the familiar story about the Protestant ethic and the spirit of capitalism: Puritanism's unbridled individualism broke up the corporate bodies and 'common-good' ethics that hindered economic change. Martin Luther's defiance of his Emperor and his Pope ('Here I stand, God help me, for I can do nothing else'), like the capitalists' appeal to the principles of universal law (the invisible hand) or progress (survival of the fittest) were the ego-driven engines of economic change, ego-driven because they respected no established social-economic situations. The immediate effect of this egoism was, as Johannes Hirschmeier and Tsunehiko Yui wrote, to 'shrug off the social costs' and the need for immediate socially responsible behavior, in the interests of entrepreneurial acquisitive desire.[3]

Westerners hitched industrialization to the bandwagon of the bourgeoisie, with their liberal ideals of individualism, formulating thereby teleological conceptions of modernization that made the destruction of 'feudalism' a prerequisite for modern industrialization: social, political, and economic reality intertwined in a teleological spiral wherein changes in modes of production created realignments in social classes and political-ideological superstructures. Karl Marx is probably the most famous exponent of these specific beliefs, but non-Marxists often employ similar ideas about socio-economic teleology. One of the most recent examples of teleological thinking appeared in the Wehler school of German historiography. Hans-Ulrich Wehler argued that Bismarck's creation, the Second German Empire (1871–1918), was a historical anachronism because it saddled a military-feudalistic monarchist superstructure on a modern industrial society. The Wehlerian argument is a perversion of the Marxist view since Germany *did* industrialize during the Second Empire, but it is no less teleological because the Wehlerians argue that a 'normal' industrial society should have developed into a liberal parliamentary democracy; the fact that Germany did not evolve 'normally' in this respect meant that Europe, and the world, had to suffer a violent fate at the hands of an atavistic, highly industrialized feudal state.[4]

These arguments are labeled 'mistaken' not because of a belief that any preindustrial society could or can undergo capitalist industrialization. Obviously this was not and is not the case. But the creation of a politically and socially liberal institutional structure and ideology did not occur in Germany, and is not a necessary part of the industrial process.[5]

Japan's Modernization

D. Eleanor Westney, who has written about the transfer of Western organizational patterns to Japan during the Meiji era (1868–1912), notes that in such great periods of modernization the specific organizational structures and functions 'derived from traditional patterns are less likely to survive than general attitudinal patterns'.[6] To this observation she adds the corollary that the government, the dynamo behind change, principally dealt with the transfer of specific Western organizational structures. Major cases of specific organizational emulation in Meiji Japan, 1869–82, were: from Great Britain, the navy, telegraphy system, postal system, and postal savings system; from France, the army, primary school system, Tokyo *Keishi-cho* (police), judicial system, and *Kempeitai* (military police); from the United States, the national bank system and the Sapporo Agricultural college. After 1878, the Japanese government began to change the specific models emulated: a switch from the French to the German army model in 1878, a switch in 1879 to an American model in primary education, and then again in 1886 to a modified German model, a switch to a Belgian-modeled central bank, and a switch in 1888 to German models of municipal and prefectural government.[7]

Besides specific organizational borrowings, the Japanese also leaned on the West for 'general models' which 'incorporated at the outset fewer "new" organizational features', that is, because they borrowed specific foreign models less, they embodied more Japanese features.[8] Among the 'general models' in Meiji Japan were newspapers, factories, incorporated enterprises, railways, and the Tokyo Stock Exchange. Westney's point is that Japanese borrowing underwent a two-phase process. In the first phase, the early Meiji era, Western models provided both 'inspiration and legitimization'. In their initial enthusiasm towards things Western, Japanese reformers imbibed the ideology of liberalism. Masanao Nakamura's (1832–91) translation of Samuel Smiles's *Self Help* and John Stuart Mill's *On Liberty*, which epitomize the liberal view, became enormously popular in Japan along with other works about rugged individualism. Former samurai were on 'the front line of enterprise, conspicuous in the establishment of national banks but also in some fields like cotton spinning'.[9] By 1872 the old caste system had been abolished, and behavior and occupation groups were no longer controlled; new social groups (the shift from farm to factory, from the land to the city) and new governmental functions (i.e. in education, in national defense) were being created in order for Japan to compete as a modern nation state. Japanese sought legitimization in Western ideology as well as inspiration in Western models.

In the later Meiji era (after 1880), Western models still inspired, but the Japanese reformers increasingly searched to legitimize them 'in Japanese tradition and environment'.[10] When, therefore, genuine reform precluded the perpetuation of pre-Meiji organizational structures and functions, the Japanese borrowed foreign models. But when they did, they carefully selected those that conformed to Japanese attitudinal patterns. Accordingly, when reasserting 'Japaneseness' after 1880, the conservatives in government consciously shifted from French or American to German models. They knew precisely the anti-liberal choice they made because Bismarck's 'modernization' of Germany had not been liberal. Hence the Imperial Constitution promulgated in 1889 was, like the German, given to the Japanese people by the Emperor (not drafted by representatives of the people); it provided for the cabinet to be responsible, as in Germany, to the Emperor, not the legislature; it left the military free from parliamentary control (as in Germany it took an oath of personal allegiance to the Emperor: it was 'His' military).[11] Subsequent to a thorough study of Western legal codes, Japanese authorities, after flirting with a Japanese version of the French civil and criminal codes, adopted heavily German-influenced legal codes, the family law provision of which (the civil code adopted in 1898) codified the prevailing custom of the patriarchal family system. These laws established family precedence over the individual, men over women, and so forth.

The redefinition of tradition, and of what constituted Japanese patterns, through selective borrowings from the past, reinterpreted in terms of present needs, was, then, the renegotiation in which Meiji Japanese engaged when organizing the developmental process. In the governmental sphere the newly created agencies rejected the liberal-democratic spirit for the ethos of traditionalism. This happened in the two ethos-building institutions, education and defense, that emerged in the modernizing Japanese state, although both institutions had to be completely invented.

Educationally, Tokugawa Japan (1603–1867) had not been a backward society. Ronald Dore figures that $c.1870$, about 40–50 percent of the boys, and 15 percent of girls, received some sort of formal schooling.[12] Commoners in the privately run village schools, especially the children of wealthier villagers and townspeople, got a practical training in the three Rs, along with some moral instruction. The samurai class, about 7 percent of the population, attended a well-developed school system, too. They learned practical subjects of use to an administrative elite, but the samurai children principally studied the Chinese Confucian classics, an instruction meant to provide this ruling class with proper moral values. Tokugawa schooling in general gave 'individuals [an] education according to their place in society, enabling each to fulfill the role assigned to him by class'.[13]

Meiji modernizers sensed that a new education system had to be established that would 'mobilize the talents of the whole nation, regardless of class'.[14] Hence they turned to specific Western models which had themselves been formulated as nation-building institutions. They drew up plans for a greatly expanded education system that would provide compulsory elementary education (four years) for all boys and girls, and a network of middle schools and national universities. The policy by 1900 resulted in almost universal elementary education, which the Ministry of Education extended in 1907 from four to six compulsory years. It was a remarkable achievement, one which astonished George C. Allen, arriving in the Japan of the 1920s from class-conscious Britain. '[A]lthough it did not then claim to be democratic,' the distinguished economic historian wrote,

> children from all classes attended the same primary schools. A Japanese friend was surprised that I should have found this a matter for remark. Though he was well-to-do, he thought it natural that the people who were now his servants and the local farm workers should have attended the same primary school as he.[15]

Above elementary levels, the Japanese implemented a multitrack system of education, that is, they followed the European elitist example in secondary education rather than the single-track American idea. Beyond elementary school, then, Meiji education remained undemocratic, for the Japanese decision to emulate the Germans expressed a firm belief in social hierarchy, even if the specific hierarchy had in the modern era to be profoundly modified from that of the Tokugawa. The Imperial Rescript on Education of 1890, which Japanese school principals read out in full at periodic ceremonies until 1945, testifies to this decision to invigorate the new educational system with inherited Japanese attitudinal patterns. It proclaimed:

> Ye, our subjects, be filial to your parents, affectionate to your brothers and sisters; as husbands and wives be harmonious, as friends true; bear

yourselves in modesty and moderation; extend your benevolence to all; pursue learning and cultivate arts; and thereby develop intellectual faculties and perfect moral powers; furthermore advance public good and promote common interests; always respect the Constitution and observe the laws; should emergency arise, offer yourself courageously to the State; and thus guard and maintain the prosperity of Our Imperial Throne coeval with heaven and earth.[16]

Japanese educational reformers distinguished fundamentally between scholarship and education. For them, 'education was not intended as an individually liberating experience, nor necessarily as an intellectually enlightening one, but rather as a socializing one with a very specific purpose in mind—the cultivation of persons who would be of service to the state'.[17] Meiji reformers, no less than Tokugawa educational officials, wanted the educational systems to inculcate people with socially conservative ethical values. Only they wanted the school system to act also as an instrument of modernization. That was new. Therefore, although they swept away the educational specifics of Tokugawa, the moral tenor of traditional Japanese education remained.

Military reform breathed this same ethos. During Tokugawa the samurai almost exclusively monopolized the military function. Therefore, they opposed the Imperial rescript in January 1873 that deprived samurai of their prerogatives. The introduction of the new conscript army, by opening the military to all social classes, fundamentally changed Japan. With the old caste system abolished, the designation of warrior family, *shizoku*, now only referred to family origins. But reformers made every effort to imbue this new army with the samurai spirit. The new officer corps inscribed the four characteristics of the ancient warrior code (*bushido*) in its heart: (1) self-sacrifice and loyalty to an organization, (2) stoicism and patience, (3) heavy responsibility for leaders, and (4) emphasis on self-improvement.

Field Marshal Sir William Slim, who drove the Japanese from Burma, gives one instance of just how much the Japanese army, in this case the 33rd Japanese division, breathed this *bushido* spirit:

[Its] penetration attacks were remarkable in their boldness and in the desperation with which the enemy fought to the death. . . . There can have been few examples in history of a force as reduced, battered, and exhausted . . . delivering such furious assaults, not with the object of extricating itself, but to achieve its original offensive intention. . . . Whatever one may think of the military wisdom of thus pursuing a hopeless object, there can be no question of the supreme courage and hardihood of the Japanese soldiers. . . . I know of no army that could have equalled them.[18]

Before the attack began, the Japanese commander told the troops: 'You men have got to be fully in the picture as to what the present position is. [On this attack] the success or failure of the Greater East Asia war' depends. Their own deaths were to be considered 'lighter than a feather'.

The Management Heritage

In classic Western capitalism the workers and the bourgeoisie shared no moral space. Between the two there has been simply the no-man's-land of bitter exploitation. Tough-minded historians have applied this formula to labor relations during Japan's industrialization in the late nineteenth and early twentieth century. William W. Lockwood, for one, observed that workers suffered terribly in the initial phases of industrialization. There was, consequently, a huge turnover of personnel in the large firms. In this period an industrial proletariat emerged, which consisted of former samurai, artisans, and merchants who had failed to adapt to the drastically altered socio-economic environment, and of unskilled workers who were drawn to urban centers from poverty-stricken rural areas.[19] Andrew Gordon concluded that 'the relationships of industrial production [in Japan] most resembled those in the West at the outset'.[20] Bitter strife and strikes erupted in large Japanese firms as Japan underwent intense industrialization (1890–1940). In Gordon's work we find ourselves on the familiar ground of conflict of interest and exploitation.

Yet the sources also paint quite different social scenarios. Equally tough-minded thinkers claim that different technological and economic factors created moral spaces in Japanese factories that did not resemble those in American firms. Because Japanese industrialization occurred late, it made relatively high technological knowledge and skill demands on the country, demands that Japan was ill-prepared to meet. Since the Japanese had to catch up with the West, they did not need, nor could they have provided, creative scientists. They needed engineers. The engineers, moreover, had to have a special brand of education that differed from the education received by engineers in the West. Japanese pioneers in technology-transfer had learned that formal and tacit knowledge are essential to manufacturing and that Japan lacked both. As Professor Ken'ichi Yasumuro explained,

> Theories could be taught in higher educational institutes, and machines could be imported from Western countries. Foreign advisers and teachers usually lacked practical knowledge, because a strict division of labour between the engineer and the skilled workers was already established in Western societies. [Western engineers] could not instruct the Japanese how to operate the machines.[21]

To be successful, Japanese engineers not only had to learn the formal engineering that the Western engineer possessed, but they had to spend time in a Western workshop acquiring the 'non-verbal knowledge and technical skills' which Western craftsmen possessed but Japanese workers did not. Then the Japanese engineers, returning to Japan, had to teach workshop skills to Japanese workers as well as carry out routine Western-style engineering tasks.

The requirement to transfer both knowledge and skill inevitably affected the evolution of Japanese management–labor relations. Yasumuro pinpointed one result. The necessity for the Japanese engineer to teach craft skills promoted the well-known closeness in the plant between Japanese engineers and skilled craftsmen. Technical needs cemented the working union in Japanese factories between engineers and skilled labor. Technical needs, too, might help explain why in Japan, unlike the U.S.A. and the U.K., the introduction of Taylorist ideas in the 1920s and 1930s did not produce a rigid separation between planning and tasks, nor foster social fragmentation.[22]

Japanese firms were immensely interested in Taylorism at the time, for they fully realized that their management needed to become more efficient if Japan were to stay abreast of world competition. So, it was not the degree of interest in Taylorism that made Japanese management behavior between the wars different from management in American firms, but the way the interest was pursued. Kenji Okua points out that Japanese industrialists created a Production Management

Committee which put together work-study groups that investigated Taylorism between 1932 and 1941. But '[u]nlike the views of workers in Taylor's scientific management [in America],' he observed,

workers [in Japan] were accepted as co-researchers in a work study. In the selection of survey subject, it was considered necessary not to choose 'first class men' but to choose not only persons capable of realizing the genuine purpose of the work study, but those who would be readily acceptable by coworkers. This is, it was agreed, because there was a need to see to it that the results of work study would be acceptable to a broad segment of workers. Such rectification of the views of workers in the scientific management system [was necessary] 'to develop concepts and methods of the kind which is in line with the reality of Japanese industry'.[23]

Whereas American management presumed to know, and hence treated 'scientific management' as an objective form of knowledge that could be imposed on the workforce by those who understood it, that is, management, the Japanese believed that those whose lives it would affect had to accept and develop the scientific management process. This Japanese approach to 'scientific management' resembled German co-determination of the postwar years much more than American managerialism.

If some observers believe this cooperative spirit emerged because of Japan's technological backwardness, others trace it to more remote sources in Japanese history. Scholars find it embedded in the work practices inherent in wetland rice cultivation. Paddy cultivation, Shuji Hayashi argues, encouraged group endeavors in village (*mura*) life. 'The *mura* work is', he noted, 'decided by the group as a whole. Farmers work so close together that cooperation becomes second nature. . . . When paddy fields are irrigated water pumped in is allowed to flow by gravity, the entire village field is worked at the same time. Even fertilizer had to be cooperatively applied because the water flow carried it everywhere.'[24] Dominique Turcq, using the same metaphor, notes that 'Japanese culture is a culture of water. The study of the Japanese economy cannot be based on structures but on the flows existing between these structures.'[25] Chie Nakane, for her part, stresses the non-kinship basis of Japanese groupism in her well-known work, *Japanese Society*. Observing that kinship ties, especially those of the extended family, are prevalent in societies of horizontal groupings (like India), she notes that in a vertical-group society, like Japan, people are bound closer to non-kinship primary vertical groups than to family. And she traces non-kinship vertical grouping again to the *mura*, the early Japanese village.

Finally, still other authorities, looking at Japan's intermediate past, explain how ideas that emerged during the Tokugawa era took Japanese modernization into paths seldom trod in the West. Eleanor M. Hadley, in her excellent work *Antitrust in Japan*, describes the quite different effect that the presence of either an Enlightenment or a 'feudal' past has on people's attitudes towards the firm during subsequent periods of high industrialization. 'Japan's early capitalists', she wrote,

> did not stand for any injection of fresh thinking into the hierarchical world which they entered. They organized their businesses on the hierarchical institution of the 'house', and externally expected to operate as superiors and inferiors, as those favored and not favored . . . It was a paternalistic hierarchy of people taught to think in terms of superiors and inferiors. As for external relations among businesses, there were no voices to suggest that all should have an equal chance, that businesses should be treated equally. In other words, there was no Adam Smith, for there was no John Locke. There was no public policy of competition, for competition is a democratic doctrine. Competition radically asserts, 'let all compete and may the best man win'. Among Japan's bureaucrats, as among Japan's political leadership, the ideology was that of superior and inferior. It should surprise no one that Mitsui, Mitsubishi, Sumitomo, and Yasuda were the superiors of Japan's business world.[26]

Hadley also noted the effect that Japan's non-Enlightenment tradition, in the Western sense, had on conceptions of macroeconomic process. 'The low esteem in which the market mechanism is held', she stated,

> and the absence of fear of abuse of power are but facets of the different orientation to political economy that one finds in Japan. Inasmuch as in Japanese conservative opinion the market mechanism is regarded as incapable of providing direction to the economy, no importance is attached, from this point of view, to market form. And inasmuch as efficiency is uncritically associated with larger and larger firm size, there tends to be the view that the higher the market concentration the greater the effective use of resources. In Japanese conservative opinion it is the government which steers, with producers the vital agents. . . . In the

liberal tradition of the West a nation's growth can be left largely to market forces. The government's role . . . is seen as primarily that of promoting through the use of monetary and fiscal policy an environment in which business can operate and prosper. Because different market structures are regarded as producing different results, market form is important. In the liberal [American] view, competitive markets are to be preferred to concentrated markets on a number of counts: 1) allocation of resources and efficiency of production; (2) consumer responsiveness; (3) diffusion of power; (4) accommodation of the 'right to entry'.[27]

Such a myriad of scholarly opinion, if it does not confuse, at least appears inconsistent to those seeking to understand Japan's industrialization process. How can it be that, as Andrew Gordon says, Japanese workers suffered class exploitation in a society characterized, as Chie Nakane says, by vertical integration? Is somebody wrong, or is it just possible that both can be right within the Japanese context? Actually, the evidence Gordon gives himself suggests that the latter might be the case. He emphasizes that, despite the commonality of conflict, the Japanese workers never developed strong industry-wide or horizontally connected trade unions—labor unions in Japan grew up centered on the firm. Conflict was not avoided, but conflict took place in status, not in class terms. As Shinji Sugayama observes in 'Business Education, Training, and the Emergence of the "Japanese Employment System"',

> [An] examination of labor disputes in the course of Japan's industrial revolution indicates that workers' anger over status discrimination lay at the heart of many of these incidents. The labor movement in Japan was thus a movement aimed at the elevation of the status of workers rather than one built on class consciousness. For the Japanese labor movement, staff employees—treated by the company as 'regular' members of the enterprise community—constituted the 'reference group', the model for the workers' status aspirations.[28]

These two management–labor relation peculiarities (enterprise unionism and vertical group status consciousness) colored the interaction between management and labor throughout Japanese industrialization.

Historical examples suggest, therefore, that, if past actions provided their own anti-liberal constraints when 'renegotiating' the institutional creations of the modern state, the same process occurred in the evolution of Japanese management. Here care must be exercised not to look too far into the past for the sources of current Japanese management practices. Scholars writing about Japan point this out quite frequently, noting that such 'typical' Japanese phenomena as lifetime employment or the seniority system hardly predate the war. It is important when discussing Japanese management, therefore, to break management down into its 'rudiments', its 'basic structures', and its 'methods'. It is, following Westney, the rudiments, 'the general attitudinal patterns', that have the sense of permanency; they change slowly and with difficulty. The basic management structures, however, and, above all, the methods of management can and must change quite readily as events and situations command. The rudiments set the limits within which the basic structures and methods adapted and changed.

Usually when management rudiments are considered, they can be boiled down to some fundamental view of life or human action. The Germans relied on the state and the law to secure rights. Which groups turned to the state and the legal system depended on the historical situation, but the fact that they did set the patterns of behavior for future actions. For instance, the creation of co-determination in 1951 set the stage for the legislation and codification of co-determination rights later. Since American rudiments differed from German (the American ideas of freedom reject the state as an instrument for its attainment), the same sort of codification did not occur in America, and probably never will.

In the Japanese case, the management rudiments can be simply stated: Japanese management has a sense of group consciousness compared with the West's ego-centered consciousness of individualism. Robert J. Smith points out that 'there is a relative absence in the Japanese language of anything remotely resembling the personal pronoun'. Consequently, the use of the personal referent 'is one of the most difficult features of the language to teach Americans, for whom the apparently irreducible "I" presents a major stumbling block to the easy adoption of the constantly shifting, relational "I" of the Japanese, which is not detached from the other, and thus stays immersed in the world.'[29] Critics of Japan, who value egocentricism, even claim that in Japan the individual ego almost disappears. This is true because Japanese organizations are not made up of a collection of individuals, as individuals, but of a 'relatum, of contextuals'.[30] Japanese ethics, then, is social-situational rather than fixed, say, like that of Martin Luther, in a transcendental source. Luther rendered unto Caesar only that which God permitted and, for the rest, let his conscience be his guide. Because of its contextual nature Japanese ethics consists of what Joseph Adams has called 'moral spaces, . . . areas encompassing an established order, or closure, of reciprocal obligations and trust implicit and explicit in the social relations of the space'.[31]

The same lack of categorical imperative (Kant's doctrine that one's acts should be determined only by principles that one wills to be binding on all men) covers the Japanese approach to logic. Thomas P. Rohlen observed that 'theoretical debates and logical dialogues are simply not part of the [Japanese] approach to education' and that 'Western observers, including myself, find reason to be amazed at the Japanese tolerance for contradictory and even ludicrous explanation and meaning [given by others] . . . '.[32] Robert J. Smith, echoing these sentiments, observes that Japanese regard people who argue 'with logical consistency as immature', and that the pejorative term *rikutsuppoi* ('reason freak') is a part of the Japanese lexicon.[33] This anti-rational impulse is implanted firmly in Japanese history.[34] Social situations, not reason, guide interpersonal actions.

Accordingly, Japanese behavior is characterized much by role-playing (presenting an appropriate face). The young Japanese studies an assigned role, and perfects it; indeed it is much prized, this perfection, for the Japanese have a word (*rashisa, rashii* in adjectival form) that can be attached 'to the name of a role or status, the very model of a student, wife, soldier, etc.'[35] The person not conforming to the idealized role or status is frowned upon. To Westerns this role-playing has always had a superficial, Zelig-like, chameleon quality that reeks of insincerity at best, at worst of the absence of personality. Japanese defend themselves from the charge of insincerity by noting that they always distinguish behaviorally between *tatemae* (the formal public self) and *honne* (what lies behind the public self), the latter, the real person, being the epitome of sincerity.

Champions of Japanese culture and society also dispute the charge that Japanese people lack strong personalities, in two ways: (1)

Japanese people, they argue, outside the organization and the public sphere, devote much time to the cultivation of the arts, painting, music, or some artisanal activity where the expression of individual worth and succinctness of personality takes place; (2) where people in the West think that one is born with a personality (which must be protected from outside menaces), the Japanese view the personality as a product of experience wherein role-playing is a natural part of the maturation process, especially for young people whose experiences are too limited for their personalities to have developed very much.

Whether one believes role-playing reveals insincerity or absence of personality, it certainly has not created the lack of conviction which the charge of superficiality implies. This is confirmed by the countless stories of deep loyalty and sacrifice that lie at the heart of Japanese life, stories which, because Japanese ethics is socially contextual, have didactically strengthened social responsibility. Janet Hunter points out, for instance, that the stress on the virtues of loyalty, filial piety, obedience to seniors, courage, and self-sacrifice in the Tokugawa neo-Confucian *bushido* code strengthened social order.[36] Chinese Confucianism espoused these virtues, too, only on transference to Japan they underwent modifications to fit Japanese social circumstances. In Japan, as a warrior society, the supreme virtue of loyalty to one's immediate superior, one's lord, one's ruler, took precedence over the paramount Chinese virtue of filial piety. Blood in this instance was not thicker than water. Although ethical behavior in Tokugawa Japan required absolute obedience to the head of household, when filial piety came into conflict with duty to lord, the latter took precedence. This led the Japanese to extend primary group consciousness far beyond the boundaries of kinship, a tendency reinforced by the legal ability, as early as the eighth century, to bestow the family name and emblem on people without blood ties that the family wished, to assure succession, to take into its bosom.[37]

Comments about the Japanese living in a status hierarchy of contextuals should not mislead, for they do not imply voiceless compliance with the commands of a superior. Magorah Maruyama argues that the traditional Japanese 'mindscape' really belies thoughtless submissiveness within the formal hierarchy. Americans, he says, have binocular vision. They believe that each lens in a bifocal compensates for deficiencies in the other to bring a true (focused) picture. But the

Japanese are 'poly-ocular' in that they think that each lens has a different view of reality. Translated into a social setting, this means that different people have different views, legitimate ones, of the same objects or problems.[38]

Robert N. Bellah traces Japanese proactive behavior to another social-contextual source. Japanese have a strong consciousness of the *on*, received from parents, teachers, superiors, or society and nature in general. Repayment of the *on*, a feeling of indebtedness rather than consciousness of rights one could claim, form the basis of moral action. With a lack of universally defined norms and with each being dependent on the limited human nexus as reference, Shintoism appeared to provide the ultimate ethical basis with its demands to repay the *on* (graces) received from the ancestors and from the community. Whereas 'guilt' drove Protestants to strive for never-assured signs of salvation, a sense of indebtedness that is never completely repayable drove Japanese. And just as the Protestant drive could be transferred to 'entrepreneurialism', so could obligation-engendered drives. Martin H. Sours has observed that many of the motivational values of Japanese traditional society underwent the same sort of transfer. Loyalty, which had been directed to the feudal lords, was redirected to the corporation; the concept of *giri* (notions of duty), of *ninjo* (human feeling)—ultimately the entire modernizing society—acceded to the pre-industrial system because general societal values accepted the notion of hierarchy and privilege as long as these ideas expressed legitimate behavior in the new contexts.[39]

Such 'mindscapes' encouraged within the Japanese group disciplined, participatory decision-making. Whatever the explanation or metaphor employed, most literature sets the Japanese off as group decision-makers who have developed processes that achieve this end. Among them is the famous *ringi sei* system, which dates from the seventeenth century. A *ringisho* (document) might be considered a recommendation sent by staff to top management concerning measures that should be taken, not just within a specific workplace but throughout the organization as a whole. Only people in responsible positions have the authority to write one and then only after painstaking study and discussion within middle management and below. Moreover, the person preparing the *ringisho* must have a clear understanding of the thinking of top management and have a good grasp of the internal situation within the enterprise so that he can skillfully evaluate the possible results of proposed policies. And the word 'policy' is used advisedly, for a *ringisho* is not a report (simply providing information for policy formulated at the top) but a documented proposal for a change of policy; it is participatory policy formulation.

Another process, which actually can start *ringi sei*, is called *nemawashi* (root-binding), which is nothing else than a thorough discussion at the grass roots about possible initiatives—a touching of bases with people potentially affected, about their attitude towards actions that could be proposed. Even if an idea originates at the top, it is dropped to the bottom of the managerial hierarchy to work its way up through a process of group discussion back to the top. Stephen Graves observes that *ringi sei*, *nemawashi*, and other forms of consensus decision-making found in Japanese organizational traditions are not 'management tools within the structure of Japanese organizations. . . . They are not prerogatives [attributed to management]; there is a distinctly passive and anti-structural quality about them. Properly understood, they are elements of and inextricably linked to processes . . . .'[40] No formal hierarchical structure held the organization together, but the members' commitment to 'embrace and support the group completely (*marugakae*)'.[41] Commitment and loyalty based on experience produced the high-density environment in which tacit communication prevailed, as opposed to a low-density one in which conditions in agreement have to be stated explicitly in writing. Implicit understanding made consensus decision-making among such committed group members genuine and comparatively easy.

Chie Nakane claims that Japanese business modernized quickly and without great upheaval because a vertical-group social system was already in place before the start of the modernization process. This implies two things: (1) that management operating in a vertical-group social context was just as capable of fomenting business and industrial change as management operating in one driven by ego-centered individualists, and (2) that this change could express very different assumptions about the economic and managerial process a transforming economy needed. Hirschmeier and Yui give one example of the complex dynamics involved under point one. They assert that even the

Japanese flirtation with Western individualism really expressed situational values.

Meiji Japanese, unlike nineteenth-century Americans, never separated secular government from personal and spiritual matters. Moral codes and religion blended together in ways that made public and private inseparable. Japanese adopted the universal ethics of individualism from the West because Japanese leaders thought it was good for the nation. Neither reason nor conscience brought Japanese to embrace a universal ethic, only role-playing suggested by the government's modernization policy. Once the government established an official line, and the public followed that line,

> behavior could be reinforced by sheer pressure of expectation which nobody could escape. . . . Pressure from above, exemplified by the will of his superiors; pressure about him, represented by the common will of his fellow and equals; pressure from below, represented by the general sentiment of his inferiors, explain enthusiasm for things Western, including individualism, during the period of Civilization and Enlightenment (*bunmei kaika*).[42]

Later, when governments abandoned Western liberal ideas, the role-playing, social-contextual Japanese quickly turned from them to the newly officially sanctioned values.

Thus the Japanese and the American management heritage differed considerably at mid-twentieth century. The distinguished political philosopher Masao Maruyama describes just how widespread and significant this difference could be, for it manifested itself not just in financial, industrial, and commercial management circles but also in the government and military. And it produced sometimes tragic misperceptions within each nation's elite about the other nation's principles of managerial behavior. Maruyama describes how Japanese and American misperceptions of each other plagued the war trials. The issue was responsibility. The Americans blamed Japan's vanquished leaders for having conspired to wage war and for having committed crimes against humanity. Maruyama, when discussing the trials, focuses on one principle of Japanese organizational behavior known as 'the rule of the higher by the lower'. This rule forces leaders to accept policy formulation and actions taken by their 'subordinates'.[43] Whereas in American organizations those at the top would be held accountable for their subordinates' acts of indiscipline, in Japan, where the rule of the higher by the lower prevailed, those at the top would not be. The issue was important. In numerous acts of what many in the West would consider a lack of discipline, including the Manchurian incident and the Rape of Nanking, '[i]nstead of punishing the conspirators', their leaders, because of the organizational dynamics implied in the rule of the higher by the lower, 'had to approve of their [subordinates'] illegal *faits accomplis* and make a suitable compromise'.[44]

Maruyama also touched on another phenomenon that has become familiar to students of Japanese corporate management. During the war, weak vertical authority in organizations, which the rule of the higher by the lower creates, affected horizontal organizational relationships. '[T]his decline in vertical authority within the armed forces', he specified,

> was used to great effect by the military when it came to imposing their will in horizontal relations. Thus, when the War Minister wished to advance or oppose a certain measure in a Cabinet meeting or at an Imperial Conference, he would invariably argue: 'In that case the department (i.e. the military) won't put up with it', or: 'In that case I can't guarantee to keep the forces under control'.[45]

Here, it is not the specific organizational history that Maruyama relates that is of interest but the general question of Japanese managerial practice, in this case the strong horizontal relationships that weak vertical hierarchies permit. These practices, which reflected traditional Japanese attitudinal patterns, persisted, despite the great social, economic, political, and institutional changes wrought in the country, after the Meiji Restoration (1868).

Long-standing attitudes could express themselves in the most unexpected places. Maruyama described the curious conversion of Kono Hironaka to liberalism. Or rather, he lets the Liberal Party leader himself relate the story of his transformation.

> I was riding on horseback when I first read this work [John Stuart Mill's *On Liberty*]. In a flash my entire way of thinking was revolutionized. Until then I had been under the influence of the Chinese Confucianists and of the Japanese classical scholars. . . . Now all these earlier thoughts of mine, *excepting those concerned with loyalty and filial piety*, were smashed to

smithereens. At the same moment I knew that it was human freedom and human rights that I must henceforth cherish above all else.[46]

Obviously, as Maruyama himself pointed out, Kono even at his moment of liberal enlightenment did not abandon traditional morality, despite the fact that any 'reason freak' could see the inconsistency of his position.

Despite Maruyama's remarks about the rule of the higher by the lower, Chie Nakane's comments about Japan being a vertical society, and many other statements about the dynamics of Japanese group consciousness, Japan did not evolve into a harmonious, conflict-free society during its long history. George C. Allen's remark about the democracy of Japanese elementary education not withstanding, after as well as before the Meiji Restoration, Hadley's characterization of Japan, as a nation of inferiors and superiors, remained true. In the multitrack educational system only 10 to 15 percent of the pupils in each age cohort got on a middle school track that led to higher education. Of them, few were women. In 1930 only fifty-one women could be found in institutions of higher education in the country.[47] Although workers might identify with the firm rather than with their proletarian brothers, few had any status in a company. They were inferiors that management excluded from governance. In Japanese commercial and industrial organizations there were so many blockages to upward economic and social mobility that only a few in the firm actually could invoke the famous rule of the higher by the lower.[48]

Postwar Occupation and Reconstruction

Postwar Japanese management is complicated. It is complicated because Japan's conqueror had a profoundly different social-political and ideological outlook from the defeated enemy, one that the American occupier believed should be adopted by the conquered nation for its own good and for the good of mankind. The story is also complicated because the interaction between the Americans and Japanese occurred during the Cold War. Global tensions caused the Americans to modulate considerably the democratic-radical aspect of the proposed Japanese transformation. The American thesis and the Japanese anti-thesis which worked itself out in the postwar synthesis resulted in a management that, although deviating from both American desires and Japanese wishes, partook a bit of both. The effect that the American-inspired and partially directed 'democratization' of Japan had on postwar Japanese management is the subject to be explored.

Probably, the best place to start is with the democratic idea, the great clarion call of America. To give people more voice in their affairs meant something different in an ego-centered individualistic society like America than it did in a status- conscious society like Japan. But democratization did take place within the Japanese context. And from a managerial perspective, the achievements of democratization turned out to be more profound in Japan than in America. Consequently, democratization of Japanese management produced something considerably different from what was offered in the American model. A look at the 'renegotiation' of Japan's socio-economic life after the Japanese defeat clarifies the nature of the Japanese management alternative to American managerialism.

When American occupation authorities decided to democratize Japan, they began with Japanese big business. Among the punished were the famous financial cliques, the *zaibatsu* families, on the grounds that their combines had supported Japanese militarism and aggression. Family-controlled *zaibatsu* had been important in the Japanese economy up to 1945, the biggest of which were Mitsui, Mitsubishi, Sumitomo, and Yasuda. Of diverse origins, the older ones had benefited from contacts within Meiji governments and the patronage they dispensed. Very often government protection had enabled them to achieve near monopolies in certain business sectors. *Zaibatsu* families used such methods as strategic marriages and 'feudal' personal relationships to maintain ownership control. In their developed forms, by the turn of the century, the various concerns within a *zaibatsu* were organized on a pyramidal basis, with a holding company controlling the group. Shares in the holding company normally remained in the hands of the family, although nonowners increasingly did the actual management. *Zaibatsu* holding companies exercised power within the group financially but they also established control over small independent companies that fell into a *zaibatsu* orbit.

124

The occupation authorities sponsored a number of measures to eliminate producer monopolies that had been so much a part of prewar Japanese economic conceptions. Under Allied tutelage the Japanese government introduced legislation to forestall excessive concentrations. The Anti-Monopoly Law of April 1947 prohibited holding companies, private monopoly, cartel agreements, unfair dealings and competition, shareholding above certain designated levels, and other such provisions. The act created a Fair Trade Commission to supervise enforcement. The government put through a Law for the Exclusion of Excessive Concentration of Economic Power, which disbanded existing organizations, held to be dangerously monopolistic. Under its provisions a Holding Companies Liquidation Commission found 325 companies to be excessive concentrations of economic power and split them up into their constituent parts or controlled them in other ways.[49]

Obviously, the Americans sought to impose their 'democratic' business forms on the Japanese, in Hadley's sense, that is, easing entry for individual entrepreneurs into a forest of firms competing openly and fairly in a consumer-driven market economy. And clearly, too, the Americans had much success. The destruction of the *zaibatsu* and the liquidation of the stockholdings of large conglomerates, by making stocks available on the open market, did reduce the influence of financial families in the economy. Inasmuch as corporations bought most of the stock, individual stock ownership did not especially result.[50] But this ownership was not concentrated in few corporate hands, since most companies habitually purchased some stock in companies with which they did business. The anti-monopoly measures also fostered a highly competitive environment within Japan from which consumers worldwide have clearly benefited. One of the reasons frequently cited for Japanese leadership in product development, variety, and quality is the intensely competitive nature of the postwar Japanese domestic market. The postwar anti-concentration measures not only created this competitive environment, more significantly, it also opened up career opportunities for professional managers within firms.

Hidemasa Morikawa argues that professional management had started to replace family management in *zaibatsu* well before the war.[51] The postwar dissolution of *zaibatsu* reinforced the trend, so that 'the ownership and management of companies in Japan is now more distinctly separate than in most other capitalist countries in the world'.[52] Professional management in Japanese corporations, moreover, came to mean 'employee management', in that corporate personnel departments and company boards promoted people to the top from within the firm (see Table 3.1).

Table 3.1. Origin of full-time directors of Japanese companies, 1977

Origin	Companies		Persons	
	Number	%	Number	%
Employees of the company	134	100.0	2,398	91.0
Owner/stockholder	23	17.2	64	2.4
Bank executives	36	26.9	56	2.1
Public officials	48	35.8	73	2.8
Others	36	26.8	45	1.7

Source: Keizai Doyukai (1977); taken from Taishiro Shirai, 'A Supplement', 374

Since American reformers prompted the Japanese to institutionalize a New Deal version of management–labor relations, they also set about, after legalizing trade unions, to reform Japanese labor law. Consequently, William B. Gould writes, 'Japan and the United States have labor laws that resemble one another and in some respects, appear identical.'[53] Consequently, too, it is not surprising to find today American conceptions of labor–management relations legally established in Japan. Like American, Japanese law excludes supervisors from union membership, thereby accenting the adversarial relationship between labor and management characteristic of American managerialism. Like American, Japanese law defines unfair labor practices and provides for agencies (labor relations commissions) that, like the American National Labor Relations Board, adjudicate disputes.

During the occupation, authorities changed curricula and modified the structure of Japanese education along American lines. The 1947 Basic Law on Education set down concepts and set out goals for a democratic education, with a new 6-3-3-4 system, based largely on the American one. It provided compulsory education for six years of primary school and three of intermediate, followed by a non-compulsory three years of senior high school, and four at college. Legally

Japan moved to a single-track system. Twenty-five years after the reform, over 90 percent of children, after completing nine years of compulsory schooling, entered a senior high school. The postwar demand for higher education followed suit. In 1945 there were forty-eight universities with over 100,000 students, in 1979 there were 443 universities with four-year courses and 518 sub-university institutions of higher education, with in all nearly two million students. Well over 30 percent of high school graduates proceeded into higher education.

School attendance, therefore, illustrates how occupation reforms heralded the 'democratization' of Japan.[54] Besides augmented numbers, there was the 'psychological disarmament', the elimination of ultranationalism and militarism from school lessons, and the introduction of a curricula that would prepare the pupils for democratic participation.[55] Civic and political concerns most exercised the minds of American reformers but, as important as they are, these concerns must give way here to a question that is more focused: what did this educational reform have to do with the development of Japanese management? Again, the numbers tell a story: from the 1860s to 1905, the greatest growth in Japanese education took place in elementary education. From 1900 to 1945, the expansion occurred primarily in the first three years of secondary education, especially vocational schools. From 1945 to 1970, however, the total enrollment, as a percentage of the population, in elementary and middle school (together the first nine years of education) hardly increased at all. Before the war, then, the Japanese population already fully participated in elementary and intermediate school education. The significant educational transformation of the postwar years, therefore, occurred in senior high school and university education, when Japan switched from a multiple to a single-track system.[56]

The universities not only witnessed a numbers explosion but a shift in the subjects students studied. Prewar, 90 percent of private university students, 81 percent of two-year college students, and 55 percent of students in national universities majored in the fields of liberal arts, law, and the social sciences. There were no graduate schools worthy of the name in the country. In the immediate postwar period the imbalance in favor of the liberal arts and social sciences disappeared. In 1970, 'out of the total of 1,669,740 university and college students, 828,096 were majors in social science, law, and liberal arts, representing forty-nine percent of the total'.[57] Between 1950 and 1965 the biggest percentage increase happened in physics and engineering at the university level, a rate of increase of 272.7 percent and 260.7 percent, respectively. With the postwar organization of graduate studies, the number of graduate schools jumped from four in 1950 to 131 in 1965, the number of graduate students from 1,052 to 40,000.[58]

Kenneth Bok Lee established some interesting correlations between the growth of Japanese New National Product (total national income) and total student enrollments at universities and colleges (see Table 3.2). At the same time, there was no unemployment problem in Japan (only about 1 per cent of the population between 1950 and 1970). Among university and college graduates, moreover, the unemployment numbers greatly improved compared with prewar years (see Table 3.3). In the fifteen years from 1951 to 1965, furthermore, the average income of Japanese families increased 400 percent, an

Table 3.2. Correlation between Japanese New National Product and university enrollment

Year	NNP (billion ¥)	Student enrollment
1953		511,124
1954		565,453
1955	6,718.8	601,240
1956	7,617.6	624,367
1957	8,285.9	637,591
1958	8,519.0	649,314
1959	10,037.3	673,384
1960	11,937.3	709,878
1961	15,775.1	763,553
1962	17,729.8	834,818
1963	20,607.2	916,392
1964	23,329.3	980,476
1965	25,977.4	1,085,119
1966	30,442.7	1,239,293
1967	36,233.2	1,395,173
1968	42,869.6	1,525,451
1969	49,856.7	
1970	59,048.0	

Source: Kenneth Bok Lee, 'The Postwar Reforms and Educational Development in Japan, 1945–1970', Ph.D. thesis (University of Southern California, 1974), 421

'improvement which [was] rarely matched by other countries in the world' (see Table 3.4). The information contained in these tables correlates the socio-economic development of postwar Japan positively with increases in higher education, and correlates the general well-being of the Japanese people positively with the development of their occupational skill and knowledge levels.

Table 3.3. Employment situation of university graduates (of those who wanted a job)

1931	1956	1959	1962	1965	1967
32.2%	64.9%	83.4%	94.8%	95.6%	93.2%

Source: Lee, 'The Postwar Reforms', 405

Table 3.4. Improvement in Japanese family monthly income (¥360 = U.S. $1.00)

1951	1954	1957	1960	1963	1965
¥24,807	¥41,017	¥47,105	¥59,658	¥83,186	¥100,670

Source: Lee, 'The Postwar Reforms', 412

Employees in Japanese firms, as a result of the postwar democratization of education, and among them those who rose in the managerial hierarchy, were better educated than ever before. After the war, getting a good education proved to be a good way to move into and up the professional management hierarchy that, after the *zaibatsu* dissolutions, controlled the Japanese corporation. School attendance also speaks about the spirit of 'democratization'. Studies indicate that the more education people had, the more self-assured they became and the more independent in their thinking. More highly educated employees, as in the German case, fostered greater effective democratic participation.

Thus, the Americans sponsored democratic measures to break up economic concentrations, to restore the rights of trade unions to engage in collective bargaining, and to improve educational opportunities for the Japanese people. Beyond these initiatives, with the very important exception of land reform, the occupiers, in the economic sphere, were not prepared to go. Indeed, as the Cold War deepened, they became preoccupied with the Communist menace. The Left likes to think that this happened because the socialists seriously threatened to take over Japan immediately after the war. And the occupation authorities obviously agreed. Hence the Americans become the bogeymen. They helped quash radical trade unions after first encouraging them; they urged, successfully, the Japanese authorities to outlaw the Japanese Communist Party.[59] They supported Japanese conservatives during the Red Purge (in late 1950 some 11,000 workers in private concerns and 1,200 in government service lost their jobs). The anti-Communism of the occupation authorities ended any possibility that Japanese business and industry would fall prey to a socialist takeover and, therefore, guaranteed that they would remain under capitalist management.

But what kind of 'capitalist' management? That proved to be the much more important question. Here the story has a somewhat familiar ring because it has overtones of the German. Hideo Otake points out that immediately after the war a strong employee participation movement arose in Japan.[60] It was strong, as in Germany, in the burgeoning trade unions, but it was also, as in Germany, supported outside labor, including even in management circles. The business leaders had been so discredited by their association with the defeated regime that many felt employee participation would forestall the outright socialization of private firms. But management acted for genuine as well as tactical motives, especially the young professional managers who believed participation morally right and managerially useful. So, just as the professional manager Heinrich Dinkelsbühl worked out *Mitbestimmung* in the German steel and coal industry, right after the war, Otsuka Banjo, his professional manager counterpart, 'organized in January 1947 within the *doyukai* a group to study enterprise democratization'.[61]

Plans to organize employee participation at the national level mirrored the actual creation of managerial councils (composed of management and union representatives) happening at the enterprise level. Although in Japan, as in West Germany, managerial councils had prewar origins, they really came into their own after 1945. According to a survey of the Minister of Labor, by the end of 1948, 'the number of unions having managerial councils amounted to 15,055 or forty-four percent of the total number of unions. [The Japanese trade unions] valued highly management participation through managerial councils.' That so many came into existence shows that management, too, was predisposed after Japan's defeat to cooperate.[62] Details of managerial council empowerment, however, often had not been settled at their creation. The unions wanted true co-determination, management to restrict the managerial councils' role primarily to consultation.

Nationally, the employee inclusion movement peaked with the establishment of an Economic Recovery Conference. This body, which assembled union and employer representations, met to promote co-determination throughout Japan. After three difficult national committee meetings, however, the managerial side withdrew, thereby, despite union desires for it to continue, dissolving the Economic Recovery Conference (28 April 1948). With the formation of the Japan Federation of Employers' Association (*Nikkeiren*) that same year, Japanese management turned its back on co-determination at the company board level. This attempt to democratize management went the way of socialism: it fell victim to a resurgence of Japanese managerial capitalism.[63]

The defeat of board-level co-determination, however, did not signal a victory of American-style managerialism. Just as democratization affected other aspects of Japanese life, it guided the 'renegotiations' of labor relations within the Japanese enterprise in ways that perpetuated traditional Japanese attitudinal patterns. Again the issue is not managerial method or technique but management itself, as a realized concept that deals with people. Because Japan's moral codes and religions (Confucianism, Shintoism, and Buddhism) blended public with private, Japanese management tended to believe that it must employ social and spiritual means, to look after 'the whole person's needs' within the subculture of a company before that person could make a full contribution.[64] Whereas classical Western management theorists have made human resource management one subject among many within management, and not necessarily the most important, '[t]he Japanese perspective of management, placed almost total reliance on the human factors within general management theory and then assumed other elements (planning, control, organization) would logically follow'.[65]

The departure point for Japanese enterprise management in 1945, then, differed from American. Within the firm's human resource management core, top Japanese business and financial leaders did not behave like Americans, not in their relationship to stockholders. Whereas in American capitalism the 'outsiders' engaged in leveraged buyouts, hostile takeovers, and claimed, as major shareholders, a say on the board of directors of firms in which they played no organizational part, in Japan they did not. James Abegglen and George Stalk note that

> Japanese companies . . . differ significantly from the Western pattern. The essence of the Japanese company is the people who compose it. It does not, as the American firm, belong to the stockholders and the managers they employ to control it, but it is under the control of the people who work in it, who play limited attention to stockholder's wishes. The company personnel, including directors, who are themselves life-time employees and executives of the company, are very much part of the company. . . . [P]ersonnel have a very real control over company decisions.[66]

The attitudinal patterns affected in numerous ways personnel inter-relationships within large postwar Japanese corporations. Little of American managerialism could be detected after the war in Japanese leadership style and method. 'Classical American management', in Philippe d'Iribarne's words,

> operates on the following behavioral principles: to define precisely and explicitly the responsibilities of each person, formulate his/her objectives clearly, give the person freedom in the choice of methods for meeting objectives, evaluate the results carefully, and reward or sanction the person according to his/her successes or failures.[67]

These principles call for a management where a 'high degree of formalization, standardization, and centralization' reigns, where managers possess good conflict-resolution skills, 'good top-down decision-making abilities', good problem-solving, analytical skills, and a capacity to devise good externally imposed evaluation systems.[68] This is Taylorism *par excellence*.

Japanese management by contrast continued to emphasize the group leadership qualities that the Tadao Kagono-led group of Japanese scholars identified in their study. Lacking the normal, standardized, externally imposed modes of work customary under

American managerialism, postwar Japanese corporate leadership espoused group-oriented consensus-making, 'control by sharing of values and information', the cultivation of 'relational skills', and 'broad consultation before acting'.[69]

The postwar democratic 'renegotiation' of Japanese organizational life transpired within this inherited managerial framework. Nonetheless, there was a renegotiation. The labor settlements of the 1950s, even after the defeat of union-sponsored managerial councils, fostered employee participation. To use the words of Professor Gordon, hardly a friend of Japanese capitalists, '[managers] conceded the status of "employee", the respect and security of a monthly wage, and the right to use all facilities to an expanding pool of [blue-collar] workers. And they worked out an implicit system of job security and livelihood wages acceptable to most employees.'[70]

Because of this recognition, the denigrated status of prewar blue-collar workers began to disappear. In unionized firms it was not uncommon for the professional manager to spend a stint as a union official before resuming a managerial career in the firm's hierarchy. Imagine senior corporate executives at General Motors or Ford doing time as officials in the United Auto Workers before returning to the corporate management ladder! While it would be perfectly acceptable for a Ford executive to have been at General Motors (not done in Japan), moving in and out of union management positions would have been inconceivable. Surveys of major Japanese firms show that members of Japanese corporate boards have often been union officials during their careers. Rodney Clark calculates, for example, 'of 313 major Japanese companies 74.1 percent had a least one executive director who once served as a labor union leader. The figure was 66.8 percent in 1968. In Japanese management, executive directors are the top day-to-day decision makers.'[71]

From an American perspective, this interlock between union and company officials looks like managerial manipulation of docile workers. One observer of Japanese participative management claims that Japanese workers are 'happy remaining in basically a suggestive mode with respect to members of higher management'.[72] But as Paul Lillrank and Noriaki Kano observe, 'in light of the turbulent and often violent history of labor relations in Japan, there is no reason to believe that Japanese employees are basically docile and submissive'.[73] Japanese scholars, moreover, not only defend the enterprise union's willingness to look out after the interest of employees but its record in so doing.[74] Perhaps disagreement about the effectiveness of enterprise unionism arises from a misunderstanding. Comparing Germany with Japan, Yoshiakiu Shimabukuro observed: 'There is nothing to match Japan's trade unions except Germany's management consultation boards (works councils). If one were to seek a corresponding system in this country to Germany's workers' management participation through the management consultation board, it would have to be workers' management through labor unions.'[75] Germany has a dual if intertwined system of management–employee relations: unions deal with employer associations outside the firm, employee-elected works councils with management within the firm. German works councils represent employees in German firms but they are not labor unions. Japanese enterprise unions should be judged in works-council, not trade-union, terms, that is, as employee representatives in the vertically structured firm.

Besides, because of the vertical cohesion within Japanese enterprise, management exhibits weaknesses similar to those of labor. Management just like labor submits to the needs of the enterprise as a whole. A 1993 estimate of the average pay ratios (income ratios) between the highest paid and the lowest in U.S. firms were 110–160 to 1, in Japan 17–18 to 1, and in Germany 23–25 to 1.[76] Taishiro Shirai compiled another table, from *Nikkeiren* surveys of private industry, that states the salary differential between company presidents and newly hired graduates (see Table 3.5). They have been gradually narrowing over time, from a differential of 110 to 1 in 1927 (before taxes) to 14 to 1 in 1980.

In America, the private corporation is a wealth source that people have felt free to abuse and on occasion pillage for 'outside' personal advantage. Stockholders want high dividends, workers high wages, managers big rewards and emoluments. Society is rich and the corporation relatively poor. Under American managerialism, top executives have garnered an uneven, nearly disreputable share.[77] In Japan, the corporation, generally characterized, is rich and society relatively poor. Both labor and management serve the corporation and their interrelationship is conditioned accordingly. That relationship is dif-

Table 3.5. Comparison of the annual earnings of company presidents and newly hired university graduates, 1927–1980 (yen in thousands)

	1927	1963	1973	1980
A. Company presidents				
Before tax	165	6,082	15,675	23,593
After tax	151	3,013	7,181	11,543
B. Newly hired employees				
Before tax	1.5	257	825	1,623
After tax	1.5	152	797	1,546
Difference Between A/B				
Before tax	110	23	19	14
After tax	100	11	9	7

Source: *Nikkeiren* (1982), 2, cited in Taishiro Shirai, 'A Supplement', 377

ferent, therefore, in form and content from what is implied by 'labor' and 'management' in America.

This said, qualifiers are in order. Despite the deepening of vertical social order brought on by the postwar democratization of Japanese firms, the inferior–superior social legacy persists. For it is important to recollect Professor Rohlen's corrective to Chie Nakane's claim that Japanese firms have a vertical social order: the characterization only applies to those with 500 or more employees (which contain but 20 percent of the workforce).[78] Eighty percent of the work force, therefore, does not have the benefits of association enjoyed by the other 20 percent.

Even within the large corporation, a status difference between 'permanent' and 'temporary' employees, moreover, divides the 20 percent. The difference between the inside group and the outside group is expressed in wages, bonuses, seniority-based promotions, and benefits. Considering that status is not determined by individual merit (women, for example, are rarely made 'permanent' employees), the projection of Japanese conceptions of inferior–superior social groupings into the postwar world has severely limited the outcomes of democratic 'renegotiations' inside the firm.

Status differences also operated inter-firm up the economic order from the smaller to the greater concern. Japanese start-up companies faced the same market-distribution disadvantages vis-à-vis older producers, with established outlets, as did foreign firms exporting into Japan. Some famous postwar firms (Sony, Honda) found it easier to expand sales in America than in Japan where the older firms (e.g. Toyota, Matsushita) controlled distribution outlets in such an exclusive way as to make entry too costly and hence prohibitive. Firms sought protection not in anti-trust legislation but in countervailing groups, the *keiretsu*.

Despite reform, therefore, the Japanese economy emerged from the war as a status hierarchy of professionally managed firms associated in business groupings. There are two kinds of *keiretsu*, horizontal and vertical. The six prominent horizonal *keiretsu* retain prewar *zaibatsu* names (Sumitomo, Mitsubishi, Mitsui, Dai-ichi Kanyo, Fuyo, and Sanwa). Between them they group 12,000 companies with sales mounting to 25 percent of Japan's GDP.[79] The vertical *keiretsu*, or supplier *keiretsu*, are composed of layered sub-contractors, which frequently have interlocking directorates. Toyota Motor Company is the obvious example of a vertical *keiretsu*.

Japanese competitiveness developed between firms located in different *keiretsu* (i.e. Nissan in one group competing with Toyota in another). Within the *keiretsu*, which gathered together a wide variety of firms (banks, trading companies, manufacturers, etc.), there emerged a pecking order, in which large, prestige firms dominated, in an unstructured chain downward, uniting firms within certain industrial sectors. In 1984, for instance, Japan had eleven assemblers employing 155,000 workers in the automobile industry, prestige firms in different *kereitsu*. Feeding these assemblers were 7,000 parts manufacturers employing 360,000 workers.[80]

The hierarchy of firms within each *keiretsu* produced corresponding wage differentials and working conditions: in small, sub-contracting companies, wages were lower and working conditions poorer. Table 3.6 gives the wage differentials by firm size as of 1978. The economy, although competitive domestically, exhibited the competitiveness of feudal barons, with their retainers gathered around them, rather than the free-for-all of independently owned and managed enterprises, which trust nobody, in the give-and-take of American consumer-driven capitalism.

Traditional Japanese patterns of managerial behavior, therefore, clearly frustrated American postwar democratic reforms. The Occupation sponsored anti-combination measures did not end 'feudal' habits in the Japanese economy. In the immediate postwar period high

Table 3.6. Japanese manufacturing industry wage differentials (1978)

Company size (no. of employees)	Wages as % of 1,000+ firms	% of workforce
1–9	33.8	
10–49	54.8	46.6 combined 1–49
50–99	60.3	
100–499	73.4	32.9 combined 50–499
500–999	85.5	
1,000+	100.0	10.5 combined 500–1000

Source: Nick Oliver and Barry Wilkinson, *The Japanization of British Industry: New Developments in the 1990s*, 2nd rev. ed. (Oxford: Blackwell Publishers, 1992), 59

tariffs and government regulatory policy discouraged foreign imports and stopped foreign high-tech manufacturers from settling in Japan. When foreign pressure forced the Japanese to eliminate legal protectionism, Japanese-monopolized distribution outlets stopped foreign firms from penetrating Japanese markets.[81]

American-favored labor legislation suffered a similar fate. In effect, a startling gap developed between the intent of the American-influenced labor law, adopted after the war, and actual Japanese behavior. Although legally forbidden, supervisors in firms have joined labor unions; although the law sets up an adversarial conflict-resolution process, it has been mostly avoided. 'In the United States', William B. Gould explains, 'the case load of the National Labor Relations Board, which has responsibility for unfair labor practice, has become a major labor law problem (40,000 cases a year), but in Japan [the number of cases brought before labor relation commissions] is minuscule.'[82] Even though Japanese law provides for arbitration to settle conflict between employees and employers, it is a rarely used procedure. Japanese prefer joint-consultation groups where informality and behind-the-scenes discussions take place.

American trade unionists consider joint consultation to be a direct attack on the principle of collective bargaining, but collective bargaining in America and Japan does not mean the same thing. Issues like dismissals, discipline, and transfers, which in America are often dealt with through collective bargaining, are usually worked out in Japan by management, in consultation with unions or a majority of the workers in nonunion plants, and then promulgated by management as the firm's 'rules of employment'.[83] If Japanese management resembled

American, this procedure would amount to managerial dominance. But the degree to which management and employees are interlaced within the Japanese firm makes 'consultation' a much more effective process, from the employees' viewpoint, than in America. Law and social practice vary considerably in Japan but this bothers not the Japanese, as it would the German, because 'the very precision of the law is alien to the Japanese [mind]'.[84] The legal relationships that the American occupation authorities tried to introduce into postwar Japan, therefore, succumbed to Japanese-style human resource management.[85]

Attempts to copy American education also succumbed to Japanese attitudinal traditions. Gary H. Tsuchimochi contends that prewar Japanese educational reformers had already embraced most of the recommendations the U.S. Education Mission brought to Japan in 1946, and that Japanese postwar reforms were the work of the Japanese much more than the Americans.[86] Although true, this claim does not negate the significance of the American presence because (1) the Japanese reforms clearly followed American recommendations, and (2) they could never have gotten through without silencing Japanese conservatives. The Occupation gave progressive Japanese educationalists their opportunity. Nonetheless, the Japanese educational system that emerged bifurcated. Education K through 9 developed into an essentially egalitarian system; senior high school and university education, on the other hand, despite the adoption of the single-track structure, turned out to be, even with increased numbers, profoundly undemocratic.

The anti-democratic impulse can be partially attributed to conservative university administrators who clung to highly selective admission standards. But the personnel recruitment policies of large Japanese firms are probably mostly responsible for derailing the single-track secondary educational reform. Personnel departments in large businesses and even certain government agencies designate a few universities as 'universities of fame' (*tokutei daigaku*), accepting only graduates from these universities as new employees.[87] The Japan Federation of Corporations (*Keidanren*) reported in 1957 that of its member firms, 270 (out of 321 companies responding to a questionnaire) limited their white-collar recruitment search to graduates 'from a preferred group of universities'. Sixty-one of these corporations recruited the graduates of five schools or less, and over half screened graduates of no more than ten schools during their recruitment drives.[88]

Selective recruitment policies within prestige firms put pressure down the educational ladder, leading to the creation of 'high schools of fame' (*tokuteiko*), high schools, that is, which produce the students who gain entry into the 'universities of fame'. In 1963 only about 400 high schools out of 4,847 in Japan produced graduates who were admitted into the nation's two prestige universities, Tokyo and Kyoto. Twenty high schools furnished thirty-five to forty-seven of the students entering these two universities (see Table 3.7).

Table 3.7. Share of 'high schools of fame' graduates admitted at Tokyo and Kyoto Universities

	Tokyo		Kyoto	
	1961	1963	1961	1963
Total freshmen admitted	2,371	2,559	1,965	2,170
From top 20 schools	1,111	1,211	725	812
% of admitted	45	47	37	37
From top 100 schools	1,847	1,995	1,422	1,638
% of admitted	78	76	72	76

Source: Yoshihiro Shimizu, *Gendai Nihon no Kyoiku* (Modern Japanese Education) (Tokyo: Tokyo University Press, 1968), 233; and Table 38 of the study. Quotes in Kenneth Bok Lee, p. 383

Thus, 'universities of fame' and 'high schools of fame' serviced firms of fame within the hierarchized Japanese economy. Specifically, because of the importance attending a 'university of fame' had for a person's career, university entrance examinations spawned a special group of students called *ronins*. The *ronins*, who usually came from families with means, repeat the entry examination two, three, or more years, until they obtain entry into the 'right' universities. Between 1955 and 1967, 30 to 40 percent of university applicants belonged to this group.[89] The examination hell and cram schools (*juku*) this system has spawned have made a mockery of postwar efforts to advance social equality through education.

There is nothing particularly anti-American about educational elitism. American higher education is elitist, too; one need think only of prestige American universities for a pertinent example. But Japanese and American higher education, if elitist, still developed differently, and in no education sector has this been truer than management education. Large Japanese firms recruit management candidates directly out of school based on their suitability to company culture (will they fit in?), not their functional management expertise. Once recruited, moreover, management specialties do not matter: people move about from job to job, department to department within the enterprise, so that they become company people rather than occupational specialists. Since the whole process of recruitment, training, and promotion within a vertically organized Japanese firm differed from America, so did the education to sustain it.[90]

In America the graduate generalists, with MBA holders at the forefront, promoted a managerialist consciousness. Undergraduate business education flourished in postwar Japanese universities, but this education only introduced students to business, namely by passing on general knowledge about business systems, business firms, organizations, and some analytical methods plus elementary instruction in accounting and computer operations.[91] Employer associations repeatedly ask for more and better higher education in Japan. But they asked for scientists, engineers, computer specialists, and technicians, for technical research facilities, and for the establishment of closer cooperation between universities and industry. The words 'management education' never appeared in these requests.[92] Since business and industrial spokesmen have expressed no real and persistent demand for this education, no American-style management education of the MBA type materialized.[93]

This does not mean that Japanese schools forgot about managerially useful education. It only means that the Americans and Europeans would not call what the Japanese do in public institutions management education. If the Japanese make human relations, not methods and techniques, the educational centerpiece; if they seek to promote group consciousness within a vertically integrated enterprise, then the management education required needs to be quite different from the American, not only in content but also at the level, within the educational system, where it is delivered. That level in Japan encompasses grades K through 9.

In postwar Japanese education academic subjects obtained an honored place. The high comparative scores Japanese participants obtain in international mathematics and verbal tests offer sufficient testimony to this fact. But in modern times educational bureaucrats have insisted that schools carry out the moral education of the nation. Before the war moral education (*shushin*) inculcated nationalistic, anti-internationalistic, and militaristic values in Japanese school children. The Occupation, therefore, eliminated *shushin* from the curriculum.[94] Indeed, Americans wanted to take the schools out of the moral education business. When the Japanese state regained control over its destiny, the Ministry of Education, at the urging of the Japanese Employers' Association (*Nikkeiren*), reinstated moral education. But it changed the educational content from an ethic of militant nationalism to one of civic virtue. This moral education fosters cooperative, family, and community values. 'Moderation' (*Setsudo*), Joseph Adams relates in his study of Japanese primary education, 'not asserting yourself too much in group relations', is the chief value taught.[95]

But the educational significance of this moral education is that it is process- not results-oriented. Process involves a continuous change in time, a moving progressively from one point to another in a continuing development towards a contemplated end. Process education stresses the process through which results are obtained, not the results themselves. W. Edwards Deming emphasized process as opposed to individual performance. He advocated making improvement in the process in which the individual's work is immersed, not trying to eliminate individual 'mistakes'. Kaoru Ishikara's famous fishbone diagrams illustrate process orientation in manufacturing; they show the people involved how the entire process in which they work produces the results, so that they can learn to think of their work in terms of process improvement.

Joseph Adams observed in a Japanese classroom that manuals for second-grade teachers contain illustrations similar to Ishikara's fishbone diagrams. They stress process modes of collective learning. Just as it is not unknown for Japanese managers to remove a worker from a production process to see how the others learn to cope with the irregularity, so it is not unknown for supervisors in schools to short the food for lunch in order to let pupils learn how to deal on the spot with the unexpected shortages. 'Japanese educators', Cummings points out, 'have never paid much attention to the innate abilities of learners. They have tended to assume that anybody can learn a task given a determined effort.'[96] Process modes of education emphasize the process, not individual abilities, and are perfectly suited to group cooperative forms of education.

Japanese educators and Japanese businessmen recognize that the cooperation essential to an integrated organization is learned, not spontaneous behavior. William K. Cummings observed that Japanese teachers spend an inordinate amount of time at the beginning of the school year just establishing order in the classroom, so that learning subsequently can take place. This happens when there is a minimal amount of classroom disorder and disturbance. Order is not established authoritatively but systemically through a learning experience that teaches cooperation. 'Classroom order', Cummings affirms, 'is . . . developed by having students cooperate in groups that prepare contributions for the rest of the class.'[97]

From K through 9 the education is organized to instill cooperative group behavior in the children. This is done, for instance, through extra-academic activities of a pleasant (organizing clubs, i.e. sports, art, etc.) or an unpleasant sort (food service and cleanup, in which teacher and pupil participate). The groups involved contain children from different age and class levels, as in after-school clubs, which promotes vertical school cohesion.

Classrooms break into groups, with teachers sitting by rather unobtrusively. Bright students work with slow learners whose performance they help raise to the group pace. Teachers and administrators do not discipline individuals, by, say, sending a student to the office, but let the group to which the problem student belongs decide and administer 'punishment'. Assertive discipline, Joseph Tobin affirmed in his study of Japanese preschools, is 'antithetical' to the Japanese style of student management. Japanese teachers even at the preschool level defer discipline authority to pupils.[98] Small work groups are held collectively responsible for homework assignments, so that if a group member does not do his work the others receive demerits.[99] Groups are assigned tasks, sometimes too difficult, just to see how well they can handle them—they are stretched.

Within the system moral education is taught by experience as well as precept. 'Regardless of students' preferences', Adams writes, '[they] are supposed to do the work their group is assigned to do, not out of preference, but out of an understanding of their "duty" and the "importance of the job".' Moral education is, in fact, an important aspect of group work tasks, including food service and clean-up. Cummings comments:

> This lunch routine contains several moral messages: no work, not even the dirty work of cleaning, is too low for a student; all should share equally in common tasks; the maintenance of the school is everyone's responsibility. To underline these messages, on certain days each year the entire school body from the youngest student to the principal put on their dirty clothes and spend a couple of hours in a comprehensive cleaning of the school building and grounds.[100]

This process, group-work education serves the personnel needs of Japanese enterprises much better than American management education. Firms, in non-technical spheres especially, recruit no specialists. Almost every firm of any size makes job applicants take a written examination and then those short-listed undergo intensive interviews. The written examination tests general knowledge (history, mathematics, geography, art, etc.). The interview is designed to establish a candidate's compatibility with firm culture. And why not, since job rotation makes flexibility gained through general knowledge (literacy and numeracy) a more important qualification than a specialist capability.[101]

Hence, after the postwar democratic 'renegotiation' the Japanese outcomes differed considerably from that set by the American example. There were reasons for the American reformers to rejoice, for the general upgrading of skills and knowledge within the population and the broadening of opportunity, which proceeded from American-supported educational and social reforms, changed the organization climate of Japanese business and industry in fundamental ways. However, the persistent 'feudal' character of the Japanese economic environment would disturb those weaned on American managerialism, as opposed to those raised in a society permeated with status distinctions. The Japanese refusal to accept the American-inspired labor laws, and to reform their educational structures in ways that would accommodate the needs of an American style of managerialism, mark the limits of American influence.

By adopting a people-oriented, 'organic management', the large postwar Japanese firm enlisted the brains and energies of the whole enterprise, management and shop floor, much more than American management. It clung in the large firm to the 'mechanistic' methods of managerialism. Summing up, the words of William Lazonick and Jonathan West seem most appropriate:

> [t]he Japanese corporations have elaborated American managerial capitalism of an earlier era into a more collective capitalism by developing long-term relations with employees not only in the managerial structure but also on the shop floor. . . . Japanese enterprises are more *organizationally integrated* than American enterprises . . .[102]

Japan's Management during High Growth Industrialization and Globalization (1960–1985)

This last section covers the period when Japanese management moved from obscurity in the era of American hegemony to prominence in a period of high growth and globalization. I propose to explain how the peculiarities of Japanese management that resisted Americanization immediately after the war manifested themselves in the period of dynamic growth and were, indeed, associated with it. It is important for the analysis to focus on certain industrial sectors because of the tendency, in recent years, to let general comparisons about productivity performances assume too much significance. Recent McKinsey and Company-sponsored surveys, for instance, report that American productivity in manufacturing and, above all, in service industries, is far superior to Japan's.[103] If, for example, American productivity is given the benchmark number 100, the corresponding productivity figure for Japan in manufacturing (1993) is 80, and in general merchandise retailing, 44 (1987).[104] Such evidence hardly supports a view that Japanese management performs well.

But Dominique Turcq, himself a McKinsey and Company consultant, pointed out a flaw in such comparisons. He observed that the Japanese productivity in general merchandizing is comparatively insignificant because in this service sector Japanese choose not to compete in a free market. That was the point of Turcq's comment about closed Japanese distribution outlets. Because Japanese distribution networks effectively exclude American products, and American distribution outlets are open to the Japanese, favorable American productivity performance figures in the retail sector do not translate in practice into an actual American comparative trade advantage. The real loser is the Japanese consumer who must pay much higher prices for items that could be more cheaply imported from America. But to look at the subject from the consumer's point of view is very 'un-Japanese'. Hadley's point, remember, is that the Japanese view the economy from the producers' perspective; their welfare matters more than that of the consumer. Since producers are also consumers this is not a completely callow view. But the emphasis is different, one that puts the protection of business and jobs ahead of consumer welfare, one that denies the primacy of the market in economic reasoning. If high-cost family-farm-grown rice, or inefficient small-shop retail distribution cost consumers more, the Japanese pay the price in order to protect their social fabric from the inevitable dissolution that a policy of mindless consumerism would entail. It is Listian as opposed to Smithian economics.[105]

On the other hand, postwar Japanese government and business recognized that the only way a resource-poor, overpopulated island could prosper would be through earning a trade surplus, based on the export of high-quality, modestly priced goods and the import of low-priced raw materials and food commodities. To develop a competitive high value-added export industry, Japan required an intelligent, selective industrial policy. The Japanese found their comparative advantage in 'fabricating industries [that] requir[ed] a skilled or semiskilled, well-motivated, and disciplined work force'.[106] To say, therefore, that the Japanese attained good levels of productivity in certain high value-added export sectors (automobiles, electronics, even steels) while performing poorly in other sectors like retail trade and farming is misleading. It does not acknowledge the success of their high value-added strategy. And to concentrate on those industries that the Japanese selected in this strategy, to explain why they flourished and what this success had to do with management, is to apprise more accurately Japanese competitiveness than to look at general studies on comparative productivity, like those produced in the McKinsey reports.

Productivity measurements can also be questioned in terms of the measurement itself. In a recent publication, entitled *L'Après-Taylorisme*, Pierre Veltz, a labor sociologist, asserted that the concept of 'productivity' has undergone change because of new approaches to production. He observes that productivity measurement is as much a result of the production system as of some externally contrived standard.[107] 'Under Taylorism,' he noted '[productivity is measured in terms of the] local optimization of human work in manufacturing' and this work is evaluated 'additively', each isolated work unit considered in itself and added to the next to form a process. This concept of 'productivity' measurement corresponds best to the classical American management idea defined by Iribarne, wherein each individual's duties are clearly demarcated and defined. The new idea of productivity, Veltz wrote, emphasizes 'the coherence and integration of the diverse steps in the cycle of production, intra- and inter-enterprise'. With this idea the yardstick for measuring productivity has to be extended from the workplace, for example, from Taylor's famous time-and-motion studies, to the enterprise level. If an accurate appraisal of Japan's national performance requires us to concentrate on the big firm within the export industries (automobiles, electronics, etc.) because that was the Japanese strategic choice, the way competitiveness is measured within these firms requires us to think, as did Japanese management itself, in holistic, systemic terms.[108]

The fame of Japanese management grew during this era because people believed that its strategies, techniques, and methods caused the high growth and globalization of the Japanese economy. The strategic vision has often been mentioned. Japanese firms emphasize market share over profitability. They gain markets by relentlessly exploiting core technologies, capitalizing on the possibilities of multiple product spin-off and constant product improvement. The techniques and methods that Japanese managers prized controlled and improved manufacturing process enterprise-wide. This resulted in maximum quality production at minimum costs.

There was nothing particularly Japanese about the strategy or the methods. Eiji Toyoda's statement to the head of Ford Motor Company (Philip Caldwell) in 1982, that Toyota had learned its famous 'lean' production system from observing Ford's plant at the River Rouge, was perfectly true.[109] H. Thomas Johnson explained that Ford's River

Rouge plant worked like clockwork but that it only produced a standardized product:

> Ford spoke proudly of turning iron ore, silica, and latex into finished vehicles in less than three and a half days, at the lowest cost in the world. And proud he could be, for the lead times and costs achieved in his River Rouge plant by 1925 had never been equaled before—nor have they been equaled since. . . . [But] Ford's system . . . was not designed to deal with variety. . . . [I]n his original system there was virtually no variety . . . , only one car in one color—the black Model T. In addition he produced one model of a farm tractor, the Fordson, a centerpiece in his River Rouge system. . . . [T]he low costs [were] achieved by repetitively producing homogeneous output, and Ford Motor Company led the way in designing systems to do just that.[110]

Since continuous, linked production requires that every process operate virtually at the same balanced rate, it could best be achieved by making one product. But people wanted variety. And so American manufacturers after 1950, 'to cope with the complexity of variety . . . decoupled the line, allowing different processes to operate at independent rates'. They created inventory buffers to handle imbalances appearing between the decoupled processes. 'Henry Ford did not require inventory buffers at the River Rouge in the early 1920s. Most American manufacturing plants could not operate without such buffers by the end of the 1950s.'[111]

To mount successful export industries the Japanese also needed to figure out how to produce variety with low-cost volume production. They solved the problem differently from the Americans. Since accumulating inventory increased costs, Taiichi Ohno at Toyota, who was deeply impressed by Ford, decided to keep Ford's no-inventory, continuous-production system but to gear it to customer demand. Actual demand determined the pace of production. To introduce variety the production line had to be stopped to allow for the die change-overs needed for different products. The success of this strategy, therefore, depended on minimizing waste, both in terms of quality and in the time required to make the necessary change-overs, since down-time reduced volume and raised costs.

Professor Mashiko Aoki describes how the production process adopted in the Japanese automobile industry worked:

The central production planning office drafts quarterly and monthly production plans for each factory, based on its market demand forecast, and presents corresponding procurement plans to outside suppliers. Those prior plans provide only a general guideline, however. The integrated production-delivery plan for a ten-day period is prepared by the commodity-flow office on the basis of orders from regional and overseas dealers. In response to this plan, the engineering office of each factory prepares a sequence of daily production schedules. The daily schedule is then adjusted two days prior to actual production in response to actual customers' orders transmitted from dealers to the factory through the on-line network system (the 'daily adjustments').[112]

Unlike the American system, in which production schedules, reflecting expert market forecasts, 'pushed' cars through the factory in long-run, big-volume spurts, in this Japanese system actual customer demand 'pulled' the product through the factory. Therefore, instead of long standardized production runs, on the final assembly line, wagons, two-door hatchbacks, and four-door sedans with red, beige, and white bodies, with left-hand and right-hand steering wheels, with a variety of transmissions, engines, and options, rolled one after the other along the line 'seemingly at random' in response to the customer orders flowing on computer printout into the factory from dealers. A just-in-time supply delivery system, which avoided inventories of parts, and a total quality control, which eliminated the losses involved in the withdrawal of defective products from the line, kept production costs to a minimum.[113]

Fine-tuning of production to actual market demand, just-in-time delivery from suppliers and from factory division to factory division, and total quality control demands the closest cooperation and coordination within and between groups involved. And a highly motivated workforce. This was true in preproduction (making the production system) and in production (constantly making improvements on the floor in the existing system), where customer orders, because of their variety, required a highly flexible response. To achieve it, Professor Hajime Yamashine remarked, Japanese manufacturers use a greater number of engineers in preproduction and production process than do Western manufacturers. More highly skilled and knowledgeable, engineers can constantly improve the process because they understand it. And Japanese engineers work closely with production workers as well as preproduction workers and people in sales.

The use of engineers on the factory floor, Professor Yamashine observed, resulted in the remarkable superiority that Japanese firms achieved in 'average setup times' involved in the die changes needed to achieve manufacturing variety. Whereas, one study shows, it took Japanese plants in Japan 7.9 minutes to change, it required Japanese plants in the United States 21.4 minutes, American plants in the United States 114.3 minutes, and European plants 123.7 minutes to change dies. Greater speed in changing dies allowed the Japanese firm to have more frequent setups, thereby permitting much greater manufacturing flexibility.[114] Because Japanese engineers not only developed and designed products, but also went to the shop floor and worked with regular employees to solve problems, they gained firsthand knowledge of the manufacturing process and obtained the quick feedback necessary for close and continuous study of the relationship between machine design and the die-change process. This allowed the Japanese production people to achieve their great success in manufacturing after the war. Keeping costly down-times to a minimum permitted continuous improvement, fine-tuning, and product variety.[115]

Just as Toyota learned production flows from the River Rouge, so did Japanese engineers borrow the quality-control techniques used in manufacturing from American experts. Walter Shewhart developed statistical process control (SPC) in the 1930s at Bell Laboratories, then, assisted by W. Edwards Deming, applied these methods to production during the war. Kaoru Ishikawa, who helped transfer quality-control methods to Japanese industry, maintains that SPC may have helped the United States win the war:

America's wartime production was quantitatively, qualitatively, and economically very satisfactory, owing in part to the introduction of statistical quality control, which also stimulated technological advances. One might even speculate that the Second World War was won by quality control and by the utilization of modern statistics. Certain statistical methods researched and utilized by the allied powers were so effective that they were classified as military secrets.[116]

Japanese Self-Absorption

Eager to improve manufacturing process, JUSE (the Japanese Union of Scientists and Engineers, founded in 1949) invited a number of quality experts to Japan. W. Edwards Deming visited in 1951 and then went to Japan repeatedly thereafter, Joseph Juran came over in 1955, and Armand V. Feigenbaum in 1960. They helped spread the quality-control idea in Japanese industry. Japanese experts made management contributions of their own. Shingo Shigeo, mechanical engineer at Toyota and Mitsubishi shipbuilding, Kaoru Ishikawa, professor at the University of Tokyo, and Genichi Taguchi, a statistician, improved SPC for shop-floor employee use. Shingo promoted the 'zero defects', or *poka yoke* objective, advancing worker-based total management control systems; Ishikawa simplified SPC theory, creating the 'fishbone' cause–effect diagram, which could be used in process analysis as part of the continuous improvement (*kaizen*) system. Taguchi formulated the 'Quadratic Loss Function', which measured the multiplier effect of minute quality losses along the process line. Because of the efforts of these statistical and industrial specialists, Japanese industries transformed the largely technical SPC methods, imported from America, into highly efficient shop-floor, process-control management systems.

As Japanese manufacturers learned to fine-tune process, comparative excellence developed steadily over years. At Toyota, quality had become an integral part of management by 1954, and the famous quality control circles had been introduced by 1962.[117] Indeed, W. Mark Fruin and Toshihiro Nishiguichi claim that the Toyota production system evolved through three stages. Immediately postwar it operated like the American Taylorist managerial model (flows of information about structures and processes top-down, flow and control of transactions predictable and managed, managerial prerogatives exclusively in the hands of Toyota's managers). Then in the early 1960s a network production model emerged; this turned into a learning model during the two decades after 1970.[118] They also claim that the Toyota system set the standard for domestic as well as foreign competitors.

If they moved slightly behind the improvement curve set by Toyota, large Japanese export firms also turned themselves during these boom years into highly productive, quick response, learning organizations. In this JUSE helped. By 1960, it sponsored three statistical quality control-related journals. In the late 1960s and 1970s Japanese process management became 'Total Quality Management' (TQM).

The story sketched here could be fleshed out in greater detail. But the point would be the same. Japanese attitudinal patterns described in the first two sections of this chapter shaped management strategies and methods during this period of high growth. There is no need to reopen debates about cultural determinism in the matter. This chapter began with the contention that each generation renegotiates the managerial conditions appropriate to its experiences—economic and social realities disciplining cultural contingencies. Many Japanese firms that have permanent employees, follow *ringi sei* decision procedures, and exhibit group consciousness did not develop Just-In-Time production process, Total Quality Control, or continuous improvement. If necessity is the mother of invention, no doubt a desperate postwar economic situation (limited capital and resource availability and overpopulation) prompted firms to implement the production innovations. Dominique Turcq, for example, cites four non-cultural reasons for the Japanese adoption of Toyota's system of 'lean' production: Japan's lack of capital (less money to put in immobile material flows, inventories); Japan's concentration in technologies that did not inventory well; Japan's lack of resources, forcing the maximization of value-added production; and Japan's need in these industries to get these products out quickly in order to compete well.[119]

But I also added a corollary at the chapter's beginning: people do not have *carte blanche* in making choices. Perception of problems and how to deal with them are to a large extent prescribed by attitudinal patterns inherited from the past. This restriction applies to the choices Japanese management made during the era of high growth and globalization.

At the corporate level the strategic decision to maximize market share certainly can be accounted for in this fashion. All firms need to protect themselves from the vicissitudes of the outside world. In America, they rely on the courts to guarantee equal access to business opportunities, and, by restraining monopoly, to protect each business from unfair competition. As so aptly described earlier in Eleanor Hadley's quotations, Japan's feudal habits created different behavioral patterns in Japanese business. Japanese firms sought security in association, which after the war assumed the form of horizontal and vertical *keiretsu*. Firms in a *keiretsu* bond through mutual ownership of stock. But the stock is purchased because of the affiliation, not the affiliation engendered through the ownership of stock. The *keiretsu* affiliation, not the actual amount of the stock held, which is usually quite small, is the crucial link. Stock held by firms in the *keiretsu*, regardless of dividends paid out or market valuation, is not sold.

Shirai pointed out that employee managers, who have spent their life in a firm, usually seek to secure the firm's long-term future by following a market-share strategy. Their ability to ignore profit maximization stems from their relationship with 'outside' stockholders. These 'outsiders', firms within the *keiretsu*, profit most from business dealing with the companies in which they hold stock. Because the 'outside' stockholders earn more through increased business with a fellow firm as it expands market share, that firm's management is not threatened by a stockholders' revolt when market expansion does not translate immediately into high profits, big dividends, and higher stock values. In America, where individuals and institutional investors (insurance companies and pension funds) predominate among the 'outsiders', stockholders are purely interested in immediate return on investment, through higher dividends and stock values. If capital depends on equity finance, specifically on the stock market, then a short-term outlook is often forced on a company—to keep the company's stock prices up, profitability must be high, hence the quarterly balance sheet drives the management.

Similar historical reasoning explains the emergence of Total Quality Manufacturing in Japan. Success depended on the uninhibited flows of information and people that Dominique Turcq and others trace to Japan's wetland forms of work organization. Japanese firms are formally among the most hierarchical in the world; formally decision-making in them is very centralized. But informally, they are much less hierarchical, with decision-making in practice 'made at lower levels in Japanese firms than in their Western counterparts'.[120] The shift to a high-technology, information-intensive work environment required the elimination of structural and organizational barriers to communications. Open-floor office plans, the common dining facility, the company uniform, the absence of reserved parking for top management, all manifested a concern for accessibility, just as the free flow of information within the firm, except for information about new technology, fostered full participation.

Blockages, moreover, could not exist in management–labor relations. Shunzo Ueda describes how, compared with an American company, Japanese organizations promote intra-firm fluidity in this respect. He calculated that the Tokyo Gas Company union enrolled 12,900 of the 13,000 people in the company, but in the Southern California Gas Company only 6,500 out of 9,000 employees belonged to unions.[121] The discrepancy could be explained mostly by the failure of the American firms to let management people into unions and by their inclusion in the Japanese company union. The Japanese firm hired university people into management-track jobs but they did not become management people until they reached the position of section head (*Kacho*), about age forty. Then they automatically withdrew from the union.

The fluid management–labor relations that resulted in the Japanese gas company contrasted sharply with antagonistic labor–management relations in the American. Informal discussions went on at various levels within Tokyo Gas Company, which resolved conflicts prior to formal labor–management negotiations. Disputes at Tokyo Gas could be settled at lower levels because upper management kept union members well informed about the national economy, the performance of the gas industry, and the situation of the company. Labor and management at Southern California Gas exchange no information prior to formal negotiations, whereupon, Shunzo Ueda observed, both sides engaged uniquely in a 'money war.'[122]

The Tokyo Gas microcosm exhibits Japanese attitudinal patterns writ large. When Masao Maruyama wrote about the effect that weak vertical hierarchies had on horizontal relations inside Japanese organizations, he looked to the past from the vantage point of 1949. Scholars describe the same organizational traits when explaining the success of Japanese Total Quality Management.[123] In 'lean' production, for instance, the ability to change dies quickly enhances the production process, but the speed depends on close cooperation between those who design, manufacture, and install the dies. That requires excellent horizontal inter-organization communications. The same cooperation is necessary throughout the chain from research, through design, preproduction, production, to marketing, each function feeding forward and backward into the other but also reaching out into the intra-firm and *keiretsu* network. In such circumstances the ability to carry on strong horizontal relations is a major reason for success.

Total Quality Manufacturing broke down communication barriers. The famous Quality Control Circles enlisted employees, equipped with statistical control techniques, into the process of continuous improvement. Whereas individual accountability in American firms fostered 'turf wars' that inhibited the sharing of ideas and limited creative interaction among employees, the Japanese stressed collective accountability in these Quality Circles. Usually, supervisors assumed leadership, but in many firms leadership rotated through the quality circle group 'to bring the abilities of all the participants into free play, to respect the personality and concerns of each member, and to create a pleasant and cheerful atmosphere for working and problem solving'.[124] Other process innovations acted like the quality circles as communication enhancers. Job rotation, multiple-skilling, small group work—each fostered information-sharing and worker involvement, the aim of which was to organize a social system that fed the production process.

Communication networks extended outside the firm proper into the *keiretsu*. Japanese firms realized that it was almost impossible in the postwar environment to keep abreast of, much less control, the new technologies. So larger producers found it expedient to acquire product ideas from abroad, and prudent to call upon outside specialists within the *keiretsu* networks for significant portions of production and development technology. This is what Toyota did in its relationships with suppliers. The *kereitsu* in the developed Toyota Production System operated as a supplier 'club', an arena for information exchange between buyers and suppliers (as well, of course, as a source for capital). Suppliers worked closely with their customers in product development to meet their specific needs, that is, suppliers did their own product research and development, calling on the know-how and information network of their customers in these efforts. This produced Toyota's learning organization, which allowed the firm, despite reliance on thousands of suppliers over which they had little ownership control, to obtain the highest standards in quality and price and product variety, in the shortest delivery times.[125]

American management during its great industrial boom (1880–

1929) adopted a low-dependency strategy, one where management carefully spelled out job descriptions, without much worker input, and implemented control techniques that permitted management to measure performance accurately against specified expectations and to take actions accordingly. Such a strategy seemed appropriate when dealing with the heterogeneous, largely immigrant workforce that peopled American industry. But, after the Second World War Japanese corporate leadership realized that if the rigidity of managerial structures could be erased and the discipline of managerial control eliminated, creative energies would flow. So they followed a high-dependency human resource management strategy that parted from Western concepts of ownership and control. American management depended on itself for success, Japanese depended on its employees. Why would the Japanese take such a risk? Human foibles make a high-dependency strategy very uncertain. Why would Japanese managment 'trust' its employees when the American low-dependency control mechanisms operate well?

It has been said that not enough policemen exist actually or potentially to stop crime if there is no compulsion within people to follow the laws. Confucius remarked about himself:

> At fifteen I thought only of study; at thirty I began playing my role; at forty I was sure of myself; at fifty I was conscious of my position in the universe; at sixty I was no longer argumentative; and now at seventy I can follow my heart's desire without violating custom.

Confucius talked about the creation of a moral order within himself which, somewhat like the German Idea of Freedom, results in a free person choosing to do the right thing. The moral order is not inborn; in a civilized society it is consciously, conspicuously, and effectively taught to citizens. It is, therefore, the very opposite of the popular Western idea of the noble savage, whose moral concepts *are* inborn, only—to use the Rousseauian image—to be dissolved through the influences of a corrupting society.

The existence of a moral order within each employee, coupled with completely fluid intra-firm and *keiretsu* communications, prevents a society, when the external controls of managerialism are removed, from degenerating into disorder in a high-dependency environment. On the contrary, instead of degenerating, as Fruin and Nishiguichi said of Toyota's 'learning' production system, 'individual experience and commitment are translated into organizational learning and this pushes system characteristics to new heights of performance'.[126]

Hiroshi Komai points out that 'Japanese workers have a stronger sense of job dissatisfaction than Americans (or Europeans), while at the same time, they have achieved, in their large export industries, excellent rates of constantly improving productivity'.[127] He believes that dissatisfaction increased among Japanese workers during the era of high growth because of the tremendous pressure put on them to raise productivity. In other words, the dissatisfaction induced by the productivity innovation of high growth (JIT, TQC, *kaizen*) offset the satisfaction that accompanied democratization in the postwar period (blue collar–white collar equity, long-term employment, job benefits, seniority systems, and so forth).

If true, job performance obviously is not to be correlated with work-satisfaction. Not surprisingly, therefore, just as U.S. Marines could attribute the conquest of Iwo Jima to *esprit de corps*, not job satisfaction, Hiroshi Komai says that the core element of Japanese managerial success is 'groupism'.[128] Ryushi Iwata adds that, because of group consciousness, the dysfunction of specialization found in American organizations does not surface in Japanese firms. Japanese employees do not permit themselves to adopt an attitude of 'no concern for any area other than one's own'. 'Responsibility for quality [resides] in its "natural" place, namely where production is performed.'[129] Whereas, therefore, Japanese have a weak individual but a strong group sense of responsibility, the American employees' sense of responsibility is the reverse.

Postwar Japanese faced a vastly different world from the one people had known in prewar Japan. The Empire, the colonies, were gone, the country subjected to occupation and demilitarization. Japan, through its participation in the *Pax Americana*, learned much from the Americans—technologically and managerially—as it inserted itself into the American security system and actively participated in the commerce of the 'free' world. But it has been argued here that, like the German, the Japanese dissent from the American management way began during this age of American hegemony. This was true because people in their continual search for meaning create rules and values that set the terms of each generation's 'renegotiations'.

The Japanese adopted a high-dependency strategy. But to have adopted a high-dependency strategy meant that Japanese management had to have confidence that it would work. It is the confidence factor that requires the group-consciousness explanation of Japanese behavior. The Japanese stress it in almost everything they write; the Americans do too, even when they are trying to deny its influence. Where did this group consciousness rudiment of Japanese management come from? The answer given here is that group consciousness is firmly rooted in Japanese historical experience and that it constantly reasserted itself despite efforts to dissolve it, in the Meiji period, the postwar period, and recent periods of high economic growth and globalization. There was nothing automatic about the perpetuation of 'groupism'; it has always been a conscious decision that each generation made, under the influence of its value system, about the future of its value system. We saw it emphasized in the postwar reforms of Japanese education, which, as comparative educational studies attest, rejected the ethics of American individualism. We saw it, too, in the failure of the Japanese to set up business schools, which, steeped in the values of American managerialism, would have undone the group-consciousness policies so carefully cultivated in big Japanese firms. Had the Japanese economy not flourished, 'groupist' ideologies might have been abandoned, but the economy flourished, beyond even the most sublime dreams of the most optimistic Japanese. It was the Americans who had, as a consequence, to undergo agonizing reappraisals.

Chapter Four

The Mystique Vanishes

THIS chapter deals with the actual collapse of the American management mystique. Three evaluative perspectives can be excluded from the analysis at the outset. One is the radical Leftist critique. Marxists might agree that a certain management 'mystique' can exist within capitalism because of management's ability to manipulate symbols, media, and government policy. But they would not consider the 'mystique' genuine because of management's exploitative function within the capitalist system. To them the whole exercise this book has undertaken is senseless.[1] The collapse of the management mystique, therefore, has to be treated from the viewpoint of those who generally support privately owned and managed, market-oriented business and industry. The purpose of the chapter, then, is to describe and analyze how America's management mystique has vanished within the citadel of capitalism itself.

The second excluded category pertains to government regulation of, and interference in, the economy. American managers love to blame government for their problems. Waking up to the Japanese challenge, CEOs emphasized government's meddlesome interference for their inabilities to compete. The subject is discussed in the English-speaking world, ad infinitum, ad nauseam. But it is ignored here, except where the interpenetration between government and business defines the essence and function of management itself, for this interpenetration has much to say about the collapse of the American management mystique.

The third ignored category is economics. Economists who write about American decline generally overlook management. In other words, if American manufactures or commerce decline, the reasons for it have little to do with management; it is not a causal agent but one that works within macroeconomic environments that really determine economic events. Even when economists recognize that business success depends on entrepreneurial skill, they usually assume that the pool of entrepreneurial talent is about the same in all industrially advanced countries. Therefore, if one nation performs better economically than another, the cause cannot be attributed to a comparative national advantage in managerial capability. In any event, whether the economists' explanations are right or wrong is immaterial, since the 'mystique' of performance, not actual management performance, is the subject here.

Something also needs to be said at the start about evidence. It might not matter whether yardsticks accurately measure management performance, but the evidence observers provide about performance is important because the shape it takes and its impact make 'mystiques'. Since the American collapse is not absolute, moreover, evidence of decline means decline relative to the perceived performance of German and Japanese management, and opinions about managerial performance in these two countries differ.

Simply stated, the American management mystique persisted vis-à-vis German management until after the mystique of American management vanished vis-à-vis Japan's.[2] Mystique has much to do with perceived economic threat, for, as Professor Otto Keck of the Freie Universität Berlin puts it, 'there is a general presumption that the managers of the most successful economy are considered best'.[3] Despite Volkswagen's postwar success in a mass-production industry Americans dominated, the resurgent German economy continued to excel in traditional low-volume lines. It did not, therefore, threaten American core capacities. Since the Germans did not generally challenge American-managed business and industry, there was no reason for Americans to doubt their own managerial skill. The creation of a German 'mini-management mystique' only came when Japanese economic success led to a general questioning of America's economic prowess. This evinced an appreciation of German management because it compared favorably (in some respects) with Japanese. In short, the fate of the American management mystique hinged on people's perception of the importance of economic events, not on their actually measured importance.

Outward Manifestations of Collapse

Acute Western awareness of a Japanese industrial challenge is often called the Japan 'shock' because it happened rather suddenly. The 'shock' produced a widespread conviction that the Japanese had developed the most successful economy. Evidence to support this contention piled up quickly in the late 1970s. Mark Fruin points out that the '[m]ost astonishing aspect of Japan's post-war economic recovery has been a surprisingly rapid penetration of the world oligarchy in such capital-intensive industries as automobiles and in related industries of steel, glass, and tires'.[4] The automobile story has been oft told.[5] The total number of American workers in that industry dropped from 802,800 in December 1978 to 487,700 in January 1983. Between 1978 and 1986 the U.S. vehicle market grew overall by 1.1 million units. Since imports grew by 1,800,000 units and transplanted (mostly Japanese firms) manufactured 700,000, the market share of American companies fell by 1.4 million units. By 1980 Japan had become the world's major automobile-producing nation. As Japanese replaced Americans, American automakers' world market share declined from 27.9 percent in 1970 to 19 percent in 1982.[6] That's a crisis. Reeling from the shock, Americans attributed the disaster to wage differentials; but a U.S. study in 1984 revealed that, if the wage differential between Japan and the U.S. completely disappeared, the gap between labor costs per unit of production would only shrink from $1,900 to $1,400 for hourly workers involved in subcompact assembly. This figure still decisively favored the Japanese producers.

The story in steel was even worse. According to a survey completed by *Business Week* in 1982, eighteen major steel companies recorded a combined loss in that year of $3.2 billion. Keitaro Hasegawa wrote in 1985 that American steel was an 'industry in crisis' and Robert Reich's data underscored the truth of the observation: half of the routine steelmaker jobs vanished between 1977 and 1988 (from 489,000 to 260,000).[7] To these horror stories could be added others about American failures in many other mass-production industries—transistor radios, cameras, binoculars, sewing machines, color television sets, VCRs, CD compact discs, as well as in glass and tire manufacturing, to which Fruin had referred.

160

Japan's achievements in industries deemed essential alarmed Americans even more. One was machine tools. Max Holland reported, in a frightful and frightening story about Burgmaster, that 'overall, perhaps twenty-five percent of the industry evaporated before the 1986 voluntary restraint agreement put a limit on [Japanese] imports'.[8] Another was the high-tech electronic industry, so vital to defense and future industrial leadership. Herbert A. Henzler and Lothar Späth figured that 30 percent of all industrial products by the year 2,000 would have a major electronic component in them, and that about 90 percent of the manufacturing process would depend on electronic components. By 1991 Japanese manufactures produced 41 percent of the world's integrated circuits and 29% of the computer hardware (as opposed to the U.S.A.'s 26 percent of the integrated circuits, 30 percent of the hardware). Rumors were that the industrial high-tech behind American defense depended on component suppliers in Japan.[9]

Overall, the American industrial picture was gloomy indeed. A Booz, Allen, and Hamilton survey, published in the *Japan Economic Journal*, claimed in 1985 that U.S. and Japanese managers ranked the U.S.A. first in basic technology, commercialization of new products, organizational flexibility, and management of information, but it ranked the Japanese first in application of technology, manufacturing technology, productivity, and quality control. The survey ranked management in the U.S.A., and Japan the same in their abilities to formulate a 'long-run strategic outlook'.[10] Whereas the U.S.A. provided half of the world's industrial output in 1950, by the mid-1980s the number was 21 percent as compared to Japan's 19 percent. American manufacturing exports rose from 9 percent of domestic production in 1960 to 19 percent in 1980, but imports of manufactured products increased even faster, from 5 percent of domestic production in 1960 to 23 percent of domestic production in 1986.[11] Since the trends were all unfavorable, Japanese superiority over America, long-term, seemed assured. As the Cold War ended victoriously for Americans, the American Council on Competition, with a membership drawn from the top ranks of industry and higher education, reported pessimistically that the U.S.A. would simply drop out of world-wide contention in fifteen areas of technological production (of a total of ninety-four).[12] And the bad news multiplied.

There was another aspect to the developing domestic story. In the

The Mystique Vanishes

1960s American industry invested heavily overseas, so much so that it prompted Jean-Jacques Servan-Schreiber to make the following remark in his blockbuster best-seller, *The American Challenge*: 'In fifteen years' time (he was writing in the late 1960s), the third largest industrial power in the world, after the United States and the Soviet Union, may well turn out to be, not Europe, but *American industry* in Europe.'[13] Servan-Schreiber's quote is striking evidence of how management gurus get it wrong. Martin Kenney and Richard Florida record that 'during the 1980s and into the 1990s 1,275 Japanese "transplants" established manufacturing operations in the United States'—this from a country Servan-Schreiber did not mention in his economic calculus two decades earlier.[14] Between 1981 and 1986 Japanese firms invested $167 billion abroad; foreign investment that in 1977 amounted to 2 percent of the total net worth (by book value) of all the non-financial corporations in the United States, by 1988 equaled 9 percent.[15] It is true that in the same period (1981–86) American firms invested $122 billion overseas. But this latter-day American foreign investment seemed to express less the industrial hegemony of the earlier investment than America's growing industrial weakness. American firms went offshore to seek cheap-labor sources in an often desperate attempt to compete with Japanese firms. Japanese overseas investment in manufacture, by contrast, resulted from domestic industrial strength. Japanese exports to the U.S.A. were so important that Americans imposed so-called 'voluntary' import-restraint agreements on the Japanese to hold them back. Fearing outright protectionism, Japanese firms decided to jump over tariff walls by manufacturing in the United States.

The Japanese investors did not send the Americans old technology, whose profitability depended on the exploitation of cheap labor, but new technology that promised, in a high-cost labor market, to improve American productivity often in the very staple industries where America's erstwhile industrial giants now faltered. This happened in steel. Japan's major steel producers—Nippon Steel, NKK, Kobe Steel, Kawasaki Steel, and Sumitomo Metal—all invested in and operated U.S. plants. Some of this investment went into joint ventures: Nippon steel joined with Inland Steel to build a new $400 million cold-rolling mill fifty miles west of Gary, Indiana, in which the time to produce a coil of steel fell from twelve days to about one hour.[16] NKK worked to revitalize National Steel mills near Detroit, Chicago, and St. Louis. Kobe Steel brought new technology to a U.S. Steel plant in Lorain, Ohio. And Kawasaki Steel, working with Armco, refurbished two Midwestern steel mills. Nippon Steel, Sumitomo Metal, and Nisshin Steel introduced state-of-the-art steel-galvanizing lines to coat and prepare steel products for automobiles and other uses.

Automobile transplants included Honda's large assembly and manufacturing complex erected in central Ohio, Nissan's plant in Smyrna, Tennessee, GM and Toyota's joint venture (NUMMI) in Fremont, California, Toyota's assembly complex in Georgetown, Kentucky, plus a Toyota transmission foundry outside Detroit. In order to insure the quality and cost effectiveness of their manufacture, Japanese transplant assemblers drew their Japanese suppliers with them. The assemblers knew that they needed reliable suppliers to feed operations in the United States like those high-quality lines of galvanized sheet metal the transplanted Japanese steel firms produced. Japanese corporations invested heavily in American rubber and tire production, through buyouts and acquisitions. In 1983 Bridgestone, Japan's largest rubber and tire producer, bought a Firestone plant; in 1988 it purchased the entire Firestone Corporation for $2.6 billion. In 1986, Sumitomo Rubber acquired Dunlop's U.S. tire operation for $350 million and invested another $200 million to build state-of-the-art factories at the Dunlop sites. Yokohama Rubber and Toyo Tire moved into the United States either by concluding joint ventures with American tire manufacturers or by purchasing them. Japanese machine tool manufacturers, too, invaded the United States. By 1988 nine Japanese machine tools plants operated on American soil.

The Japanese firms seriously exploited the technological dimensions of their American ventures. By 1990 more than 500 scientists and engineers worked for Honda Motors in Torrance, California, another 200 for Honda in Ohio. Nissan employed 400 engineers at its plant in Plymouth, Michigan and Toyota 140 at its Technical Center in Ann Arbor, Michigan. Meanwhile, Mazda built a $23 million research center in Irvine, California where hundreds of American designers and engineers work. And nothing has been said in this litany of transplants about Japanese manufacturers of electronic products, Matsushita, Sony, Sanyo, and Sharp, who had been established in North American longer than any other Japanese firms.[17]

Although American workers might rejoice at the employment opportunities and American consumers might long for the excellent products that Japanese transplants provided, American firms were not content. No doubt many reacted like the worried Campbell Soup Company executives who, learning that a Japanese canned soup manufacturer had built a plant in Fresno, California, increasingly focused on productivity.[18] Japanese competition especially upset American suppliers who feared the competition of Japanese suppliers that followed parent firms into the American market. One executive at Ford Glass, which supplied glass to Mazda's new assembly plant in Flat Rock, Michigan, complained about the difficulties his company faced satisfying Mazda's stringent quality requirements. Despite the fact that Mazda's cost and quality exigencies eliminated Ford Glass profits, the company suffered the Mazda deal. If it had not, Ford Glass feared that Mazda would switch to its glass supplier in Japan, which, with a new production facility in the U.S.A., eagerly sought to expand its American market share. With Japanese transplants, American firms now had strong domestic competitors from which they could not hide behind tariffs or voluntary-restraint agreements.

Finally, events in Europe conspired to undermine faith abroad in American managerial leadership. American influence, paramount there since the war, waned as Europeans by the late 1970s faced pressures quite similar to those Americans experienced. A 1989 survey (see Table 4.1), which compared plant performance in the American, Japanese, and European automobile industries, provided discouraging news. The numbers showed that the Europeans had less reason to be satisfied with performance than the Americans. But they also indicated that for Europeans le défi américain had turned into le défi japonais. The threat to Europe had to be grasped in global terms. Japan had become the key player. In automobile production, for instance, one-third of Japanese exports went to America, one-third to Asia, and a fifth to Europe. Japanese firms operated in America, in Asia, and in Europe. They had become truly global operations. American firms with transplants manufacturing in Europe operated in two important global regions. But the European firms manufactured mostly in Europe alone.

Europeans, like Americans, turned increasingly to the Japanese for the secrets of success. The recent agreement between Volvo and

Table 4.1. Comparative plant performances in automobile industries (1989)

	Japanese American 'Transplants'	U.S. plant in America	Europe in Europe
Productivity	21.2	25.1	36.2
Quality (defects per 100 vehicles)	64.0	82.3	97.0
Inventories (days of for 8 sample parts)	1.6	2.9	2.0
Size of repair areas (% of assembly space)	4.9	12.9	14.4
Absenteeism	4.8	11.7	12.1
Training of new workers (hours)	370.0	46.4	173.3
% of workers in teams	71.3	17.3	.6
Number of job classifications	8.7	67.1	14.8

Sources: J. D. Powers: Initial Quality Survey and the MIT, IMVP, Survey of World Assembly Plants, given in Robert R. Rehder, 'Building Cars as if People Mattered: The Japanese Lean System vs. Volvo's Uddevalla System', *Columbia Journal of World Business*, 26/2 (1992), 57–69

Mitsubishi is perhaps the most painful example of the new orientation. Volvo had pioneered group work techniques to replace Taylorism; now, awash in red ink, they turned to Mitsubishi to learn Japanese work process methods.[19] Japanese industrial know-how arrived through Japanese transplants like the greenfield factories of Nissan and Toyota in the United Kingdom. It came through buyouts like Sumitomo's acquisition of Dunlop, Fujitsu's of ICL, and Asahi Glass's of Glaverbel. It arrived through joint ventures like the Mitsubishi–Mercedes deal and the just mentioned Mitsubishi–Volvo–Holland agreement. And Japanese know-how arrived through even more circuitous routes like the NUMMI–Opel connections.[20] Toyota taught production methods to GM in America at their joint-venture NUMMI plant, then GM transferred the NUMMI methods to GM's Opel operations in Germany.

Japanese direct investments in Europe simply confirmed the great historical reversal occurring in Europe's global fortunes. Volkswagen's exports to North America halved between 1965 and 1975 (down from one million vehicles) as the Japanese took over America's small car market.[21] During the 1980s the European Economic Community's share of the U.S. automobile market fell from 10 to 4 percent. Germany exported more to tiny Austria (eight million inhabitants) than it did to all of East Asia. Indeed Germany's exports to non-European countries during the decade did not grow.[22] Europe, deprived of world market share, found itself falling back on European markets, which they protected, like the Americans did, through tariffs and voluntary-restraint agreements. American industry in Europe still counted, but, since the Japanese manufacturing dynamic had changed the world, Europeans stopped talking about the American challenge.

After 1980 Americans confronted three new economic realities: an inability to compete with Japanese imports in many important industrial sectors, an unprecedented invasion of Japanese transplants, and a diminished American influence in Europe. Together they precipitated the great crisis in confidence that resulted in the collapse of the American management mystique. The collapse can be easily documented. Pioneering prognosticators may have touted Japanese managerial capacity before America's problems took on crisis proportions.[23] But the sea change from self-confidence to self-doubt came within the managerial world at the end of the 1970s. It expressed itself in various forms.

One was the near panic that broke out in American management about its ability to survive, much less compete. Since the Americans really did not know what to do, this panic resulted in a hasty search for the secrets of Japanese success. American firms that had close contact with the Japanese could learn the easiest and the quickest. The Xerox experience illustrates how a firm could exploit its Japanese connection. In 1960 Rank-Xerox, the U.K. subsidiary of the American firm, founded a fifty-fifty joint venture with Fuji Films in Japan. Although this company, Fuji-Xerox, prospered throughout the 1960s, when its patents expired it rapidly lost market share in Japan to Japanese competitors. Responding to the challenge, Fuji-Xerox instituted Total Quality Control manufacturing in 1975 and won the Deming Prize for quality in 1976. The impetus for recovery had come from the Fuji people who moved to the Fuji-Xerox joint venture, many of whom had been at Fuji Film when it had won the Deming Prize in the 1950s. Moreover, the same consultant that helped Fuji Film to implement TQC helped the Fuji-Xerox people, too.

In the 1980s, Japanese competition threatened Fuji-Xerox's parent firm, Xerox U.S.A.'s American market. Xerox U.S.A. revamped production processes using the same Total Quality Control methods employed by Fuji-Xerox. Xerox U.S.A. won the Baldrige National Quality Award in 1989, thirteen years after Fuji-Xerox had won the

Deming Prize. The point is that the learning process about Total Quality Manufacturing extended from Fuji Film to Fuji-Xerox, to the parent company in America.[24] American firms with Japanese branches (another was Hewlett-Packard, whose Japanese subsidiary also won the Deming Prize) could and did tap Japanese management quickly and knowledgeably when the crisis came.

American firms without subsidiaries in Japan but with close relations with Japanese firms could also learn quickly. One noncarbon paper manufacturer, the Nashua Corporation, had such a relationship with Ricoh, whose copiers Nashua sold worldwide outside Japan.[25] In 1975, Nashua executives visited Ricoh. When they returned, one vice-president complained to Nashua's President, William Conway, about the way the Japanese had behaved. The American delegation had been ignored. 'It seems the Japanese hosts', the executive explained,

> were furiously engaged in preparations for something they called the 'Deming Prize'. The Americans had no idea what they were taking about. . . . On hearing this story, Conway's curiosity was piqued. 'Prize? What the hell is the Deming Prize?' The Nashua vice-president told Conway that as far as he could tell 'it was all about statistics and charts, and geez they're all nuts, they're all crazy. They're all working on it.' 'Who's working on it?,' asked Conway. 'Everyone', replied the vice-president. 'The president of Ricoh is involved . . . , sales managers, administrative people, engineers, manufacturers, everybody's working on the Deming Prize.'[26]

Conway tracked Deming down in March 1979 and invited him to the company. After lunch, he decided to hire Deming and Deming installed statistical quality control in Nashua's operations. Nashua 'conversion' is especially significant because of the company's influence on other American corporations.

With the broadcast (24 June 1980) of the NBC White Paper, 'If Japan Can, Why Can't We', Americans learned much more about the Japanese challenge. It was reputedly one of the more successful documentaries in television history. The last fifteen minutes of the program highlighted Dr. Deming's work at Nashua Corporation. But the documentary seems to have come off most casually. The producer, Clare Crawford-Mason, had heard from a faculty member at American University about 'this guy named Deming' who had done a lot of work in Japan. 'She contacted a high-ranking economics official from the

Carter Administration and asked if he knew W. Edwards Deming [who lived only five minutes from the White House]. He didn't.' But her contacts with Deming led to five interviews, consuming twenty-five hours. If the episode resulted in a successful program, it nonetheless confirms the incredible ignorance of Americans about the rest of the world in matters of extreme national importance.

After the NBC White Paper some Americans quickly climbed a rather steep learning curve. William E. Scollard, in charge of automobile manufacturing at Ford, saw the NBC White Paper on Deming and asked him to visit the company.[27] Ford President Peterson got on well with Deming. Hired as a consultant, Deming recommended installing statistical process methodology and for Ford to adopt his fourteen points of managerial behavior. Thus a reform impulse moved from Ricoh, through Nashua, to Ford, and then to other corporations. But the information-flow pattern was complicated. For example, Robert A. Lutz, Ford's European head, challenged by Japanese imports into Europe, sent 'dozens of executives and engineers to Japan' on factory tours in 1979.[28] Thus began an 'After Japan strategy' in Ford of Europe, entailing employee and customer involvement and quality enhancement. Whereas, then, at GM the knowledge moved from Toyota to NUMMI in California to European Opel, at Ford it moved in reverse, from Japan to Ford of Europe and then to Ford North America, where it mingled with a counterflow of information reaching America from Japan transmitted through the news media (the NBC White paper and other programs) and Dr. W. Edwards Deming. Robert Lutz and other European Ford executives eventually took command of the U.S. parent company.

It might well be asked, since he had a key role in the scenario, what was particularly Japanese about learning from Deming. After all, he taught statistical process control (SPC) to the Japanese. But, as one of Deming's disciples, Professor Kosaku Yoshida, observed, statistical process themes constituted only a small part of Deming's view of management.[29] Deming formulated a mature view (his famous fourteen points) in the late 1970s, after many visits to Japan. His management philosophy, therefore, was as informed by observing Japanese work processes as the Japanese work processes were informed by Deming's statistical techniques.[30] Ford Motor Company obviously realized this, too. Although they had hired Deming as a consultant for the Taurus project (1980), the project leader also looked to the Japanese for instruction. One of Ford's major supplier's, Smith, at Ford's urging, sent four of its people to Japan to study the supplier relations that Ford sought to emulate.[31] And Ford hired Kaoru Ishikara as a consultant.

Deming obviously benefited personally from this explosion of curiosity about things Japanese. His classes on statistics at New York University in the early 1970s had been sparsely attended; indeed as late as 1979 Deming's four-day seminar at George Washington University only drew fifteen people. However, a few months after the NBC White paper, between three and four hundred of the alarmed managers trooped into each seminar. The movement of opinion took on institutional dimensions. Older institutions, waking up, spun off special groups to deal with industrial innovation. This happened, for example, when (1983) the Greater Philadelphia Chamber of Commerce sponsored the creation of PACE, the Philadelphia Area Council for Excellence, which brought together businessmen, union leaders, and civic dignitaries concerned about the de-industrialization of their region. It happened, too, with the creation of the Growth Opportunity of Alliances of Greater Lawrence (GOAL), composed of the same sort of people as PACE, which met for the same reason. These associations and others provided venues for Dr. Deming's seminars to which the executives now flocked. At a PACE-sponsored Deming Seminar in Philadelphia (1983) executives from Campbell Soup Company or its vendors made up a quarter of the four hundred participants. Deming societies popped up in every region of the country, more than fifty of them by the late 1980s, eagerly involved in propagating the master's ideas about statistical quality control and process management.

In the rust belt, concerned people organized the Association for Manufacturing Excellence (AME), headquartered in Wheeling, Illinois. Formally chartered in 1985, AME concentrated initially on manufacturing improvements. They investigated JIT, TQM, and employee participation schemes on shop floors. Then AME broadened its interests to more team-based issues.[32] Growing from a Midwestern base into a national association with 5,000 members, AME organized regionally, like the Deming societies, with branches in the Northeast, the Mid-Atlantic, the Southeast, the Midwest, the West, the Southwest, and Canada. Each region, besides organizing its own activities, participates in national and international events. Originally, AME just mounted workshops, generally lasting one and a half to two days, almost always conducted at a host work site, often a production plant. Since the host was an acknowledged production innovator, workshop participants learned about improvements, goals, and practices first hand. Later AME sponsored seminars and conferences on topics in which regional members expressed an interest. It also started two serial publications for its members. *AMEN* focuses on AME activities and on ways to become involved in the 'excellence' process. The second periodical, *Target*, publishes interviews, articles, and reports about manufacturing innovations, designed to meet its members' needs. The management guru, Tom Peters, called *Target* 'the best business publication in America'.[33]

Recently *Target* printed a comprehensive index of articles published since the journal's inception in 1983. It verifies the Japanese impact. Some of the influence is direct, for example, articles on Japanese manufacturing or Japanese management techniques; most, however, is indirect in that the innovative firm is American. But the American firm has been directly influenced by Japanese production methods.[34] The atmosphere at AME, especially in the first few years, resembled Western Europe after the Second World War, only the transfer of management know-how was not sponsored by a massive government program like the Marshall Plan and was quite modest in scope. And the borrowers were not progressive European businessmen, manufacturers, or academics eager to learn about American managerialism but American businessmen, manufacturers, and academics ready to absorb good, effective management practice from Japan.

Finally, the Japanese challenge sparked the transformation of old organizations and inspired the foundation of new. In the quality control area, for example, both occurred. The American Society for Quality Control (ASQC), founded in 1946 with 1,000 members, was the first such society in the world. Although membership grew steadily over the years (24,000 in 1970, 32,000 in 1979), it rose spectacularly to 57,000 in 1988, a result, as Robert Cole phrased it, of 'the growing recognition by American management that continuous quality improvement is critical to competitive success'.[35]

The ASQC shifted emphasis to small-group activity, in the form of Quality Control Circles. Although American quality experts like

Joseph Juran developed the idea, especially in Japan after his first trip there in 1954, small-group activity did not take hold in the United States until much later, primarily because of its success in Japan. Cole observed:

> Ironically, it was only with the remarkable success of the Japanese in competing in American export and domestic markets that a more general reevaluation of small-group activities began. Suddenly in the early 1980s managers and the media were looking for the key to Japanese success, and participating work practices based on small-group activities were identified as part of the package.[36]

Whereas the ASQC journal, *Quality Progress*, hardly mentioned quality circles for years after publishing Joseph Juran's first article on them in 1968, the number of QC articles had jumped to four or more a year by the early 1980s.[37] In 1976 the ASQC devoted an entire conference 'track' to quality circles; that same year a ASQC Quality Motivation Technical Committee (QMTC), which had been established in 1965, outlined a three-year program on quality circles that included conferences, case-study research, development of educational materials, and training packages. Although JUSE had sent Japanese quality circle teams to the United States yearly since 1968, talk about quality led ASQC members finally in the late 1970s to strengthen contacts with these Japanese visitors.

The quality emphasis led in 1978 to the formation of another quality control organization, the International Association of Quality Control (IAQC), whose budget grew in just nine years from $100,000 to $1.5 million. Dramatic membership growth at ASQC and IAQC during the 1980s confirmed the intense interest that Japanese success in quality manufacturing evoked in the minds of American managers.

Although some hearty souls might still believe in it, and others not readily accept a Japanese version of it, the evidence clearly indicates that the American management mystique mostly vanished in the late 1970s and early 1980s. It is important, however, to distinguish between management and management expertise when making this point. After the war American management experts and management schools flourished. American consultancies and American management periodicals almost monopolized the subject nationally and internationally; everybody, including the Japanese, had to learn English in order to keep abreast of new management ideas and techniques. When the American management mystique collapsed, the mystique of American management 'science' did not. Indeed, and quite ironically, the American experts themselves contributed to the collapse of the American management mystique, not only in America but worldwide, for the best-sellers about Japanese management were to a great extent written by Americans.

Womack, Jones, and Roos's *The Machine that Changed the World* has probably had the greatest impact.[38] Its description of Toyota's 'lean' production systems dismayed European managers everywhere because of the challenge it presented.[39] But it is only one spectacular example of a literature with a ten-year lineage.[40] American management publications continued to predominate, only the subject handled shifted from American to Japanese management themes.[41] This transformation is readily discernible through a content analysis of relevant periodicals. Here is an analysis of a serious academic journal, selected at random, the *California Management Review*. In 1978–79, no articles appeared on Japan, in 1980–81 only one, and then in 1981–82 again none.[42] In 1982–83, out of forty-six articles published, three covered Japanese management. Then, in 1983–84 the number of articles about Japan increased to eight out of forty-nine; in 1984–85, to eighteen out of forty-five. In 1985–86, the journal indexed 'Japan' as a special category. Names that have subsequently become familiar to students of Japanese management began to appear regularly, including William Ouchi, Chalmers Johnson, and Richard Pascale. Articles not classified or classifiable under Japan discussed themes in ways that revealed Japan's impact on American management culture.[43]

To this content analysis of an academic journal can be added one of a randomly selected popular business weekly, *Fortune*. In 1980 *Fortune* published six articles on Japan, only 2.4 percent of its article content. This marked the end, however, of disinterest in the Japanese, for during the next three years slightly more than 12 percent of the magazine's articles covered Japanese business and manufacturing or American subjects related to the Japanese challenge (1981, 13%; 1982, 9%; 1983, 15%). During these three years, pessimism deepened in this normally extremely, if not to say nauseatingly, self-confident American business publication. Again, even when the Japanese were not mentioned, a Japanese presence haunted the issues (for example, in articles on the death of a steel town, or Ford's drive for quality). When articles praised American performance, they usually used Japanese standards as a benchmark. Europeans who habitually read this American management literature abruptly learned much about the rise of Japan.

To some extent, the American 'scientific' dominance expressed the essence of American managerialism. Japanese firms had not worked closely on management problems with the Japanese academic community (it was not the habit of management or academia). In fact, Japanese firms turned to American experts for many of the useful ideas they implemented. Moreover, with English the *lingua franca*, Japanese could not play the proselytizing role internationally that American experts did, even when discussing management events in Japan. So the lot of interpreting Japanese management to the world fell primarily to the Americans.

Professor Horst Wildemann's Japanese 'education' illustrates the American role. Robert Hall of AME described Wildemann as 'the repository of nearly all the history of the coming of "manufacturing excellence" practice to Germany, . . . a part of it, almost from the beginning'.[44] Without Japanese language skills, Wildemann depended on the Americans when trying to 'make sense' of Japanese experience with JIT and TQC.[45] Although especially strong at the beginning, this dependency has continued to the present. Wildemann states that he formulated the ideas for a recent paper on how to measure the quality of behavior when observing practices in twelve Japanese transplant factories in the United States.[46] If, however, the dominance of the English language helped perpetuate the reputation of American management science abroad, it could not save the American management mystique. As Karel Williams, Itsutomo Mitsui, and Colin Haslam concluded, 'Japanese manufacturing now [1994] has the same international status as American manufacturing in the first half of this century; its factories are sites of international pilgrimages and its manufacturing practices are objects of emulation.'[47]

Perhaps resistance to foreign influences is perfectly normal, although it is not particularly healthy.[48] Unabashedly self-confident about their management until the late 1970s, Americans have reluctantly criticized it thereafter. The nature of the American reaction, however, has varied. Some believed nothing was wrong with American management while others thought that, despite its excellence, Japanese management had cultural roots so different from American that to copy it would bring disastrous results. Still others felt that Japanese management techniques could and should be imported.[49] Borrowers were more or less 'selective' in their opinions about what could be borrowed; nobody really believed that Japanese management could be transferred to an American firm *in toto*.

The cultural argument against importing Japanese management seems somehow bogus, however. The American expert on Japan did not exist in a world apart from his American client. Management expert and manager had grown up together; they shared the same values and had similar vested interests. This limited the ability of American management experts to appreciate, much less to adopt, Japanese management when it parted company from American practice. Statements about cultural incompatibility look, therefore, like the 'good' argument people give when they are reluctant to discuss the real source of resistance. Japanese management ideas threatened vested interests.

The threat and resistance varied according to where people stood within a company's personnel hierarchy, from CEO down to unskilled worker. Japanese managers working in North America quickly learned about these states of resistance. For the most part, the Japanese transplant firms have been union-shy in the United States. They disliked trade and industrial unions because they forced management to deal with non-enterprise people. But mostly they disliked the adversarial mentality that had developed in American unions within the context of American managerialism. To the Japanese the ethos of the American industrial relations system was simply 'unsuitable'. Even so, transplant managers got American workers to accept Japanese arrangements much more easily than they did American managers. Martin Kenney and Richard Florida emphasize this point in their study: 'In nearly every plant we visited, Japanese managers voiced concern about the manner by which American managers operate. An executive at Honda of America Manufacturing told us that his greatest problem was teaching American managers the Honda way.'[50]

Japanese criticized U.S. managers pointedly for their lack of 'commitment' and their abuse of power. The American managers, in American firms bought by the Japanese, resisted assimilation. In these firms, the new managers from Japan complained about their American colleagues' lack of loyalty to the company, about their higher salary claims, and about their inability to forget Taylorist modes of command-management. In addition, the Kenney and Florida canvass turned up 'reports from Japanese executives, American shop-floor workers, and clerical staff, of American managers, who refer to their Japanese counterparts in derogatory, even racist, terms'. Japanese transplants, therefore, have preferred to cultivate their own managers, by promoting from shop floor or office, as they do in Japan, rather than hire them from the labor market. This suggests that American difficulties with Japanese management techniques stems less from incongruities between American and Japanese work cultures in general than from an incompatibility between the way American and Japanese management behaves.

The Crumbling Epistemological
Foundation of American Managerialism

At this juncture it is necessary to change perspectives. I have looked at the collapse of the American management mystique in three ways: (1) how the bad news about America's economic performance undermined confidence in American management, (2) how the good news about Japan's economic posture increased the despair, and (3) how the American management expert acted as a catalyst in the transformation process. But what about American management itself in an epistemological sense: Epistemology considers the methods which are used to acquire knowledge and the grounds upon which this acquisition is based. It is one thing to say that American management did not do well in the marketplace, another to say that it did not do well because its assumptions about knowledge acquisition led it astray. Here I am not concerned with the limits or the validity of the epistemological assumptions that American managers and management experts used to justify their actions, indeed, their very *raison d'être*. Since we deal in mystiques, the question can be left to philosophers to debate. I only ask, did American management experts in the 1980s start to question the epistemological assumptions of American managerialism? If the experts, who had once embraced the epistemology of American managerialism, came to believe that these assumptions were no longer valid, then, coupled with the poor performance record, the foundation of the mystique would have completely collapsed. Even more significantly, if people abandoned the theory of knowledge underpinning American managerialism for some other set of assumptions, and if they judged Japanese modes of management better suited to the new epistemology, then American management experts would themselves be transformed into the Japanese mode. During the 1980s for certain experts this transformation took place.

I cannot thoroughly discuss the transformation. The subject is too big for this book. I just want to show how this transformation could actually happen. And to do that I shall use a particular device: examine the transformation through the evidence presented by one management expert. That expert is H. Thomas Johnson. In 1980 Johnson was a professor of management accounting, teaching at a respectable university; in 1990 Johnson taught at another respectable university but he was no longer a professor of accounting; he had become a Professor of Quality Management. This change did not result from a quick jump onto some bandwagon of faddists; it was the consequence of a considerable pilgrimage during which Johnson came to question the value and usefulness of what he had been doing in his professional life. Along the way Johnson spent three years studying the Toyota Production System, took a seminar with W. Edwards Deming and even investigated new developments in physics.[51] Johnson mentions three books in particular that influenced him during his metamorphosis: Peter M. Senge's *The Fifth Discipline: The Art and Practice of the Learning Organization*, Robert W. Hall's *The Soul of the Enterprise*, and Fritjof Capra's *The Turning Point: Science, Society, and the Rising Culture*.

Two of the three books are about management, but the other, Capra's, is not a management book at all, for it deals with a reevaluation of the foundations of science. Taken together, the three books permit the reader to construct a fantasy about the epistemological collapse of American managerialism. It is not, it must be cautioned, necessarily a fantasy about the specific intellectual and psychological transformation through which Professor Johnson went. He never said precisely how the books affected his thinking, he only wrote to me that they did. But if the books do not reveal the actual process of transformation experienced by anyone, not even Professor Johnson, they do offer one representative insight into the process of Everyman who changed his view of American management during the 1980s. The story begins with Capra's *The Turning Point*. For a few pages the reader must bear with what, at first impression, might appear to be a digression into science. But be reassured, it is not a digression, for Capra's discussion of the turning point in science is at the heart of the management matter.

In the book Capra plants an intellectual and psychological seedbed in which the Japanese view of management, in contrast to American managerialism, can thrive and grow. Capra asserts that a systemic crisis in Western science not only has questioned its intellectual foundations but raised doubts about the ability of science to solve pressing human problems. The book begins with a statement about how people in 'think tanks' and 'brain trusts', expressing 'mainstream academic views', have been unable by their own admission 'to solve the nation's most urgent policy problems'.[52] Capra traces this impotence to what Alfred North Whitehead called 'the century of genius', the seventeenth, when Isaac Newton worked out the mathematical basis of exact physics, René Descartes its dualist philosophy, and Francis Bacon the experimental method that has led it from triumph to triumph. Descartes proclaimed that 'all science is certain, evident knowledge, we reject all knowledge which is merely probable and judge that only those things should be believed which are perfectly known and about which there can be no doubt'.[53]

The experimental method that brought 'certain' results in physics is called reductionism. Reductionism assumes that matter is 'the basis of all existence' and that the material world is composed of 'a multitude of separate objects assembled into a huge machine'. Consequently, these complex phenomena can best be 'understood by reducing them to their basic building blocks and by looking for the mechanisms through which these interact'.[54] Although physics led the way, the reductionist methodology eventually permeated all the sciences by the start of the twentieth century.

Capra contends, however, that this Western view of scientific method has come tumbling down and that the first to tumble has been physics, where the Cartesian philosophic foundation and the reductionist methodology had seemed most secure. He begins with Heisenberg's statement that 'every word or concept, clear as it may seem to be, has only a limited range of applicability', a twentieth-century assertion that plays havoc with Descartes' 'certainty' principle. Capra claims that two discoveries of modern physics have fundamentally challenged the Newtonian world. First, quantum theory proclaimed not only that subatomic particles—electrons, protons, neutrons—are not the solid objects of classical physics, but that they are very abstract entities which have a dual aspect:

> depending on how we look at them, they appear sometimes as particles, sometimes as waves; and this dual nature is also exhibited by light, which can take the form of electromagnetic waves or particles. . . . The more we emphasize one aspect in our description the more the other aspect becomes uncertain, and the precise relationship between the two is given by the uncertainty principle.[55]

The second discovery pertains to the nonlocal connections of individual events. We can never predict the jump of an electron from one atomic orbit to another, we can only predict its probability because the behavior of the electron is affected by the nonlocal and unknowable connection to the whole. Nonlocality stops us from being able to determine cause and effect precisely—we have to fall back on statistical probabilities. 'The concepts of non-locality and statistical causality', Capra affirms, 'imply quite clearly that the structure of matter is not mechanical . . . , [but that] the universe [is] more a great thought than a great machine'.[56]

The new physics abolished Descartes' separation of Mind from Matter. The result of this abolition, Capra observed, is manifest in scientific investigation itself:

> Human consciousness [in quantum physics] plays a crucial role in the process of observation. . . . My conscious decision about how to observe, say, an electron will determine the electron's properties to some extent. If I ask a particle question it will give me a particle answer. The electron does not have objective properties independent of my mind.[57]

This discovery overthrew the Newtonian epistemology, it meant that the patterns scientists find in nature connect intimately with the patterns of their minds; with their 'concepts, thoughts, and values'. Consequently, the universe is perceived as a dynamic 'web of inter-related events'. Since none of the properties of any part of the web is independent, reductionism is devalued. Since all the parts follow the properties of the other parts, 'the overall consistency of their inter-relations determines the structure of the entire web'.[58]

In subsequent chapters Capra observes that all of modern science realizes that 'scientific theories are approximations to the true nature of reality; and that each theory is limited to a certain range of phenomena'. Moreover, researchers have questioned the reductionist method over and over again in other sciences. Biology, which Capra discusses in detail, where life, under the reductionist theory, 'had to be understood in terms of its cells', now increasingly studies 'the organism as a whole. [B]iological functions . . . [are] seen as the results of the interactions between the cellular building blocks.'[59] The contention, then, is that the really interesting questions are about how the cells interconnect, how the cell must be understood in terms of the whole organism, not the individual cell itself. If the cell alone is examined, the observer might come up with a view of cell processes that would not fit the whole organism. Capra extends the same anti-reductionist theme to the psychological and social sciences, where he singles out behaviorialism and economics for special criticism.

Throughout, Capra adopts a systems view of knowledge, wherein systems are defined as 'integrated wholes whose properties cannot be reduced to those of smaller units'.[60] Within systems 'the behavior of the individual part can be so unique and irregular that it bears no sign of relevance to the order of the whole system'.[61] For our purposes, Capra's choice of an organic metaphor to illustrate the social aspects of systems theory is particularly interesting:

> Bees and ants are unable to survive in isolation, but in great numbers they act almost like the cells of a complex organism with a collective intelligence and capabilities for adaptation far superior to those of its individual members. This phenomenon of animals joining up to form larger organismic systems is not limited to insects but can also be observed in several other species, including, of course, human species.[62]

Capra's systems approach undermines nineteenth-century social Darwinian ideas about individual competition. The individual is not only imbedded within a system but is directly involved in that system's self-organization. 'The tendency of living systems to form multilevel structures whose levels differ in their complexity is all-pervasive throughout nature and has to be seen as a basic principle of self-organization.'[63]

The application of systems ideas to human organizations makes them fundamentally different in their patterns from the consecutive 'stacking of building blocks', or the hierarchy of command-power relations so familiar to the Newtonian outlook. Borrowing Arthur Koestler's concept of the 'holon', Capra points out that 'every subsystem is a relatively autonomous organism while being a component of a larger organism'. And he extends the idea of dual identity—a relative 'autonomous organism while being a component of a larger organism'—to the mind. 'In the systems concept of mind, mentation is characteristic not only of individual organisms but also of social . . . systems. As Bateson has emphasized, mind is immanent in the body and also in the pathways and messages outside the body. There are larger manifestations of mind of which our individual minds are only subsystems.'

This statement has radical implications for an understanding of group mental activity and the individual's place in it. It also revolutionizes our view of social order. Capra's comments on this subject deserve, despite the technical language, to be quoted at length because they describe a fundament shift in our views about organizational behavior:

> The multileveled structure of living organisms, like any other biological structure, is a visible manifestation of the underlying processes of self-organization. At each level there is a dynamic balance between self-assertive and integrative tendencies, and all holons act as interfaces and relay stations between systems levels. Systems theorists sometimes call this pattern of organization hierarchical, but that word may be rather misleading for the stratified order observed in nature. The word 'hierarchy' referred originally to the government of the Church. Like all human hierarchies, this ruling body was organized into a number of ranks according to levels of power, each rank being subordinate to one at the level above it. In the past the stratified order of nature has often been misinterpreted to justify authoritarian social and political structures (From the Greek *hieros*, 'sacred', and *arkhia*, 'rule'). To avoid confusion

we may reserve the term 'hierarchy' for those fairly rigid systems of domination and control in which orders are transmitted from the top down. The traditional symbol for these structures has been the pyramid. By contrast, most living systems exhibit multileveled patterns of organization characterized by many intricate and nonlinear pathways along which signals of information and transaction propagate between all levels, ascending as well as descending. That is why I have turned the pyramid around and transformed it into a tree, a more appropriate symbol for the ecological nature of stratification in living systems. As a real tree takes its nourishment through both its roots and its leaves, so the power in a systems tree flows in both directions, with neither end dominating the other and all levels interacting in interdependent harmony to support the functioning of the whole.[64]

These, then, were the ideas that Professor Johnson encountered in one of the three seminal books. Well might it be asked what connections Capra's study has with the management books (by Hall and Senge) that Professor Johnson also mentions among those that most influenced his 'migration'. The answer is that both works exhibit the transformed outlook that Capra traces from the Newtonian, mechanistic, reductionist view of science to the organic, systemic view. Robert Hall, for instance, in *The Soul of the Enterprise*, calls for a new 'holistic' form of manufacturing in which companies do not preach teamwork between customers, employees, and suppliers, while management makes decisions that profit only the owners. 'We need a more challenging, holistic view of the purposes of enterprise, something beyond balancing the conflicts between fiduciary duties (for profitability), customer satisfaction, purifying the environment and the like . . . ', which 'cannot cope with holistic considerations'.[65] And he presents a schema (see Table 4.2) which contrasts the old hierarchical spirit with the 'new Soul of Enterprise.'

People upset about the 'dehumanization' of work might be pleased with Hall's approach. But Hall thinks systemically, not philanthropically, that is, like Capra he realizes that all elements within a thriving system are integral to the entire system's well-being, are interconnected. The systems metaphor for Hall's new management dynamic is not the machine, the power hierarchy of classical American managerialism, but Capra's tree, with the roots and leaves, all parts sustaining the life of the system.

Table 4.2. Hall's new and old soul of enterprise

Old	New
1. Mass production, business as usual	Lean manufacturing
2. Economy of scale	Economy of time
3. Assets are things	Assets are people
4. Profit is #1	Customer satisfaction
5. Owners, managers, and staff are thinkers, separated from doers	Doers are thinkers, thinkers are doers
6. Organizations controlled by hierarchies; functional departments separated	Weak hierarchies; organized based on teamwork; numerous cross-teams
7. Suppliers kept at arm's length, and contracted by bid and negotiation	Suppliers are partners integrated into many customer operations
8. Performance measurement for control (financially dominated)	Performance measurement for improvement (broader measures)

Source: Robert W. Hall, *The Soul of the Enterprise*, 281–82

The same is true of Peter Senge's book, *The Fifth Discipline*, in which the author combines systems theory with processes of continuous improvement. Senge's fifth discipline is the learning organization. He describes it in the following way:

> Systems thinking leads to experiencing more and more of the interconnectedness of life and to seeing wholes rather than parts. Whenever there are problems, in a family or in an organization, a master of systems thinking automatically sees them as arising from underlying structures rather than from individual mistakes or ill will. Likewise, personal mastery leads to an increased sense of 'beingness', awareness of the present moment, both what is happening within us, and to heightened experience of 'generativeness', of being part of the creative forces shaping one's life. At the level of essences, the disciplines start to converge. There is a common sensibility uniting the disciplines—the sensibility of being learners in an intrinsically interdependent world.[66]

Senge recognizes different goals in this learning process. He writes about them in terms of personal mastery (connectedness), systems thinking (interconnectedness), shared visions (commonality of purpose), and team learning (alignment). But he talks too about the differences being increasingly subtle.

Just as Capra notes of the physicist, 'ask a particle question, you get a particle answer', Senge notes of the manager, if you ask a systems question you get a systems answer. And the opposite is implied. The phrases and reasonings Senge uses echo Capra's views—the metaphor of the tree, the values and thought patterns of the observer coloring reality, the web of interconnectedness of the single unit with the whole, the extra-corporeal extension of the mind to group 'thinking'. The connections between both Hall's and Senge's systemic modes of perception and Capra's are obvious just as they are multiple.

So are the connections between Capra's work and the Japanese production system. Capra does not mention Japanese management, but certain beliefs dwelt upon in the book are central to it. One is the limited 'rationalism' that was mentioned as a Japanese trait in the last chapter, another is the Yin–Yang philosophy which Capra discusses at length, another a 'holistic', systems, contextual, non local view of life which permeates books about the Japanese mentality and how it is integral to their management.

Moreover, if Capra does not write specifically about Japanese management, those who do, if without reference to him, often do in Capra's terms. In some cases the terms are identical. The Research Team for Japanese Systems, sponsored by the Masuda Foundation, speaks of Japanese management as 'An Alternative Civilization', using Arthur Koestler's 'holon' concept to clarify its position: 'the Japanese organization is constructed from a system base of sub-whole and sub-individuum, and it may be most appropriate to view the Japanese organization as a holon made up of contextuals'.[67]

The number of books and articles on Japanese management that use Capra-like concepts are too numerous to cite. But three books at hand, Mark Fruin's *The Japanese Enterprise System*, Martin Kenney and Richard Florida's *Beyond Mass Production*, and Ikujiro Nonaka and Hirotaka Takeuchi's *The Knowledge-Creating Company* use Capra's conventions. Kenney and Florida write: 'The underlying conceptual premise of this book is that Japan is at the cusp of a new model of production organization that mobilizes workers' intelligence as well as physical skill.'[68] They stress how the Japanese enterprise uses teams and other organizational techniques that explicitly harness workers' knowledge at the point of production, thereby transforming the ordinary employee's 'knowledge and intelligence into a source of value'. Kenney and Florida insist on the integrative, organic nature of the Japanese work process. They are, as in the following passage, not talking about hierarchy, but about reciprocal action, interconnections, not Taylorism:

> We refer to this organization as the new shop floor [where] innovation becomes more continuous and the factory itself becomes a laboratory-like setting. The underlying organizational feature is the self-managing work team that enhances the functional integration of tasks. The new shop floor thus integrates formerly distinct types of work—for example, R & D and factory production, thus making the production process very social. In doing so, the organizational forms of the new shop floor mobilizes . . . the collective intelligence of workers as a source of continuous improvement in products and processes, of increased productivity, and of value creation.[69]

Behind these words and phrases looms Capra's 'non-localism', his organic values and thought patterns, and the replacement of the Taylorist pyramid of organizational life with the hierarchy of the 'tree'.

Correspondingly, Mark Fruin talks of how Japanese corporations build

> a stair-step process of give-and-take, of interaction, and integration between various production functions, and the welding of this interactive, feedback process into a product-development system. . . . Variability results in learning and learning is the basis of a strategy based on functional integration, innovation, and continual improvement in manufacturing. . . . [F]actories as architectures of innovation appeared [imbued with the] conviction that institutions can think, learn, and act for the purposes of self-improvement and self-renewal.[70]

Institutions that 'think, learn, and act'—such words clearly conjure up Capra's biological references to nonlocal connections of individual events to the whole, of the universe as a great 'thought' instead of a machine, of the 'web of interconnectedness' where the properties of parts map with the properties of other parts.

Nonaka and Takeuchi build their case about knowledge-creating Japanese companies on their ability to harness both tacit and explicit knowledge. Ken'ichi Yasumuro observed how sensitive Japanese engineers were about the necessity to learn tacitly as well as explicitly when importing Western technology at the end of the last century. (see above, pp. 112–13). Nonaka and Takeuchi relate that the interaction between these two knowledge sources, one with it locus in the skilled labor force, the other in the upper levels of management, is the dynamic of knowledge-creation found typically in Japanese but rarely in Western corporations. In the West an

> intellectual tradition can be traced back to Cartesian dualism. . . . A is pitted against B, resulting in the 'A vs. B' model. . . . The debates over subjective vs. objective, mind vs. body, rationalism vs. empiricism, and scientific management vs. human relations reflect this intellectual tradition. The danger . . . is to create the building blocks of organizational knowledge creation in the same light. In our view, tacit knowledge and explicit knowledge . . . are not opposing ends of a dichotomy, but mutually complementary entities. They interact and interchange into each other to create something new.[71]

To some extent the contrast Nonaka and Takeuchi draw between Japan and the West is false. German *Technik* combines tacit (*Können*) and explicit (*Wissen*) knowledge. The distinction, therefore, really applies to the dichotomy drawn between explicit and tacit knowledge in the Anglo-American world. The Japanese references in Nonaka and Takeuchi are organic. Although they do not mention Capra, they are not compatible with the organization metaphor of the pyramid but with his tree, with the organization receiving its sustenance from the leaves as well as the roots in the knowledge-creating interaction between them. Nonaka and Takeuchi acknowledge Peter Senge's attempt to overcome 'the Cartesian dualism' by integrating 'reason and intuition', but they also feel that Senge himself is too much caught up the Mind/Body duality characteristic of Cartesian thinking.[72] This prevents him from appreciating the importance of the body-learning aspect of tacit knowledge and hence stops him from fully appreciating the source of knowledge-creation at play within the Japanese company.

To dredge up more comparisons would be useless. They jump from the pages of these books, just as they do from those that Professor Johnson wrote influenced him so much during the 'migration of [his] thinking' from professor of management accounting to professor of Quality Management.[73] The point has been made. And it has been worth making because many Americans have so trivialized Japanese management, reduced it to some policy features (company unionism, lifetime employment, seniority pay systems) or techniques (*kanban*, quality-control circles, just-in-time deliveries) that the profound differences rather than the superficial ones require emphasis. That is what writers like Mark Fruin, Martin Kenney, Richard Florida, Ronald Dore, Thomas Rohlen, and a few others do.

And it is the profound differences, the rudiments of Japanese management, that have often blocked the adoption in America of Japanese organizational policies and management techniques. I raised this issue earlier in the chapter when discussing American reactions to Japanese management. I noted that cultural arguments against adoption of Japanese techniques were somewhat bogus since they masked the real reason for rejecting them: their adoption would threaten vested interests. Two specific techniques that have drawn much scholarly attention in the Japanization debate show why this is so.

The first debate is about the replacement of American Management Accounting Systems (MAS) with the control techniques of Total Quality Management (TQM). Professor Johnson has written about the subject.[74] His indictment of American accounting procedures echoes Dr Deming's famous statement that 15% of mistakes can be attributed to individual failure, 85% to faults in the process in which the individual works. The process, not the individual, should be blamed for mistakes. Since management installs and oversees process, it is management, not the worker, that must be held responsible when things go wrong. Johnson questioned the tools of management accounting because 'no accounting system has ever told anyone if a process is in control or if a customer is satisfied'. He advises, following Deming, to adopt in accounting's place 'the primary language of processes, statistical process control (SPC)—the language of variation'.[75]

Such radical advice inevitably aroused criticism. Mahmoud Ezzamel, Professor of Accounting at the University of Manchester Institute of Science and Technology, raises two points. Not concerned particularly with defending MAS, he conceded that much of Johnson's critique is just. He focuses instead on the shortcomings of TQM, with which Johnson wants MAS replaced.[76] First, he denies that Japanese-inspired TQM results in 'superior' consensual and humanistic work methods. TQM gets employees involved in the quality creation process. But it uses top-down 'techniques of measurement, monitoring and control to ensure that quality is achieved'. This puts the workers under tremendous pressure. The pressure is intensified when all in the factory must submit to the discipline of the market, where customers' desires have to be met. Continuous improvement and employee involvement in this pressure cooker ends up being employee hell.[77] Secondly, Ezzamel argues that TQM does not get rid of management by the numbers; it reeks as much of Taylorism as MAS, except that TQM replaces 'financial' numbers with 'physical' quantities. 'Just as under the accounting calculus,' Ezzamel contends, 'the "hard" face of TQM reduces the organisation and its members to an abstraction which promulgates and celebrates economic efficiency, and scorns any form of waste irrespective of what this means for the quality of working life.'[78]

These are valid criticisms, but they are not precisely the right ones to raise when evaluating the difference between TQM and MAS. Johnson did not claim that MAS used rigorous measurement techniques and TQM did not; he claimed that TQM's techniques provided management with the information needed for correct decisions and traditional MAS did not. Shirley J. Daniel and Wolf D. Reitsperger emphasize this interpretation. Their study shows that 'Japanese companies following a zero defect quality strategy have modified their management control system' from those traditionally used in MAS.[79] And using the proper method is essential. Johnson notes:

> I once saw a 'TQM guide for team leaders and facilitators' which contained a section on American-style cost-volume-profit break-even analysis juxtaposed to a section on the Seven Statistical Tools (Pareto diagrams, histograms, control charts, etc.) that are basic to Japanese quality programs. This bizarre mismatch is comparable to placing a recipe for Molotov cocktails among recipes for healthy breads.[80]

Japanese managers familiar with American practices make similar comments. One, who had studied a large American firm, condemned their management accounting procedures as a 'joke', for they could not provide 'accurate or relevant cost information'. Williams, Mitsui, and Haslam observe that Japanese managers 'advocate physical measures because they believe [they] are more immediately intelligible than financial measures and also help to identify what has to be improved'.[81] Indeed, the difference between financial and physical measurements is profound. 'In terms of understanding,' they comment, 'Japanese managers are like Copernican astronomers disparaging their Ptolemaic precursors whose beliefs and practices they represent as crudely inferior.' But their 'Western counterparts are often in the position of Ptolemaic astronomers who may have heard of, but do not understand, Copernicus.'[82]

The controversy needs to be thought of systemically. Despite Ezzamel's critique, TQM techniques differ from MAS in that they require employee involvement. Workers within a statistical process control system must be directly engaged in monitoring process, using simple, easily learned statistical measurement techniques to determine whether the process is in or out of control. Moreover, they must disseminate timely information about inter-process physical performance horizontally within the organization as well as vertically up the hierarchy. But MAS, which emphasizes financial reporting, is under the control of orthodox accountants who report vertically up the organization. Accordingly, the 'orthodox finance function must always be protected as long as Western management demands the financial numbers, and it is hard to see that demand changing when financial expertise is an important qualification for senior management'.[83] TQM is not achieved just with the introduction of new techniques; its implementation challenges the authority and function of the traditional hierarchy which MAS, under American managerialism, protects. Objections to TQM arise, therefore, not from cultural misunderstandings but from narrowly construed self-interest that feels menaced. To the extent that TQM threatens their authority American management will resist its implementation or shape it so as to preserve concentration of power at the top.

The second Japanization debate focuses on the transfer of Quality Circle to American business and industry. Because American managerialism basically rejects the rudiments of Japanese management, American firms also spurn small-group activity, embodied especially in what the Japanese call Quality Control Circles (QCC) and the Americans, leaving the control out, Quality Circles (QC). Japanese firms created the first QCC in 1961. They were 'voluntary' small groups of six or seven, organized to help solve job-related quality problems in a company. QCC grew rapidly in Japan. The Japanese Union of Scientists and Engineers, which registers QCC, reported over 250,000 of them with over two million members in 1987.[84] Since a conservative estimate would put the number of unregistered QCC at five times the registered, a total of about eight million Japanese, roughly one out of every six employees, in 1987 engaged in QCC activities.

American managers reacted enthusiastically to Japanese QCC after 'discovering' them in the late 1970s. People expected these small groups to solve America's quality problem. The New York Stock Exchange national survey revealed in 1982 that overall, 19 percent of reporting manufacturing firms had adopted quality circles (but only 9 percent of non-manufacturing firms). In firms with more than 500 employees quality circles grew more rapidly than any other human-resource activity at the time. The movement had been of quite recent vintage. Seventy-five percent of the quality circles surveyed (firms with more than 500 employees) had existed for less than two years, 85 percent for less than five.[85] Then, in the mid-1980s, American interest in quality circles quickly diminished. The comparative growth data is instructive. What for the Japanese developed into a mature movement, for the Americans turned, as so often before, into a passing fad. Why did the QCC movement succeed so thoroughly in Japan, but fail in the United States?

Two points can be made quickly. Considering that the Japanese QCC movement began twenty years before the American QC surge, the two are not easily compared. Secondly, there is the question of 'voluntarism'. In America the decision to join a QC *was* purely 'voluntary'; in Japan joining was *de rigueur*, but the way one participated was 'voluntary'. These two factors alone would explain lower density of QC membership in America. But they do not explain the recent decline in QC membership density in the United States.[86]

Cole describes QCC growth systemically. JUSE, taking up the cause, advocated them relentlessly through their many chapters in the country. Top management got involved early; so did middle management and foremen. 'In a stroke of organizational genius,' he continued, 'they created a corporate association with a mass constituency. Therein lies one of the central roots of Japanese success and their ability to avoid a faddish succession of management panaceas.' JUSE, although heavily involved in the propagation of QCC, did not work alone. The *Nihon Kantokushi Kyokai*, Japan Supervisors' Association (JSA) joined in. Through local chapters nationwide, JSA taught its first-line foremen members a variety of managerial skills. After 1975, it added small-group activities to its training program, including the management of QCCs. JSA even claims to have developed the QCC initially on its own. 'Thus,' Cole concluded, 'we see an unconscious patterning of organizational responses to the task of mobilizing and training mass constituencies for Japanese industry.'[87]

If a mass constituency fostered QCC success in Japan, the absence of one hindered America's ability to follow suit. Robert Cole writes that the American QC movement never attracted the support of top management. Since it also did not involve foremen or worker organizations, QC advocacy turned out primarily to be a middle management project. This news is not surprising. But the reasons why the mass constituency failed to materialize are interesting, for they reveal the substance and express the limitations of American managerialism. American managers like to think of themselves professionally. They are people in charge because they possess the knowledge, skills, and experience to 'manage' the other employees. Alongside working managers, there exists a corps of managerial consultants that act like doctors, called in when the patient is sick to prescribe cures from their bag of management remedies. But like doctors, their services are expensive, for management consultants operate in the marketplace, selling their knowledge and skill to the highest bidder.

Thus, because the consultant is financially interested, he has trouble convincing top management about the virtues of adopting a particular management technique such as quality circles. It might just be another useless and expensive management panacea that consultants constantly push and distrustful executives resist. In Japan, JUSE, Robert Cole acknowledged, 'stood above the pursuit of private economic interests in a way that was not possible for either consultant, firms, or individual corporations' in the United States. Neither could the quality control associations that took up the Quality Circle idea (The AQCA and the IQCA) fulfill JUSE's role in America. The IAQC did 'develop grass-roots activities' (although the AQCA never did), but they were conducted 'by middle and lower-level managerial officials responsible for circle efforts in their firms'.[88] Local IAQC chapter members were quality experts. Remember, too, in Japan not only JUSE but the Japan Supervisors' Association developed small-group training programs for first-line foremen, independently of, but in close association with, JUSE. With this sort of cooperation, if not enthu-siasm, at the foreman level, QCCs could be transferred to the shop floor. American managers interested in small-group activities did not and do not bring employees in as full, active partners in their planning and implementation. There is an exclusivity about American manage-rialism that prevents it, without undermining its position, from including a mass constituency in management process.

Robert Cole claims in his comparative study that American and Japanese small-group management differs from Swedish. Whereas small groups are quite independent in Sweden, with employee parti-cipants conceded decision rights in matters of work process and work implementation, in America and Japan decisions to implement small-group recommendations have remained a managerial prerogative. Cole seems to say that compared with Sweden employee participation in America and Japan is a bit of a sham. Yet this view is surely misleading if not incorrect. The important difference between the Japanese and Americans, as Cole himself stresses in his book, is not managerial prerogatives but the presence or absence of the mass constituency that made the pursuit of small-group activities possible. Because American managerialism operated in hierarchical command-control rather than organic-systemic terms, the small-group activity it sponsored could not, to stay with Fritjof Capra's metaphor, take sustenance from the employee leaves of the organizational tree as well as from the manage-ment roots. American managerialism hobbled the American firm's ability to transfer quality circle activities into the American office and plant just as it did the adoption of TQM in place of MAS. Both required employee cooperation for implementation, but American managerialism, with its predilection for making employees the object of, not part of, management, could not alter its behavior sufficiently to allay fears within the labor force that quality circles were just another form of managerial manipulation.

Thus, as the recent odyssey of American management shows, the epistemological and psychological assumptions upon which American managerialism built its house collapsed. American capitalists, man-agers, and management scientists turned to Japan for help. But they were ill-prepared to adopt alternative techniques, developed during Japan's period of high-growth globalization. To adopt fully and imple-ment these process techniques would have required the acceptance of rudiments of Japanese management that were, despite the newly argued validity of their scientific underpinnings, inimical to American management's self-interest, as understood in the tradition of American managerialism. Certain American firms in recent years have made determined efforts to transform their organizational cultures along Japanese lines, but the jury is still out on how successful these efforts have been in transforming the outlook of the American managerial community *writ large*.

Factoring in the German Mini-Management Mystique

Since, to repeat Professor Keck's assertion, most people would equate best management with the best economies, German management's part in the story of the collapse of the American management mystique differs from Japan's. Actually, if stress is placed on future-oriented growth industries, German management's 'mini-mystique' itself has vanished during the past decade. Abundant statistics support this claim. Herbert A. Henzler and Lothar Späth, in *Sind die Deutschen noch zu retten?*, offer three sets of statistics to make a case.[89] In a chart entitled 'Future Market Information Technology—Where is Germany?' they pointed out that Japan produced 41 percent of the world's integrated circuits (1991), the U.S.A 26 percent, and Germany 9 percent; in hardware the corresponding figures were Japan 29, the U.S.A. 30, and West Germany 8; in software they were Japan 13, the U.S.A. 49, and West Germany 9. Considering the increasing importance of the electronic component in modern manufacturing, the German future in these three significant product lines is not promising. India, a newcomer in software manufacture, threatens to overtake German producers.[90]

A second chart, entitled 'Technologically on the Way to the Minor Leagues', portrays the relative position of Germany and Japan, 1970 and 1990, in world export of high- and low-tech products. The West Germans outstripped the Japanese in high-tech exports, 16 percent to 12 percent, in 1970, but the Japanese exports exceeded the German,

19 percent to 15 percent, in 1990. The third chart, entitled 'Invention Enthusiasm Wanes in Germany', illustrates how, beginning in 1975, with 20 percent of international patents, the German share fell to 18.5 percent in 1982, and to 16 percent in 1990. The Japanese position, by contrast, improved from under 14 percent in 1975 to rival the West German in 1982 (18.5%), and then to equal the previously leading Americans at 26 percent in 1988. Germans in 1990 patented more than the Americans and Japanese in only one industry, machine tools; in pharmaceutical, chemicals, and automobiles the Japanese and American firms patented more than West Germany; in growing industrial branches like biotechnology and electronics, Japanese researchers registered four times as many patents as their German colleagues.[91]

These numbers raise questions about the German entrepreneurial spirit. Even when numbers seem somewhat promising they hide uncomfortable trends. German export prowess is proverbial. The West Germans have had solid trade surpluses throughout the postwar period. But these surpluses have been in products of the second industrial revolution. Moreover, the German trading surplus increasingly has been a regional phenomena, indicating that, although Germany remained a trading powerhouse within the confines of a protected European Economic Community (EEC), its world trade position has really deteriorated. Two-thirds of West German foreign trade on 31 December 1992 was with EEC states; on 1 January 1993, when all intra-EEC trade ceased to be designated foreign, Germany's part of world exports shrank to 7 percent compared with Japan's 12 and America's 16. Germany scarcely traded with Asia, the world's fastest growing economic region.

Still, there is no need for unremittent gloom. Germany is a regional economic powerhouse, in a region, moreover—with, since the fall of the Soviet Union—considerable expansion potential. Professor Manfred Perlitz, after an evaluation of German competitiveness published in 1993, calculated that German private firms are richly endowed with capital, which is 'surely a competitive advantage for the German economy'.[92] German firms have managed to provide favorable balance-of-trade and balance-of-payment positions for their country, despite trade difficulties resulting from the strong D-Mark. The inability of American management to achieve comparable results, with the constant devaluation of the dollar—indeed, to have persistently high trade deficits—is somewhat shocking. German managerial capacities, then, reflected in the business and industrial accomplishments of the German enterprise, are, if mixed, still enviable when measured against world-class standards.

But the reputation of German management is not built uniquely on economic achievement. The American management mystique did not itself arise after the war just because managers made lots of money for their firms and paid excellent dividends to stockholders. Such a greedy, narrow accomplishment could not have fathered a mystique. In fact, as described in Chapter 1, the mystique emerged out of the great postwar competition between capitalism and communism. Postwar advocates of American capitalism claimed that it was different, that this unique brand of capitalism had turned a zero-sum into a win-win economic game. In America capitalists no longer won at the expense of the workers but both now benefited from the material riches generated under the guidance of American managerialism. This was the model American Marshall Planners and others peddled as an alternative to the old European zero-sum exploitative form of capitalism, and, of course, as an alternative to communism.

But statistical evidence that is uniformly cited in recent studies discloses unfulfilled promises. Michel Albert, a capitalist executive in France, observed in a critical study of American 'casino' capitalism that forty million Americans at the lower end of the scale saw their incomes drop by 10 percent in as many years (the 1980s). If, he observed, poverty is defined as 'living on a disposal income less than half the national average', 17 percent of Americans were poor in 1990 compared with 5 percent of West Germans (8 percent of Swiss, and 10 percent of the British).[93] Robert Reich reported the same trend: between 1977 and 1990 the best estimate is that the average income of the poorest fifth of the U.S. population declined by 5 percent while that of the richest fifth increased by 9. The richest fifth had 50 percent of national income, the top 5 percent commanded 26 percent.[94]

An analysis based on people who work in corporations produces similar results. Bureau of Labor Statistics data, in 1982 constant dollars, revealed that the earnings of American industrial workers, which peaked in 1978 at $9.11 an hour (it had been $7.00 in 1958), fell by 1988 to $8.44, and then steadily declined in 1989 to $8.29, and in 1990 to $8.05 an hour.[95] Hourly wages in manufacturing industries in 1990 were $10.48 in America, $12.42 in West Germany, and $12.37 in Japan. With social benefits added, the disparities between the Americans ($15.39 total compensation hourly) and Germans ($24.36) is even greater.[96] Compared with the normal forty-hour week of American industrial workers, Germans worked 37.6; annually Germans worked even less, 1,499 days a year, Americans 1,847. Americans received twenty-three paid holidays and vacation days in the year, Germans forty-two. Germans, compared with working Americans, also receive excellent severance pay and health care. And Michel Albert remarked that the gap between the best-paid and the lowest-paid worker is not as wide in Germany as in America, 'making Germany a far more egalitarian society'.[97]

Income statistics on top corporate earners confirm Albert's contention. He reported the differentials between CEO salaries and that of the lowest-paid workers in U.S. *Fortune* Five Hundred corporation at 110 to 1, compared to 23 to 1 in Germany. Robert Reich traced a progressively widening gap in America: whereas in 1960 an executive in a *Fortune* Five Hundred corporation at $190,000 a year received forty times (twelve times after taxes) the wage of an average American factory worker, by 1988 the difference had increased to ninety-three times (seventy times after taxes).[98] In 1990 CEOs in American corporations earned 90 percent more total compensation than German CEOs ($543,000 to $287,000). The real disparity is greater, considering the purchasing power of the German CEO's income. The mark purchased in Germany only half what the dollar did in America.[99] Although the postwar win-win prediction could be said to have been realized under West Germany's brand of capitalism, the predictions for America have certainly missed the mark. In America it looked very much after 1980 like a zero-sum game.

People give many reasons for these comparatively unhappy American results: the growth of American government fiscal irresponsibility, the economic dislocations of the Cold War, and the bureaucratization of the national government are probably the most frequently cited. But two management-related causes must be mentioned: (1) trade union policies, and (2) the West's reaction to the Japan 'shock'. German and American management handled both issues somewhat differently, with results that contributed to the collapse of the American management mystique.

As to trade union policies, Robert Reich calculates that the number of non-agricultural U.S. workers in trade unions fell steadily from 35 percent in 1960, to 25 in 1980, to 17 percent in 1989. Excluding unionized government employees from the 1989 count, the percentage was 13.4.[100] During the same period German trade union membership did not fall—it even increased slightly to over 40 percent of nonagricultural workers. Serious structural changes in America partially account for the American decline, for example, the move of manufacturing to nonunion Sunbelt states or offshore and the rapid growth of the nonunionized service sector. The fact that manufacturing retained a greater share of German GDP might explain some of the sprightliness in German trade unions. But American management, unlike German, never overcame a long history of anti-unionism. It devoutly wished and actively sought to foster the decline of unions; indeed this attitude contributed to union-disadvantaged decision-making that produced geographical relocations and structural change.

Ray Marshall, President Carter's Secretary of Labor, commented that even in the 1950s and early 1960s American employers had remained 'hostile to unions and collective bargaining, but most stifled overt opposition' then. In the 1970s a group of 'human resource management professionals helped anti-union employers develop alternatives to collective bargaining'.[101] A 1979 study by a management-supported organization, the Conference Board, admitted the policy. 'It is no secret that management would prefer to operate without a union. Indeed, in many ways, all aspects of supervision of personnel relations might be subsumed under "union avoidance".'[102] Mounting employer opposition made unionization increasingly difficult. Paul Weiler of the Harvard Law School calculated that unions won certification elections in 80 percent of potential bargaining units in the late 1950s and concluded agreements in 90 percent of the certified units; in 1980 unions won certification in less than 40 percent of potential bargaining units, and actually concluded contracts in just half of them.[103]

Employers claimed the nonunion model gave them greater flexibility in job design and work reorganization that had to be done to bring about the productivity enhancement required in the new, ferociously competitive global economy. But studies generally affirm higher productivity in union rather than in nonunion plants. These same studies also show that there is less profitability in unionized plants. American employers, therefore, in their nonunion strategies, really pursued profits instead of productivity, profits gained at the expense of their employees. Reich states that in the United States the gap between the average wages of union and nonunion U.S. workers widened significantly from a 14.6 percent difference in 1973 to a difference of 20.4% at the end of the 1980s.[104] Remembering that the percentage of unionized workers in the nonagricultural labor force fell from 30 to 17 percent within the same time frame, the employers' antiunion campaign contributed directly to the impoverishment of working people.

During the same period the differential in pay between German unionized and nonunionized workers remained insignificant. This was true because the employers of nonunion workers accepted the wage rates negotiated regionally between German trade union and employer federations. Inasmuch as wage differentials were slight, little incentive existed for German employers, on the money issue alone, to engage in antiunion campaigns. The laws, moreover, guaranteed nonunion German workers a minimum three-week annual paid vacation. It is true, 70 percent of those working under collective bargaining agreements got six weeks, but the actual minimum annual paid vacation for nonunion workers was four weeks and about a third of them got five.[105] Because German high-wage policy has been accompanied by high levels of unemployment in recent years, economists, with their equilibrium logic, like to say that it is just a matter of choice. America trades high wages for jobs, Germany jobs for high wages. Considering the excellent unemployment benefits in Germany, however, the trade-off from the workers' perspective is not equal.[106]

Nonetheless, German wage and benefit disparities do raise questions about efficiency. And this leads to the second point. The Germans hardly worried about their ability to compete throughout most of the postwar years. Predictions about the managerial incompetence of labor-elected members of Supervisory Boards proved to be manifestly absurd; on the contrary, reports accumulated about managerial superiorities achieved through co-determination. But management also did not fear co-determination, especially at the Supervisory Board level, because it really posed no threat to management's control of the work

197

process. Lowell Turner observed, after studying GM Opel in West Germany, that management would, as the German co-determination law required, notify the works councils of work changes, but then, in the best Taylorist tradition, put them through top down. Because of imperious managerialism the 'Humanization of work' movement stagnated. Unions more or less supported the government-sponsored Quality of Working Life projects, but management resisted any humanization of work project that did not promote its idea of efficiency. The co-determination laws did not eliminate management's control prerogatives in a Taylorist work environment.

Sometime in the 1980s, the idea of humanizing work ran straight into the movement to 'Japanize' work process. Since Total Quality Management, Just-In-Time, *kaizen*, indeed, all the techniques so well known to those currently reading management literature, required extensive communications with employees, and their participation in task-related decisions, only worker involvement could produce the commitment, loyalty, and job satisfaction that successful 'Japanization' demanded. In America, an all-powerful management called the shots and implemented the policies. Under its guidance there could be no doubt that the purpose of 'Japanization' was higher productivity, profitability, and dividends for stockholders. With unions marginalized in America, the 'Japanization' movement became just another expression of American managerialism.[107]

Because German law established mandatory employee participation in the governance of the firm, German management could not dominate work-process reform as did American. Here the distinction between trade unions and works councils must be recalled. Trade unions had nothing legally to say about the management of work process. German employers had fought adamantly and successfully to prevent such union interference. Their attitude towards works councils was different. Since they were elected uniquely by and from a firm's employees, they were not outsiders. Management always felt closer to works councils than to unions. Dr. Dieter Kirchner, of Gesamt-Metall, expressed a widely held view in his employer association when he stated that management disliked co-determination at the Supervisory Board level because it was union-dominated but had very positive feelings towards works councils.[108]

Still, it is well to remember that the division between unions and works councils is somewhat fluid. Although a firm's employees elected the works councils, unions have taken a very active part in these elections, so that union members frequently dominate works councils. But the union members have to win support among employees and must adjust their behavior towards management to fit this context in ways that an employee-delegate coming from a union central would not. It was easier, therefore, for management to work with works councils, even if dominated by union shop stewards, in changing work process. It was indeed the works councils rather than the unions with which the co-determination laws made management work.

Although the first 'Japan shock' arrived in the late 1970s, the full impact of 'Japanization' really hit the German workplace in the late 1980s. This arrested reaction occurred because German manufacturing had, unlike American, continued to perform rather well in the 1980s, well after performance numbers in American industries (automobiles, steel, rubber, machine tools, electronic appliances, etc.) dramatically plummeted. If a single event could be said to have triggered this somewhat belated reaction to the Japanese challenge in the German managerial consciousness, it was the publication of the Womack, Jones, and Roos book on 'lean production'. Dr. Kirchner's claim that this book changed German management thinking, and not just in the automobile industry, is echoed from behind every management desk. Nevertheless, for German 'Japanization' pioneers like Professor Horst Wildemann, the change process had started earlier. Wildemann's awakening came in 1978 in Brussels at the European Foundation for Management (EFM). He recalls that a Japanese colleague, also an EFM visiting professor, introduced him to JIT, *kanban*, and other Japanese techniques. Wildemann began to read more deeply in the literature on Japan and became, with his associates, an important part of the work-process innovation story in Germany.

Wildemann's activities provide a useful reference from which to gauge Germany's response to the same Japanese challenge with which Americans struggled. Since 1989, he has been Professor of Business Economics, *mit Schwerpunkt Logistik*, in the Technical University of Munich. Here he teaches courses on work-process innovation, primarily to engineering students. It is a substantial group, for he presides over one hundred people, including thirty-five graduate assistants

(30% with business degrees, 50% with degrees in economics-engineering, and 20% with engineering degrees). The operation is heavily oriented to mathematic modeling and computer simulations. Wildemann produces five to ten Ph.D.s a year; about 120 of his current students and assistants are active consultants with firms; former students have moved to consulting agencies mostly in Germany (Boston Consulting Group, Arthur D. Little, etc.). Before Munich, Wildemann worked in quality-management programs at other universities, some of which were new institutions (Passau and Bayreuth) and others old and famous, for example, St Gallen in Switzerland. Although the Munich operation is by far the largest, the others also had money and people; at Passau, for instance, he had fifteen graduate assistants.

Like any German professor Wildemann must publish; he has many books and articles, including a work done in 1983 on the 'focused-modular factory'. The knowledge contained in these publications, however, is not 'book' knowledge—knowledge acquired, that is, from reading books. It is knowledge derived, in the best empirical tradition, from hands-on experience gained while implementing new process-production technology in European, but mainly German, manufacturing. There are, to name a few, books on 'Strategic Investment Planning', 'Creating Synchronized Production', 'Factory Planning', 'The Just-In-Time Concept', 'Work-Time Management', 'Optimization of R & D Time', and 'Enterprise Quality: Introduction of Continuous Quality Improvement'. Their bibliographies are filled with references to English-language publications by Americans and Japanese as well as to work by Germans. His acknowledgments in the books thank famous consultancies.[109] And his introductions contain statements like 'this book mirrors the research results of a two-year industrial project on investment planning for new production technology', or 'the following report encompasses the research results of eight years, introducing and implementing Just-In-Time Production in over 120 European firms', or, in a later edition, after twelve years' experience 'in over 200 European firms'.[110]

The professor has in fact been at the cutting edge of international work-process reform throughout the 1980s. In 1988, for example, he attended a special seminar at the Massachusetts Institute of Technology, sponsored by Volkswagen, at which Womack, who was finishing the co-authored book, talked about 'lean' production. Real innovators, Wildemann affirms, are not up on the latest publications; they know about its contents *before* it appears. Wildemann has taught the new work-process methods to active managers; at Passau in 1981 he held three seminars with an attendance of about sixty; by 1983 attendance at a seminar, with managers from all over Europe, had grown to 1,500. To date, he and his colleagues have implemented work-process change in plants of some very famous firms, including Mercedes-Benz, Grundig, Philips, and Volkswagen. At Volkswagen he spent three years teaching small-group quality-control management techniques in five-day courses to over 2,500 managers.

The question is, then, has German management's efforts to 'Japanize', to modernize work processes along Japanese lines, succeeded? If so, how did the German management system contribute to the success? As to the first question, although 'Japanization' is a serious movement, it is also a recent one. Americans started earlier and, despite the constraints American managerialism impose, their 'Japanization' is farther along. Factors that have very little to do with shop-floor process can cloud judgments about the skills of German managers in this regard. German employers themselves complain constantly that high social costs significantly reduce the competitive capacities of German firms. And the statistics, which depict gross disparities between Germany and its chief rivals, support the claim. The decision of the German people to pay heavy social overheads unquestionably places German industry at a competitive disadvantage. The collapse of the Soviet system, moreover, added to the burden because it created a skilled, cheap labor source at Germany's door.[111] To the extent that social cost and wage disparities reduce the profits of German firms, they limit their ability to finance work-process reforms, a limitation which, therefore, cannot be attributed to German managerial ineptitude.

Nonetheless, work-process reform moves along quickly in Germany. No doubt work forces in former West Germany offer great resistance to change perceived to be harmful to workers' interests, but unions are fully involved in the implementation.[112] The pace of change in the new federal states (the former East Germany), moreover, moves well, especially on greenfield sites. West German-based chemical firms have quickly settled into the new federal states, especially into Sachsen-

Anhalt.[113] But the most famous success story in the former East Germany has probably been the new Opel factory at Eisenach. The oft-repeated witticism about this factory, that it has 'American managers, Japanese management methods, communist workers, and German automation', is caricature but it contains the truth that, under new management, East Germans are quite adaptable. The Eisenach plant is the most efficient in Europe.[114] Professor Wildemann estimated in 1994 that 30 to 50 percent of German industry has successfully implemented TQC, JIT, *kaizen*, or other work-process techniques.[115]

Much success can be claimed, but the answer to the second part of the question is more germane to this study. How did the German management system contribute to this success? Wildemann states that in four years at Volkswagen he worked closely with works councils and shop stewards. The works councilors he dealt with at VW were, as he phrased it, 'very intelligent people' who fully appreciated the necessity to improve work process but also understood the impact the changes would have on jobs in the workplace, in reducing work time and pay. Wildemann's group taught the new techniques to shop stewards at the same time as they did to management. The fact that at Volkswagen, the union, IG Metall, dominated works council and shop steward elections highlights another of Wildemann's points: IG Metall promoted the implementation of JIT and other new work processes. The institutions of co-determination, therefore, abetted Volkswagen's attempt to reform work process. Wildemann's comments about the usefulness of works councilors and shop stewards in carrying through change at Volkswagen are uniformly positive; indeed, often, he states, these employee representatives led management instead of following.[116]

This affirmation raises the question: how does co-determination compare with American managerialism in the 'Japanization' process? The question is particularly intriguing because American companies with operations in both countries have implemented work-process reform under both German and American managerial systems. This happened and is happening in the automobile industry, at Ford and General Motors plants in the U.S.A. and Germany. Lowell Turner, who studied labor–management relations in Germany for one year, 1989–90, observed that Ford of Europe, after the wake-up call from Japan in 1979, started reorienting its work processes in Germany. For General

Motors the big change had occurred at the Toyota–GM NUMMI plant in California, where management, with UAW cooperation, installed a team-production system, a model that became 'The New Shrine in the West'.[117] The NUMMI model spread to other GM plants in the United States, and in Germany to Opel's greenfield plant site in Eisenach, and to the older Opel plants in Bochum and Rüsselsheim.

At Cologne's Ford plant, management and works council had cooperated with each other under the provisions of the 1952 and 1972 Works Constitution Acts; at Opel the relations were less friendly, although formally correct, as the laws required. As a social settlement German co-determination rested on the employer's right to determine the nature of the workplace in return for recognition of unions and works councils as partners in industrial relations and as a power in the labor market. Since co-determination never applied to the management of work process, even the Ford plant functioned under an authoritarian Taylorist regime, with 'drill-sergeant foremen completing the chains of command'.[118]

For management the 'big difference between the [new] bargaining for team work and past rationalization initiatives [was] that this time management very much need[ed] the cooperation and participation of shop-floor workers'.[119] Since group work processes had to be established cooperatively, the German experiences in co-determination gave the German plants advantages over their U.S. counterparts. At Ford in Cologne 'a cooperative tradition and framework' meant that when Ford sought 'organizational reform through Employee Involvement (EI) beginning in the late 1970s and established Mission Values Guiding Principles (MVGP) in the mid-1980s, Ford managers in West Germany were already one step up.'[120] Wolfgang Streeck studied labor relations at the Opel Rüsselsheim plant between 1975 and 1977. He concluded that a leftist works council, dominated by IG Metall stalwarts, taking a tough stance with management, obtained the same results with Opel as the more conservative and cooperative works councils did at Volkswagen. It was not ideologies or radical strategy that determined outcomes but the institutional framework of industrial relations.[121] Streeck's observation covered a period before GM's 'Japanization' movement. But the observation appears as valid after 'Japanization' as before. One manager at Opel-Rüsselsheim observed that, because of the institutions and history of co-determination, his plant had advanced further than GM plants in the United States in the implementation of cooperative labor–management relations and a team form of shop-floor organization.[122] Co-determination was the main determinant.

Co-determination's force resided in institutionalized behavior not ideology. Lowell Turner concluded that the UAW at NUMMI, which installed Japanese work process in California, 'does not have a strategy of its own for work organization and industrial relations (beyond cooperation). This is definitely management's game. . . '.[123] The point made in Chapter 2 about co-determination is that it prevents management from being uniquely 'management's game'. German employee cooperation, therefore, unlike American, is not a disguised sigh of acquiescence as workers knuckle under to management imperatives. Works councils have acquired considerable sophistication, 'as younger, well-educated works councilors are brought in and expanded use is made of hired experts (the *Referenten*), who advise the works councils at company expense on issues such as new technology. . . '.[124] German trade unions, in addition, have developed considerable expertise in work shop management. Rooted in the 'Humanization of Work' movement, group work methods, based more on the Swedish than the Japanese model, had long drawn the interest of the German unions. IG Metall composed its own twelve principles of group work, which it presented to Ford and GM management before they showed much interest in group work. When the Japan shock belatedly converted management to the idea of Employee Involvement, the works councils and the unions carefully and fully prepared group-work counter proposals to those offered by managers at Ford and GM. Consequently, in an American-owned automobile firm in Germany, as Lowell Turner remarked about the Opel-Bochum plant, 'the works council, for its part, has what plant-level union representation at U.S. plants lack: an independent, well-articulated vision of the shape of new work organization, along with considerable leverage to negotiate for its implementation'.[125]

U.S.–German comparisons show that despite cross-national similarities, the German plants of American multinational firms must be classified 'squarely within the distinctive West German national framework of industrial relations'.[126] Managers cannot easily lay off workers and have to 'concede rationalization protection measures to the work councils, that are unparalleled in the United States'. German managers have to give full information in advance about technological and organization changes that affect personnel. They must outsource suppliers only after allowing works councils to study proposals and suggest alternatives. They must negotiate terms of change, including no layoffs and full pay protection. They have 'no formal or practical authority to impose teams on a reluctant work force without extensive negotiations and substantive agreement with the works councils'. Works councils are provided with full information, are drawn into shop-floor production discussions concerning the introduction of new technology, work reorganization, and model changes. And they do so not as suppliants, as is so often the case in America, but as partners, if perhaps unequal partners, in the plants.[127] In short, in this era of 'Japanization' works councils in German firms are more deeply involved in the management of work processes than ever before.

Such statements immediately raise questions about efficiency. The 'humanizing of work' program, after all, broke down on that issue. What did it matter, reorganizing work processes, if the transformed firm could not compete? Two group-work substitutes for Taylorism, Volvo's Kalmar and Uddevalla plants, pioneers in 'sociotechnical principles of design and union ideas of "good work"', have closed because they did 'not evolve to the point where they [could be] considered a substantial alternative in the global battle of "best practice"'. Hence Volvo's partnership with Mitsubishi at its Netherlands plant.[128]

Indubitably, too, many American managers chaff at co-determination because they think it impedes technological change. But the evidence even in old industries where co-determination parity has existed since 1951, in coal, iron, and steel, proves the contrary. Two experts, Kathleen Thelen and Alfred L. Thimm, although opponents in a debate, agreed that

> co-determination has been, on balance, an asset to German society, and
> . . . furthermore, good management and heavy investment in labor-saving
> equipment has enabled [the steel firms] Thyssen, Krupp, and Kloeckner
> [to maintain] their international competitiveness. . . . Management strat-
> egy of combining intensive rationalization with a new emphasis on the
> production of high value-added, price inelastic products could not have
> been accomplished without the support of the works councils and, at least,

initially, the tacit approval of the steel union, *IG Metall* and its representatives on the supervisory boards.[129]

What a striking contrast between the story of American managerial ineptitude and the skill of co-determined German management during each nation's steel crisis!

Professor Wolfgang Streeck does not believe such results fortuitous. He argues that management by co-determination, compared with management freed from employee participation, speeds up technological change. In Germany union- and works council-imposed high salaries have prevented employers from utilizing cheaper labor, thereby forcing employers upmarket into diversified high-quality production. The works councils' insistence (the price of their cooperation in management's work-process reform) that management constantly upgrade the skills of the labor force has meant that the German firm has had the manpower needed for this high-quality production strategy.[130] Americans often speak of the need to improve skills so that the nation, by shedding mass production, low-skill, low-paying jobs, can retain a high standard of living. But the inability of American labor unions to force employers to invest significantly in employee training defeats this policy. Streeck's argument is that co-determination has had positive results for German competitiveness, and the decline of American unionism negative ones, in those spheres of high-quality production where both countries, if they are to avoid sinking to Third-World standards of living, must compete.

One issue remains: how the German mini-management mystique has fared against the Japanese management mystique. In Japan, work-process reform occurred in a cultural context that differed from the American. Although the efforts to improve productivity have put great pressures on both the Japanese and the American workforce, surveys of American and Japanese employees indicate that among the latter there is a much greater trust in management. Two studies permit us to follow workers' attitudes in each country over twenty years. In 1960 Arthur Whitehill and Schin-Ichi Takezawa published *The Other Worker* a comparative survey of Japanese and American workers; in 1981 they published the results of a second comparative study, following the same format and surveying the same firms.[131] The second survey showed that during the very period (1969–80) of work intensification in Japanese firms, associated with JIT, TQC, *kaizen*, and other work-process reforms, the employee's trust in management actually increased. Some of this trust probably reflected confidence in a management that had presided over sustained economic success. Some might be attributable to the security of lifetime employment and a confidence, induced by equitable wage and qualification systems, that the rewards gained from work intensification would be fairly distributed in the firm.

But the penetration of Japanese work-process reforms into American work culture has not brought people together. Womack, Jones, and Roos, and Kenney and Florida maintain in their books that the structure of Japanese management could be transferred to the American workplace both in American-owned firms and Japanese transplants. Once the 'restructuring of the basic conditions unique to the Japanese model', takes place, through the introduction of work teams, task rotation, worker quality control, and just-in-time inventory control, the American firm could 'harness the collective intelligence of workers for continuous improvement' and delegate managerial authority and responsibility to the shop floor.[132] However, close study of the actual conditions of work suggests that such a transformation of the American work environment is not taking place. This is true even in Japanese transplant operations. Both the Fucini and Fucini and the Laurie Graham studies show that in Japan's American plants 'even though the structures of Japanese management are present, the way in which these structures are mediated by the workforce does not indicate the successful transference suggested by Kenney and Florida'.[133]

Such critiques of 'Japanization' have prompted people to look for alternatives to Japanese management systems. Karel Williams, Itsutomo Mitsui, and Colin Haslam, after studying work process in three Japanese and one large British car body press shop, came up with a suggestion directly of interest to this study.[134] 'The problem for British and many other European firms', they argue,

is not that they are technically too far from Japan; the problem is that they are geographically not far enough from West Germany. In manufacturing terms, West Germany is a regional superpower in Europe as Japan is in East Asia.[135] Academics, who are fixated on the superiority of the Japanese, have neglected the persistent and significant differences in competence between national manufacturing sectors inside Europe and America. German success is particularly interesting because German management combines technical efficiency with a limited social prerogative over labour.[136]

Alfred L. Thimm observed in 1987 that co-determination was 'on both economic and moral grounds superior to a spurious policy of "maximizing stockholders wealth" on the basis of Wall Street reactions to quarterly reports'.[137] '"Germanization"', Williams, Mitsui, and Haslam have added, 'would certainly represent a more congenial and appropriate future for the Western countries, and the implication is that research into the possibility of Germanization should be given much higher priority'.[138]

This quotation is a fitting place to end a chapter about the collapse of the American management mystique. Whether 'Germanization' is indeed a better path to follow for U.S. or European management is open to debate, but nobody seems prone these days to talk much about an 'Americanization' of their management.

Chapter Five

Quo Vadis

THIS final chapter is about the future more than the past, or rather, it is an attempt to consider the future with the segment of the past covered in this book in mind. Some time ago I had occasion to learn about the futility of such an exercise when leafing through issues of *Fortune* magazine for the year 1955. I discovered that the magazine's editor had commissioned a series of articles to be written by distinguished Americans, with the task of predicting what the world would look like in a quarter century. Looking back at 1980 from 1993, I was in a good position to evaluate how those trying to look forward to 1980 from 1955 had carried out their assignment. They were not a mean list of people: the heads of RCA and of Dupont, the Secretary of Commerce, and the head of the biggest labor union in America, the AFL-CIO. It will come as no surprise, I think, to learn that they really got it very wrong. Everybody suggested that technology would expand, but nobody really anticipated the revolution in information technology (IT), not even the head of RCA. Much more stress was laid on atomic energy. But the main 'miss' in forecasting was the failure to foresee the rise of Japan as an economic juggernaut. Nary a word about Asia, just the assumption that the U.S. would continue to run the world, set the pace, and that the Cold War would continue.[1]

But prognosticators of 1955 should not be condemned. Historians especially, but most thinking people generally, realize that human beings living at a particular point in time do not understand the significance of contemporary events; that is why historians fifty years or so later have the last word, although by then few nonhistorians give a damn. But there is also no particular reason to despair about our inability to predict accurately and precisely. Some years ago the Institute for Job Market and Occupational Research in Nuremberg concluded that 'it is illusory to believe that quick changes can be made in the training structure, the educational curricula, or in continuing education in order to keep them synchronized with the sudden and constantly changing work world'.[2] Institutional inflexibility would prevent adjustments even if the future were known. But the same study also concluded that, had educational institutions been flexible, our inability to predict size and shape of future job demand would nonetheless stymie useful planning.[3] However, neither institutional inflexibility nor poor powers of predictability, the experts at the Research Institute concluded, really mattered. '[P]ositions offered can be filled by people of quite diverse training. . . . [I]n numerous cases a complete elimination of bottlenecks and surpluses on the labor market occurs, even if calculation about future educational and occupation structures are wrong. The imminent elasticity of the system is important.'[4]

The lessons to be learned from these two stories are clear: because you cannot predict the future do not spend much time and money training prognosticators for employment in 'think tanks'; do, however, spend money and time creating flexible people and organizations, and the management integral to them, that can quickly adapt to the unforeseen. So the question is, as we face the uncertain future, what can we learn from Germans and Japanese about how to make American firms flexible and responsive?

Confronting Real Issues in a False Way

Although the focus here is management in private capitalist firms, a good place to begin is with the firm's relationship with the state. This is true because the American firm and its management confronts the state at every turn: as potential economic and/or industrial policy-maker, as regulator of health, safety, and the environment, as labor arbitrator in courts of appeal in labor grievances, as taxing authority, etc. It would be presumptuous and fruitless to rehash the debate on this familiar ground. Industrial policy, for example, the presence of MITI in Japan—indeed the role the state has played in modern Japanese development and America's need to follow suit—have been much and inconclusively discussed.[5] Nothing can be added here. The same sort of swirling debate surrounds other questions, fiscal and taxation policies, tariffs, and the like—to which also nothing said here can contribute very much. Americans are obsessed about government. They resent its cost and fear its interference in their personal lives and private businesses. About all that can be said on the subject of government has been said or is currently being said in Washington.

This study, however, can make one point about the interaction between the state and the management of private enterprise. Everybody knows that government regulations hamstring managers in significant ways; indeed the not unreasonable claim is that government interference causes management to dysfunction, thereby damaging the nation's competitive posture. But the private firm's relationship with government cannot be separated from questions of what Germans call the 'Constitution of the firm'. If we think of the firm as a community within which there are common but also mutually antagonistic interests, then the constitution of the firm must provide the rules through which mutual antagonisms are satisfactorily resolved, or the workplace community dissolves. It is important, moreover, to think about the firm's socio-economic embeddedness. Capitalist firms have employers (owners and top managers) and employees but they also have customers; it is this three-cornered relationship (employer, employee, and customer) that the postwar Japanese business experience has particularly emphasized. But the relationship is not just historical, in that it expresses one nation's particular experience; it is implicit in the theory of capitalism itself.

Willard F. Enteman reminds us that Adam Smith in his great work on capitalism was much less concerned about protecting private property (the owners) than developing the market system, and he did so for moral as much as for utilitarian reasons.[6] From an ethical perspective private property rights are, at times, indefensible; after all slaveholders defended slavery in the name of property rights. Far from letting property owners run the economy, 'Smith wanted to put consumers in charge. He believed that if the consumer [really commanded] the rapacious temptations of business people would be curbed by the operations of the economy . . . Smith believed his view did not force a choice among the interests of merchants, laborers, and landowners. Capitalism required them all to serve . . .

the consumers.'[7] Since everybody is a consumer, to subject the owners and employees in the firm to the discipline of the market is a moral act because it is in the interest of everyone. The market mechanism promotes an ethical end. Here morality coincides with efficiency, for the market mechanism serves everyone well.[8]

Most Japanese leaders place customer satisfaction high on the list of their firm's 'mission' statement. Ethically, owners and employees should not pursue their particular advantages at the expense of the customers; practically, to do so, when the market provides customers' with alternatives, is to place their firm in peril. The lesson that Japanese exporters have taught American management and labor in the past forty years is that in Japan such mission statements were not empty rhetoric. That an international study could report that 'American companies had caught up with and overtaken their Japanese competitors in terms of quality' indicates that this Japanese lesson has been, by some and for the moment at least, learned.[9]

But Japanese firms, if they stress customer satisfaction, have not neglected the interests of employers and the employees. Nobody has sermonized about customer satisfaction more than the quality expert Kaoru Ishikawa. But in his book *What is Total Quality Control: The Japanese Way*, he affirms:

> In management, the first concern of the company is the happiness of people who are connected with it. If the people do not feel happy and cannot be made happy, that company does not deserve to exist. The first order of business is to let the employees have adequate income. Their humanity must be respected, and they must be given an opportunity to enjoy their work and lead a happy life. The term 'employees' as used here includes those employees of subcontractors and affiliated sales and service organizations. Consumers come next. . . . The welfare of shareholders must also be taken into consideration. Japan is a capitalist society, and each company must make sufficient profit to provide stock dividends for shareholders.[10]

Within the Japanese firm the constitution is largely 'unwritten', within the German it is written out in the Co-Determination Laws and Works Constitution Acts, but whether written or unwritten the postwar constitution of the firm in both countries has made all stakeholders (employers, employees, and customers) within these working communities—to rephrase the title of Professor Ray Marshall's book, 'Heard Voices'. That is the chief lesson for American management.

If government regulation and oversight jurisdictions are vexatious, inefficient, unfair, and often just plain silly, their abolition, from the perspective of a firm's employees in America, could be quite unacceptable. American firms, in this land of democracy, are not democratic communities. Part of the reason for the state's interference with the firm's management is probably a direct result of managerialism: lacking democracy, the employees have turned to the state and the courts to seek redress. It might be said that the erection of the lawyer-plagued, suit-ridden edifice within which today's American management operates is, to some extent, a direct consequence of the undemocratic constitution of the American firm. The Japanese reaction to the importation of American procedures after the war would support this contention. Under American managerialism American employees have had to turn to labor relations courts to redress their grievances; under Japanese management employees preferred to work out their problems within the firm, rather than deal with the newly established American-inspired labor courts. In Germany, although the law provides for appeals to outside labor courts, most employee grievances are settled through talks between management and works councilors. Japanese and German experience indicates, therefore, that dismantlement of government interference in the life of the firm must be carried out with the successful development of employee participation, especially after the decline of labor unions in recent years. Otherwise the employees will end up without power or rights.

The Information Technology revolution, however, has enormously complicated the industrial democracy issue. Its impact on working people is indeed the theme, sometimes stated, sometimes not, of works frequently cited in this study. Sometimes, an author voiced concern about how the globalization of IT affected the living standards of Americans. Robert Reich dwells on this subject a great deal in *The Work of Nations*. Other authors (Senge, Hall, Johnson, and Quinn) concentrate their analysis on the effects that globalization and IT have on the structure of the firm and its management. But whatever the emphasis, the arguments are quite similar.

Reich notes that IT and globalization have fundamentally transformed the working lives of people. Nowadays they are involved in three activities: 'routine production services, in-person services, and symbolic-analytic services'.[11] Among the three the symbolic analysts, who hold about 20 percent of American jobs, have seen their incomes rise, sometimes dramatically, in recent years. College graduates for the most part, those working in this service group possess highly demanded skills. They are people who 'solve, identify, and broker problems by manipulating symbols'.[12] Reich puts many high-paid occupations and professions in this group.[13] He calls the other two occupational groups 'Routine Production Services' and 'In-Person Services'. Routine Production Services 'entail the kinds of repetitive tasks performed by the old foot soldiers of American capitalism in the high-volume [production] enterprise'. The occupations covered include traditional blue-collar jobs but also lower management positions, including foremen, line managers, clerical supervisors, and sections chiefs. Routine Production Services also encompasses a number of new information-processing jobs linked to world-wide data banks. In-person servers also do 'simple and repetitive tasks', but they differ from routine producers in that they must provide services person-to-person and are, therefore, not, like the routine producers, competing with other routine producers worldwide.[14] Unlike the symbolic analysts, people in the other two service groups suffer economically, although they have different occupational fates.

The routine producers in 1990, Reich tells us, held about 25 percent of America's jobs, but their numbers were dwindling. The in-person servers that same year had about 30 percent of the jobs and their numbers were rapidly growing. Globalized labor markets and the IT revolution dictated these trends. Since in-person servers are among the lowest paid and routine producers, especially in unionized blue-collar jobs, among the best-paid workers the shift to in-person jobs impoverished Americans. Because in-person service people are less unionized than routine producers, the trend also provides a structural explanation for the de-unionization of America's non-agricultural workforce.

There is no reason to quarrel with these employment categories or the numbers. Problems arise only when considering causes. In effect, Reich, if he sympathizes as a human being with the suffering of the working poor, offers scant hope as an economist for the future. This is true because he considers American employment trends to be the

unavoidable consequences of both the IT revolution and the globalization of the labor market. Globalization started to affect American jobs
when Japanese competition challenged American corporations in the
1970s. They often responded to invasions of foreign products by
themselves becoming foreign producers for the American market.
Going off-shore for cheap labor exposed American workers to global
competition. And not just in manufacturing.

The exposure resulted from IT's impact on American service-sector
workers. Reich gives some spectacular examples of its effect. He noted
that by 1990 'American Airlines employ[ed] over 1,000 data proces-
sors in Barbados and the Dominican Republic to enter names and
flight numbers from used airline tickets . . . into a giant computer
bank located in Dallas', how 'Chicago publisher R. R. Donnelley [sent]
entire manuscripts to Barbados for entry into computers in preparing
for printing', how 'The New York Life Insurance Company dis-
patch[ed] insurance claims to Castle Island, Ireland, where routine
producers, guided by simple directions, entered the claims and determined the amounts due, then instantly transmitted the computations
back to the United States'.[15] The availability of routine producer
services worldwide forced American service workers into a tough
labor market.

The IT revolution also induced workforce helplessness through the
hollowing out of the American corporation. James Brian Quinn
observed that '[v]irtually all public and private enterprises . . . are
becoming predominantly repositories and coordinators of intellect,
i.e., "knowledge based"'.[16] IT permits the symbolic analysts at the
core to reduce a corporation's size and transform its shape. In fact,
organizational specialists like Quinn and Reich argue that IT has made
obsolete the old managerial pyramids, 'with strong chief executives
presiding over ever-widening layers of managers, atop an even larger
group of hourly workers, all following standard operating procedures'.[17] Quinn notes that the multidivisional corporation, namely a
large headquarters staff, is disappearing. '[H]eadquarters in multibil-
lion dollar firms', he wrote, 'are shrinking': Apple and Compaq have
two of 'the flattest organizations in the computer industry', Philips's
staff costs have fallen from 30 percent of personnel costs to 13, Nucor,
America's seventh largest steel company, has become an 'extremely flat
organization'. It recently reported but seventeen people in its corpo-

215

rate headquarters. The seven billion dollar Burlington Industries could count only seventy-seven people in its headquarters, and giant ASEA Brown Bovari but one hundred and fifty.[18]

The high value-added enterprise does not need to control directly vast resources or disciplined armies of production workers. It does not need to impose upon its minions predictable, managerially devised routines. 'Instead of a pyramid', Robert Reich opined, ' . . . the high-value enterprise looks more like a spider's web'.[19]

Both Reich and Quinn specifically use the term spider's web. And the organizational idea it embodies fits the new global environment. In particular, the concept of a spider's web explains Reich's employment dynamic. The symbolic analysts sitting at the center of the webs are the movers and shakers. From their small headquarters, these 'strategic brokers' continually spin out 'all sorts of connections. . . . At each point of connection are a relatively small number of people—depending on the task, from a dozen to several hundred; [e]ach point of the "enterprise web" representing a "unique combination of skills".' In this organization in-person servers and routine production workers of the old pyramidal corporation have no place. The speed and agility afforded by electronic networking permits the high value-added enterprise to dispense with large overhead costs like office buildings, plant, equipment, and payroll. Whereas 'in the old high-volume enterprise', as Reich wrote,

> fixed costs such as factories, equipment, warehouses, and large payrolls were necessary in order to achieve control and predictability, [in the new] high-value enterprise . . . [o]ffice space, factories, and warehouses can be rented; standard equipment can be leased; standard components can be bought wholesale from cheap producers; secretaries, routine data processors, bookkeepers, and routine production workers can be hired temporarily. . . . At the web's outer edges, suppliers of standard inputs (factories, equipment, office space, routine components, bookkeeping, janitorial services, data processing, and so forth) contract to provide or do specific things for a certain time and for a specified price. Such arrangements are often more efficient than directly controlling employees.[20]

The shift from the high-volume mass-production corporation to the high value-added, globalized firm precludes the possibility that routine producers could protect their wages and achieve social justice by engaging in the great union–employer battles of confrontation that characterized industrial relations in the past. In the spider's web the key players at the hub can outsource the routine production services needed domestically or overseas, to firms whose workforce lacks the social benefits, the permanent employment guarantees, the security of union protection that were regular features of the old systems of industrial relations. Because the spider's web organization, or something like it, is imperative for survival in the dynamic global high-tech economy, organizational theorists have argued that the routine producers have lost the security of the old high-volume American corporation pyramid structure forever. Marginalized, most American working people are left unprotected to struggle for a living against the forces of world capitalism.

There is something quite compelling about this scenario of footloose, buccaneering symbolic analysts making lucrative deals throughout the global village. There is also something quite depressing about it as well, for the symbolic analysts are the only ones to profit from the system. With this analysis, therefore, we have moved far away from the original mystique about American managerialism. It is fostering no people of plenty now. Whether the story is true or not, or rather, whether the results are inevitable, is another matter. The spider's web may be less a fact of global reality than these management experts depict. In any event, like most hypotheses, theirs is probably easier to disprove than prove. But we are less concerned about the predicted pace of change from the old pyramidal to the new spider's web organization. The analytical assumptions behind the predictions hold our interest.

The American organizational expert, if he or she thinks about working Americans, hardly seems to know what to do about their plight. Since the problem source is the globalization of consumer and labor markets, the standard solution would be to wall off America from the rest of the world. But this solution, to those who believe in the superiority of market mechanisms (and that is about everybody), is unacceptable. And with market mechanisms operating freely, the economic future of America's routine producers is bleak. Dilemmas abound. What seems to be amiss is that the analysis is conducted within the mental straitjacket of American managerialism. In other words, if the experts invariably take American managerialism as a sort of universal given, then the scenario just described is inevitable. Only a state-imposed solution to the plight of workers can be discussed and rejected.

American management literature does not, therefore, explore the possible behavior variations that different managerial systems occasion within the global environment. Law and custom, for example, protect Japanese and German corporations from the sort of hostile takeovers that, if it provided windfall profits and big bonuses to corporate management and deal-doing brokers, did so much damage during the 1980s to the interest of bondholders and employees in American corporations.[21] German co-determination, too, provides ample evidence of how a different constitution of the firm stops global market mechanisms from rendering the workforce helpless. German law gives works councils the leverage with which to 'persuade' management to upgrade workforce skills. Because under American managerialism employee leverage is so limited, American management can outsource without being forced, like German, to make a concomitant decision to upgrade employee skills, as a concession to workers who lose their jobs. Without skill upgrading, outsourcing has a particularly devastating effect on the American labor force that, because of skill upgrading, it does not have on the German. Both countries will see their low-skilled and unskilled jobs outsourced to cheap labor firms. But German workers, because their skills have been upgraded, will retain high value-added manufacturing jobs at home, while Americans, in the long run, will see both low value and high value-added production go overseas. That was the argument made by Professor Wolfgang Streeck. To avoid such economically and socially undesirable results, Japanese management also selectively outsources. A firm cuts costs by manufacturing simple components in low-wage facilities offshore, but it keeps the research, development, and manufacture of high-tech, high value-added products or product components at core facilities in Japan.

Two stories illustrate the sense of responsibility to employees and community that Japanese management assumes and that American management shuns. The first is about 'The Mazda Turnaround'.[22] Toyo Kogyo, the maker of Mazda cars, for a number of reasons, suffered huge losses which brought the company to near bankruptcy in the mid-1970s.[23] With 37,000 direct employees and 23,000 people employed by independent suppliers, the company accounted for 25 percent of total manufacturing employment in the Hiroshima region. For the firm to disappear, therefore, would have been a blow to the regional economy. Kogyo's turnaround was dramatic. 'By 1980 debt had been reduced considerably. Cash and deposits had grown by 100 billion yen. Revenues from sales had more than doubled and, most critically, production per employee had risen from 19 to 43 vehicles per year. Profits as a result of these improvements doubled from their pre-oil shock levels.'[24]

So, how did the peculiarities of Japanese management save the situation? First, in finance, Toyo Kogyo could rely on its *kereitsu* relations for support: Sumitomo Bank, the company's leading banker, Sumitomo Trust Company, another major lender, the Hiroshima Bank, major bank of Mazda suppliers, and other less important banks. Sumitomo Trust Company let it be known that it would continue to provide Mazda whatever loans it needed. Sumitomo could assume this risk because it 'knew' that the government, although it might let an insolvent car manufacturer go under, would not let a major *kereitsu* bank perish.[25] The 600-member Sumitomo Group also rallied behind Mazda. The bank, trust bank, and Sumitomo Fire Insurance Company switched all their automobile purchases to Mazda cars and asked all group members to do the same (a total of 18,000 vehicles in six years, 1975–81). Members of the Hiroshima City Chamber of Commerce formed an association of company presidents that sought to increase the purchase of Mazda cars. They were able to talk the taxi companies, the city government, and the prefecture into converting to Mazdas. Company support organizations sprang up in other cities of the region (over 600 local companies were involved, including the telephone company, and the gas and electricity utilities). Pascale and Rohlen figure that the total sales impact of all these hometown efforts improved company sales by one percent which, combined with the Sumitomo group's purchase of another one percent, was marginally significant to the hard-pressed company.[26]

But the most significant changes occurred within Mazda itself. Sumitomo Bank, 'without any involvement from courts or lawyers', put Mazda into a sort of 'quasi-receivership', which allowed the bank's experts a direct say in overhauling operations and management. Sumitomo delegated a troubleshooter, Tsutomu Murai, to join the

Toyo Kogyo management team. He took four executives with him, whom he placed in marketing, finance, and cost-control functions. Pascale and Rohlen note that Sumitomo Trust 'gave Murai no deadline or fixed plan'. Murai himself did not go instantly into action. 'While his colleagues from Sumitomo gathered facts on the financial and marketing picture, he went about building relationships, trying to improve the climate of communications and problem solving.'[27] As Murai told the story,

> I spent almost no time by myself at Toyo Kogyo. If there was any extra time, I went out to union offices. My secretary worked on the principle of scheduling as many meetings as possible. I spent a lot of time with Hiroshima business leaders, with the press, and with managers and workers at the education and training center. In two years, I met every manager personally and with at least 2,000 of our hourly employees.[28]

Since the company had stockpiled unsold automobiles, Mazda had cash-flow problems. Nonetheless, management issued a no-layoff pledge to the union. Inasmuch as the company needed to sell cars, not produce them, Mazda, with the approval of its 'independent' dealers and the company union, converted factory workers into car salesmen. To set the good example, management did not just foist the sales assignments off on newcomers. Senior middle managers and older workers 'volunteered' first. Over a seven-year period this 'dispatched worker' program, which could not have worked without employee cooperation, saved the company $120,400,000 in labor costs, while, through this temporarily augmented sales staff, the dealers sold an additional 400,800 automobiles.[29]

To the temporary measures management added permanent ones. Its experts reexamined all the old 'givens' of production. Despite 'the massive debt' management introduced automation throughout the motor assembly plant and installed robots in auto assembly. Group work was revitalized and with it the capacity to identify problems. By 1978 each first-line supervisor had been 'retrained and rotated through different jobs to stimulate their perception of problems'.[30] In 1979 employees submitted 600,000 suggestions (22 per capita) and the numbers thereafter continued to climb each year. Workers achieved dramatic improvements in 'change over times for dies and cutters', and reduced part inventories in manufacture from a 6.8 to a 2.5 days supply. Most of the improvements were 'initiated at the shop floor level through the interaction of plant management and workers. Toyo Kogyo sources confirm that fully 80 percent of the improved productivity came from small, incremental improvements in processes and quality control.'[31] And these improvements required little or no capital outlay.

Finally, the suppliers responded to calls on them to make the necessary sacrifices and contributions. Mazda management asked for significant price reductions, proposing a two-year program, but they also proposed 'to work with each supplier to achieve these goals through more productive manufacturing processes and better coordination of design work, to lower costs'.[32] At the time more than 250 Toyo Kogyo engineers worked full-time with suppliers in the pursuit of improved manufacturing, instituting small process improvements, achieved over months of examination and adjustment. The results were significant: an average reduction of about 14 percent in supplier prices over thirty months.[33]

The Mazda turnaround engaged almost all the elements of Japanese management that have been discussed in this book. The government, the *kereitsu*, top and middle management, the dealers, the suppliers, the hourly employees were involved, and involved in ways that illustrate the substance of Japanese management ideology. Japanese banks, unlike American creditors who often seek debt reduction at any cost, lent more money to the cash-strapped company to buy time. But the management did not try to save the firm through infusions of money. A no-layoff policy meant that Mazda would be 'long on people' and short on cash. The company would not, of course, sacrifice its long-term future in order to protect workers' jobs and pay. Company survival came first. But instead of devising and imposing some heavy-handed top-down scheme that would have involved drastic downsizing, Mazda's management really believed that its people were the company's greatest resource. The no lay-off policy enlisted labor cooperation, the intensity and breath of communications allowed the interested community to work out and implement the turnaround.[34] Everybody gained, including the consumer, for Mazda's success had to be consummated on the market.

Advocates of American managerialism might tend to argue that the efforts of unions to hinder plant closures, or works councils to delay outsourcing, or communities to save corporations could, by stopping management from making 'correct' decisions, prove economically detrimental to the community in the long run. In Japan, however, there is every reason to believe that the firm's embeddedness in community and *kereitsu* does not stop it from acting with speed and flexibility.

Mark Fruin's story about how Mitsubishi Motors mobilized its resources underscores this point. Its 'Galant' won the car-of-the-year award in 1988. The 'Galant' embodied a full assortment of high-technology features—four-wheel steering, four-wheel drive, integrated transmission, anti-skid brakes, an electronically controlled suspension system, and much more. But Mitsubishi Motors only had 3,500 people on its Research and Development staff. On its own, it lacked the capacity to develop the car. How did they do it? The answer: they exploited the resources within their *kereitsu*. Mitsubishi Heavy Industries, one of the most advanced engineering firms in aircraft engine design, contributed; so did Mitsubishi Electric, whose knowledge of process-control technology enabled them 'to design the sensor and relay systems of the steering, suspension, integrated transmission, and engine control systems'.[35]

When costs can be easily estimated in advance, outsourcing parts and components is a low-risk activity, in which case Mitsubishi like any American major manufacturer could simply buy from the lowest cost producer. But when 'close coordination between different steps in the development sequence is critical and, therefore, when ease and speed of effective communication in product development are of primary importance, the tacit, implicit, and sometimes explicit ties of cooperation based on inter-firm affiliation are irreplaceable'.[36] Coalitions like the Mitsubishi *kereitsu* can mobilize resources as quickly as any spider's web organization, and American management scientists recognize it. Their writings frequently praise Japanese firms for their innovative organization structures: the small size of their 'big' firms, compared with the old high-volume pyramidal American corporation, their tendency to spin off units into independent entities, their ability to form alliances which permit them, as in the Mitsubishi Motors case, to achieve strategic aims.

But Japanese firms possesses one crucial advantage over the new American spider's web organizational form. The moral order that is the *kereitsu* assures that, without the leverage of control exercised by ownership or legal contract, the intense cooperation needed for a success like the 'Galant' project would be forthcoming. This is such an important advantage that it is surprising that American management books do not discuss seriously the process through which this cooperative interaction is activated. To be sure, Reich and Quinn, and so many others, in the tradition of American managerialism, talk about intelligence; the heros of the global economy, the symbolic analysts, are manipulators of symbols. It is their intelligence and knowledge, therefore, that justify the wealth and power symbolic analysts accumulate, for they are just as essential to the dynamics of the spider's web organization as they were to the successful functioning of the managerial hierarchies in the pyramidal organizations of America's capitalist heyday.

But intelligence alone does not activate people. Fear might; American managerialism, with its surveillance and control mechanisms, has been based, to a large extent, on fear. Yet Reich proclaims that the 'standard operating procedures and other bureaucratic structures' used to coordinate large numbers of people in the old high-volume corporation have been swept away in the spider's web organization.[37] If that is true, then, why should employees be afraid if not watched? And if not afraid, why should they work?

The answer is that those who manage in a spider's web organization have to place their faith less in instruments of surveillance than in trust. The word trust is often heard when speaking about Japanese organizations. Trust is emphasized constantly when discussing parent company relations with suppliers within the *kereitsu* (an important factor when it is remembered, for example, that Toyota has 40,000 suppliers contrasted with Fiat's 4,000 and Volvo's 1,500). Americans and Japanese who write about the implementation of Total Quality Control, Just-In-Time, or Flexible Manufacturing Systems, Americans who describe the rise of the spider's web organization, also talk about the need for trust. With the police systems of the old pyramidal organization removed, trust is just as important to the organization's well-being as Intelligence. One must trust others to honor agreements, work, and do right.

The trust issue, however, seems to raise the hackles of American managers and workers, particularly when they discuss the Japanese.

The Americans are quick to remark that the Japanese use all sorts of information systems with which to control their workers. The usual Japanese response is that the systems are used for information rather than surveillance. Remember, one characteristic of organizational dynamics, in the water-based civilization, is barrierless information flows. Workers as much as managers need information about how they are doing when they are involved in the management process. That is Deming's point. He counseled using SPC information systems. But, if integral to quality process control, Deming insisted that management not utilize these information systems to police individual performance. So, the issue is not whether information is collected but how it is used. The lesson is trust.

This lesson has probably been the hardest for American executives, including those who have become Deming disciples, to learn. Indeed, trust, the one element that seems to be missing in the American corporation and American workplace, is also the element that management experts, even those who say trust is needed, write the least about in procreational terms. And yet, without trust, no matter what its intelligence quotient, the American organization cannot thrive socially and economically. Instilling trust, therefore, should be a top priority task for every firm.

The issues are as old as civilization itself; there can be no trust without moral order. But where does it come from? Perhaps one can do no better to answer this question than repair to the wisdom of the sages. Confucius observed, Huston Smith points out, that in traditional societies, the 'cake of custom' provided the intelligence and moral cohesion that kept the community intact. People imbibed these traditions, so to speak, in their mothers' milk. But Confucius also knew that the growth of individualism, self-consciousness, and reflectiveness undermines 'spontaneous traditions'. The American response has been to make a virtue out of egoism. Economists do it, with their philosophy of the invisible hand which assures that maximum individual greed increases the general welfare. Politicians do it, with preachments about the creative dynamics of individualism. Managers do it, with their stress on entrepreneurial genius. But the collapse of the moral order in America, the ensuing crisis in civic society, and unprecedented Asian successes rob American philosophies of individualism of verisimilitude.

Confucius, confronting disorder in state, society, family, and firm, five hundred years before Christ, responded differently than Americans to the disruptiveness of individualism. If spontaneous traditions can no longer hold their own against the 'eroding wash of critical self-consciousness', Confucius advised people consciously to reinforce the belief system that cements the moral order. He called this consciously reinforced tradition 'deliberate' tradition, whose aims had to be consciously formulated within a community and carefully taught in public education.[38] Confucius did not try to put the genie of individualism back into the bottle. But he knew if free people were to make 'correct' choices they had to be educated to it. There was nothing about 'natural' man that made him a moral being. And, translated into the terms of this book, there is nothing about the intelligent enterprise that makes it a moral association. Left on their own, people will not feel compelled to behave ethically.

The point at issue, then, is not the individual merits of people. Japanese managers or workers are not inherently more moral than their American counterparts. The differences are systemic, not individualistic. For order and commitment to exist they have to be based to some extent on (1) a fear of legal punishment if one violates rules that are accepted as sensible and just in the community, and (2) a fear of social disapproval for breaking the community's rules. But they must also arise from the individual's positive acceptance of his or her community's codes of conduct, work behavior, and values. This acceptance is the moral order.

The contention is that American managerialism, heavy on top-down imposed rules and sanctions, has been unable systemically to get the enterprise, as a community, to internalize commonly held codes of conduct and work values, and to induce a broad spectrum of community members, as individuals, to make moral commitments to the group. If Confucius is right, education in the broadest sense of the word, inside and outside the firm, is the critical public issue. What can Americans learn from Japanese and German postwar management about the process of building the moral order on which trust is based? This question needs an urgent answer because ample evidence is accumulating that, as Americans thrash about in a despairing search for solutions, wrong choices are being made instead of right ones.

Education Outside the Enterprise

The outside educational experience affects everybody entering and working in the firm. Usually when the subject comes up young people are criticized. The blacks in the ghetto, the high school dropouts, underachieving elementary school children are the targets. It is indeed distressing, since they are society's notables, to see the managerial elite shed responsibility for the moral and intellectual condition of the children. So before considering the education of the people, what about the education of the leaders, the managers themselves? People praise their education mostly because they consider the American universities and business schools that managers attend to be the best in the world. But the evidence cited in this study suggests that American managers are not the best in the world. They can, of course, hold their own in terms of intelligence, including a knowledge of the highly sophisticated techniques at the heart of managerialism. American symbolic analysts are second to none.[39] But in every category discussed in this book—salaries and bonuses received, attitudes towards subordinates on the job, receptivity to employee benefit schemes, etc.—all essential to the cultivation of moral order, the American manager compared with the Japanese and the German drops to the bottom of the ethical scale. Since American managers are a dominant elite, since their cooperation is critical to the success of any long-term management reform, and since their ethical behavior is doubtful at best, it is well worth reconsidering their education. The focus is on business schools.

Business Schools

Business schools, as noted in Chapter 1, have been a growth industry, in America and internationally. Indeed, they have continued to grow dramatically even after the collapse of the American management mystique. A close look at the Fall 1994 issue of a publication called *The MBA Career Guide* confirms their current and continued popularity. In a subtitle the magazine calls itself an 'International, a Truly Global Publication', and its articles cover MBA careers in Banking,

Pharmaceutical Companies, Financial Services, Industry, Technology and Information, Consumer Products, Media, and Consulting, in Asia, Latin America, Europe, and America. This periodical also presents an extensive review of business schools which reads like the global triumph of American managerialism. But careful study of the guide turns up some not so surprising absences from the MBA bandwagon. American presence is massive; so in Europe is British and French. But there is only one MBA program (WHU Koblenz) listed for Germany under full-time European MBA programs, and none, for Germany, under part-time MBA programs. The guide provides no lists of MBA programs in Asian countries; the only one in Japan that is discussed is at the Graduate School of International Management. But it is not very Japanese; it is headed by an American, Dean Melvyn R. Copen, who works with 'a first-rate international MBA curriculum, based upon that of the top-rated Tuck School at Dartmouth'.[40] Evidently, the German and Japanese refusal to emulate American business school education persists right up to the present. This suggests, considering the success of these two countries, that Americans need to take a good comparative look at the education of German, Japanese, and American managers. Education for 'intelligence' will be dealt with first, and then education for 'trust'.

Recently, a few dissenting voices, although not many, have criticized the research achievements of the American business schools. Research is a pillar of modern academic science, since it purportedly expands knowledge. In business schools research also pretends to improve the firm's intelligence. Their 'enormous commitment to research', business schools maintain, not only 'is necessary to keep abreast or ahead of business development' but contributes to the competitiveness of American firms.[41] But Robert S. Kaplan, former Dean of Carnegie-Mellon Business School and a Harvard Business School professor, observed that American business school research and teaching have contributed almost nothing to the most significant development in the business world during the past half century—the quality revolution. After reviewing articles published in leading operations management journals and examining research and teaching in top business schools, he found that only one to two percent of the schools had 'truly been affected, as of early 1991, by the TQM revolution that has been creating radical change in many U.S. and worldwide businesses. . . .

227

[Business schools] completely missed the quality revolution in management'.[42] H. Thomas Johnson, quoting Kaplan, added: 'Kaplan believes his conclusion applies equally to any subject that is germane to competitiveness in the global economy. In general, American business schools have completely missed the information-based management revolution.'[43] This powerful indictment echoes elsewhere in the halls of academe. Reviewing almost a hundred years of research in German business economics, I concluded in a comparative study of management education that 'business does not need academic research'.[44]

This conclusion, however, should not be misunderstood. It means neither that research is useless to management, nor that academics should not be involved in research. It simply signifies that the firm rather than the academic institution should be the place where research problems are identified and innovations implemented. That was the point Professor Huchzermeier made about how German firms use academia: they draw technical expertise from all sorts of academic institutes (physics, mathematics, etc.) whose raison d'être might have nothing to do per se with management. Lillrank and Kano, after studying the development of Japanese Quality Control Circles, remarked about the role of academic research in this work-process reform:

> We believe that a lack of sociological sophistication was one of the major strengths of the Japanese QCCs. Too much analysis can lead to paralysis, as with the Western job reform and Quality of Working Life (QWL) movements. Social science might come in later and describe what has already emerged in practice, but it seems that social science simply is not powerful enough to have a constructive role in the design of new systems.[45]

Engineers, not social scientists, in a long series of trial-and-error experiments, based on common sense and practical experience in the workshop, created Japanese small-group activity. Academic consultants got involved (Deming, Juran, and Feigenbaum), but the firm itself and professional groups composed of people from praxis, like those in JUSE, set the agenda and carried it out.

Then what role do business schools play in the education of American managers? Lori Bongiorno, in a 1993 issue of *Business*

Week, reported that corporate America demands that 'executive education achieve specific, real-world goals'.[46] That indicates a certain dissatisfaction with the academics. But she went on to note that firms also showcase star business school professors at conferences and seminars, attended almost exclusively by top executives:

> Critics argue that at rates as high as $20,000 per day, these profs rush in for guest appearances, seldom getting to know the company or its problems . . . . The savvier companies, such as Champion International Corp., favor experts with less marquee value, figuring they're more likely to study the company and play an instrumental role in implementing changes. These professors typically charge $5,000 to $12,000 per day, depending on how much preparation and travel they must do.[47]

If Kaplan's and Johnson's views are correct, then, even at $5,000 to $12,000 per day, these corporate executives are not getting any bargain. The German and Japanese alternatives demonstrate quite convincingly that stars from glamorous business schools constitute no indispensable research or teaching resource for the management of the intelligent enterprise.

Yet big bucks paid to professors of dubious value, and the moral outrage this engenders, is probably the business school's least objectional educational function. Certainly the community-disruptive, elitist, classical American management image that business schools project into praxis is more detrimental. This is true not only because of what the schools teach (indeed they might talk up community), but because of the way their graduates are received and treated in the corporate world, with high starting salaries and fast-track promotions. Any doubts about this assertion can be easily dispelled by a quick read of one popular publication, *Business Week's Guide to the Best Business Schools*. The aggressiveness of MBAs, especially from the top schools, which this publication reveals disrupts community in any organization into which they are introduced. To avoid this disruptiveness, the Japanese firm hires people right out of school, trains all of them in various jobs through a carefully worked out system of job rotation, supplementing this on-the-job training with short in-firm or extramural courses. German firms hire functional specialists but do not consider management itself a specialty. In neither country are there many MBAs to claim privileged 'management' capability. Everybody in the firm learns about management, beginning at the bottom with a broom, and then, based on performance on the job, moves up.

Should, then, graduate schools of business administration be abolished? Probably not, for they are established American institutions that teach useful managerial functions. But they need to be refocused in two ways. First, they must be more fully integrated into the university. American firms have, in American universities, a rich resource from which to draw. In areas of technical need, science, mathematics, and engineering, the university's usefulness is obvious. But American universities have among them the world's finest Sinologists, Japanologists, linguists, cultural anthropologists, and other culturally knowledgeable experts, tucked away in history, religion, and philosophy departments, in area study programs and institutes. No American corporation need send a delegation to Tokyo, Jakarta, or wherever, with everybody in it unable to speak the appropriate language or understand the religious customs or cultural mores of their hosts. No American firm need welcome foreign customers without the appropriate cultural and linguistic resources immediately at hand. The potential is in the universities waiting to be tapped.

Since most universities have no idea how to shape and package their knowledge in forms business people can appreciate, and because busy businessmen lack the time to deal with academic configurations, the business school is in an excellent position to facilitate the interaction between the university community and firms. During the 1950s and 1960s business schools ignored culture. But a cultural emphasis has invaded MBA education in recent years. Actually, thirty years ago the American Graduate School of International Management (Thunderbird) integrated foreign languages, history, comparatives courses in the humanities, foreign internships, and exchange studies into its programs.[48] Although for a long time Thunderbird was an educational exception, after the Japan shock these programs blossomed. Some of the cultural interests reflected regionalism. Hawaii's Pacific-Asian Management Institute (PAMI), Texas (Austin)'s preoccupation with Mexico are examples. Others responded to the economic challenge from Japan (The joint MBA–Asian studies degrees offered at Cornell, the University of California at Berkeley, Michigan, and Wharton). Some assumed a global outlook. The Joseph H. Lauder Institute of Management and International Studies, founded at Wharton in 1983, is the best example of this tendency. It grants joint MBA/MA degrees to highly linguistically qualified, internationally recruited groups of students. The 1988 Trade Act, which authorized the U.S. Department of Education to found sixteen Centers for International Business Education and Research (CIBER), has added government support to this cultural approach, for the twenty centers that have been created in the past five years—all with one exception in business schools—stress foreign languages, regional studies, foreign business internships, and study exchange programs. No graduate school system rivals the American in cross-cultural management study programs.

If, to carry through these programs, the business schools have had to reach out into the university community in unprecedented ways, the contacts have nonetheless been quite superficial. Emphasis on the required core subjects (accounting, finance, marketing, etc.) remains the business school's chief educational preoccupation; they are usually taught by professors without any foreign language skills or interests. Moreover, the international study programs that have been adopted are sideshows. Business schools, almost invariably, still have no foreign language requirements for mainline MBA students. The neglect of foreign languages compares unfavorably with what has been going on in some other countries. In France, for example, students in French business schools (*Grandes Ecoles de Commerce*) in the 1960s used to be as unilingual as Americans. In the best schools all students now have to pass an entrance examination in two foreign languages (oral and written). During their studies, they attend regular courses sometimes taught in a foreign language (usually English but not exclusively). In their final year, they have to write a report in the foreign language of a non-French-speaking company in which every student is required to do an internship.[49] If *every* American MBA student did the same, great educational repercussions would reverberate through the university community, whose area studies and foreign language competencies would be tapped, and within industry, which would have to arrange the internships. It would also have an impact on language programs in secondary schools.

Business school professors and staffs need to learn more about what is going on in universities. To do that they must stop thinking of themselves as repositories of managerial knowledge and start thinking of themselves as facilitators, for the former attitude builds barriers

231

within the university and the latter increases the information flow between active managers and the entire university. But this attitudinal change requires that American business schools abandon certain pretensions. This is a touchy subject but it must be broached. As professional educational institutions, American management schools tend to claim, as such, exclusive rights to deal with American management. Since business school professors earn from consultancy, as well as receiving a much higher regular salary than other university professors, their indifference towards university colleagues outside the business school might be a way to defend vested interests. But some of the indifference results from the professional ethos of American managerialism itself. Because business schools think they are the guardians of management knowledge, they are reluctant to act as a clearinghouse that facilitates the establishment of close relationships between praxis and other parts of the university. In Germany and Japan, where business schools do not exist, facilitators continually bring people in praxis into contact with a broad range of educated people.[50] Often the facilitator organizations in these countries are not academic institutions. JUSE, for example, brings praxis and university together in Japan. So do the Frauenhofer institutes in Germany. They, in contrast to the more famous Max-Planck institutes, work closely with industry on problems industry brings to them. Although engineers predominate on Frauenhofer institute staffs, they also include business economists.[51]

Secondly, American management schools need to refocus their education in order to promote trust in American firms. As a first step, the American business school must stop sending out MBA students indoctrinated with the self-serving elitist ideology of American managerialism. Then, the schools have to extend education further down the social and educational ladder than they do today. It is not necessary for business schools to sever or sharply curtail their special relations with top executives, so perfectly illustrated by the high-priced get-togethers between CEOs and professor-stars. But slogans and exhortations from the top cannot create the moral order in the firm upon which trust rests. Only through employee empowerments, giving them authority, bringing them into management's confidence, training them to comprehend work process, and involving them in surveillance of their work, can moral education be done.

Kaoru Ishikawa related that JUSE started publishing the journal *Statistical Quality Control* in 1950; it disseminated information about TQC to management. But JUSE also sponsored the publication of *Quality Control for Foremen*, starting in April 1962, which broadcast the TQC message to shop workers and their foremen.[52] Through the educational function JUSE promoted the managerial capability and harmony that was essential to the successful implementation of modern work systems. Chapter 2 recorded similar developments in German management education: employer associations organizing courses for works councilors, trade unions working out courses with universities for management, and works councilors, university professors, and active managers teaching short courses to *Meister*.

American management schools could participate in this extended educational mission. Admittedly the project would be difficult, if for no other reason than because the necessary outside groups and institutions, with which business schools would have to affiliate, do not exist. There are no works councils, as in Germany, with which business schools could collaborate on short courses, or active, vigorous associations of low-level managers, supervisors, and foremen with which management schools could work.

But if the American business school wants to strengthen moral order within the firm, its management education *has* to be made more inclusive. Courses must not only investigate how labor is a management problem but how management is a labor problem, or rather, how good management requires the creation of a third dimension, which includes the customer, to whose needs conflicting interests within the firm must submit. The quality revolution that is happening in American firms, which asks labor and management to work closely together, might provide the business school an opening, belatedly, to expand its clientele. At NUMMI, the American Federation of Labor local, whose headquarters is now inside the plant, cooperates with management in work-process design and implementation. A business school could focus on this innovation process—in a short course specifically designed for all participants, in publications meant for workers and management at all levels, and in regular MBA courses that view the process inclusively. Drawing nonmanagerial as well as managerial people into the educational process rather than teaching courses on business ethics is the principal way to increase trust. It is the brand of management education that America's leadership elite should experience.

Mass Education and Management

If business school reform is important, reform of mass education in elementary and secondary schools, as German and Japanese experience has shown, is even more necessary. Reform does not just mean throwing money at educational institutions. Americans spend far more on education per capita (just as they do for health) than the Germans or Japanese. The money, moreover, is not spent just on elaborate sports facilities (although there is far too much spent there). Comparatively, American schools lay out more on textbooks and equipment like foreign language labs and computer installations than Japanese or German schools do. Larry Rhodes observed that '[F]ew "ordinary" schools in Japan are equipped with computers or other sophisticated equipment to give students hands-on experience in technically oriented fields before sending them out into the professional world. Even Japanese vocational schools may seem surprisingly behind American expectations.'[53] So what do these countries do that America could emulate? Again, the answer will be given under two rubrics, 'intelligence' and 'trust', but under 'intelligence' both skill and knowledge acquisition will be discussed, for both are needed, often in the same person.

Intelligence and Skills

So much has been said about the need for teachers to be respected that it is not necessary to repeat it here, except to conclude that no serious reform of American mass education can succeed unless authority (not authoritarianism) is returned to the classroom teacher. Managerialism in American schools, in the form of school administrators, is the principal culprit here, and it must be ended. Once education can proceed under the authority of the teacher, what shape should it take? Before reviewing the lessons for America in German and Japanese mass education, a few words should be said about how education best prepares the minds of young people for work.

Research conducted at Nuremberg's Institute for Job Market and Occupation Research established that the inability to predict occupational demand did not lead to an over- or undersupply of people in the labor market because people learn jobs quickly and well for which they had not been specifically trained. This immanent flexibility is not, however, inherent in people; it depends on education. The Nuremberg study showed that an individual, in order to learn a job rapidly, has to acquire what Professor Mertens called key qualifications (*Schlüssel-qualifikationen*). According to Mertens the key qualifications subdivide into two groups, basic and lateral ones. Basic qualifications facilitate learning. Lateral qualifications permit the individual, who is properly equipped with basic qualifications, quickly to tap information that is available in society. Tables 5.1 and 5.2, which are much abridged from the original source, outline the two sets of qualifications. Even a cursory glace at the tables confirms that these 'key qualifications' are not really 'qualifications' in the sense that they qualify people for a particular job or occupation, like accountancy, bricklaying, or hairdressing. Rather, they equip people with the capacity to learn quickly the 'intelligence' part of any job after it is assumed. The distinction here is the one encountered in German education between making people *berufsfähig* (job capable) and *berufsfertig* (job ready).

Table 5.1. Basic qualifications for learning

As educational goals	Expressed concretely	Acquired through
logical thinking	logical conclusions	formal logic, algebra
analytical procedures	technical analytical processes	linguistics, analytical geometry
critical thinking	capacity to discuss and dispute	dialetics
structural thinking	classification skills	priority ordering of phenomena
managerial thinking	leadership	organizational theory, principles of economics
conceptual thinking	strategic calculations	planning techniques

Source: Harmut Wächter, 'Praxisbezug des wirtschaftswissenschaftlichen Studiums', *Expertise für die Studienreformkommission: Wirtschaftswissenschaften* (Sept. 1980)

Table 5.2. Lateral qualifications for learning

As educational goals	Expressed concretely	Acquired through
capacity to acquire information	nature of information	semantics, information science
	acquisition of information	library science statistics, media science
	understanding of information	speed reading, acquisition of specialized vocabularies elimination of redundancy and repetition

Source: Wächter, *Praxisbezug des Wirtschaftswissenschaftlichen Studiums.*

Obviously people need good language and mathematical knowledge, key qualifications, if they are to learn the jobs of the symbolic analysts.[54] But at the technical- and skilled-worker level, this knowledge component has become increasingly important, too. For example, to implement the Statistical Process Control, which is integral to TQC, workers have to learn the elementary statistical techniques needed when they check the quality production process in which they are involved. Japanese and German manufacturers stress that the labor force that understands the process in which it is immersed can best fine-tune it to maximum effect. The higher the employees' key qualifications in information acquisition and calculating skills, the quicker they will be able to learn how to engage in continuous process improvement once on the job.

The complaint, then, is that American elementary and high school education teaches key qualifications poorly. The low scores of Americans on science, math, and foreign language tests, compared with Japanese and German students and students in other advanced countries, provide worrisome testimony to this fact. The answer, therefore, is not to spend money on computer equipment but to teach language, math, and science seriously step by step throughout the educational process. As the Japanese and German examples also indicate, the educational process functions best when the schools work closely with the parents. In German and Japanese schools, the law requires that a standard amount of material be taught to pupils at each grade of instruction; in Germany, students repeat the grade if tests show that they have not assimilated this material. In Japan the high school entrance examination funnels achievers and underachievers into different schools. Since academic performance very much determines their children's future, the parents seriously supervise homework. Parent–teacher relationships, since teachers are important, are just that, meetings between teachers and parents, where the teacher outlines what the child must do to succeed, and the parents take notes and ask questions about how they can help. School administration does not, as in America, get between teacher and child, teacher and the child's parent. Without similar teacher empowerment in America no serious improvement in academic instruction can take place.

Japanese and German employers and their associations play an active part in the educational process. This happens in Germany through justifiably renowned apprenticeship programs which allow a student, usually after ten years of school, to learn the cluster of skills for a particular calling on the job while still taking classes in academic subjects. Sixty percent of German youth enter these highly structured apprenticeship programs that last for three years (beginning between ages sixteen and eighteen).[55] During the apprenticeship they work three or four days each week in a company, learning on the job. But two additional days are spent during the week in a public vocational training school learning academic subjects—German, English, mathematics, and so forth. The program is supervised by unions, works councils, employers associations, and the quasi-public Chambers of Commerce and Industry. The works councils monitor how effectively the training is carried out within a company, the Chambers of Commerce and Industry administer the system on the local level. This apprenticeship program, with more than four hundred apprenticeship options, is a sterling instance of German co-determination management in action.[56] Through it people without academic inclination or talent are streamed into useful occupations.

Like America, Japan has no apprenticeship system similar to Germany. Students in Japan's commercial or technical high schools take regular academic courses. But Japanese educational conceptions resemble German in that they distinguish between education to make people job-capable and education to make them job-ready. Japanese job-ready training occurs on the job; but employers are very interested in hiring school-leavers who are capable of easily being trained. That is why they test each job applicant's key qualifications. Even in modest-size firms, personnel uniformly requires all job applicants to sit an examination. These tests emphasize general knowledge, even for those who come from vocational schools, for, as Larry Rhodes observed, the candidates' 'ability to read, write, and perform basic math at relatively high levels means that they can easily be trained (and retrained whenever necessary) to do many kinds of work'.[57] To discover whether the job applicant, to use the German terms again, is *berufsfähig* (job-capable) not *berufsfertig* (job-ready) is the aim of the employer's examination.

To emulate the German apprenticeship system would require a major overhaul of American secondary education. If, however, all American employers asked all job applicants to take a general knowledge test and hired people based on results, it would, as in Japan, concentrate the minds of teachers and students. Firms could work out such tests with the schools; the implementation of the program should not create much fuss. The educational challenge, however, is formidable. Remember one-fifth of American high school graduates are functional illiterates. Only by making the acquisition of key qualifications a serious part of an educational system that honors knowledge can the woeful educational inadequacies of American youth be repaired.

Aside from borrowing ideas from the Germans and the Japanese the following goals must also be set: discipline established in the classroom; teachers given authority; student 'troublemakers' who disrupt the learning process removed from the classroom; and students and their parents held responsible monetarily for defacement or destruction of school property. Students, employers, parents, civil servants, and teachers have to be actively involved in order to raise the key qualifications within the population. Such gimmicks as the privatizing of schools provide no answers. Both the Japanese and the Germans have quality public school education. In fact, in Germany, private schools are academically substandard. The educational process can be good or bad under public or private forms of ownership. The issue, therefore, is educational process, not ownership status. Nor is it a matter of getting tough with students. As Deming emphasized, it accomplishes little to blame individuals and criticize results. Reforms have to start with the administration that currently dominates public schools. Ask a systems question, get a systems answer: eliminate the top-down professional managerialism, which, aping triumphant post-war American managerial capitalism, took over our schools.

Trust

As moral order cannot be based on a philosophy of unbridled individualism, so can an educational system not exalt individualism too far without creating a dysfunctional society. This issue surfaced when considering business school education; it disrupts community in the workplace. Because of the importance of contextual ethics to the Japanese, groupism is implanted through their educational process. Japanese emphasis on group work, especially in grades K–9, obviously prepares Japanese people for group work practices on the job. This is the 'deliberate tradition' Japanese pedagogy inspires. Because Japanese teachers generally reject the notion that students are innately different in ability, they attribute different results to motivation, work, and pedagogy. If one forgets IQs it is also easier to forget about grouping students by capacity and intelligence at the beginning of their education. The students, therefore, learn to work within groups composed of quick and slow learners, the former helping the latter. Such pedagogical policies should be adopted in America, in order to promote mutual reliance and 'trust'. But because of a deeply ingrained preference for one-on-one teacher–student relations in American schools, changing pedagogical practice in the United States would not be easy.[58]

If, however, Americans have anything to learn from the Germans and Japanese in popular education, it is about how to educate ordinary people so that they can lead useful lives. Brilliant children and children whose parents are wealthy fend very well for themselves. Ordinary people need the most help. Their education and proper placement in jobs has as much to do with trust as intelligence. It is in fact the most important step a society takes to instill moral order. As many American educational experts readily point out, German and Japanese secondary education are quite elitist; students are grouped by achievement (in Germany beginning in the fourth grade, in Japan in the eighth), and the top groups streamed into programs leading to university studies. But the systems do not, as is so often the case in

America, relegate ordinary pupils to the educational and hence social dung heap.

If a society wants young people to take education seriously, it also has to be serious about finding good jobs for them when they need them. Otherwise, the youth will become cynical and discouraged. For high school students who choose not to go on to college or who cannot go, planning for the future is just as necessary as for the college-bound. Therefore, a carefully scheduled process of job entry is essential to the moral order. The Germans do so in the apprenticeship programs. At the end of apprenticeship, jobs usually await, often in the firms where people have been apprentices.[59] The success rates of job placement for Japanese high school graduates is even more impressive than the German. Unemployment among Japanese youth has been extremely low.[60] Although much of the success can be attributed to the consistently strong demand of the postwar Japanese economy for workers, job placement is not left to chance. In Japanese high schools homeroom teachers chart students for three years, the last of which involves the rather intensive networking needed for job placement success. It takes hard, serious cooperative work, between homeroom teacher, student, local employers, and civil servants to achieve the excellent placement results.

Since nothing is perfect, there are complaints that students get stuck in uninspiring jobs that are really chosen by the system rather than by them. To ideologues, too, all this job placement activity sounds anti-free market and 'un-American'. But none of the placements is done by government fiat or bureaucratic heavy-handedness. It is brought off by information sharing among interested parties and there is nothing anti-free market about information sharing because the market functions best when informed. The parties involved, on the other hand, have to consider community interests as well as their own. But when the American alternative, high percentages of unemployed teenagers, or teenagers with no-opportunity low-paying service jobs, is remembered, the Japanese system of job placement is worth trying to imitate.

Since Japanese firms are accustomed to working closely with schools, directors of major Japanese transplants have had similar inclinations when they moved to America. One company, when it built a plant in Scott County, Kentucky, sent local leadership, including the school superintendent and other school officials to Japan to expose them to the Japanese system. Based on these experiences, the school system is now implementing new teaching approaches emphasizing group work skills over individual effort. . . . [The school superintendent] lamented the traditional emphasis on individualized learning (i.e., the fact that in American schools group activity is labelled 'cheating'.).[61]

No doubt this Japanese plant perceived the need to foster good public relations with the community. Sending the hometown notables on an expensive free trip to hospitable Japan would counter local hostility to having a foreign plant in their midst. But the trip served an equally serious purpose. If this Japanese firm were to recruit its workers locally—which is the firm's desired policy—it had to work actively with the schools to assure an appropriate supply of qualified workers. American firms could follow this line of behavior, too, rather than rely on the 'invisible hand' of the free labor market to cough up people from the annual pool of ill-prepared, mostly to be disappointed, and hence demoralized school-leavers. By providing jobs for ordinary students, through well-organized job placement systems, American firms could encourage trust in ordinary people. For the moral order does not just sustain trust, it is sustained by trust—engendered when young people have confidence that firms and schools will not leave them in the lurch on graduation.

Change inside the Firm

On their own, piecemeal reforms of outside educational institutions will never bring about the demise of managerialism within American organizations. In reality, the transformation of outside education requires more enlightened management inside the firm that is willing to connect with the outside environment in new ways. Unless business leaders take a direct interest in the project, high school graduates cannot be placed, and unless firms include workers and foremen in management training schemes, the business schools cannot serve this clientele. The goals must be clearly stated and assimilated, and then pursued by all Americans, but especially the business elite.

David Coates observed that today's successful economies have low-

or high-wage strategic options.[62] Low-wage strategies are market-driven, high-wage strategies are driven by the state in partnership with private producers, in that the partnership fosters high-skill, value-added production. Clearly, the goal Americans want to pursue is the high-wage option, otherwise they will not be a people of plenty.[63] The thesis here has been, however, that American managerialism compared with the Japanese and German modes of management frustrates the development of the highly skilled, morally cohesive organization on which the high-wage policy depends. So, what lessons can Americans draw from Japanese and German experience about the restructuring American firms need in order to pursue high-wage strategies?

Masahiko Aoki, quoting G. C. Archibald, states that currently the most popular theory of the firm, espoused especially by Anglo-American economists, is agency theory. 'According to this theory, the firm is conceived as a "nexus of contracts".'[64] Aoki counterpoises two additional models to agency theory. One is the H-Model, the other the J-Model, the H and J standing respectively for Hierarchy and Japan. Aoki's comparative description of the three models is a good place to begin to answer the question posed at the end of the last paragraph.

As an economist Aoki conducts the discussion scientifically. He describes managerial behavior in terms of how management (1) motivates its people and coordinates the work processes, (2) deals with external sources of finance, and (3) deals with its employees in the decision-making process. Although three models are mentioned, the article really compares two, the J-Model with the H-Model. It describes how each copes with the three managerial functions just mentioned. The point of Aoki's exercise is that management in the two models behaves differently.

Aoki formulates that difference in general principles. First, he establishes a general rule: 'In order for firms to be internally integrative and organizationally effective, either their coordination or their incentive mode needs to be hierarchical, but not both.'[65] Put into plain English, this means that the way the firm goes about coordinating activities is one thing, the ways it rewards its employees (pay, status, promotions) is another. He postulates that J-Model firms have weak vertical hierarchies in the coordinate mode and strong hierarchies in their incentive systems. H-Model firms have the reverse (strong vertical hierarchies in the coordinate mode and weak hierarchies in their incentive systems). This means that the vertical chain of command is strong in American firms and weak in Japanese, but that Americans do not have to wait their turn, as do Japanese, when it comes to pay, promotions, and status positions. The same difference between the J- and H-Model characterizes their relations with financial institutions: those who finance the J-Model firm exercise much weaker control over its management than those who finance the H-Model firm. Under the third point (employee involvement), stockholders in the H-Model do not share power with the firm's employees, while in the J-Model they do; there is dual control.

Despite the theoretical cast of Aoki's discussion, there is nothing really very theoretical about it, not in the sense that the models emerged from didactic reasoning about the inherent characteristics of firms. These models really result from ex post facto reasoning about the historical phenomena that has been examined throughout this book. Viewed from the historical perspective, Aoki's H-Model is nothing less than the pyramidal high-volume manufacturing American corporation that Chandler's work has so carefully described.[66] Therefore, Aoki's decision to compare the J-Model with the H-Model firm is to do battle with a straw man. Few, since high value-added strategies have replaced high-volume ones, believe that an H-Model firm is anything but *passé*. Nobody today would counsel Americans interested in pursuing a high-wage strategy in high value-added manufacturing to cling to the top-down management structures of the H-Model. Although somewhat hidden within the scientific language of self-restraint and economic jargon, that, too, is the message of the Aoki article.

For contemporary Americans, then, the real choice is between the J-Model and the agency theory of the firm. Once again, the comparisons are not theoretical but historical, for agency theory, as William Hecht wrote, 'reflects the dramatic restructuring of [management] work [in recent times]. Companies may now simply retain a core professional competence and seek the remainder of traditional in-house skills, including research and development, design, and even manufacturing and marketing, among people outside the conventional corporate boundaries.'[67] Agency theory sounds suspiciously like the American version of a spider's web organization in which American managerialism still reigns supreme.

Structurally and legally, since there is an absence of managerial hierarchies in the agency model and weak vertical control and coordination in the J-model, they resemble each other. Both, for example, outsource operations, thereby reducing core size. This makes the J-Model and the agency theory of the firm different from the H-Model which is burdened by the pyramidal organization. But the J-Model also differs significantly from the firm described in agency theory in that independently owned Japanese firms are tied together, informally, in group associations, the *kereitsu*. These are missing in the American corporate scene. It is, then, this informality of association, characteristic of the *kereitsu*, and of in-house horizontal as well as vertical coordination, that differentiates J-Model firms from firms covered by agency theory.

Only informal behavior within the Japanese firm permits Aoki to characterize the J-Model in terms of a duality management principle. Formally, no power or control duality exists in these firms. Each is legally independent; its management is not legally compelled to cooperate with other firms in a *kereitsu*. Banks can legally call in loans, just like American banks, top management has all the formal power, and the vertical hierarchy is, just as in the American firm, formally strong. Considered formally, the J-Model hardly differs from the American corporation. The countervailing power-modulating influences within the J-Model are carried out informally.

This book has cited many historical examples of how these informal checks on management work: how the bottom-up *ringhi-sei* corporate decision-making process results in weak vertical coordination modes, how weak vertical hierarchy enables people in Japanese firms informally to coordinate horizontally. Aoki summed up the advantages the J-Model derived from the dual behavioral structure in terms of knowledge flows. 'In the Japanese case,' he notes,

> . . . knowledge sharing and the horizontal co-ordination based on it are often informal and based on verbal communications (even tacit understanding) . . . . Such undocumented communications may generate information value by the finer use of on-site information that is too subtle or cumbersome to document usefully [in the formal American management system].[68]

Aoki is obviously interested in the greater efficiency brought on by the flexible response capabilities of the J-Model firm. He makes this case easily against the old H-Model. But the spider's web organization makes that case, too. This chapter has already presented the argument that the J-Model's organizational advantage over the spider's web organization resides in the element of trust. America is a society characterized by conflict: it is in the language, the movies, the court room, it permeates politics, and labor–management relations in firms; it is the very essence of informal American behavior that American formality, in a constitutional-legal sense, attempts to regulate. Agency theory, the idea of a firm as a 'nexus of contracts', reflects the need for formalizing managerial arrangement in a world in which, informally, there is so much distrust.

This distrust gives the spider's web organization one great advantage over the J-Model. The spider's web organization can eliminate people and units with less restraint and regret than management in the J-Model. The Americans can quickly downsize. But the element of trust, whose retention inhibits downsizing in a Japanese firm, gives the J-Model greater ability to mobilize resources in an intense and flexible manner. The dual nature of its managerial structure, moreover, forces it to pursue a high-wage strategy.

American managerialism has created a great myth about itself, that it knows what is best for the firm. It might know best how to maximize profits in the short run for the stockholders, but no evidence exists that American management knows how to look after the well-being or long-term interest of a firm. On the contrary, an abundant commentary proclaims that the Japanese firm does a much better job in this regard and that it does it because of the duality embodied in its management system. Unless some restraint is put on American management, it will simply pursue high profits through low-wage strategies, refuse to invest sufficiently in the skills and talents of its people, and go off-shore. In principle, the restraints embodied in the J-Model firm could benefit the American people. But could the J-Model actually be adopted?

The answer, I believe, is no. Borrowing the J-Model is not a problem because of the duality principle embodied in its management but because it is expressed informally. Even the Japanese have trouble maintaining employee participation within their system. This does not mean that Professor Aoki's J-Model is a fiction. The J-Model characterization is based on a 'considerable economic and management literature' supplemented by field studies of fifty or so Japanese 'manufacturing firms and banks'.[69] It correctly characterizes Japanese management. Nonetheless Japanese executives, subject to the same globalization pressures as the Americans, find it easier to whittle down the prerogatives of their employees in management matters because they are informal. W. Edwards Deming, who perceived the trend during his last visits to Japan in the 1980s, warned Japanese managers to resist the siren of American managerialism. Professor Hideo Totsuka, who 'has long studied industrial relations' within Japanese corporations, agrees. He thinks that augmented managerial powers have come to threaten the integrity of trade union and workers' participation in the Japanese firm.[70] He laments 'the death of shop floor activities by labor unions' in Japan. But then he rather curiously adds:

> Although it is not possible to find examples of groups in Japan [who resist managerial encroachments], the struggles of U.S. workers under Japanese management [in the transplants] can serve as a convenient reference. U.S. workers have fought against Japanese management by altering the meaning of the symbols management has used as tools to integrate them.[71]

Professor Totsuka's quote is sobering but still a comparatively good sign for the Japanese. If they cannot find an example of Japanese unions resisting management's demands, it could mean Japanese management is still restrained in its relationship with unions by the tacit understanding that Aoki states explicitly in the duality principle. Japanese employees still share power with management. But the quote is not very good news for Americans. For it suggests that most of the Japanese work processes Americans adopt like JIT, TQM, and FMS have been turned, under American managerialism, into a sort of jumped-up Taylorism that the duality principle of informal control prevents from happening in Japan. So, it does no good to import Japanese work processes into American firms without the simultaneous adoption of the informal Japanese behavior patterns that go with them. Unfortunately, borrowing the mores and values that have driven nonlegally specified behavior in Japan is not easy, because they are so much at variance with American mores and values. In fact, it is well-nigh impossible, which makes the J-Model difficult for Americans to imitate.

But what about the German model? Americans have trouble borrowing anything from Germans, of course, whom they suspect of having incurable if currently latent fascist tendencies. But the German system of management is the antithesis of fascism; indeed the enabling acts of the German system were passed when, fascism and authoritarianism discredited, the German elites, in a brief and unprecedented postwar moment of humiliation and contrition, conceded to working people and their unions a voice in the governance of firms. The second chapter described the process of recognition, formally embodied in the various co-determination laws and works-constitution acts, legislation that created works councils in almost all firms and allowed for employee representation on the supervisory boards of all large firms. The duality of the German model is explicitly stated, and because of its very formality, potentially easier for Americans to understand than the J-Model. The key is not democratization alone, but democratization carried out within the tripartite framework which, through mutually interacting rights and obligations, serves the interests of customer (society), employee, and stockholder. Just as the Germans, therefore, Americans could legislate co-determination, with management and employees, through elected works councils, running the firm, subject to the discipline of the market system. This would be a desirable result since the German managerial model, it has been argued in this book, has followed a high-wage strategy better than American firms under the guidance of American managerialism.

But legislation means government intervention, something Americans particularly detest. Two things can be said about that: (1) there is a larger state bureaucracy involved in the current litigious and dysfunctional American system of industrial relations than in German co-determination, and (2) in conflict-ridden societies, like postwar Germany and the United States, a legal framework is essential for change. In the German experience legislation itself did not constitute the change; it only acted as the lever which initiated the change process and the channel through which it, formally and informally, took shape within the German firm and its environment during subsequent decades.

Could similar reforms be carried out inside the American corporate world? The answer to this has more to do with will than capacity. Writing almost five hundred years ago, Niccolò Machiavelli astutely observed:

> There is nothing more difficult to carry out, nor more doubtful of success, nor more dangerous to handle than to initiate a new order of things. For the reformer has enemies in all who profit by the old order, and only luke-warm defenders in all those who would profit by the new order. This lukewarmness arises partly from fear of their adversaries, who have the law in their favor; and partly from the incredulity of mankind, who do not truly believe in anything new until they have had actual experience of it. (*The Prince*, 1513).

There is little doubt about the attitude of the enemies of reform, American managers and stockholders. They would be enemies, as they have been in the past, of the G-Model. Only the threat of imminent collapse would prompt them to modulate their ownership and control claims. This happened in the late 1970s when the Japanese challenge provoked serious reform. W. Edwards Deming and his disciples, groups like the Association for Manufacturing Excellence, and progressive American corporations like Xerox, Motorola, and General Electric started a quality revolution in American manufacturing and service industries that has had important repercussions for management. But even in the most wretched years of the Japanese challenge, the most reform-minded management never thought in terms of sharing power with employees. Certainly they never thought to sponsor passage of an American version of German co-determination laws and works-constitution acts. Stockholders in corporate America see any attempt to give employees a voice in the selection of management as a violation of their property rights; and American managers still perceive attempts formally to give employees a say in management as an assault on managerial prerogatives.

Already the timid reform steps falter. Record profits and the evident success of the quality campaign have seemingly dampened management's reformist ardor. As *The Economist* recently wrote: 'The American Quality Foundation has been disbanded. And, tellingly, applications for the Baldrige award, America's prestigious prize for quality, have slumped. . . . In 1994 only 71 firms vied for a Baldrige, a fall of a third in three years.'[72] The return to profitability, moreover, seems to have resulted from rigorous downsizing and cost-cutting measures as the new spider's web organizations slough off middle managers from their now abandoned H-Model hierarchies, and contract out, to get cheaper labor and avoid paying employee benefits.[73] Despite the fact that German firms, under co-determination, have also returned to profitability, American CEOs are content to attribute signs of resiliency essentially to themselves, to the abilities of an unreformed American managerialism.[74]

But Machiavelli's comment is less interesting for what it says about the attitude of those with vested interests in American managerialism than for what it says about those who resist changes from which they would gain. Truly, the 'incredulity' of people prevents them from believing 'in anything new until they have actual experience of it'. Despite the evidence from Europe about co-determination, the American worker and American unions have been lukewarm about demanding participation in management. As for the middle classes, they accept American managerialism; that is, they complain about their economic decline but they do not attribute it, in any way, to the effects of managerialism. There is no movement at present to pass the appropriate participatory legislation. Indeed, ongoing efforts pretend to take even more power away from workers and unions and increase the prerogatives of management.

What about the future? This chapter began with rather scathing comments about prognosticators and prognostications. There is no reason to alter those remarks at the end. But prognostication is most accurate when the parameters that prevail in the present can be projected into the future. What are the trends? The issue is not private ownership of property but American managerialism, which the evolution of the firm in the conditions of global capitalism has shown to be inadequate to the needs of the American people. Since recent rises in corporate profitability have been accompanied by a continued fall in the wealth of American households and a widening of the gap between rich and poor, there are scarcely any grounds for renewed optimism about the general efficacy of American managerialism in the future.[75]

Japanese and German stockholders have enjoyed excellent dividends for decades. They are fat, happy capitalists. If the favorable balances of trade and constantly appreciating values of their currencies are taken into account, the blessings of capitalism to the citizens of these two countries have been truly great. During the 1970s and 1980s the tourist signs at the *Place de l'Opéra* in Paris gradually turned away from American English to Japanese. Japanese buy vacation and retirement homes in Vancouver, Seattle, and Honolulu, for prices that are, by their standards, exceedingly cheap. Meanwhile middle-class Americans struggle to pay for the no-fringe trips to Europe, Tokyo, and Hong Kong. American scholars, who once roamed these places in droves, find their dollar stipends cut, as revenues fall, and the unfavorable exchange rates prohibitive for study and research abroad.[76] No nation's people can call themselves prosperous if they live in the world with a debased currency that does not permit them to pay their way. No nation's community of scientists can pretend to lead the world if they lack sufficient funds to promote and attend conferences everywhere.

Although this managerialism—which subjects those in the workplace to the authority of a professionally dominant and aggressive career elite—has not properly tended to the upgrading of employees' skills, its principal failing has been an inability to foment the trust which must exist, experts universally acknowledge, for the development of high-wage, high value-added work processes in a post-Taylorist world. If this failing persists, then the proposition that more Americans will work increasingly in low-paying, low value-added, market-driven firms, or not work at all, will be true. If this happens, then perhaps those who would benefit from a new order of things— and that is most Americans—would be able to face the green-eyed monster of this outmoded American managerialism and enact the sort of reforms that recent German and Japanese experience indicate work. That is, after all, what happened in Germany and Japan after the war. They changed. Then, the mystique of a reformed American management could take on new life.

Notes

INTRODUCTION

1. Peter D. Anthony, *The Foundation of Management* (London: Tavistock, 1986), 30. Child's definition is quoted there.
2. Ibid. 29.
3. Alfred Vagts, *A History of Militarism: Romance and Realities of a Profession* (New York: Norton, 1937), 11.
4. Ibid.
5. In answer to a questionnaire I sent to him.
6. Thomas J. Peters and Robert H. Waterman, Jr., *In Search of Excellence* (Cambridge, Mass.: Harvard University Press, 1981).
7. Shirley J. Daniel and June Y. Aono, 'A Framework for Comparing International Auditing Practices and an Examination of Auditing in the U.S.A. and Japan', unpublished paper, School of Accountancy, University of Hawaii, 2404 Maile Way, Honolulu, HI 96822.
8. He adds, 'Perhaps we can understand why there is no controversy [in management education]. It would be hard to find another field of educational activity in which intelligent, and sometimes educated minds, were so harmoniously disposed. There may be occasional disagreement about educational methods, never about doctrine': Peter D. Anthony, *The Ideology of Work* (London: Tavistock, 1977), 262.
9. Paul Krugman, 'Technology and Changing Comparative Advantage in the Pacific Region', in Hadi Soesastro and Mari Pangestu, *Technological Challenge in the Asia-Pacific Economy* (London: Allen & Unwin, 1990), 25–37.
10. Ibid. 35.
11. Shari Kimoto, an economics student at the University of Hawaii, observed, in response to a question about what economists would think of the cultural-historical approach to economics: '[economics classes at the University of Hawaii do not] take culture into consideration, do not ever mention any countries'. But she perceptively remarked about a

visiting professor from Japan, whose course she took in the department of Economics in Hawaii: 'Right from the beginning of this economics course, he took more of a historical perspective and took cultural factors into consideration.' The universal mode of thinking in economics seems to be universal in some countries but not in others.

12. Manfred Perlitz, 'Culture and Strategy', *European Business Journal*, 6:2 (1994), 55–62 at 56. In a table (p. 57) he lists seventeen of these 'Japanese' management techniques with references to their Western antecedents. The seventeen are: (1) suggestion systems, (2) shortening of processing time, (3) avoidance of dissipation, (4) Just-In-Time delivery (JIT), (5) make or buy, (6) statistical quality control, (7) multiple-machine work, (8) teamwork, (9) shortening of change-over time, (10) continuous improvement process, (11) project management, (12) inclusion of staff in decision-making, (13) market-oriented thinking, (14) business processes across functional areas, (15) zero-defect method, (16) motivation by participation, and (17) simultaneous engineering.

13. See, for example, the essays in John Hassard and Martin Parker (eds.), *Postmodernism and Organizations* (London: Sage, 1993). Rarely do authors mention specific countries when discussing organizational behavior, and when they do, the countries are cobbled together in the most superficial manner. For example, Paul Thompson notes that 'Japan and Sweden are held by Clegg to offer the main contrasting postmodern futures', but Japan and Sweden have such profoundly different organizational cultures that this statement explains very little.

14. One exception is the work done by the Canadian historian William Lazonick, but this work has appeared rather late. See, for example, William Lazonick, *Business Organization and the Myth of the Market Economy* (Cambridge: Cambridge University Press, 1991), in which, especially in ch. 1, pp. 36–43, the author deals with the shortcomings of American management as a system.

15. See, for instance, the essays in Charles S. Maier (ed.), *The Marshall Plan and Germany: West German Development within the Framework of the European Recovery Program* (New York: Berg, 1991).

16. Richard F. Kuisel points out that in the immediate postwar period 'We [the Americans] did not confine our role to that of a rich uncle providing material assistance, but also acted as Europe's mentors who gave advice and even reprimands to backward pupils. We tended to patronize Europeans after the war. We tried to sell what we called, the "free enterprise system"': comments in the discussion, Part II, Stanley Hoffman and Charles Maier, *The Marshall Plan: A Retrospective* (Boulder,

Colo.: Westview, 1984), 13. Charles L. Mee, Jr., *The Marshall Plan: The Launching of the Pax Americana* (New York: Simon & Schuster, 1984), 251, echoed: 'What Hoffman (the head of the Marshall Plan agency, the Economic Cooperation Administration, ECA) knew he was right about was productivity: growth, raising output by 30 percent, 50 percent, and more and more. He staffed his Washington office with fellow business-men, investment bankers, corporation lawyers, automobile salesmen . . . , and pep-talked them into a froth. America with a population of 150,000,000 turned out $300 billion worth of goods a year. Europe, with a population of 260,000,000 turned out only $150 billion worth of goods. If Europeans could be made as productive as the Americans, Europe would turn out three times as much as it did.' The most positive book about America's leadership role is probably Michael J. Hogan, *The Marshall Plan: America, Britain, and the Reconstruction of Western Europe, 1947–1952* (New York: Cambridge University Press, 1987). The work of Alan S. Milward offers, from the viewpoint of an economic historian, a healthy corrective to this ebullience.

17. Charles S. Maier, *In Search of Stability: Explorations in Historical Political Economy* (Cambridge, Mass.: Harvard University Press, 1987); id., 'The Politics of Productivity: Foundation of America's International Economic Policy after World War II', in Peter J. Katzenstein (ed.), *Between Power and Plenty: The Foreign Economic Policies of Advanced Industrial States* (Madison: University of Wisconsin Press, 1978).

18. Id., 'Society as Factory: Postscript, Ideologies of Industrial Management Since the Depression', in id., *In Search of Stability*, 67.

19. Ibid. 68.

20. See Alfred D. Chandler, Jr. and Fritz Redlich, 'Recent Developments in American Business Administration and their Conceptualization', *Business History Review*, 35:1 (1961), 1–27, which gives an early version of the Chandler thesis. Also Alfred D. Chandler, Jr., *Strategy and Structure* (Boston: MIT Press, 1962).

21. Chandler's students set out to prove this convergence in Europe, but with limited success. See Gareth Dyas and Heinz T. Thanheiser, *The Emerging European Enterprise: Strategy and Structure in French and German Indus-try* (Boulder, Colo.: Westview Press, 1976), and Derek Channon, *The Strategy and Structure of British Enterprise* (London: Macmillan, 1973).

22. Alfred D. Chandler, Jr., *The Visible Hand: The Managerial Revolution in American Business* (Cambridge, Mass.: Harvard University Press, 1977).

23. Id., *Scale and Scope: The Dynamics of Industrial Capitalism* (Cambridge, Mass.: The Belknap Press, 1990).

24. Winston Churchill, *The Second World War*, v (London: Cassell, 1952), 95.
25. Howell John Harris, *The Right to Manage: Industrial Relations Policies of American Business in the 1940s* (Madison: University of Wisconsin Press, 1982).
26. Lenard R. Berlanstein (ed.), *Rethinking Labor History: Essays on Discourse and Class Analysis* (Urbana: University of Illinois Press, 1993), 'Introduction', 6.
27. Among these useful labor studies, consult, including their bibliographies, Lowell Turner, *Democracy at Work: Changing World Markets and the Future of Labor Unions* (Ithaca, NY: Cornell University Press, 1991); Thomas A. Kochan, Harry C. Katz, and Robert B. McKersie, *The Transformation of American Industrial Relations* (New York: Basic Books, 1986); Wolfgang Streeck, *Industrial Relations in West Germany: A Case Study of the Car Industry* (New York: St. Martin's, 1984); id., 'Industrial Relations and Industrial Change: The Restructuring of the World Automobile Industry in the 1970s and 1980s', *Economic and Industrial Democracy*, 8 (1987): 437–62; and Richard Hyman and Wolfgang Streeck (eds.), *New Technology and Industrial Relations* (Oxford: Blackwell, 1988).
28. Quoted in Paul Thompson, 'Postmodernism: Fatal Distraction', in Hassard and Parker, *Postmodernism and Organizations*, 183–203 at 197. Michael Reed adds: 'In a curious way . . ., [Michel] Foucault seems to have repeated the same classic error of totalizing thinking with which he taxed classic theory. . . . Not only does he give us a vision of the world in which humans are caught within imprisoning structures of knowledge and practice, but he offers no hope of escape': Michael I. Reed, 'Organizations and Modernity: Continuity and Discontinuity in Organization Theory', in Hassard and Parker, 163–82 at 168.
29. Christofer Norris, *What's Wrong with Postmodernism: Critical Theory and the Ends of Philosophy* (London: Harvester Wheatsheaf, 1990), 147. The second quote is from Berlanstein, *Rethinking Labor History*, 'Introduction', 6.

CHAPTER I

1. Joseph A. Litterer, 'Systematic Management: The Search for Order and Integration', *Business History Review*, 35 (Spring 1961), 450–73 at 467.
2. Robert Hall, *The Soul of the Enterprise: Creating a Dynamic Vision for American Manufacturing* (New York: Harper Collins, 1993), 15.
3. Ibid. 16.

4. H. Thomas Johnson, *Relevance Regained: From Top-Down Control to Bottom-Up Empowerment* (New York: Free Press, 1992), 36.

5. Henry Ford (in collaboration with Samuel Crowther), *Today and Tomorrow* (New York: Doubleday, Page, 1926), 114.

6. Hall, *The Soul of the Enterprise*, 17.

7. Edward Lorenz and Frank Wilkinson, 'The Shipbuilding Industry 1880–1965', in Bernard Elbaum and William Lazonick (eds.), *The Decline of the British Economy* (Oxford, 1986), 109–34.

8. Anthony, *The Foundation of Management*, 34.

9. See Frederick W. Taylor, *Principles and Methods of Scientific Management* (New York: Harper, 1911) and Frank B. Gilbreth, *Motion Study* (New York: Van Norstrand, 1911). Also, for the long-term effects of these work-study techniques see Keith G. Lockyer, John S. Oakland, and Clive H. Duprey, 'Work Study Techniques in UK Manufacturing Industry', *OMEGA: The International Journal of Management*, 11:3 (1983), 293–302.

10. Anthony, *The Ideology of Work*, 51.

11. The classic study of Taylorism's effect on labor is Harry Braverman, *Labor and Monopoly Capital: The Degradation of Work in the Twentieth Century* (New York: Monthly Review Press, 1974). Braverman (10–14) writes that Lenin believed, as did also Clark Kerr and other American labor sociologists, that all modern industrial societies, capitalist or socialist, are subject to a 'scientific management' which of necessity divides the managers from the managed. But, as Braverman avers, Lenin misunderstood Marx, i.e. it was not inevitable, as Lenin believed, that socialist societies borrow Taylorist modes of management and production. Also see Clark Kerr, John T. Dunlop, Frederick Harbison, and Charles A. Myers, *Industrialism and Industrial Man* (Cambridge, Mass: Harvard University Press, 1960).

12. Chandler and Redlich, 'Recent Developments in American Business Administration'. This article was also published in the March 1961 issue of the *Weltwirtschaftliche Archiv*, a periodical, published by the Institut für Weltwirtschaft, Kiel University, that has appeared since 1913.

13. For instance, the 1806 campaign which led to Napoleon's victories at Jena-Auerstädt demonstrated the superiority of the Multi-Division organization's command structure over the functionally organized and centralized management that prevailed in the Prussian camp (the U form). See F. Loraine Petre, *Napoleon's Conquest of Prussia—1806* (London: John Lane, The Bodley Head, 1907), ch. 2, 'The Armies of the Contending Powers', 18–47.

14. Bruce Kogut and David Parkinson, 'The Diffusion of American Organiz-

ing Principles to Europe', in Bruce Kogut (ed.), *Country Competitiveness: Technology and the Organizing of Work* (New York: Oxford University Press, 1993), 185–205 at 191.

15. Anthony, *The Foundation of Management*, 52.

16. Ibid. 39.

17. The first test done at Western Electric's Chicago (Hawthorne) plant took place in Nov. 1924. They continued until 1936. See Elton Mayor, *Human Relations in Industrial Society* (Cambridge Mass.: Harvard University Press, 1933).

18. Examples, from an abundant literature, of this emphasis: Daniel Katz, Robert L. Kahn, and J. Stacy Adams (eds.), *The Study of Organizations* (San Francisco: Jossey-Bass, 1980), and A. J. Marrow and G. David, 'The Turnover Problem: Why do they Quit', *Personnel Administration*, 1951: 3–27.

19. Luc Boltanski, *The Making of a Class: Cadres in French Society* (Cambridge: Cambridge University Press, 1987), 129. First published as *Les Cadres: La formation d'un groupe social* (Paris: Editions de minuit, 1982).

20. The comments of one corporation vice-president indicate how substance as opposed to method hardly changed: he reportedly said, 'Psychology shows apparently that people produce more if happy, if they would produce more when furious, we would make them so.' Quoted in Pierre Fraisse, 'Les Perspectives des relations humaines', *Revue de psychologie appliquée*, Revue trimestrielle, 4:1 (Jan. 1953), special number devoted to the report of the French Psychotechnique mission to the U.S.A. (Oct.–Nov., 1952), 144. Also see in the same volume, Pierre Rennes, 'La Sélection des ouvriers et des employés', 23–37. Contemporary works describing the Human Relations Movement include Georges Friedmann, *Problèmes humains du machinisme industriel* (Paris: NRF, 1946) and Michel Crozier, 'Human Engineering, les nouvelles techniques "humaines" du Big Business américain', *Les Temps Modernes*, 7:69 (1951), 44–75.

21. Ivan Prashker (ed.), *Duty, Honor, Vietnam: Twelve Men of West Point* (New York: Arbor House, 1988), 12.

22. Chandler, *The Visible Hand*, 95.

23. Keith W. Hoskin and Richard H. Macve, 'The Genesis of Accountability: The West Point Connections', *Accounting, Organizations and Society*, 13:1 (1988), 37–73.

24. Charles de Gaulle, 'Mobilisation économique à l'étranger', reprinted in *Trois études* (Paris: Editeur Edito-Service, 1973), 125–6, 131.

25. Boltanski, *The Making of a Class*, 129.

26. For information and bibliography on British wartime Operational Research see Robert Locke, *Management and Higher Education since 1940: The Influence of America and Japan on West Germany, Great Britain, and France* (Cambridge: Cambridge University Press, 1989), 117–18.

27. Corelli Barnett, *The Audit of War: The Illusion and Reality of Britain as a Great Nation* (London: Macmillan, 1986) writes of this eclipse of Britain by the American partner.

28. Bertold Gamer, 'Planung und Einsatz elektronischer Datenverarbeitungsanlagen in einer chemischen Grossunternehmung', *Zeitschrift für betriebswirtschaftliche Forschung*, 13 (1961), 353–67 at 353.

29. American Management Association (eds.), *Operations Research: Mittel moderner Unternehmensführung* (Essen, 1958), 20.

30. John E. Jeuck, 'Business Education: Some Popular Models', *The Library Quarterly*, 43:4 (Oct. 1973), 281–92 at 287.

31. Tadao Kagona *et al.*, 'Mechanistic vs. Organic Management Systems: A Comparative Study of Adaptive Patterns of U.S. and Japanese Firms', reprint from Kobe University's *Annals of the School of Business Administration*, 25 (1981), 119–41 at 136.

32. Gilbert Burck, 'The Transformation of European Business', *Fortune* (Nov. 1957), 145–52 at 147.

33. Heinz Hartmann, *Amerikanische Firmen in Deutschland: Beobachtungen über Kontakte und Kontraste zwischen Industriegesellschaften* (Cologne and Opladen: Westdeutscher Verlag, 1963), 149.

34. David M. Gordon, 'Chickens Home to Roost: From Prosperity to Stagnation in the Postwar U.S. Economy', in Bernstein and Adler (eds.), *Understanding American Economic Decline* (Cambridge: Cambridge University Press, 1994), 34–75 at 56–7.

35. Reported in *Fortune* (Sept. 1950), 43. Cited in Robert Reich, *The Work of Nations: Preparing Ourselves for 21st-Century Capitalism* (New York: Knopf, 1992), 43.

36. Anthony Carew, *Labour under the Marshall Plan: The Politics of Productivity and the Marketing of Management Science* (Manchester: Manchester University Press, 1987), 42–3.

37. Ibid. 41.

38. Donald Duncan Gordon, quoting Gibney, in *Japanese Management in America and Britain: Revelation or Requiem for Western Industrial Democracy?* (Aldershot: Ashgate, 1988), 142.

39. Reich, *The Work of Nations*, 63.

40. 'In 1929, the highest-paid five percent of Americans received thirty-four percent of total individual incomes, but by 1946 their share was down to

eighteen percent. . . . The top one percent of income earners fell from nineteen percent of income to 7.7% in 1946. By the mid 1940s, almost half of all American families fell comfortably within [the] middle group': Reich, *The Work of Nations*, 49.

41. Ibid. 44.

42. Robert J. Koehne, *Co-Determination in Business: Workers' Representatives in the Boardroom* (New York: Praeger, 1980), 14. On the Scanlon plan and its successes, also see F. G. Lesieur and E. S. Puckett, 'The Scanlon Plan has Proved Itself', *Human Relations*, 19 (1966), 3–19.

43. Daniel Bell, 'The Language of Labor', *Fortune* (Sept. 1951), 86.

44. Carew, *Labor under the Marshall Plan*, 58.

45. Ibid. 56. He notes: 'These case studies were used in university teaching, as models for further research and provided extensive source material for popularized accounts in newspapers and magazines.'

46. Ibid. 57.

47. 'Co-determination: When Workers Help Manage', *Business Week* (16 July 1975), 160–7.

48. Besides Howell John Harris's *The Right to Manage*, see the appropriate essays in Nelson Lichtenstein and Howell John Harris (eds.), *Industrial Democracy in America: The Ambiguous Promise* (Cambridge: Cambridge University Press, 1993), and the abundant bibliographical references given in both publications which affirm management's insistence on its prerogatives.

49. George Meany, 'What Labor Means by "More"', *Fortune* (Mar. 1955), 92–5, 272–9 at 93.

50. Hence the value of the postmodernist stress on language analysis when considering work culture. Harris's focus on language illustrates how, against the background of the Cold War, the force of language itself shaped American belief systems in which labor's future became bleak. See *The Right to Manage*.

51. And they were easily recognized as such. See the sharp criticism of Human Resource Management as a sham democracy from the French social scientists who observed it in action in America, in Paul Fraisse and Yves Guibourg, 'Human Relations: Progrès ou mystification?' *Esprit* (May 1953), 783–804 and Michel Crozier, 'Human Engineering'.

52. See Michael A. Bernstein, 'Academic Reconstruction and the Pax Americana: Notes on Imperial Legitimation after World War II', paper presented at the conference on 'Knowledges: Production, Distribution, Revision' held at University of Minnesota (Minneapolis, Apr. 1994). This world systems literature, Bernstein reminds us, includes Immanuel

Wallerstein, *The Modern World System: Capitalist Agriculture and the Origins of the European World-Economy in the Sixteenth Century* (New York: Monthly Review Press, 1976); André Gundar Frank, *Capitalism and Underdevelopment in Latin America* (New York: Monthly Review Press, 1967); Celso Furtado, *Development and Underdevelopment: A Structural View of the Problems of Developed and Underdeveloped Countries* (Berkeley: University of California Press, 1964; and T. Dos Santos, 'The Structure of Dependence', *American Economic Review*, 60:5 (May, 1970), 235–46.

53. François Etner, *Les Ingénieurs-Economistes français (1841–1950)*, Doctoral thesis 'sciences économiques', option: économie appliquée, Doctorat d'Etat, U.E.R. Sciences des Organisations, Université de Paris (Paris IX-Dauphine), 1978.

54. The results were published for working managers to consult in a civil engineering journal, the *Annales des Ponts et Chaussées*. This periodical probably hid this and subsequent articles from economists who did not read technical journals. The economists' discovery of Dupuit was delayed until the 1930s when five of his articles were reprinted in a book (1933) edited by an Italian economist, and when Harold Hotelling's article appeared (1938) in *Econometrics*. J. R. Nelson (ed.), *Marginal Cost Pricing in Practice* (Englewood Cliffs, NJ: Prentice Hall, 1964), p. vi.

55. Reprinted as Maurice Allais, *Traité d'économie politique*, no. 2 (Paris, 1952).

56. Richard F. Kuisel, *Capitalism and the State in Modern France: Renovation and Economic Management in the Twentieth Century* (Cambridge: Cambridge University Press, 1981), 219.

57. Corelli Barnett's *The Audit of War: The Illusion and Reality of Britain as a Great Nation*.

58. Alistair Mant, *The Rise and Fall of the British Manager* (London: Macmillan, 1977), 41.

59. F. J. Gosselink, 'Marshall-aid and Organization/Management Sciences', the Centre for Research in Business Economics, Department of Organization and Management, Erasmus University Rotterdam, Report 8205/0 (May 1982), 16. For the Marshall Plan in Holland see also Peter J. van Baalen, *Management en Hoger Onderwijs* (Delft: Eburon Delft, 1995), 241–4.

60. One example: Although armies might have adopted MD structures during the French Revolution, the adoption of MD corporate structures in Europe really did not happen until the 1960s. Also before the Second World War there had still been much interest in America in European

management techniques. The *Journal of Accountancy*, for instance, published articles regularly until 1941 about accounting methods in Germany. After the war, the management periodical literature is purely American.

61. Carew, *Labour under the Marshall Plan*, 3.
62. The ECA was the formal name of the Marshall Plan agency.
63. Carew, 100.
64. Ibid. 148.
65. Ibid. 59.
66. Ibid. 197.
67. Ibid. 193.
68. Hogan, *The Marshall Plan*, 207.
69. Carew, 13.
70. See the chapter 'Continuities and Discontinuities, 1940–1960', in my *Management and Higher Education since 1940*.
71. Charles L. Mee, *The Marshall Plan: The Launching of the Pax Americana* (New York: Simon & Schuster, 1984), 251.
72. Carew, 137.
73. Mant, *The Rise and Fall*, 41.
74. Quoted in Carew, 137.
75. Gosselink, 'Marshall-aid', 30. For France, see Luc Boltanski, 'America, America . . ., le plan marshall et l'importation du "management"', *Actes de la recherche en sciences sociales,* a publication of 'La Maison de l'homme', 38 (1981), 19–41.
76. Ibid.
77. Luc Boltanski, 'America, America . . . le plan marshall', 38. The French name for the Productivity Association: *Association française pour l'accroissement de la productivité.*
78. Among the travelers Boltanski mentions J. Stoetzel, D. Anzieu, J. and M. Van Bockstaele, R. Pagès, M. Pagès, Cl. Faucheux, J. Maisoneuve, G. Palmade, and Bize.
79. The Rand Corporation ran Defense Policy Seminars at U.C.L.A., University of Chicago, Columbia, Dartmouth, etc.; Bruce L. R. Smith, *The Rand Corporation* (Cambridge, Mass.: Harvard University Press, 1966).
80. Bernstein, *Academic Reconstruction and the Pax Americana*, 13. Also see Tessa Morris-Suzuki, *A History of Japanese Economic Thought* (New York: Routledge, 1989).
81. Bernstein, 33.
82. Carew, *Labour under the Marshall Plan*, 192.
83. Ibid. 196.

84. Locke, *Management and Higher Education since 1940*, 176–87.

85. Richard Whitley, Alan Thomas, and Jane Marceau, *Masters of Business? Business Schools and Business Graduates in Britain and France* (London: Tavistock, 1981), 45.

86. Ibid. 46.

87. Marc Meuleau, 'Les HEC: D'un diplôme marginal à la célébrité scolaire et professionnelle (1881–1980)', paper delivered at the Colloquium on History of Management, Paris, 11–12 March 1988, 48.

88. Consult Yvette Ménissez, *L'Enseignement de la gestion en France* (Paris: La Documentation française, 1979).

89. Locke, *Management and Higher Education since 1940*, 209.

90. In French, the *Fondation Nationale pour l'Enseignement de la Gestion*.

91. The results of the program are clearly discernible in the *Annuaire des Enseignements de Gestion* where the educational backgrounds of French professors of management are given (although not consistently, thereby precluding using the reference as a source for a statistical analysis of the extent to which these French professors had American educations). This *Annuaire*, which is published by FNEGE, shows that the first French professors of management had American educations to a very large extent.

92. In French, *College Interuniversitaire d'Etudes Doctorales dans les Sciences du Management* (CIM).

93. For American influence on Swedish management education, see Lars Engwall, *Mercury Meets Minerva: Business Studies and Higher Education, the Swedish Case* (Oxford: Pergamon, 1992).

94. Pierre-Alain Schieb, 'Des modèles nationaux ou un modèle européen?' *La Revue Française de Gestion* (Mar.–Apr.–May 1990), 105–10.

95. Boltanski, 'America, America . . . le plan marshall', 20.

96. Luc Boltanski reproduces a sketch of this manager and his/her management style that is given in Jean-Louis Servan-Schreiber's *Le manager exemplaire*, which is well worth reading. Ibid. 24.

97. The year in parentheses is when the periodical was founded.

98. Luc Boltanski, 'America America . . . le plan marshall', 30.

99. Hogan, *The Marshall Plan*, 429.

100. Octave Gélinier, *Morale de l'entreprise et destin de la nation* (Paris: Plon, 1965), 155. Luc Boltanski, who studied the Americanization phenomenon, added: 'it remains true that during the years of the Marshall Plan the United States was widely acknowledged as a model: most Europeans were passionately attracted by everything America stood for. And what American stood for was first of all scientific management, technical

competence, and industrial might. The American landing in Europe, the liberation, and the victory over Germany brought an influx of all kinds of American-made items—not only airplanes, trucks, and tanks but also food and clothing ('American surplus')—into Europe. The American system, which had been a matter for ideological debate and polite conversation in the 1920s, now became a physical presence, an overwhelming force, for millions of people': *The Making of a Class*, 133.

101. Donald Gordon, *Japanese Management*, 170.

102. Philip F. Nind, *A Firm Foundation: The Story of the Foundation for Management Education* (London: Foundation for Management Education, 1985), 80.

103. Ibid.

104. Robert J. Samuelson, 'What Good are B-Schools', *Newsweek* (14 May 1990), 45.

105. 'Management Education', *The Economist* (2 Mar. 1991), 2.

106. Stanley Hoffmann and Charles Maier (eds.), *The Marshall Plan: A Retrospective*, 84.

107. See Leslie Hannah, *Delusions of Durable Dominance Or The Invisible Hand Strikes Back: A Critique of the New Orthodoxy in Internationally Comparative Business History—1980s*, unpublished book manuscript, available through Professor Hannah.

108. See the quotation from Anthony above, Introduction. The spread of American-bred social science methods can be explained by a historical rationale. Haruo Shimada, speaking of the 'functional analysis approach' of American social scientists, remarked: 'The prevalence and far-reaching influence of this approach are not unrelated to the fact that the postwar prosperity of the United States made money and places available to bring together scholars from all over the world and to foster major centers of social research': Haruo Shimada, 'Japanese Industrial Relations—A New General Model? A Survey of the English-Language Literature', in Shirai, *Contemporary Industrial Relations*, 3–27 at 13. The implication is clear: a historical situation, not the persuasive power of the science itself, is responsible for the postwar dominance of American social science.

109. *Webster's Third New International Dictionary, Unabridged.*

110. Haruo Shimada notes: 'Until around 1960, the time when the Japanese economy began its extraordinarily rapid growth, the majority of the scholars in the industrial relations field believed that the seeming peculiarities of Japanese industrial relations could be attributed simply to the backwardness or immaturity of Japan's capitalist development.'

For Japan to be competitive it had to convert to the American management model. Shimada, 'Japanese Industrial Relations', 9. For authors
who held this view see Masaki Imai, 'Shukko, Jomukai, Eingi—the
Ingredients of Executive Selection in Japan', *Personnel*, 46:4 (July–
Aug. 1969), 20–30; Kunio Odaka, 'Traditional Democracy in Japanese
Industry', *Industrial Relations: A Journal of Economy and Society*, 3:2
(Feb. 1964), 95–103; and Michael Yoshino's book *The Japanese Manage-
rial System* (Cambridge, Mass.: MIT Press, 1968) for English language
examples of Japanese writers who, before 1970, tended to evaluate
Japanese management critically and to advocate convergence on the
American model.

CHAPTER 2

1. The Liberal Party, FDP, was the coalition partner. Because FDP votes were
   needed to pass legislation, its presence in the Federal government mod-
   erated SPD reforms.
2. Eleanor M. Hadley, *Antitrust in Japan* (Princeton: Princeton University
   Press, 1970), 391–2.
3. Leonard Krieger, *The German Idea of Freedom: History of a Political
   Tradition* (Boston: Beacon, 1957).
4. Bismarck (1815–98) expressed this view best himself: 'That the State
   should interest itself to a greater degree than hitherto in those of its
   members who need assistance, is not only a duty of humanity and
   Christianity—by which State institutions should be permeated—but a
   duty of State-preserving policy, whose aim should be to cultivate the
   conception—and that, too, amongst the non-propertied classes, which
   form at once the most numerous and the least instructed part of the
   population—that the State is not merely a necessary but a beneficent
   institution. These classes must, by the evident and direct advantages
   which are secured to them by legislative measures, be led to regard the
   State not as an institution contrived for the protection of the better classes
   of society, but as one serving their own needs and interests': 'Official
   Justification of the First Accident Insurance Bill of March 8, 1881',
   trans. and reprinted in *Introduction to Contemporary Civilization in the
   West* (New York: Columbia University Press, 1961), taken from Otto von
   Bismarck's *Gesammelte Werke*, xii (Berlin, 1929).
5. Specifically therein the famous 19th-c. German reformers Friedrich Nau-
   mann, Franz Hitze, and Friedrich Lange, who talked about the creation of
   a 'constitutional factory'.

6. Abraham Schuchman, *Co-determination: Labor's Middle Way in Germany* (New York: Public Affairs Press, 1957), 14.

7. Erberhard Schmidt, *Die verhinderte Neuordnung, 1945–1952* (Frankfurt am Main: Europäische Verlagsanstalt, 1970), 81.

8. A Historical Clarification: After four years of war, 1914–18, uprisings within Germany brought the collapse of the Second Empire. The organization of a Republic took place in the city of Weimar, where a Constituent Assembly met and drafted a new constitution. This Constitution created a new legislature, the Reichstag, which sat during the Weimar Republic, 1919–33.

9. It also called for the workers to elect one to two members of supervisory boards. In the German corporation there is a two-tier board system at the top: (1) the Supervisory Board (*Aufsichtsrat*) and (2) the Managing Board (*Vorstand*). The Supervisory Board has considerable power. It elects the Managing Board, which runs the firm's daily operations. Moreover, the Supervisory Board's approval is necessary in all basic decisions affecting the firm (long-term planning, lay-offs, major investments in new plant and equipment, plant closings, new equity capital issues, etc.). The works council (*Betriebsrat*) is an employee-elected plant-level committee. For a good short discussion of the subject see Thomas Raiser, 'The Legal Constitution of Business Enterprises in the Federal Republic of Germany,' *Annals of the Institute of Social Science*, 34 (Mar. 1993), 27–46.

10. Frankfurt am Main, 1928.

11. Schmidt, *Die verhinderte Neuordnung*, 62.

12. Ibid. 81. He refers to the conservative counter-offensive when the Weimar Republic began, 1919–22.

13. Schuchman, *Co-determination*, 101.

14. Ibid. 110.

15. George Meany, 'What Labor Means by "More"', 93.

16. Gloria Müller, *Mitbestimmung in der Nachkriegszeit: Britische Besatzungs-macht—Unternehmer—Gewerkschaften* (Düsseldorf: Patrios-Schwann Verlag, 1987), 53.

17. The Marshall Plan historian Michael J. Hogan says this of General Clay: 'He had little sympathy with the German trade unions or with the Social Democrats. . . . [Trade unionists] complained bitterly about the wage-price differential in German industry, the delays in returning union property confiscated by the Nazis, the lack of labor representation on Clay's staff and various bizonal agencies, and the general's strong opposition to co-determination and all German trade unions': Hogan, *The Marshall Plan*, 201–2.

18. For example, Jack Raymond, *New York Times* correspondent in Germany, reported: 'Hundreds of thousands of workers demonstrated in Hessen in a double-barrelled protest against high prices and the refusal of the U.S. Military Government to accept . . . measures passed by the State Parliament months ago. There appeared to be universal popular support for the demonstration. Newspaper editorials approved of the Trade Union League calling demonstrations . . . in at least 20 towns and cities. . . . In Frankfort 20,000 persons, probably the largest gathering since the war, packed the Römerberg, the old city square. . . . [Max Bock, vice president of the Trade Unions League], called for lower prices and higher wages, price control and the right of workers to participate in management policies. . . . The third of these points referred to the Works Council Law, which was adopted in the State Parliament by an overwhelming majority but requires the approval of General Lucius D. Clay': *New York Times*, 13 Aug. 1948.

19. It seems the other allies were less reticent about speaking out. The *New York Times* (21 Mar. 1951), 11:3 wrote that the governments of France, Belgium, the Netherlands, and Luxembourg 'have protested strongly against . . . legislation on co-determination. Tacit in the protests is the threat, openly voiced by some private concerns, that investment capital would be withdrawn from the affected enterprises and the possibility for the fresh inflow of investment money, sorely needed by the West Germany economy, would be shattered. André François-Poncet, French High Commissioner, personally intervened. . . . Representatives of the Belgian steel firm Arbed ". . . declared that the Luxembourg industry believes the present draft for a co-determination law is equal to expropriation. . . ."'.

20. 12 Apr. 1951, 32:3.

21. Gilbert Burck, 'Can Germany Go Capitalist?' *Fortune* (Apr. 1954), 114–22, 247–52 at 250.

22. Id., 'The German Business Mind,' *Fortune* (May 1954), 111–14, 219–20 at 220.

23. Hoffman and Maier, *The Marshall Plan: A Retrospective*, 64.

24. Werner Link, 'Building Coalitions: Non-governmental German-American Linkages,' in Maier, *The Marshall Plan and Germany*, 282–330.

25. Bernd Dornseifer and Jürgen Kocka, 'The Impact of the Preindustrial Heritage: Reconsiderations on the German Pattern of Corporate Development in the late 19th and Early 20th Centuries,' *Industrial and Corporate Change*, 2:2 (1993), 233–48 at 234.

26. Chandler, *Scale and Scope*, Part IV: Germany: Cooperative Managerial Capitalism gives pertinent information.

27. Dornseifer and Kocka, 'The Impact', 236.

28. Robert R. Locke, *The End of the Practical Man: Entrepreneurship and Higher Education in Germany, France, and Great Britain, 1880–1940* (Greenwich, Conn.: JAI, 1984), ch. 2.

29. Decades after the Second World War, the importance of the *Fachschule*-trained engineer persisted. A 1980 survey showed that 51 percent of German managers had degrees from these *Fachschulen* compared with 41 percent with university degrees (technical *Hochschulen* for the most part). A disproportionate number of *Fachschule* graduates were in lower and middle management positions (lower 56% *Fachschulen*, 34% University; middle, 55% *Fachschulen*, 40% University), but even in higher management *Fachschulen* graduates were strongly represented (29% *Fachschulen*, 61% University level, mainly from technical *Hochschulen*).

30. Dornseifer and Kocka, 'The Impact', 245.

31. I am indebted for this information on the German army to my student, a retired Marine Major who prepared a Master's thesis on the subject. Donald W. Wilson, 'The German Soldier: Social Origins of Prowess', Thesis, Master of Arts in History, Dec. 1989, University of Hawaii at Manoa.

32. U.S. War Department, Military Intelligence Division (eds.), *German Training Methods* (Washington, DC, 1946), 57.

33. Ibid.

34. Wilson, 'The German Soldier'.

35. Rick Atkinson, *The Long Gray Line: From West Point to Vietnam and After—The Turbulent Odyssey of the Class of 1966* (New York: Simon & Schuster, 1989), 442.

36. Link, 'Building Coalitions', 312.

37. Burck, 'The Transformation of European Business', *Fortune* (Nov. 1957), 296.

38. Booz, Allen, and Hamilton, 'German Management', *International Studies of Management and Organization. Report* (White Plains, NY: Arts and Science Press, Spring/Summer 1973). Also see 'German Management: Challenges and Responses—A Pragmatic Evaluation', in J. J. Boddewyn (ed.), *European Industrial Managers* (White Plains, NY: International Arts and Science Press, 1976), 251–338, and Heinz Hartmann, 'Appraisal of the Report "German Management: Challenges and Responses"', ibid. 237–50. Hartmann wrote extensively and intelligently about German management during this period of the American management mys-

tique, pointing out the many differences. See Heinz Hartmann, *Authority and Organization in German Management* (Princeton: Princeton University Press, 1959) and Heinz Hartmann, *Amerikanische Firmen in Deutschland.*

39. *Handbücher, Management Weiterbildung in Deutschland.* Publications of the Wuppertaler Kreis. Post-experience education means the education one gets after starting to work.

40. Locke, *End of the Practical Man*, ch. 2.

41. Quoted in Locke, *Management and Higher Education*, 167.

42. 'Betriebswirtschaftslehre, Theorie und Praxis im Streitgespräch', *Der Volkswirt—Wirtschafts- und Finanz- Zeitung*, 19 (9 July 1965), 1426–8 at 1427.

43. To be a professor a person had to get a first degree, usually the Dipl.-Kaufm., then do a doctorate, and then the difficult *Habilitationsschrift.* If a doctorate would have sufficed for a university professorship lots of people in praxis would have been able to move to university positions because the doctorate is a much coveted and held degree among businessmen and industrialists in Germany.

44. Quoted in Joachim Kienbaum and Peter Paschek, 'Das beste Sprungbrett ist ein breites Wissen', *Deutsche Universitäts-Zeitung* (1981), 854–7 at 857.

45. The German name for the Wuppertaler Kreis (the Wuppertal Circle): *Deutsche Vereinigung zur Förderung der Weiterbildung von Führungskräften.* The RKW (*Rationalisierungs-Kuratorium der Deutschen Wirtschaft*) is the Efficiency Committee of the German Economy. The VDI (*Verein Deutscher Ingenieure*) is the German Engineering Society. REFA (*Reichsausschuss für Arbeitsstudien*) is the Reich Committee for Labor Research.

46. Specifically, TWI (training within industry, used so effectively during the war), American intrafirm communications methods, profit-sharing inducements, entrepreneur-trade union partnership ideas, and concepts of common risk-sharing.

47. Hartmann, *Amerikanische Firmen*, 113.

48. Ibid. 173.

49. Ibid. 197.

50. Ibid.

51. Within the works council there is a committee called the *Wirtschaftsausschuss* (economics committee). The Works Constitution Act of 1972 empowered it to receive information on the company's economic position—sales, orders, profits, prospects—and to treat this in confidence. Management must provide this information, even the most sensitive kind, about the firm's performance. This arrangement, Peter Lawrence

comments, 'has traditionally induced an element of well-informed and economically responsible realism into the consciousness of employees and their representatives': Peter Lawrence, 'German Management: At the Interface between Eastern and Western Europe', in Roland Calori and Philippe de Woot (eds.), *A European Model of Management: Unity in Diversity* (New York: Prentice Hall, 1994), 133–64 at 141.

52. In firms with more than 20,000 employees.

53. See article in *New York Times*, 29 May 1975 on the attitude of the American Chamber of Commerce in Germany. Henry Ford II voiced his opposition to the coming 1976 law in a speech delivered during ceremonies celebrating Ford's fiftieth anniversary in Germany. Reported in *New York Times*, 17 Oct. 1975.

54. All institutions of higher education, whether universities or not, are called *Hochschulen*. This, not university, is the generic term.

55. Remember, in German *Hoch* + *schule* makes it a university-level institution.

56. Of the others, 30 percent were children of college graduates, 30 percent from white collar management families (half of these from fathers with 'leading positions'), and 30 percent from civil servant (*Beamte*) families. Sylvia Verdier, 'Studenten und Gewerkschaften', in Bamberg, Kröger, and Kuhlmann, *Hochschulen*, 415–22 at 23.

57. Verdier notes, in the oil industry, '30% of the *gewerbliche Arbeitnehmern were Hochschulabsolventen, 30% Tarifansgestellten und bereits 40% ausser-tarifliche Angestellten*': ibid. 421.

58. Hans Mätthofer, *Humanisierung der Arbeit und Produktivität in der Industriegesellschaft* (3rd edn., Cologne: Bund-Verlag, 1980), 34.

59. Gerhard Leminsky, 'Erfahrungen bei der Verwertung und Umsetzung von Wissenschaft im Arbeitsnehmerinteresse', in Bamberg, Kröger, and Kuhlmann (eds.), *Hochschulen und Gewerkschaften*, 367–77 at 368.

60. In German the *Bundesministerium für Forschung und Technologie*.

61. Leminsky, 'Erfahrungen', 370.

62. David Soskice and Ronald Schettkat, 'West German Labor Market Institutions and East German Transformation', in Ulman, Eichengreen, and Dickens, *Labor and an Integrated Europe*, 102–27 at 113. There were also supplemental wage agreements at the plant level, but the regional agreements were the important ones.

63. *Humanisierung der Arbeitswelt*; taken from a long passage cited in Mätthofer, *Humanisierung*, 185.

64. Hans Preiss, 'Gewerkschaften und Erziehung', in Bamberg, Kröger, and Kuhlmann, *Hochschulen und Gewerkschaften*, 501–3 at 502.

65. Kurt Johannson and Jürgen Weissbach, 'Zusammenarbeit von Gewerkschaften und Hochschulen in der Weiterbildung', in Bamberg, Kröger, and Kuhlmann, *Hochschulen*, 115–30 at 119.

66. Turner, *Democracy at Work*, 100.

67. Johannson and Weissbach, 'Zusammenarbeit', 126.

68. Preiss, 'Gewerkschaften und Erziehung', 501.

69. Ibid.

70. Johannson and Weissbach, 'Zusammenarbiet', 119.

71. Ute Cabarusm, Jürgen Jöns, and Gerd Syben, 'Kooperation von Hochschulen und Gewerkschaften bei der Hochschulausbildung', in Bamberg, Kröger, and Kuhlmann, *Hochschulen*, 89–114 at 94.

72. Jörg Virchow and Jochen Flarup, 'Zusammenarbeit zwischen Gewerkschaften und Hochschulen in Berlin', in Bamberg, Kröger, and Kuhlmann, *Hochschulen*, 183–99 at 190.

73. USW = *Universitätsseminar der Wirtschaft*.

74. ACHI = *Arbeitsring der Arbeitgeberverbände der Deutschen Chemischen Industrie*; BBW = *Bildungswerk der Bayerische Wirtschaft*; BWHF = *Bildungswerk der Nordrhein-Westfälischen Wirtschaft*; BWRP = *Bildungswerk der Rheinland-Pfälzischen Wirtschaft*.

75. STFG = *Studien- und Fördergesellschaft der Schleswig-Holsteinischen Wirtschaft*; IMA = *Institut zur Weiterbildung von Führungskräfte*.

76. BJU = *Bundesverband Junger Unternehmer*.

77. DGFP = *Deutsche Gesellschaft für Personalführung*.

78. Mario Helfert and Gundrun Trautwein-Kalms, 'Die gewerkschaftliche Auseinandersetzung um Arbeitsbedingungen und das Forschungsprogramm der Bundesregierung zu Humanisierung des Arbeitslebens', Bamberg, Kröger, and Kuhlmann, *Hochschulen*, 378–96 at 396.

79. The Booz, Allen, and Hamilton report, discussed in the text, exuded this American managerial attitude.

80. Lawrence, 'German Management', 146.

81. Reijo Luostarinen and Tuija Pulkkinen, *International Business Education in European Universities in 1990* (Helsinki: European International Business Association, 1990).

82. Peter Turnbull and Malcolm Cunningham (eds.), *International Marketing and Purchasing: A Survey among Marketing and Purchasing Executives in Five European Countries* (London: Macmillan, 1981), 123.

83. He is holder of a *Dipl. Wirts-Ing.* (Karlsruhe) and a Ph.D. from the Wharton Business School. The *Dipl. Wirts-Ing.* is a very respected degree in Germany, which, because its study program is divided between management and engineering subjects, takes more time to complete

and is more demanding than the normal first degree in business economics (*Dipl.-Kaufm.*).

84. Huchzermeier's observations here reported are taken from an interview, Koblenz School of Corporate Management, 26 July 1994.

85. This is not Huchzermeier's observation but my own, which is based on talks with numerous American professors of management.

86. Lawrence, 'German Management', 146.

87. Ibid. 144.

88. In Lawrence, *Managers and Management in West Germany* (London: Croom Helm, 1980). Lawrence belongs to a group of people who have stressed the difference between the German idea of *Technik* and Anglo-American ideas about applied science. These include S. Hutton, Michael Fores, Ian Glover, and Arndt Sorge.

89. Interview, Schloss Mannheim, 19 July 1994.

90. Interview, Munich Technical University, 23 July 1994. Professor Wildemann heads a very large institute in the Munich Technical University. Research institutes and seminars exist throughout German academia. Those useful to management are not, therefore, concentrated in business schools. This is the dispersed knowledge and talent that Professor Huchzermeier spoke of when comparing the manner in which the American business school and German institutions of higher education interrelate with business and industrial management.

CHAPTER 3

1. Andrew Gordon (ed.), *Postwar Japan as History* (Berkeley: University of California Press, 1993), 'Conclusion', 457.

2. Peter L. Berger and Thomas Luckmann, *The Social Construction of Reality* (New York: Doubleday, 1967), 72.

3. Johannes Hirschmeier and Tsunehiko Yui, *The Development of Japanese Business* (London: Allen & Unwin, 1981), 133.

4. The literature is vast, but one could start with Hans-Ulrich Wehler's *The Second German Empire* (Leamington Spa: Berg, 1985). Also see the 2nd edn. of V. R. Berghahn, *Germany and the Approach of War in 1914* (New York: St. Martin's, 1993), the introduction to which offers a brief discussion of the issues and cites the literature.

5. See my *French Legitimists and the Politics of Moral Order in the Early Third Republic* (Princeton: Princeton University Press, 1974), in which I argue that the political-social conflicts between French divine-right monarchists and republicans c.1870 were a projection of unresolved 18th-c. and early

19th-c. conflicts which, since they came from a pre-industrial society, had nothing much to do with industrialization. That is why divine-right monarchists could be financiers and industrialists and radical republicans could represent economic retrograde groups in late 19th-c. France. The fact that industrialization coincided with the ideology of liberalism in the Anglo-American world has more to do with pre-industrial heritages than the nature of the industrial process.

6. D. Eleanor Westney, *Imitation and Innovation: The Transfer of Western Organizational Patterns to Meiji Japan* (Cambridge, Mass.: Harvard University Press, 1987), 218–19 at 219.

7. Ibid. 14.

8. Ibid. 221.

9. Hirschmeier and Yui, *The Development of Japanese Business*.

10. Westney, *Imitation and Innovation*, 219.

11. Here I adopt the standard view about Prussian influence. The subject, however, is somewhat controversial in Japanese historiography, since some historians argue that the constitutional reforms followed the British idea of a constitutional monarchy, where the Emperor reigns but does not rule, where he is not responsible. The controversy is interesting but it does not touch the substance of my argument that the Japanese justified their borrowings in terms of their customs and habits of thought. See George Akita and Hirose Yoshihiro, 'The British Model: Inoue Kowashi and the Ideal Monarchical System', *Monumenta Nipponica*, 49:4 (Winter 1994), 413–21, where appropriate references are given.

12. Ronald Dore, 'The Legacy of Tokugawa Education', in Marius Jansen (ed.), *Changing Japanese Attitudes toward Modernization* (Princeton: Princeton University Press, 1969), 100.

13. Leonard J. Schoppa, *Education Reform in Japan: A Case of Immobilist Politics* (London: Routledge, 1991), 24.

14. Ibid. 25.

15. George C. Allen, *The British Disease* (London: Institute of Economic Affairs, 1979), 68.

16. Quoted in Robert J. Smith, *Japanese Society: Tradition, Self, and the Social Order* (Cambridge: Cambridge University Press, 1983), 10–11.

17. Mike Bottery, *The Ethics of Educational Management* (London: Cassell, 1992), 133.

18. Sir William Slim, *Defeat into Victory* (London: Cassell & Co., 1956), 331.

19. Lockwood, cited in Yoshino, *Japan's Managerial System*, 73.

20. Andrew Gordon, *The Evolution of Labor Relations in Japan: Heavy*

Industry, 1853–1955 (Cambridge, Mass.: Harvard University Press, 1985), 413.

21. Ken'ici Yasumuro, 'Engineers as Functional Alternatives to Entrepreneurs in Japanese Industrialisation', in Jonathan Brown and Mary B. Rose (eds.), *Entrepreneurship, Networks and Modern Business* (Manchester: Manchester University Press, 1993), 89–90.

22. Ryushi Iwata, *Japanese-Style Management: Its Foundation and Prospects* (Tokyo: Asian Production Organization, 1982), 1.

23. Kenji Okuda, 'Comment', on paper by Andrew Gordon, 'Araki Toichiro and the Shaping of Labor Management', in Tsunehiko Yui and Keiichiro Nakagawa (eds.), *Japanese Management in Historical Perspective* (Tokyo: University of Tokyo Press, 1989), 195–6. The quote within the quote comes from Yamashita Okiie, who chaired the Production Management Committee in 1938. Also see comments of Hashimoto about Japanese rejection of 'Taylorist ideas', in Juro Hashimoto, 'The Japanese System of Divisions of Labor: The Combination of a "Flexible" In-House Division of Labor and a "Planned" Inter-Company Division of Labor', *Annals of the Institute of Social Science*, University of Tokyo, 35 (1993), 195–228.

24. Shuji Hayashi, *Culture and Management in Japan* (Tokyo: University of Tokyo Press, 1988), 68.

25. Dominique Turcq, *L'Inévitable Partenaire japonais* (Paris: Fayard), 55.

26. Hadley, *Antitrust in Japan*, 34–5.

27. Ibid. 391–2.

28. Published in Nobuo Kawabe and Eisuke Daito (eds.), *Education and Training in the Development of Modern Corporations* (Tokyo: University of Tokyo Press, 1993), 156.

29. Smith, *Japanese Society*, 74.

30. The Research Team for Japanese systems, Masuda Foundation, *Japanese Systems: An Alternative Civilization?* (Yokohama: Sekotac, Ltd., 1992), 15.

31. Joseph Adams, 'The "British Disease" and the "Japanization" of British Industry: Conjuncture or Continuity in World History', Master's thesis (University of Hawaii at Manoa, 1995), 38.

32. Thomas P. Rohlen, *Japan's High Schools* (Berkeley: University of California Press, 1983), 261, for the first quote. The second is cited in Smith, *Japanese Society*, 59.

33. Ibid. 58.

34. An example: the importation of the Neo-Confucian doctrines of Wang Yang-ming (*Oyomei*) ideology, a branch of Neo-Confucianism originally introduced in Japan by Nakae Toju (1608–48) that emphasized the

importance of personal intuition and moral sense over rationality and intellect, an idea that received official sanction during the Tokugawa period because of the government's interest in Neo-Confucianism as a social ethic.

35. Smith, *Japanese Society*, 81.

36. Janet E. Hunter, *The Emergence of Modern Japan* (London: Longman, 1989), 66.

37. Edward T. Hall, *The Hidden Dimension* (New York: Doubleday, 1990), 175.

38. Magoroh Maruyama, 'Mindscapes, Workers, and Management: Japan and the U.S.A.', in Lee and Schwendiman, *Japanese Management*, 53–71. Maruyama says that the Americans have a 'homogenetic mindscape', the Japanese a 'heterogenic' one. Homogenetic minds 'tend to attribute disagreements to errors, noises, lack of education, or opposing interests in a zero-sum game. They often say: "Let us disregard the areas on which we disagree and stick to the areas on which we agree."' The areas of agreement are supposed to be objective and real, while those of disagreement are considered as subjective, political, and immaterial. The 'heterogenic' mind, on the other hand, takes 'it for granted that different persons have different views of the same situation. . . . In the Japanese culture, the notion of "objectivity" does not exist and is even now unimportant. When the foreign word "objective" had to be translated, the Japanese invented the expression *kyakkanteki*, which means "the guest's point of view," while "subjective" became *shukanteki* or "the host's point of view"', 59–60.

39. Martin H. Sours, 'The Influence of Japanese Culture on Japanese Management Systems', in Lee and Schwendiman, *Japanese Management*, 27–38.

40. Stephen Graves, *Corporate Flexibility in Japan* (Sophia University, Tokyo: 1989). Business series, Bulletin, No. 126. ISBN 4–88168–126–5.

41. Chie Nakane, *Human Relations in Japan* (Tokyo: Ministry of Foreign Affairs, 1972), 10.

42. Hirschmeier and Yui, *The Development of Japanese Business*, 131.

43. Masao Maruyama, 'Thoughts and Behavior Patterns of Japan's Wartime Leaders', in Masao Maruyama, *Thought and Behavior*, 84–135 at 109–10. This article was originally published in May 1949.

44. Ibid. 110–11.

45. Ibid. 111. It should be noted that Maruyama himself was trying to explain, not justify, behavior. 'The fact remains that', he commented, 'if the *faits accomplis* created by the "lower echelons" or "local agencies" had actually run counter to the interests and sense of values of the upper

strata of the ruling class, or to the fundamental direction of Japanese imperialism, they would never have reached the stage of becoming national policy': ibid. 109 n.

46. From Biography of Hironaka Kono, quoted in Masao Maruyama, 'Theory and Psychology of Ultra-Nationalism', in Masao Maruyama, *Thought and Behavior*, 1–25 at 4–5.

47. Kenneth Bok Lee, 'The Postwar Reforms and Educational Development in Japan, 1945–1970', Ph.D. thesis (University of Southern California, 1974), 430.

48. Maruyama maintains in fact that the '[p]rinciple known as "the rule of the higher by the lower" . . . can occur only in a society in which power from below is not officially recognized. It is, so to speak, an inverted form of democracy . . . when the rulers . . . are guided by their subordinates and by other people who are theoretically subject to their rule': 'Thoughts and Behavior Patterns of Japan's Wartime Leaders', ibid. 113.

49. T. A. Bisson, *Zaibatsu Dissolution in Japan* (Berkeley: University of California Press, 1954); Hadley, *Antitrust in Japan*.

50. Taishiro Shirai reports that, in 1980, companies owned 70 percent of the stock of companies listed on the stock exchange. Shirai, 'A Supplement: Characteristics of Japanese Managements and their Personnel Policies', in Shirai, *Contemporary Industrial Relations*, 369–82 at 369.

51. See Hidemasa Morikawa, *Zaibatsu: The Rise and Fall of Family Enterprise Groups in Japan* (Tokyo: University of Tokyo Press, 1992).

52. Shirai, 'A Supplement', 370.

53. William B. Gould, *Japan's Reshaping of American Labor Law* (Cambridge, Mass.: MIT Press, 1984), xiv.

54. See William K. Cummings, *Education and Equality in Japan* (Princeton: Princeton University Press, 1980) for a positive appreciation of this postwar educational social engineering.

55. The 'democratic' intent of the victors was stated in the Potsdam Declaration of 26 July 1945: 'The Japanese government shall remove all obstacles to the revival and strengthening of democratic tendencies among the Japanese people. Freedom of speech, of religion, and of thought, as well as respect for the fundamental human rights, shall be established.' Marlene J. Mayo, 'Psychological Disarmament: American Wartime Planning for the Education and Re-education of Defeated Japan, 1943–45', in *The Occupation of Japan: Educational and Social Reform*, Proceedings of a Symposium Sponsored by the MacArthur Memorial, Old Dominion University, October 16–28, 1980, 21–127. Copies available at MacArthur Memorial, MacArthur Square, Norfolk VA 23510. Also see in the same

volume, Toshio Nishi, 'Education during the Meiji-Taisho-Showa Periods', 15–21.

56. See Kenneth Bok Lee, 'The Postwar Reforms and Educational Development in Japan', 245–445.

57. Ibid. 393.

58. Ibid. 311.

59. For the 'Turnabout' on labor see Koshi Endo, 'Reflections on the Turnabout in Labor Relations Policy in Occupied Japan', *Annals of the Institute of Social Science*, University of Tokyo, 26 (1984), 78–101.

60. Hideo Otake, 'The *Zaikai* under the Occupation: The Formation and Transformation of Managerial Councils', in Robert E. Ward and Yoshikazu Sakamoto (eds.), *Democratizing Japan: The Allied Occupation* (Honolulu: University of Hawaii Press, 1987), 366–89.

61. Formed after the war, the *Keizai Doyukai* (Economic Comrades Association) gathered two groups of businessmen, one the businessmen from the Tuesday Society of the Japan Industrial Club and the other from the Council of Key Industry Control Associations (the *Jusankyo*), that assisted government in establishing and operating industrial controls. The initial *Keizai Doyukai* paper on co-determination was called 'Economic Democratization and the Specific Measures Involved'. Otake, 'The *Zaikai*', 369–70.

62. Otake, 'The *Zaikai*', 372.

63. This is Hideo Otake's argument and it is largely the argument of Andrew Gordon in 'Contest for the Workplace', in Gordon, *Postwar Japan as History*, ch. 2, 373–93. Also see Gordon's 'Conclusion', 449–64.

64. Bottery, *The Ethics of Educational Management*, 133.

65. Taiichi Ohno, *Toyota Production System: Beyond Large-Scale Production* (1978; translated and reprinted by Productivity Press, 1988), 35.

66. James Abegglen and George Stalk, *Kaisha: The Japanese Corporation* (New York: Basic Books, 1985), 184. A group of Japanese scholars, who surveyed organizational objectives of Japanese and American corporations, confirmed this judgement. They pointed out that the list of managerial priorities in the two countries differed: the U.S. managers rated 'Return on investment' as the number one goal, the Japanese rated it number two (after 'Increase in market share'), the U.S. managers rated 'Capital gain for stockholders' as the number two goal, the Japanese as number nine on their list (at the bottom). Tadao Kagono, Ikujiro Nonaka, Akihiro Okumura, Kiyonori Sakakibara, Yoichi Komatsu, and Akinobu Sakashita, 'Mechanistic vs. Organic Management Systems: A Comparative Study of Adaptive Patterns of U.S. and Japanese Firms',

reprint from Kobe University's *Annals of the School of Business Administration*, no. 25 (1981), 119–41 at 121.

67. Philippe d'Iribarne, *La Logique de l'honneur: Gestion des entreprises et traditions nationales* (Paris: Editions du Seuil, 1989), 131.

68. Tadao Kagono *et al.*, 'Mechanistic vs. Organic Management Systems', 136.

69. Ibid.

70. Gordon, *The Evolution of Labor Relations in Japan*, 411.

71. Rodney Clark, *The Japanese Company* (New Haven: Yale University Press, 1979), 109 n. 12. William B. Gould writes: 'The Japanese pattern of mobility between labor and management means that union presidents and other high officials are sometimes (though not often) graduates of the University of Tokyo and other leading Japanese universities. It also means that most anyone who has worked for a Japanese company has been a member of a union at some point. It affects the style and attitude of trade unions in Japan by inhibiting militancy, providing expertise, and creating more contact and perhaps some egalitarianism between blue-collar and white-collar employees': Gould, *Japan's Reshaping of American Labor Law*, 5.

72. Edward E. Lawler, *High-Involvement Management: Participative Strategies for Improving Organization Performance* (San Francisco: Jossey-Bass, 1986), 59.

73. Paul Lillrank and Noriaki Kano, *Continuous Improvement—Quality Control Circles in Japanese Industry* (Ann Arbor Center for Japanese Studies, 1989), 127.

74. See Taishiro Shirai, 'A Theory of Enterprise Unionism', in Taishiro Shirai (ed.), *Contemporary Industrial Relations in Japan*, 117.

75. Yoshiakiu Shimabukuro, *Consensus Management in Japanese Industry* (Tokyo: I.S.S., 1982), 131.

76. *Honolulu Advertiser*, 11 Feb. 1993. It is worth noting, too, the 'relatively narrow differentials between blue-collar and white-collar salaries in Japan': Taishiro Shirai, 'A Theory of Enterprise Unionism', 117.

77. George Will reported that the differential between executive and worker salaries has been moving the opposite direction from the Japanese trend. In Japan the compensation of major CEOs, he reports, is 17 times that of the average workers, in Germany, 23–5 times. The American CEO/worker pay disparity is between 85 and 100-plus times. 'The disparity doubled during the 1980s—while the top income-tax rate was cut and workers' tax burdens increased because of Social Security taxes. . . . In 1990, CEO pay rose 7 percent while corporate profits fell 7 percent':

George Will, 'CEOs—Capitalist Heroes?' in *Honolulu Advertiser*, 15 May 1994.

78. Taishiro Shirai says 70 percent of the Japanese work in 'small and medium sized' firms.

79. Yanan Ju, 'Supremacy of Human Relationships: A Japanese Organizational Model', in Branislav Kovacic (ed.), *New Approaches to Organizational Communication* (Albany, NY: State University of New York Press, 1994), 67–85 at 76.

80. Nick Oliver and Barry Wilkinson, *The Japanization of British Industry: New Developments in the 1990s* (Oxford: Blackwell, 1992), 59.

81. Dominique Turcq explained how Japanese manufacturers gain competitive advantage. If the foreigner had a 10 percent cost advantage in manufacturing over the Japanese, the inability to compete inside the Japanese distribution system, where more costs are involved than in manufacturing and the Japanese firms have monopolistic advantages, effectively blocks this manufacturer from exporting to Japan. On the other hand, because the American firms have no advantages over the Japanese within the American distribution system, a Japanese firm with a 10 percent advantage in manufacturing productivity over an American firm can easily enter the American marketplace. Dominique Turcq of McKinsey and Company, Brussels, Belgium, interview, 5 July 1994.

82. Gould, *Japan's Reshaping of American Labor Law*, 15.

83. In Germany they would not be negotiated by the unions either but by the works councils.

84. Gould, *Japan's Reshaping*, p. xv.

85. This anti-legalism is a general characteristic of Japanese life. William B. Gould calculated (1984) that in Japan there are 15,000 lawyers compared with 500,000 in the U.S., a country with only twice the population (p. xiv) Thomas K. McCraw noted that America has twenty-two times as many lawyers *per capita* as Japan and Germany four and a half times as many as Japan. Thomas K. McCraw, 'From Partners to Competitors: An Overview of the Period since World War II', in id. (ed.), *America versus Japan* (Boston: Harvard Business School Press, 1986), 1–33 at 26.

86. Gary H. Tsuchimochi, *Educational Reform in Postwar Japan: The 1946 U.S. Education Mission* (Tokyo: University of Tokyo Press, 1993).

87. Lee, 'The Postwar Reforms', 380, 439.

88. Yoshihiro Shimizu, *Shiken* (Examinations) (Tokyo: Iwanami Shinsho, 1957), 123, quoted in Cummings, *Education and Equality in Japan*, 209.

89. Lee, 'The Postwar Reforms', 377.

90. Yanan Ju observes that individual job performance has become more of a

factor affecting individual pay and promotion in recent years. 'Between 1978 and 1987, the contribution of the seniority factor to pay raises systematically declined from an average of 57.9% to 46% while the contribution of the performance factor increased from 42.1% to 54%. However, the fact that seniority accounts for 46% of all pay raises is still impressive': 'Supremacy of Human Relationships', 72.

91. Katsuyuki Nagaoka notes that there is 'only one small business school [in Japan] and that it is not yet well-known': Katsuyuki Nagaoka, 'The Japanese System of Academic Management Education', in Lars Engwall and Elving Gunnarsson (eds.), *Management Studies in an Academic Context* (Uppsala: Motala Grafiska AB, 1994), 138–54 at 144.

92. Examples of business and industry's call for scientific and technical education are: 'Opinion on Technical Education to Meet the Needs of the New Era', issued 9 Nov. 1956 by the Education Section of the Federation of Economic Organizations (*Nikkeiren*); 'The Advance of Manpower Capability and Promotion of Scientific Technology', paper issued, in July 1960, by the Economic Advisory Committee; 'Request for Measures for the Establishment and Promotion of the Advance of Technical Education', document issued 25 Aug. 1961 by the Federation of Economic Organizations and Japanese Federation of Employers' Associations; and 'A Proposition from Businessmen for Educational Reform: In Pursuit of Creativity, Diversity, and Internationality', issued in July 1984 by the Education Council, Japan Committee for Economic Development (*Keizai Doyukai*). All these documents are reproduced, along with many others on education, in Edward R. Beauchamp and James M. Vardaman, Jr., *Japanese Education since 1945: A Documentary Study* (London: Sharpe, 1994). There are no documents in the collection that call for the creation of business and management schools. Indeed, there is no entry under business and management education in the index. But calls for 'moral education', issued by business and industrial support groups, abound in the collection.

93. Jean-Michel Leclercq observes that Japanese firms 'of any importance' take their employees' education in hand: 'Training workers, white collar employees, and management at every level, initiating new recruits into the life of the firm, training new office personnel, training people in research and production methods, in management techniques and in marketing, offering special courses for employees promoted to foremen, office head, or head of a lab, providing special skill instruction (computers, foreign languages, etc.). Frequently the firm has a proper school where people recruited from high schools receive additional

education, along with young people who attend from other firms.'
Higher management can go outside the firm for education, even to an
American business school, 'but only after they have received a solid
education in the firm are these external contacts permitted': Jean-Michel
Leclercq, *Le Japan et son système éducatif* (Paris: La Documentation
française, 1984), 66.

94. A memorandum from the Imperial Japanese Government, via Tokyo
Central Liaison Office from GHQ. SCAP, 31 Dec. 1945, had abolished all
'course in Morals (*Shushin*), Japanese History and Geography in all
educational institutions'. Reproduced in Beauchamp and Vardaman,
Japanese Education, 74–5.

95. Joseph Adams, 'The "British Disease"', 69.

96. Cummings, *Education and Equality in Japan*, 150.

97. Ibid. 110.

98. Cited in Joseph Adams, 'The "British Disease"', 69. See Joseph J. Tobin,
David Y. H. Wu, and Dana H. Davidson, *Preschool in Three Cultures:
Japan, China, and the United States* (New Haven: Yale University Press,
1989).

99. Irmina Hayashi, interview, Honolulu, 10 May 1994.

100. Cummings, *Education and Equality in Japan*, 117.

101. Professor Rohlen notes: 'The Japanese firm tends to hire persons rather
than specific skills. It follows that the firm trains and retrains its
workers and directs them where their talents seem most clearly to lie,
but always in accordance with its long-range goals. The great seven-
teenth-century *haiku* poet Basho taught different things to different
people, perhaps "because he wanted to cultivate his pupils" talents
rather than to impose his own theory upon them': quoted in Smith,
Japanese Society, 5. Smith himself observes: 'One reason for this flexibility is *shugyo*, the Japanese concept that people who are experts in
one specialty can demonstrate the same degree of ability in another.
This is traditional way of thinking in Japan. For example, someone who
is judged to be a first-rate exponent of classical sword combat techniques is expected to possess a certain level of knowledge and judgment
in other fields, even religion. In fact, the concept of *shugyo* insists that
he must have this kind of transferred knowledge' (ibid.). All of this fits
in well with the idea of job rotation, of the ability of people to work well
without being experts. Even in research this is done. 'Under Japanese
management, the people who work in research and development are not
necessarily there because of their specialty or abilities. Frequently, they
are people who have been through many years of job rotation and are in

an area that has no relation to their specialty at the time of joining the company. They can cram or find someone with expert knowledge to work with, gradually learning by watching the expert' (ibid. 115).

102. William Lazonick and Jonathan West, 'Organizational Integration and Competitive Advantage: Explaining Strategy and Performance in American Industry', paper presented at the Fifth International Week on the History of Enterprise, Varese, Italy, 16 Dec. 1993, p. 22.

103. McKinsey Global Institute, *Service Sector Productivity* (Washington, DC, Oct. 1991), with assistance from Martin Baily, Francis Bator, Ted Hall, Bob Solow, Eisenhower Center, Columbia University, McKinsey & Company, Inc. McKinsey Global Institute, *Manufacturing Productivity* (Washington, DC, Oct. 1993). With assistance from Martin Baily, Francis Bator, Ted Hall, Bob Solow, University of Groningen, the Netherlands.

104. The figure for Japanese Market GDP (excluding government, education, health, and real estate) was 61 in 1988.

105. Friedrich List (1789–1846), critic of English classical economics, was popular in 19th-c. America, in protectionist circles, and in Germany and Japan, where his economics fit state-building policies. Most states are Listian in behavior. They unashamedly protect their commerce and industry. America is protectionist, too, although ashamedly since it pays lip service to free market economics. Consequently Americans open themselves up to charges of hypocrisy. If Smithian at heart, the Americans are really Listian in practice. The Listian view implies furthering the national interest through rational state policy. American protectionism is created haphazardly through lobbyists defending particular interests, not the national interest. List said this about individualistic consumer-driven economics: 'However industrious, thrifty, enterprising, moral, and intelligent the individuals may be, without national unity . . . and national co-operation of productive powers, the nation will never reach a high level of prosperity and power. . . .
It is a sophism . . . that the wealth of the nation is merely the aggregate of the wealth of all individuals in it, and that the private interest of every individual is better able than all State regulations to incite to production and accumulation of wealth': Friedrich List, *The National System of Political Economy*, quoted in *Introduction to Contemporary Civilization in the West: A Source Book* (3rd edn., New York: Columbia University Press, 1961), 387 and 398. For the neglect of List in the Anglo-American World, see James Fallows, 'How the World Works', *The Atlantic Monthly* (Dec. 1993), 61–87.

106. John Dunning, 'The Governance of Japanese and U.S. Manufacturing Affiliates in the U.K.', in Kogut, *Country Competitiveness*, 203–24 at 205.

107. Pierre Veltz, 'Introduction', in Patrick Cohendet, Michel Hollard, Thomas Malsch, and Pierre Veltz (eds.), *L'Après-Taylorisme* (Paris: Economica, 1989), 6. The authors are German experts, the book in French.

108. Yanan Ju provides an example of this 'holistic' way of thinking. The central feature of Japanese trading companies is the element of trust. 'Japanese employees, just like American . . . want to get ahead. . . . On a typical day, the central office of one of the major trading firms will receive 35,000 telex messages, each one with an offer to buy or sell. Often, the firm's overall profitability will be maximized if an office takes a loss, which will be more than made up in another office. The success of the trading company depends critically upon the willingness of individual offices and employees to make these sacrifices': Yanan Ju, 'Supremacy of Human Relationships', 74–5. If productivity is measured additively, the person in the office will suffer; if it is measured 'holistically', the individual performance will be considered part of overall performance. Yanan Ju adds that Japanese individual offices and employees are willing to make sacrifices because 'the Japanese trading firm uses managerial practices that foster trust through the knowledge that such sacrifices will always be repaid in the future' (ibid. 75).

109. Quoted in David Halberstam, *The Reckoning* (New York: Morrow, 1986), 81.

110. Johnson, *Relevance Regained*, 37.

111. Ibid. 38.

112. Mashiko Aoki, 'Towards an Economic Model of the Japanese Firm', *Journal of Economic Literature*, 28 (Mar. 1990), 1–27 at 4–5.

113. Richard J. Schonberger, *Japanese Manufacturing Techniques: Nine Hidden Lessons in Simplicity* (New York: Free Press, 1982).

114. Professor Yamashine gave some comparative data. Quick die changes allow more frequent setups for different product runs, 13.8 setups in two shifts in Japan, 9.0 in Japanese-owned factories in the United States, 2.0 in American factories in the United States, and 1.83 in European factories.

115. Hajime Yamashine, Stockton lecture, 'Time and Innovation: The View from Japan', London Business School, 1991.

116. Kaoru Ishikawa, *What is Total Quality Control? The Japanese Way*, trans. David J. Lu (Englewood Cliffs: Prentice-Hall, 1985), 14.

117. Hiroshi Komai, *Japanese Management Overseas: Experiences in the Uni-*

ted *States and Thailand* (Tokyo: Asian Productivity Council, 1989), 34. Oliver and Wilkinson, *The Japanization of British Industry*, 120.

118. W. Mark Fruin and Toshihiro Nishiguichi, 'Supplying the Toyota Production System: Intercorporate Organization Evolution and Supplier Subsystems', in Kogut (ed.), *Country Competitiveness*, 225–46.

119. Turcq, *L'Inévitable Partenaire japonais*, 98.

120. Oliver and Wilkinson, *The Japanization of British Industry*, 42.

121. Shunzo Ueda, *Japanese Management in the United States: Flexibility in a Foreign Environment*, USJP Occasional Paper 89-17. The Program on U.S.–Japanese Relations (1989).

122. Shunzo Ueda's comments are interesting because he worked for nine years in union negotiations at Tokyo Gas and two years as an observer, while a trainee, at Southern California Gas. He concluded that 'Based on personal experience working for an American firm, my own view is that American management problems stem from conflict with labor unions' (ibid. 19).

123. Maruyama was, of course, complaining about this characteristic: the excuse that the army would not stand for a policy forced the civilians into adopting the military's disastrous views.

124. Smith, *Japanese Society*, 55. A 1983 JUSE survey reports that typically quality circles had five to eight members. 'Some 60 percent of the groups choose their own leaders, and some 20 percent rotate the leadership; still others have staff specialists as leaders, or leaders are appointed by the supervisor': Paul Lillrank, *Sociological Aspects of Japanese QC Circles*, Discussion Paper, Tokyo, Social Research Institute of Japan, 1984, quoted in Robert E. Cole, *Strategies for Learning: Small-Group Activities in American, Japanese, and Swedish Industry* (Berkeley: University of California Press, 1989), 18.

125. Fruin and Nishiguichi, 'Supplying the Toyota Production System', observed that Toyota by 1977 had, depending on methods of calculation, between 36,468 and 47,308 suppliers. Seventy percent of the value of motor cars carrying the Toyota badge came from supplier costs, compared with 30% at GM, 50% at Ford, and 60% at Chrysler.

126. Ibid. 234.

127. Komai, *Japanese Management Overseas*, 55.

128. Here he inserts a 'trust' rather than a 'job satisfaction' quotient, observing, for example, that 78% of Sony's American workers trust management, as opposed to 30.9% of workers at American Motors, and lots of information taken from the comparative studies of Arthur Whitehill and Shin'ichi Takezawa. Ibid. 58–9.

129. Iwata, *Japanese-Style Management*, 2. The idea is that Japanese workers will not let quality specialists assume responsibility for quality that is the responsibility of all, including each worker, in the process.

CHAPTER 4

1. As example of this Leftist critique, see the special issue, 'Myths of Japanese Management, Myths of Japanese Education', *AMPO: Japan-Asia Quarterly Review*, 25:1 and the essays in Gavan McCormack and Yoshio Sugimoto (eds.), *Democracy in Contemporary Japan* (London: Sharpe, 1986).
2. This is not totally true. Robert Ball published an article in *Fortune* (8 Dec. 1980, pp. 147–9) entitled 'Europe Outgrows Management American Style', which does not mention Japan. But such assertions of European managerial superiority were indeed rare.
3. Letter to author, 31 Aug. 1994.
4. Mark W. Fruin, *The Japanese Enterprise System: Competitive Strategies and Cooperative Structures* (New York: Oxford University Press, 1992), 294.
5. Alan Altshuler *et al.*, *The Future of the Automobile: The Report of the MIT's International Automobile Program* (London: Allen & Unwin, 1984); David Halberstam, *The Reckoning* (New York: Morrow, 1986); David Dyer, Malcolm S. Salter, and Alan M. Webber, *Changing Alliances* (Boston: Harvard Business School, 1987).
6. Ray Marshall, *Unheard Voices: Labor and Economic Policy in a Competitive World* (New York: Basic Books, 1987), 171.
7. Keitaro Hasegawa, *Japanese-Style Management: An Insider's Analysis of Corporate Success* (Tokyo: Kodansha International, 1986). Reich, *Work of Nations*, 251.
8. Max Holland, *When the Machine Stopped: A Cautionary Tale from Industrial America* (Boston: Harvard Business School Press, 1989), 274.
9. Herbert A. Henzler and Lothar Späth, *Sind die Deutschen noch zu retten? Von der Krise in den Aufbruch* (Munich: Bertelsmann, 1993), 22.
10. Marshall, *Unheard Voices*, 106.
11. Ibid. 12.
12. Michel Albert, *Capitalism against Capitalism* (London: FWEW, 1993), 55.
13. Cited, with irony, ibid.
14. Martin Kenney and Richard Florida, *Beyond Mass Production: The Japa-*

nese System and its Transfer to the U.S. (New York: Oxford University Press, 1993), 4.

15. Reich, *The Work of Nations*, 174.

16. Ibid.

17. Tetsuo Abo, 'U.S. Subsidiaries of Japanese Electronic Companies Enter a New Phase of Activity: A Report of On-the-Spot Observations', *Annals of the Institute of Social Science*, University of Tokyo, 26 (1984), 1–32.

18. Mary Walton, *The Deming Management Method* (New York: Dodd, Mead, 1986), 239.

19. See Robert R. Rehder, 'Japanese Transplants: In Search of a Balanced and Broader Perspective', *Columbia Journal of World Business* (Winter 1989), 17–28, and id., 'Sayonara, Uddevalla?', *Business Horizons* (Nov.–Dec. 1992), 8–18.

20. Turcq, *L'Inévitable Partenaire japonais*, 226.

21. Robert Ball in 'Volkswagen's Struggle to Restore its Name', *Fortune* (27 June 1983), 100–4, observed that the number of Volkswagen dealers in America fell from 1,200 to 920 in three years, and among the 920 many had become a dual dealership with a line in Japanese cars.

22. Henzler and Späth note, for instance, that West German exports to non-European countries between 1985 and 1991 declined between 3 and 10 percent each year. During this same period American exports increased 60 percent and Japanese 20. Henzler and Späth, *Sind die Deutschen noch zu retten?*, 18.

23. James Abegglen, Zbigniew K. Brzezinski, and Herman Kahn, for example, sounded their 'own early warning to other Americans that Japan had become rather more than just a non-Western developing country with a thriving economy': Boltanski, *The Making of a Class*, 171.

24. The Japanese story is told well in Yotaro Kobayashi, 'Quality Control in Japan: The Case of Fuji-Xerox', in Kazuo Sato and Yasuo Hoshino, *The Anatomy of Japanese Business* (Armonk, NY: Sharpe, 1984), 164–97. Also see Hasegawa, *Japanese-Style Management*.

25. Walton, *The Deming Management Method*, relates this Nashua story.

26. Ibid. 122.

27. Ibid. 18.

28. David B. Tinnin, 'Ford is on a Roll in Europe', *Fortune* (18 Oct. 1982), 182–91 at 185.

29. Professor of Statistics at California State University, Dominguez Hills. Professor Kosaku Yoshida, an accountant by education and work experience in Japan, came to the Sterns Business School, New York University in 1970, to earn a doctorate. There he studied under Dr. Deming. After

completing his Ph.D., he assisted Deming for six years in his four-day seminars.

30. On how American ideas on quality were 'readjusted' in Japan, in line with Japanese work principles, see Juro Hashimoto, 'The Japanese System of Divisions of Labor'.

31. They reported, 'wherever we went, much emphasis was placed on the close relationship between the Japanese auto industry and its suppliers. It was frequently referred to as an "arms around" versus an "arms length" relationship': Walton, *The Deming Management Method*, 141.

32. For example, a recent AME sponsored Seminar (10–12 July 1995) focused on 'Managing a Team-Based Organization'.

33. Cited in AME literature, for example, in its pamphlet, 'Making Excellence Routine', Association for Manufacturing Excellence, 380 West Palatine Road, Wheeling, IL 60090.

34. Examples of *Target* articles which go directly to Japanese practice, 'Manufacturing in the 21st Century: Perspective From the Japanese Manufacturing 21 Research Project', by Jinichiro Nakane, 5:1 (Spring 1989), 32–7; 'The Challenges of the Three-Day Car', by Robert W. Hall, 9:2 (Mar.–Apr. 1993), 3–7; 'Using an Environmental Measurement to Guide Strategy at Sony', by Dr. Seiichi Watanabe, 9:5 (Sept.–Oct. 1993), 15–19; 'The Power of Taguichi Methods to Impact Change in U.S. Companies', by L. P. Sullivan, 3:2 (Summer 1987), 18–22 (plus three other articles on the Taguichi Methods); 'Events Report: Unleashing the Power of *Kaizen* at NUMMI', by John Coltman, 7:4 (Fall 1991), 40–2; 'Workshop Report: Work Standardization at Toyota Auto Body of California', by Bob Dozier, 4:2 (Summer 1988), 31–5, etc. Articles on the following corporations show indirect Japanese influence: Nashua Corporation, Florida Power & Light (2 articles), Ford Motor Company (3 articles), Motorola (16 articles), and Xerox (4 articles). There are, in addition, numerous articles on TQC and JIT.

35. Cole, *Strategies for Learning*, 154.

36. Ibid. 75.

37. Stephan Konz reviewed the literature on quality circles in 1981, looking primarily at journal publications. Articles on the subject by year were, 1966: 1, 1967: 1, 1968: 1, 1970: 0, 1971: 0, 1972: 5, 1973: 0, 1974: 1, 1975: 1, 1976: 0, 1977: 2, 1978: 4, 1979: 12, 1980: 14. Stephan Konz, 'Quality Circles: An Annotated Bibliography', *Quality Progress*, 14:4 (1981), 30–3.

38. James P. Womack, Daniel T. Jones, and Daniel Roos, *The Machine that Changed the World* (New York: Rawson Associates, 1990).

39. Dr. Dieter Kirchner, the chief executive officer of the German Trade Association Gesamt-Metall, in answer to a question about influential management best-sellers, unhesitatingly pointed to his bookshelf at the German language copy of this book. This book, he explained, was not just a best-seller but an eye-opener for automobile and nonautomobile executives alike. Interview, Cologne, at the Gesamt-Metall headquarters, 18 July 1994. I asked the same question at all interviews in Germany and got the same response. In the summer of 1994, the mass circulation newspaper *Süddeutsche Zeitung* ran a series of articles on 'lean' production. This indicates the extent to which the ideas in the book by Womack, Jones, and Roos have been popularized in Germany.

40. Beginning with books like Ezra F. Vogel, *Japan as Number One: Lessons for America* (Cambridge Mass.: Harvard University Press, 1979); Richard Tanner Pascale and Anthony G. Athos, *The Art of Japanese Management: Applications for American Executives* (New York: Simon & Schuster, 1981); William G. Ouchi, *Theory Z* (Reading, Mass.: Addison-Wesley, 1981).

41. With all due respect to really fine authors like Ronald Dore.

42. Even an article on 'The Future of American Capitalism' (Spr. 1979, 5–16) did not mention the Japanese challenge.

43. Articles entitled 'The Paradox of "Corporate Culture"', 'A Reader's Guide to the Industrial Policy Debate', 'Revitalizing American Industry: Managing in a Competitive World Economy', 'Restoring the Competitive Edge in U.S. Manufacturing', and 'Who Should Control the Corporation' fell into this category.

44. Robert Hall, letter to author, 25 June 1994.

45. Prof. Dr. Horst Wildemann, interview, 21 July 1994, in Munich.

46. Horst Wildemann, 'Die "normale" Blindleistung in der Unternehmerorganisation', unpublished manuscript available from the Lehrstuhl für Betriebswirtschaftslehre mit Schwerpunkt Logistik, Technische Universität München, Leopoldstr. 145, 80804 Munich, Germany.

47. Karl Williams, Itsutomo Mitsui and Colin Haslam, 'How far from Japan? A Case Study of Japanese Press Shop Practice and Management Calculation', 60, in Tony Elger and Chris Smith (eds.), *Global Japanization? The Transnational Transformation of the Labour Process* (London: Routledge, 1994). This collection of essays is in itself a testimonial to the collapse of the American management mystique.

48. A news story by Steven E. Prokesch, *New York Times* (6 Nov. 1985), which bore the title 'Xerox Halts Japanese March', illustrates one kind of resistance, a refusal to give credit where credit is due. The article began

with the sentence 'Xerox has managed to do what hardly any other American Company has done: Stop the Japanese advance into its market.' Xerox had 'managed' to do this primarily because it had learned so much from Fuji-Xerox. In one sense, Xerox did not 'halt' the Japanese march, but was part of it.

49. Frank Gibney, Sang M. Lee and Gary Schwendiman, William Ouchi, Richard T. Pascale, and Antony J. Athos were among those who believed Japanese management techniques would be efficacious in the U.S. So did James Abegglen and George Stalk. Among those who argued that the cultural basis of Japanese management precluded borrowing were Chalmers Johnson, Thomas J. Peters and Robert H. Waterman, Jr., and Charles R. Taylor.

50. Kenney and Florida, *Beyond Mass Production*, 287. The quotation in the next paragraph is on the same page.

51. Johnson's interest in the organizational implications of physics was expressed in a paper he presented with Anders Bröms at a recent conference, 'Rich Ends from Simple Means: Three Cases of Managing from a Quantum Perspective', papers presented at the 1995 Systems-Thinking-in-Action Conference, 'Building Organizational Learning Infrastructures', Boston, 18–20 Sept. 1995.

52. Fritjof Capra, *The Turning Point: Science, Society, and the Rising Culture* (New York: Simon & Schuster, 1982), 25.

53. Cited ibid. 47.

54. Ibid. 47.

55. Ibid. 78.

56. Ibid. 86.

57. Ibid. 87.

58. Ibid. 93.

59. Ibid. 103.

60. Ibid. 21.

61. Ibid. 268.

62. Ibid. 277.

63. Ibid. 280.

64. Ibid. 281–2.

65. Hall, *The Soul of the Enterprise*, 24.

66. Peter M. Senge, *The Fifth Discipline: The Art and Practice of the Learning Organization* (New York: Doubleday, 1990), 375.

67. Research Project Team for Japanese Systems, *Japanese Systems: An Alternative Civilization?* p. 15.

68. Kenney and Florida, *Beyond Mass Production*, 9.

69. Ibid. 16.
70. Fruin, *The Japanese Enterprise System*, 214.
71. Ikujiro Nonaka and Hirotaka Takeuchi, *The Knowledge-Creating Company: How Japanese Companies Create the Dynamics of Innovation* (New York: Oxford University Press, 1995), 236.
72. Ibid. 45 and 239.
73. Quote from letter to author, 22 Mar. 1994.
74. H. Thomas Johnson and Robert S. Kaplan, *Relevance Lost: The Rise and Fall of Management Accounting* (Boston: Harvard Business School Press, 1987), constituted a big first step in Johnson's journey which was further expressed in a complete break with accounting control systems in Johnson, *Relevance Regained* (1992). In the first book Johnson and Kaplan argued that 'relevance was lost by using improper accounting information to manage', and they advocated the adoption of Activity Based Accounting (ABC). In the second volume Johnson abandoned ABC, too, arguing that 'relevance was not lost by using improper accounting information to manage: it was lost by improperly using accounting information to manage'.
75. Johnson, *Relevance Regained*, 194.
76. Mahmoud Ezzamel, 'From Problem Solving to Problematization: A Comment on "Relevance Revisited"', to be published in *Critical Perspectives on Accounting*.
77. Ezzamel supports this contention with lots of references: M. Parker and J. Slaughter, 'Managing-By-Stress: The Team Concept in the US Auto Industry', *Science as Culture*, No. 8, Free Association Books, London, 1990; C. Brooke, 'Symbols and Shambles: Quality and Organizational Change', paper presented at *The International SCOS Conference: Organizations and Symbols of Transformation*, EADA, Barcelona, July 1993; S. Hill, 'How do you Manage the Flexible Firm? The Total Quality Model', *Work, Employment and Society*, 5:3 (1991), 397–415; S. Kamata, *Japan in the Passing Lane* (Counterpoint, 1983); D. Derfoot and D. Knights, 'Managerial Evangelism?—Planning for Quality in Financial Services', paper presented at the EIASM Workshop in *Quality Management in Services*, Maastricht (May 1992); M. Ezzamel, K. Hoskin, and R. Macve, 'Managing it all by Numbers: A Review of Johnson and Kaplan's "Relevance Lost"', *Accounting and Business Research*, 20:8 (1990), 153–66.
78. Ezzamel, 'From Problem Solving to Problematization', 5–6.
79. Shirley J. Daniel and Wolf D. Reitsperger, 'Linking Quality Strategy with

Management Control Systems: Empirical Evidence from Japanese Industry', *Accounting, Organizations and Society*, 16:7 (1991), 601–18.

80. Johnson, *Relevance Regained*, 8.

81. Williams, Mitsui, and Haslam, 'How far from Japan?', 73.

82. Ibid. The authors continued with an example of how American managers do not understand TQM because they mix it with MAS. '[A]t Detroit Motors, the company had an "After Japan" programme but the managers we interviewed had not considered privileging relevant physical indicators. They had no doubts about the capacity of the financial to represent the productive and guide production; if managers get the right set of costings, the financial numbers will tell them what to do. Thus, the size and expertise of the finance function was a matter of pride; we were told that management accounting was one of the things which the company did "really professionally"' (ibid.).

83. Ibid. 76.

84. Cole, *Strategies for Learning*, 29.

85. Ibid. 27–8.

86. Cole, who has studied the subject, says the following about American attempts to borrow small-group activities: 'When one examines the adoption and diffusion of small-group activities . . . in the United States over the period 1960–85, one is hard put to say that many of the noble ideas outlined above have been institutionalized in large numbers of American corporate entities.' The noble ideas about which he spoke: end employee alienation and enhance job satisfaction through increasing employees' participation in workplace decisions and more job variety to make more effective use of workers' potential. Cole adds: 'In the 1970s self-managing teams won only very limited acceptance here. In companies like General Electric, where they had, all died out by the 1980s' (ibid. 25–6).

87. Ibid. 304. Mary Walton describes the same pattern of Japanese mass-networking in the Deming Prize competitions. What began as a modest award in 1950 'evolved into a feverish month-long celebration of quality. In 1985 more than 550 presidents and vice presidents attended the annual conference for top management at which Dr. Deming spoke. More than 2,000 middle managers and staff attended a three-day conference at which 108 case studies were presented. [It took a translator an entire evening merely to translate the titles for an American visitor.] More than 2,000 foremen attended a three-day conference where there were 150 case studies. An annual national AC-Circle competition drew 2,000 finalists. And in 1985, for the first time there was a conference for

service industries': Walton, *The Deming Management Method*, 249. Thus top management, middle management, and foremen actively participated in the Deming Prize competitions just as they did in the QCC activities that Cole describes. In these QCC and Deming Prize activities we discover the same sort of systems interconnectedness that Fruin, Kenney, and Florida found to be typical of the Japanese enterprise.

88. Cole, *Strategies for Learning*, 303.

89. The translated title of their book registers their meaning: *Can the Germans still be Saved?*

90. Henzler and Späth, *Sind die Deutschen noch zu retten?*, 22.

91. Ibid. 23.

92. Manfred Perlitz, 'Die Aufrechterhaltung der internationalen Wettbewerbsfähigkeit als Verpflichtung für Unternehmen und Gesamtwirtschaft', in E. Dichtl (ed.), *Standort Bundesrepublik Deutschland* (Frankfurt am Main: *Frankfurter Allgemeine Zeitung* Verlag, 1993), 9–49 at 37. Perlitz's evaluation is judicious and, while not uncritical of German performance, on the whole favorable. Michael Albert notes that German firms pay out a smaller percentage of GDP in wages and salaries (67% as compared with 71% in France, 72% in Italy, and 73% in the U.K.) than other leading EEC members, which means that 'German companies manage to pay out the highest wages in Europe . . . and still have more funds left over for self-financing': *Capitalism against Capitalism*, 114.

93. Albert, *Capitalism Against Capitalism*, 45.

94. Reich, *The Work of Nations*, 197.

95. 'Manufacturing, production-worker hourly earnings in 1982 dollars'; US Department of Labor, Bureau of Labor Statistics, *Employment Hours and Earnings, United States, 1909–90*, Bulletin 2370 (Washington, DC, Mar. 1991), i. 63.

96. Edward N. Luttwak, *The Endangered American Dream: How to Stop the United States from Becoming a Third World Country and How to Win the Geo-Economic Struggle for Industrial Supremacy* (New York: Simon & Schuster, 1993), 202.

97. Albert, *Capitalism against Capitalism*, 114.

98. Reich, *The Work of Nations*, 207.

99. Ibid.

100. Ibid. 209.

101. Marshall, *Unheard Voices*, 137.

102. Ibid. 138.

103. Ibid. 209.

104. Reich, *The Work of Nations*, 213.

105. Luttwak, *The Endangered American Dream*, 203.

106. Also, if unemployment is slightly higher in Germany than in the United States, it is not higher there than in other European countries where co-determination is much weaker. In 1988, in fact, German unemployment rates were the lowest in the European Economic Community: Belgium 12.3%, West Germany 8.1%, Spain 20.5%, France 10.8%, Ireland 19.2%, Italy 14.0%, Netherlands 11.5%, United Kingdom 10.6%. Jasminka Sohinger and Daniel Rubinfeld, 'European Labor Markets: The Eastern Dimension', in Ulman, Eichengreen, and Dickens, 271–85 at 283.

107. Stephen S. Roach made this point in a recent article in *The Washington Post*, which was reprinted in *Japan Times*: 'Longer Hours, Harder Lives: Battle Lines are Drawn in U. S. Productivity Clash', *Japan Times* (16 Mar. 1995).

108. Interview, Cologne, 18 July 1994.

109. McKinsey, Booz, Allen & Hamilton, Arthur D. Little, Knight Wendling, are among those thanked.

110. The German titles of Horst Wildemann's books are *Strategische Investitionsplanung* (Wiesbaden: Gabler, 1987); *Das Just-In-Time-Konzept: Produktion und Zulieferung auf Abruf* (3rd edn., Munich: Gesellschaft für Management und Technologie-Verlags, 1987); *Produktionssynchrone Beschaffung* (Munich: Gesellschaft für Management und Technologie-Verlags KG, 1988); *Arbeitszeitmanagement: Einführung und Bewertung flexibler Arbeits- und Betriebszeiten* (Munich: Gesellschaft für Management und Technologie, 1992); *Optimierung von Entwicklungszeiten: Just-In-Time in Forschung und Entwicklung und Konstruktion* (Munich: Transfer-Centrum-Verlag, 1993); *Unternehmensqualität: Einführung einer kontinuierlichen Qualitätsverbesserung* (Munich: Transfer-Centrum-Verlag, 1993).

111. Comparative hourly manufacturing wages in 1993: German DM 42, Hungary DM 4.2, Poland DM 2.3, Russia DM 0.6. *Sind die Deutschen noch zu retten?*, 52.

112. See *Die Mitbestimmung*, which the Hans-Böckler-Stiftung publishes monthly, wherein work-process reform articles have held center stage since the late 1980s.

113. See Ministerium für Wirtschaft, Technologie und Verkehr des Landes Sachsen-Anhalt (ed.), 'Chemie in Sachsen-Anhalt: Magnet für Folgeinvestitionen', *Invest* (Mar. 1994).

114. Professor Huchzermeier related the witticism during the interview, Koblenz, 20 July 1994. It is a caricature because the machine tools

are German but the robotics at Opel are Japanese, so the automation is only partially German. Videos about *Das Opel-Produktionssystem* are available.

115. Interview, Munich, 21 July 1994.
116. Ibid.
117. Lowell Turner, *Democracy at Work*, 53.
118. Ibid. 38.
119. Ibid. 131.
120. Ibid. 138.
121. Streeck, *Industrial Relations in West Germany*, 114, 135.
122. Ibid. 136.
123. Ibid. 59.
124. Ibid. 135.
125. Ibid. 133.
126. Ibid.
127. Ibid.
128. Paul Thompson and Per Sederblad, 'The Swedish Model of Work Organization in Transition', in Elger and Smith, *Global Japanization?*, 238–65 at 260.
129. Kathleen Thelen, 'Codetermination and Industrial Adjustment in the German Steel Industry: A Comparative Interpretation', *California Management Review*, 29:3 (Spring 1987), 134–48, and Alfred L. Thimm, 'Codetermination and Industrial Adjustment in February 1987: A Few Comments on Ms Thelen's "A Comparative Interpretation"', ibid. 149–53. The quotes are from Thimm, 149–50.
130. Streeck, 'Industrial Relations and Industrial Change'.
131. Arthur Whitehill and Schin-Ichi Takezawa, *Workways: Japan and America* (Tokyo: The Japan Institute of Labor, 1981). The results: '[A] striking difference persists with Japanese workers placing their company in a far more central life-role than U.S. workers. Furthermore, the willingness to at least equate work life with personal life among Japanese workers tended to strengthen during the interim between surveys. In contrast, U.S. workers, particularly the young, demonstrated an increasingly alienated, separatist view of the work-life sector' (p. 123).
132. Laurie Graham, 'How does the Japanese Model Transfer to the United States? A View from the Line', *Global Japanization?*, 123–51 at 124.
133. On the contrary, '[e]mergent patterns of shop floor behaviour indicate that Japanese management practice can result in . . . individual and collective resistance [from] U.S. workers. Workers participate in both

spontaneous and planned resistance. Whether spontaneous or planned, only collective resistance, produced the strength necessary to effectively challenge [*sic*] management's control on the shop floor' (ibid. 124). Also see J. Fucini and S. Fucini, *Working for the Japanese: Inside Mazda's American Auto Plant* (New York: Free Press, MacMillan, 1990).

134. Williams, Mitsui, and Haslam, 'How far from Japan?'.

135. With just one-sixth of the population in 1990 within the EEC 12 states, the West Germans had nearly 40 percent of EEC 12 manufacturing output. Their huge surplus in manufactured trade with the rest of Europe represents a substantial transfer of employment to West Germany.

136. Williams *et al.*, 'How far from Japan?', 88–9.

137. Thimm, 'Codetermination and Industrial Adjustment', 152. Thimm's favorable opinion about co-determination is all the more interesting because he is a management spokesman.

138. Williams *et al.*, 'How far from Japan?', 88–9.

CHAPTER 5

1. George Meany, 'What Labor Means By "More"', *Fortune* (Mar. 1955), 92–95, 272–9; Charles P. Taft, 'The Familiar Men of 1980', *Fortune* (Feb. 1955), 104–5, 214–20; David Sarnoff, 'The Fabulous Future', *Fortune* (Mar. 1955), 82–3, 114–18; George M. Humphrey, 'The Future: Sound as a Dollar', *Fortune* (Apr. 1955), 116–18.

2. In German, Das Institut für Arbeitsmarkt- und Berufsforschung.

3. 'For most jobs the bosses in a business or firm find that they want people with entirely different qualifications than those imagined when the original position was advertised'; quoted in Hartmut Wächter, 'Praxisbezug des wirtschaftswissenschaftlichen Studiums', Expertise für die Studienreformkommission: Wirtschaftswissenschaften (Sept. 1980), 34.

4. The citation is from Professor Mertens's study which is quoted in Wächter, 'Praxisbezug', 35.

5. Luttwak, for instance, in *The Endangered American Dream*, discusses the pros and cons of an industrial policy; Chalmers Johnson's *MITI and the Japanese Miracle: The Growth of Industrial Policy, 1925–1975* (Stanford: Stanford University Press, 1982) brought the subject up; Dominique Turcq, in *L'Inévitable Partenaire japonais*, criticizes MITI. Conclusions about the advisability of the Americans adopting an industrial policy seem to be determined by the ideology of the author less than by the 'facts'.

6. Willard F. Enteman, *Managerialism: The Emergence of a New Ideology* (Madison: University of Wisconsin Press, 1993). Enteman devotes most of ch. 3 to a discussion of the 'Adam Smith Problem'.

7. Ibid. 53–4. Enteman argues that American economists have done violence to Smith's views in two ways: (1) they have separated fact and value, making, in Milton Friedman's words, '[p]ositive economics . . . in principle independent of any ethical position or normative judgements'; (2) these economists have, unlike Smith, become apologists, through their discipline, of the managerial-ownership class.

8. By this logic, the suppression of the market, not private property, constituted the principal weakness of Communist regimes.

9. Cited in 'The Straining of Quality', *The Economist* (14 Jan. 1995), 65. The study was done by Boston University, Tokyo's Waseda University, and INSEAD, Fontainebleau, France, three prestigious schools.

10. Ishikawa, *What is Total Quality Control?*, 97.

11. Reich, *The Work of Nations*, 175.

12. Ibid. 178.

13. Research scientists, design engineers, software engineers, civil engineers, biotechnology engineers, sound engineers, public relations executives, investment bankers, lawyers, real estate developers, management consultants, financial consultants, tax consultants, armament consultants, strategic planners, management information specialists, advertising executives, marketing strategists, and more.

14. Included among in-person servers: retail sales workers, waiters and waitresses, hotel workers, janitors, cashiers, hospital attendants and orderlies, health-care aides, taxi drivers, secretaries, hairdressers, fast-food workers, auto mechanics, security guards, etc.

15. Reich, *The Work of Nations*, 211.

16. James Brian Quinn, *Intelligent Enterprise: A Knowledge and Service Based Paradigm for Industry* (New York: Free Press, MacMillan, 1992), 175. Also see Gunnar Eliasson, Stefan Fölster, Thomas Lindberg, Tomas Pousette, and Erol Taymaz, *The Knowledge-Based Information Economy* (Stockholm: Almquist & Wiksell International, 1990).

17. Reich, *The Work of Nations*, 87.

18. Quinn, *Intelligent Enterprise*, 375.

19. Ibid.

20. Reich, *The Work of Nations*, 90–1.

21. Reich, like so many others, dwells on this rape of corporate America by hostile takeovers. But French businessman Michel Albert, who also discusses this phenomenon, sees it not as an unavoidable feature of

the global marketplace but as a special characteristic of American 'casino capitalism', which he contrasts with the 'Rhine model' of capitalism. See his *Capitalism against Capitalism*.

22. Richard T. Pascale and Thomas Rohlen, 'The Mazda Turnaround', *The Journal of Japanese Studies*, 9:2 (Summer 1983), 219–63.

23. Pascale and Rohlen cite as reasons: (1) The Wankel (rotary) engine was less fuel efficient than conventional engines at a time of extreme fuel conservation; (2) the U.S. Environmental Protection Agency had precipitated a particularly steep revenue shortfall in the U.S. market by noting that Mazda cars only got 10 miles per hour mileage, sales immediately plummeting; (3) inventories piled up, causing a severe cash flow problem; (4) Toyo Kogyo was Japan's highest-cost producer, averaging only nineteen cars per employee annually against a Japanese average of thirty; ibid. 219–20.

24. Ibid. 220.

25. Ibid. 229.

26. Ibid. 257.

27. Ibid. 235.

28. Cited ibid. 234.

29. Ibid. 241.

30. Ibid. 245.

31. Ibid. 247.

32. Ibid. 246.

33. Ibid.

34. Ibid. 259.

35. Fruin, *The Japanese Enterprise System*, 197.

36. Ibid. 197–8.

37. Reich, *The Work of Nations*, 90.

38. Huston Smith, *The Religions of Man* (New York: Harper & Row, 1986), 237.

39. Reich devotes a chapter to describing their ascendancy.

40. Melvyn R. Copen, 'Training International Managers', *The MBA Career Guide* (Fall 1994), 19, is the source of the quote; the data on Germany is extracted from pp. 138–41.

41. Robert S. Kaplan, 'Quality in Business School Education and Research', presentation to the Annual Meeting of the American Assembly of Collegiate Schools of Business, St. Louis, MO, 22 Apr. 1991; quoted in Johnson, *Relevance Regained*, 176–7.

42. Ibid.

43. Ibid. 177.

44. My conclusion; see *Management and Higher Education*, 220–3.

45. Lillrank and Kano, *Continuous Improvement*, 2.

46. Lori Bongiorno, 'Corporate America's New Lesson Plan', *Business Week* (25 Oct. 1993), 101–7.

47. Ibid. 105.

48. More than 20,000 Thunderbird graduates populate the ranks of such companies as Citicorp, Bank of America, General Motors, American Express, IBM, and General Electric, many of whom have foreign postings or U.S. jobs with international responsibilities.

49. Robert R. Locke, 'Mastering the Lingo', *The Times Higher Educational Supplement* (4 May 1991), 23 and 25.

50. There is a sort of 'standoffishness' in American business school professors. Some years ago, a professor from a major business school who did not know German or Germany was charged with setting up a program with German professors of business economics. Since I had many contacts with German professors of BWL, I, a historian, offered to help. The offer, made twice, did not even merit the dignity of a response. Stories like this can easily be multiplied. In Europe, on the other hand, where all university professors are paid the same rate, and consultancy fees are not so high, there seems to be a much greater receptivity to nonbusiness schools academics in the business schools and faculties of business economics. Perhaps this results, too, from the general lack of prestige of European business schools within the university community.

51. There are thirty Frauenhofer Institutes in Germany. The one I visited some years ago at Stuttgart was magnificently laid out. Its director, Professor Warnecke, an engineer, noted that about 10 percent of the staff were economics engineers.

52. Ishikawa, *What is Total Quality Control?*, 5.

53. Larry Rhodes, 'Legal Bases for Vocational Mediation in Japanese Schools', unpublished paper, University of Hawaii at Manoa, Department of Political Science, n.d., 12. Rhodes is a graduate student in political science at the University of Hawaii at Manoa with much on-site experience in Japanese secondary schools.

54. See the list of specialties given in n. 13.

55. The figures for the youth in this age bracket are 60% into apprenticeships, 30% on to higher education, and 10% who leave school at age 16 without further education and training. David Soskice and Ronald Schettkat, 'West German Labour Market Institutions and East German

Transformation', in Ulman, Eichengreen, and Dickens, 102–27 at 209–12.

56. Ibid.

57. Rhodes, 'Legal Bases', 13.

58. Think, for example, of getting the American students to clean and maintain the school, to carry out food services, with all involved in the common tasks.

59. The results of such apprenticeship systems show up in comparative statistics. Lane notes, for example, that in the late 1980s university levels of educational qualifications were about the same in the West German and the United Kingdom labor force: 3.5% in Germany, 3.3% in Britain. But at the intermediate level of qualifications, a great discrepancy existed between the two: 6.8% of the German working population as compared with 28.7% of the British have no formal qualifications of the sort given in an apprenticeship program. This left 35.7% of Germans in the manufacturing sector without qualifications, and 68% of the British. 'The deficiencies in Britain are greatest at the level of technician, foreman, office clerk, and a little less, though still considerable, at the level of manual workers': C. Lane, *Management and Labour in Europe: The Industrial Enterprise in Germany, Britain and France* (London: Edward Elgar, 1989), 82.

60. Most of the high school graduates who enter the job market are from less prestigious high schools. To understand the exclusivity of the Japanese secondary education process, consider the following scheme: Japanese secondary schools divide into two groups, vocational and 'ordinary'. Vocational high schools breakdown into several sub-types. One subtype is the manual arts high schools (*kogyo*), in which courses of study break down into sub-specialties, electrical, technical, civil, etc. The best students take the electrical curriculum. A second vocational school type is the commercial school (*shogyo*), where all students take a common course. In addition to the technical and commercial schools in the vocational school category, which are the most important, there are two lesser vocational high school types: agricultural and horticultural. They have few students.

The second high school category is called 'ordinary'. But it breaks down into 'advanced ordinary' (*shingakko*) high schools and 'ordinary, ordinary' high schools. Graduates from the 'advanced ordinary' high school move up to university and into the Japanese business and administrative elite. Only a very small number of high school graduates go to university from the 'ordinary, ordinary' and the vocational schools.

Those that do usually come from the electrical section of the manual arts schools. The rest (most of those from vocational and 'ordinary, ordinary' high schools) find jobs. It is remarkable how much care is taken in these low prestige schools to place these students and not just throw them out on the street.

61. Kenney and Florida, *Beyond Mass Production*, 293–4.

62. David Coates, *The Question of UK Decline: The Economy, State and Society* (London: Harvester Wheatsheaf, 1994), 246–7.

63. Even if low-wage firms make big profits, the workers do not gain from it because of the 'suck up' effect. The profits, under American managerialism, are not shared with the workers, in pay, benefits, or further training, but 'sucked up' by the executives to fatten stockholder dividends and management pay.

64. Masahiko Aoki, 'Toward an Economic Model of the Japanese Firm', *Journal of Economic Literature*, 28 (Mar. 1990), 1–27 at 22. G. C. Archibald, 'The Theory of the Firm', in *The New Palgrave: A Dictionary of Economics*, 2 (London: Macmillan, 1987), 357–63. Also see Michael Jensen and William Meckling, 'Theory of the Firm: Managerial Behavior, Agency Costs and Capital Structure', *Journal of Finance and Economy*, 3:4 (Oct. 1976), 305–60.

65. Aoki, 'Toward an Economic Model', 13–14.

66. Aoki's description of the H-Model sounds very familiar to American business historians. The model has two features, Aoki notes: (1) 'the hierarchial separation between planning and implemental operations and (2) the emphasis on the economies of specialization. That is, planning, such as for production scheduling, manufacturing process control, and commodity development is entrusted to an office at the top level of each function.' The H-Model is defined as a firm with managerial hierarchies that subjects planning and operations to top-down control. Ibid. 8.

67. William J. Hecht, 'Challenges Ahead for White-Collar Workers', *Target*, 10:3 (May–June 1994), 6–7 at 6.

68. Aoki, 'Toward an Economic Model', 10.

69. Ibid. 1 and 3. Between Sept. 1987 and Aug. 1989, he interviewed managers and engineers from about fifty firms. He did intensive studies of many plants, including those of Nippon Steel Corporation, Matsushita Electric Industrial Co., Ltd., Sony Corporation, Honda Motor Co., Ltd., Toyota Motor Corporation, Omron Tateisi Electronics Co., Kyowa Hakko Kogyo Co., Ltd., Tonen Corporations, and many more; see p. 3.

70. Hideo Totsuka, 'Building Japan's Corporate Society', *AMPO Japan-Asia*

Quarterly Review, 25:1, 11–17. Also see id., 'Transformation of Japanese Industrial Relations: A Case Study of the Automobile Industry', *Annals of the Institute of Social Science*, University of Tokyo, 35 (1993), 69–90, and Hirokuni Tabata, 'Changes in Plant-Level Trade Union Organizations: A Case Study of the Automobile Industry', *Annals of the Institute of Social Science*, University of Tokyo, 30 (1988), 57–88.

71. Totsuka, 'Building Japan's Corporate Society', 18. For example, 'when Japanese managers proposed team work for U.S. workers, the unions made counter-proposals based on their own understanding of teamwork . . . .'

72. 14 Jan. 1995, 65. The Baldrige competition, in emulation of Japan's Deming Prize, only started in 1988. Applications of firms competing for the award were 60 in 1988, 40 in 1989, 90 in 1990, 103 in 1991, 83 in 1992, 79 in 1993, and 71 in 1994. Is the competition to be another passing fad?

73. See Robert Kuttner's comments, 'Needed: A Two-Way Social Contract in the Workplace', in which he notes that 'Even the best companies now slash benefits and dump workers'; *Business Week* (10 July 1995), 22. Also see 'The Wage Squeeze, Productivity and Profits are up a lot. Paychecks aren't', *Business Week* (17 July 1995), 54–62.

74. Wolfgang Hirn and Andreas Nölting in an evaluation of German firms reported in 1994 that 'corporate profits are about to explode': 'Not lehrt Handeln', *Manager Magazin*, 24:7 (July 1994), 84–97 at 84.

75. Gene Koretz reported in *Business Week* that 'although 1994 was a banner year for U.S. corporate profits, U.S. household wealth seems to have actually fallen', 6 March 1995, 26. Data from the U.S. Census Bureau shows, moreover, that between 1989 and 1993, the number of people below the poverty level ($14,764 in 1993 dollars for a family of four) grew from thirty-one to thirty-nine million.

76. Once, at the French National Library in 1962, Americans, struck by the extent of their presence, did an unofficial count of the Americans occupying seats in the main reading room of the library (400+ seats). Americans sat in 25 percent of the seats that day. Author's recollection.

Bibliography

INTERVIEWS

On Japan

Management

Prof. Nobuo Kawabe, Honolulu, 10 Apr. 1994
Hugh Leonard, Long Beach, Calif., 13 Apr. 1994
Prof. Tetsuo Najita, Honolulu, 5 May 1994
Mr. Dominique Turcq, Brussels, 5 July 1994
Prof. Kosaku Yoshida, Dominguez Hills, Calif., 13 Apr. 1994
Prof. Tsunehiko Yui, Tokyo, 24 May 1990

Education

Joseph Adams, Honolulu, 20 April 1994
Irmina Hayashi, Honolulu, 15 April 1994
Larry Rhodes, Honolulu, 12 Dec. 1994

On Germany

Management

Dr. Thomas Breisig, Trier, 19 Mar. 1993
Prof. Dr. Arnd Huchzermeier, Koblenz, 20 July 1994
Prof. Dr. Alfred Kieser, Mannheim, 19 July 1994
Dr. Dieter Kirchner, Cologne, 18 July 1994
Dr. Wolfgang Ollmann, Hamburg, 12 Aug. 1994
Prof. Dr. Manfred Perlitz, Mannheim, 19 July 1994
Prof. Dr. Horst Wildemann, 21 July 1994

Bibliography

PERIODICALS (Consulted for period after 1975)

Business History Review
Business Week
California Management Review
Columbia Journal of World Business
Fortune
Harvard Business Review
Manager Magazin
Die Mitbestimmung
Quality Progress
Schmalenbachs Zeitschrift für betriebswirtschaftliche Forschung
Target

ARTICLES

ABO, TETSUO, 'U.S. Subsidiaries of Japanese Electronic Companies Enter a New Phase of Activity: A Report of On-the-Spot Observations', *Annals of the Institute of Social Science*, University of Tokyo, 26 (1984), 1–32.

AKITA, GEORGE, and YOSHIHIRO, HIROSE, 'The British Model: Inoue Kowashi and the Ideal Monarchical System', *Monumenta Nipponica*, 49:4 (Winter 1994), 413–21.

ALBACH, HORST, 'Über die Praxisnähe betriebswirtschaftlicher Ausbildung: Non Universitati sed vitae oeconomicae discimus', *Hochschulnachrichten aus der Wissenschaftlichen Hochschule für Unternehmensführung Koblenz*, 1 (1992), 24–30.

ALTMANN, NORBERT, 'Company Performance Policies and the Role of the Works Council', in Tokunaga and Bergmann, *Industrial Relations in Transition*, 255–84.

'American Multinationals Want to go Home', *The Economist* (17 Nov. 1976), 85–6.

AOKI, MASAHIKO, 'Toward an Economic Model of the Japanese Firm', *Journal of Economic Literature*, 28 (Mar. 1990), 1–27.

ARCHIBALD, G. C., 'The Theory of the Firm', in *The New Palgrave: A Dictionary of Economics*, ii (London: Macmillan, 1987), 357–63.

ATLESON, JAMES B., 'Wartime Labor Regulation, the Industrial Pluralists, and the Law of Collective Bargaining', in Lichtenstein and Harris, *Industrial Democracy in America*, 142–75.

'Auszüge aus der Plenumsdiskussion anlässlich der Schmalenbach-Tagung',

Schmalenbachs Zeitschrift für betriebswirtschaftlich Forschung, 34 (Jan. 1982), 79–82.

BACHNIK, JANE, '*Kejime*: Defining a Shifting Self in Multiple Organizational Modes', in Rosenberger, Japanese Sense of Self, 152–72.

BAIN, TREVOR, 'German Co-Determination and Employment Adjustments in the Steel and Auto Industries', *Columbia Journal of World Business*, 18:2 (Summer 1983), 40–7.

BALL, ROBERT, 'Europe Outgrows Management American Style', *Fortune* (8 Dec. 1980), 147–9.

——'Volkswagen's Struggle to Restore its Name', *Fortune* (27 June 1983), 100–4.

BAMBERG, HANS-DIETER, KRÖGER, HANS-JÜRGEN, and KUHLMANN, REINHARD, 'Soziale Verantwortung und Freiheit: Wissenschaft in der Zusammenarbeit von Gerwerkschaften und Hochschulen', in Bamberg, Kröger, and Kuhlmann, *Hochschulen und Gewerkschaften*, 15–86.

BAUER, EWALD, 'Qualität als Unternehmensleitbild: Einführung des Konzeptes "Unternehmensqualität" bei einem Hersteller Technischer Keramik', in Wildemann, *Qualität und Produktivitätat*, 147–64.

BAUR, FRIEDRICH, 'Auswirkungen des Standortes Bundesrepublik Deutschland auf die Fabrik von morgen', in Wildemann, *Fabrikplanung*, 252–64.

BEDEIAN, ARTHUR, 'A Comparison and Analysis of German and United States Managerial Attitudes towards the Legitimacy of Organization Influence', *Academy of Management Journal*, 18:4 (Dec. 1975), 897–904.

BELL, DANIEL, 'The Language of Labor', *Fortune* (Sept. 1951), 86.

BENSON, JOHN, 'The Economic Effects of Unionism on Japanese Manufacturing Enterprise', *British Journal of Industrial Relations*, 32:1 (Mar. 1994), 1–22.

BERNSTEIN, MICHAEL A., 'Academic Reconstruction and the Pax Americana: Notes on Imperial Legitimation after World War II', paper, Conference on 'Knowledges: Production, Distribution, Revision', University of Minnesota, Apr. 1994.

'Betriebswertschaftslehre, Theorie und Praxis im Streitgespräch', *Der Volkswirt—Wirtschafts- und Finanzzeitung*, 19 (9 July 1965), 1426–8.

BOLTANSKI, LUC, 'America, America . . ., le plan marshall et l'importation du "management"', *Actes de la recherche en sciences sociales*, a publication of 'La Maison de l'homme', 38 (1981), 19–41.

BONGIORNO, LORI, 'Corporate America's New Lesson Plan', *Business Week* (25 Oct. 1993), 103–7.

BOOZ, ALLEN, and HAMILTON, 'German Management', *International Studies of Management and Organization* (White Plains, NY: Arts and Science Press, 1973).

Bibliography

BRANDT, GERHARD, 'Industrial Relations in the Federal Republic of Germany under Conditions of Economic Crisis', in Tokunaga and Bergmann, *Industrial Relations in Transition*, 5–20.

BREISIG, THOMAS, 'Betriebsvereinbarungen zu Qualitätszirkeln—Eine Inhaltsanalyse', *Die Betriebswirtschaft*, 51:1 (Jan.–Feb. 1991), 65–77.

——'Unternehmerische Sozialtechniken als Herausforderung an die gewerkschaftliche Interessenvertretung', *Die Mitbestimmung*, 33:22 (1987), 665–71.

BROUTHERS, LANCE E., and Warner, Steve, 'Are the Japanese Good Global Competitors?' *Columbia Journal of World Business*, 25:3 (Fall 1990), 5–12.

BURCK, GILBERT, 'Can Germany Go Capitalist?' *Fortune* (Apr. 1954), 114–22, 247–52.

——'The German Business Mind', *Fortune* (May 1954), 111–14, 219–20.

——'The Transformation of European Business', *Fortune* (Nov. 1957), 292–9.

BYRNE, JOHN A., 'Management', *Business Week* (18 Sept. 1995), 122–34.

CABARUSM, UTE, JÖNS, JÜRGEN, and SYBEN, GERD, 'Kooperation von Hochschulen und Gewerkschaften bei der Hochschulausbildung', in Bamberg, Kröger, and Kuhlmann, *Hochschulen und Gewerkschaften*, 89–114.

CALORI, ROLAND, 'The Diversity of Management Systems', in Calori and de Woot, *A European Model of Management*, 11–30.

——and SEIDEL, FRED, 'The Dynamics of Management Systems in Europe', in Calori and de Woot, *A European Model of Management*, 55–78.

——VALLA, JEAN-PAUL, and WOOT, PHILIPPE DE, 'Common Characteristics: The Ingredients of European Management', in Calori and de Woot, *A European Model of Management*, 31–54.

CHANDLER, ALFRED D., Jr., 'Corporate Strategy, Structure and Control Methods in the United States During the 20th Century', *Industrial and Corporate Change*, 1:2 (1992), 263–85.

——and REDLICH, FRITZ, 'Recent Developments in American Business Administration and their Conceptualization', *Business History Review*, (Summer 1961), 1–27.

CHILD, JOHN, FORES, MICHAEL, GLOVER, IAN, and LAWRENCE, PETER, 'A Price to Pay: Professionalism and Work Organisation in Britain and West Germany', *Sociology*, 17:2 (1983), 63–78.

CHIMOTO, AKIKO, 'Development of Personnel Management in Post-Meiji Japan', in Kawabe and Daito, *Education and Training*, 53–76.

'Co-determination: When Workers Help Manage', *Business Week* (16 July 1975), 160–7.

COPEN, MELVYN R., 'Training International Managers', *The MBA Career Guide* (Fall 1994).

CROZIER, MICHEL, 'Human Engineering, les nouvelles techniques "humaines" du Big Business américain', *Les Temps Modernes*, 7:69 (1951), 44–75.

DANIEL, SHIRLEY J., and AONO, JUNE Y., 'A Framework for Comparing International Auditing Practices and an Examination of Auditing in the U.S.A. and Japan', unpublished paper, Department of Accounting, University of Hawaii at Manoa, 1–18.

——and REITSPERGER, WOLF D., 'Linking Quality Strategy with Management Control Systems: Empirical Evidence from Japanese Industry', *Accounting, Organizations and Society*, 16:7 (1991), 601–18.

DOMBOIS, RAINER, 'The New International Division of Labour, Labour Markets and Automobile Production: The Case of Mexico', in Tolliday and Zeitlin, *The Automobile Industry and its Workers*, 244–57.

DORE, RONALD, 'The Legacy of Tokugawa Education', in Jansen, *Changing Japanese Attitudes*, 99–131.

DORNSEIFER, BERND, and KOCKA, JÜRGEN, 'The Impact of the Preindustrial Heritage: Reconsiderations on the German Pattern of Corporate Development in the Late 19th and Early 20th Centuries', *Industrial and Corporate Change*, 2:2 (1993), 233–48.

DRUCKER, PETER, 'Really Reinventing Government', *The Atlantic Monthly*, 275:2 (Feb. 1995), 49–61.

DUFOUR, BRUNO, 'Changes in Management Education and Development: A European Perspective', in Calori and de Woot, *A European Model of Management*, 236–58.

——'Management is not a Science', *Hochschulnachrichten aus der WHU Koblenz*, 2 (1992), 69–73.

DUNN, ROBERT M., Jr., 'Why do Economists Prosper more than Economies?' *The News* (26 Mar. 1993), 28.

DUNNING, JOHN, 'The Governance of Japanese and U.S. Manufacturing Affiliates in the U.K.', in Kogut (ed.), *Country Competitiveness*, 203–24.

ECKEL, GERNOT, 'Qualitätskosten—neu betrachtet', in Wildemann, *Qualität und Produktivität*, 183–200.

ELIASSON, GUNNAR, 'The Knowledge-Based Information Economy', in Eliasson et al., *The Knowledge-Based Information Economy*, 9–88.

ENDO, KOSHI, 'Reflections on the Turnabout in Labor Relations Policy in Occupied Japan', *Annals of the Institute of Social Science*, University of Tokyo, 26 (1984), 78–101.

ENSSLIN, WOLFGANG, 'Qualitätskostenüberwachung—Baustein in einem umfas-

Bibliography

senden Leistungscontrolling', in Wildemann, *Qualität und Produktivität*, 176–83.

ESSER, JOSEF, and FACH, WOLFGANG, 'Crisis Management "Made in Germany": The Steel Industry', in Katzenstein, *Industry and Politics in West Germany*, 221–49.

EZZAMEL, MAHMOUD, 'From Problem Solving to Problematization: A Comment on "Relevance Revisited"', to be published in *Critical Perspectives on Accounting*.

——HOSKIN, KEITH, and MACVE, RICHARD, 'Managing it all by Numbers: A Review of Johnson and Kaplan's "Relevance Lost"', *Accounting and Business Research*, 20:8 (Spring 1990), 153–66.

FALLOWS, JAMES, 'How the World Works', *The Atlantic Monthly*, 273:12 (Dec. 1993), 61–87.

FARRELL, STEVEN J., 'Why the Japanese Conglomerate is Globally Successful', *Jaims Journal*, 1:1 (1992), 87–98.

FELS, GERHARD, 'Internationale Wettbewerbsfähigkeit Japan, Vereinigte Staaten, Bundesrepublik—Fakten, Trends, Hypothesen', *ZfbF*, 34 (Jan. 1982), 8–24.

FISCHER, GABRIELE, and RISCH, SUSANNE, 'Unter Beschuss, Mittelmanagement', *Manager Magazin*, 8 (1994), 112–30.

FORES, MICHAEL, GLOVER, IAN, and LAWRENCE, PETER, 'Management Thought, the American Identity and the Future of European Labour Processes in 1992', 10th Annual International Aston/UMIST Conference, University of Aston, 1–3 Apr. 1992.

——————————'Professionalism and Rationality: A Study in Misapprehension', *Sociology*, 25:1 (Feb. 1991), 79–100.

FORSGREN, MATS, 'Managing the International Multi-Centre Firm: Case Studies from Sweden', *European Management Journal*, 8:2 (June 1990), 261–7.

FRAISSE, PIERRE, 'Les Perspectives des relations humaines', *Revue de psychologie appliquée*, Revue trimestrielle, 4:1 (Jan. 1953), 35–56.

——and GUIBOURG, YVES, 'Human Relations: Progrès ou mystification?' *Esprit* (May 1953), 783–804.

FRICKE, WERNER, 'New Technologies and German Co-determination', *Economic and Industrial Democracy*, 7:4 (1986), 543–51.

FRUIN, MARK W., and NISHIGUICHI, TOSHIHIRO, 'Supplying the Toyota Production System: Intercorporate Organization Evolution and Supplier Subsystems', in Kogut, *Country Competitiveness*, 225–46.

GAMER, BERTOLD, 'Planung und Einsatz elektronischer Datenverarbeitungsanlagen in einer chemischen Grossunternehmung', *Zeitschrift für betriebswirtschaftliche Forschung*, 13 (1961), 353–67.

306

GARVIN, DAVID A., 'Japanese Quality Management', *Columbia Journal of World Business*, 19:3 (Fall 1984), 3–12.

GAUGLER, EDUARD, GILLE, GERD, and WEBER, BERND, 'Die Entwicklung der Betriebswirtschaftslehre an den wissenschaftlichen Hochschulen in der Bundesrepublik Deutschland und in Österreich und in der Schweiz', *Die Betriebswirtschaft*, 45:4 (1985), 13–27.

GAULLE, CHARLES DE, 'Mobilisation économique à l'étranger', reprinted in *Trois études* (Paris: Editeur Edito-Service, 1973).

GLOVER, IAN A., 'How the West was Lost? Decline of Engineering and Manufacturing in Britain and the United States', *Higher Education Review*, 17:3 (1985), 3–34.

GORDON, ANDREW, 'Araki Toichiro and the Shaping of Labor Management', in Yui and Nakagawa, *The Development of Japanese Business*, 173–97.

———'Contest for the Workplace', in Andrew Gordon, *Postwar Japan as History*, ch. 2.

GORDON, DAVID M., 'Chickens Home to Roost: From Prosperity to Stagnation in the Postwar U.S. Economy', in Bernstein and Adler, *Understanding American Economic Decline*, 34–75.

GOSSELINK, F. J., 'Marshall-aid and Organization/Management Sciences', the Centre for Research in Business Economics, Department of Organization and Management, Erasmus University Rotterdam, Report 8205/0 (May 1982).

GRAHAM, LAURIE, 'How does the Japanese Model Transfer to the United States? A View from the Line', in Elger and Smith, *Global Japanization?*, 123–51.

GUEST, DAVID E., 'Human Resource Management and the American Dream', *Journal of Management Studies*, 27:4 (Jul. 1990), 377–97.

GÜNTHER, MAX, 'Internationale Wettbewerbsfähigkeit der Unternehmen in Japan, USA und der Bundesrepublik Deutschland', *ZfbF*, 34 (Jan. 1982), 1–7.

HANNAH, LESLIE, 'The American Miracle 1875–1950 and After: A View in the European Mirror', paper, Business History Conference, Fort Lauderdale, 17–19 March 1995.

HARTMANN, HEINZ, 'Appraisal of the Report "German Management: Challenges and Responses"', in Boddewyn, *European Industrial Managers*, 237–50.

HARTWICH, GÜNTER, 'Die neue Fabrik am Standort Bundesrepublik Deutschland', in Wildemann, *Fabrikplanung*, 221–35.

HASHIMOTO, JURO, 'The Japanese System of Divisions of Labor: The Combination of a "Flexible" In-House Division of Labor and a "Planned" Inter-Company Division of Labor', *Annals of the Institute of Social Science*, University of Tokyo, 35 (1993), 195–228.

Bibliography

HAYS, ROBERT H., 'Why Japanese Factories Work: They Succeed not by Using Futuristic Techniques but by Paying Attention to Manufacturing Basics,' *Harvard Business Review* (July–Aug. 1981), 57–66.

——and ABERNATHY, WILLIAM J., 'Managing Our Way to Economic Decline', *Harvard Business Review* (Jul.–Aug. 1980), 67–77.

HECHT, WILLIAM J., 'Challenges Ahead for White-Collar Workers', *Target*, 10:3 (May–June 1994), 6–7.

HELFERT, MARIO, and TRAUTWEIN-KALMS, GUNDRUN, 'Die gewerkschaftliche Auseinandersetzung um Arbeitsbedingungen und das Forschungsprogramm der Bundesregierung zu Humanisierung des Arbeitslebens', in Bamberg, Kröger, and Kuhlmann, *Hochschulen und Gewerkschaften*, 378–96.

HERRIGEL, GARY B., 'Industrial Order and the Politics of Industrial Change: Mechanical Engineering', in Katzenstein, *Industry and Politics in West Germany*, 185–220.

HIRAMOTO, ATSUSHI, 'Technological Changes and Rationalization in Japanese Industry Since the Oil Crisis: Characteristics of Management Strategies', in Tokunaga and Bergmann, *Industrial Relations in Transition*, 133–47.

HIRN, WOLFGANG, and NÖLTING, ANDREAS, 'Not lehrt Handeln', *Manager Magazin*, 24:7 (July 1994), 84–97.

HOFSTEDE, GEERT, 'Businessmen and Business School Faculty: A Comparison of Value Systems', *Journal of Management Studies*, 15:1 (Feb. 1978), 78–87.

——'The Poverty of Management Control Philosophy', *Academy of Management Review*, 3 (1978), 450–61.

HÖHN, SIEGFRIED, 'Materialwirtschaft als Teil der Unternehmensstrategie—dargestellt am Beispiel der Automobil-Industrie', *ZfbF*, 34 (Jan. 1982), 52–66.

HOSKIN, KEITH W., and MACVE, RICHARD H., 'The Genesis of Accountability: The West Point Connections', *Accounting, Organizations and Society*, 13:1 (1988), 37–73.

————'Understanding Modern Management', *University of Wales: Business and Economics Review*, 5 (1990), 17–22.

IMAI, MASAKI, 'Shukko, Jomukai, Eingi—the Ingredients of Executive Selection in Japan', *Personnel*, 46:4 (July–Aug. 1969), 20–30.

'Index', *Target*, Issue No. 1 (Aug. 1983) to Vol. 9, No. 6 (Nov./Dec. 1993).

IRIBARNE, PHILIPPE D', *La Logique de l'honneur: Gestion des entreprises et traditions nationales* (Paris, 1989).

IWASA, NOBUMICHI, 'Postconventional Reasoning and Moral Education in Japan', *Journal of Moral Education*, 21:1 (1992), 3–16.

JACOBY, SANFORD M., 'Pacific Ties: Industrial Relations and Employment

Systems in Japan and the United States Since 1900', in Lichtenstein and Harris, *Industrial Democracy in America*, 206–48.

JENSEN, MICHAEL, and MECKLING, WILLIAM, 'Theory of the Firm: Managerial Behavior, Agency Costs and Capital Structure', *Journal of Finance and Economy*, 3:4 (Oct. 1976), 305–60.

JOHANNSON, KURT, and WEISSBACH, JÜRGEN, 'Zusammenarbeit von Gewerkschaften und Hochschulen in der Weiterbildung', in Bamberg, Kröger, and Kuhlmann, *Hochschulen und Gewerkschaften*, 115–30.

JOHNSON, CHALMERS, 'Intellectual Warfare: The Reviews of James Fallows's Latest Book . . .', *The Atlantic Monthly* (Jan. 1995), 99–104.

JOHNSON, H. THOMAS, 'Management Accounting in an Early Multidivisional Organization: General Motors in the 1920s', *Business History Review*, 52:4 (Winter 1978), 490–517.

——'So Where do we Turn: Relevance Lost After Five Years', reprints available at Tennessee Associates International, 214 E. Broadway Ave., Maryville, Tenn. 37801.

——and BRÖMS, ANDERS, 'Rich Ends from Simple Means: Three Cases of Managing from a Quantum Perspective', paper presented at the 1995 Systems-Thinking-in-Action Conference: 'Building Organization Learning Infrastructures', Boston, 18–20 Sept. 1985.

JONES, DANIEL T., 'Measuring up to the Japanese: Lessons from the Motor Industry', *University of Wales: Business and Economics Review*, 5 (1990), 23–7.

JU, YANAN, 'Supremacy of Human Relationships: A Japanese Organizational Model', in Kovacic, *New Approaches*, 67–85.

JUECK, JOHN E., 'Business Education: Some Popular Models', *The Library Quarterly*, 43:4 (Oct. 1973), 281–92.

JUNNE, GERD, 'Competitiveness and the Impact of Change: Applications of "High Technologies"', in Katzenstein, *Industry and Politics in West Germany*, 249–74.

JÜRGENS, ULRICH, 'National and Company Differences in Organizing Production Work in the Car Industry', in Kogut, *Country Competitiveness*, 106–23.

——and MALSCH, THOMAS, 'New Production Concepts in West German Car Plants', in Tolliday and Zeitlin, *The Automobile Industry and its Workers*, 258–81.

KAGONO, TADAO, *et al.*, 'Mechanistic vs. Organic Management Systems: A Comparative Study of Adaptive Patterns of U.S. and Japanese Firms', reprint from Kobe University's *Annals of the School of Business Administration*, 25 (1981), 119–41.

KATZ, HARRY, 'Policy Debates over Work Reorganization in North American

Unions', in Hyman and Streeck, *New Technology and Industrial Relations*, 220–32.

KATZ, HARRY, 'Recent Developments in US Auto Labour Relations', in Tolliday and Zeitlin, *The Automobile Industry and its Workers*, 282–304.

KAWAHITO, KIYOSHI, 'Relative Profitability of the US Japanese Steel Industry', *Columbia Journal of World Business*, 19:3 (Fall 1984), 13–17.

KAWANISHI, HIROSUKE, 'The Reality of Enterprise Unionism', in McCormack and Sugimoto, *Democracy in Contemporary Japan*, 138–55.

KECK, OTTO, 'The National System for Technical Innovation in Germany', in Nelson, *National Innovation Systems*, 115–56.

KERN, HORST, and SCHUMANN, MICHAEL, 'New Concepts of Production in West German Plants', in Katzenstein, *Industry and Politics in West Germany*, 87–112.

KIENBAUM, JOACHIM, and PASCHEK, PETER, 'Das beste Sprungbrett ist ein breites Wissen', *Deutsche Universitäts-Zeitung* (1981), 854–7.

KIKKAWA, TAKEO, 'Do Japanese Corporations Derive their Competitive Edge from the Intervention of Government, Corporate Groups, and Industry Associations?: A Rethinking of Conventional Views', *Annals of the Institute of Social Science*, University of Tokyo, 36 (1994), 33–56.

KIKUCHI, KOZO, 'Industrial Relations at the Plant and Shopfloor Level in the British Steel Industry: A Case Study of the Bloom and Billet Mill of the British Steel Corporation', *Annals of the Institute of Social Science*, University of Tokyo, 24 (1982–3), 1–54.

————'The Japanese Enterprise Union and its Functions', in Tokunaga and Bergmann, *Industrial Relations in Transition*, 171–94.

KOBAYASHI, KAORU, 'The Global Corporation in a Global Society—Japanese Experience', *Jaims Journal*, 1:1 (1992), 2–21.

KOBAYASHI, YOTARO, 'Quality Control in Japan: The Case of Fuji-Xerox', in Sato and Hoshino, *The Anatomy of Japanese Business*, 164–97.

KOCH, JOHANNES, 'Auf dem Weg zur neuen Qualität der Arbeit?' *Die Mitbestimmung*, 33:11 (1987), 703–4.

KOGUT, BRUCE, 'National Organizing Principles of Work and the Erstwhile Dominance of the American Multinational Corporation', *Industrial and Corporate Change*, 1:2 (1992), 285–326.

————and PARKINSON, DAVID, 'The Diffusion of American Organizing Principles to Europe', in Kogut, *Country Competitiveness*, 185–205.

KONZ, STEPHAN, 'Quality Circles: An Annotated Bibliography', *Quality Progress*, 14:4 (1981), 30–3.

KORETZ, GENE, 'Economic Trends: A Poor Year for U.S. Households', *Business Week* (6 Mar. 1995), 26.

KOSHIRO, KAZUTOSHI, 'The Organisation of Work and Internal Labour Market Flexibility in Japanese Industrial Relations', in OECD, *New Directions in Work Organisation*, 113–32.

KRAUS, WILLY, 'Japanisch-deutsche Beziehungen und Zusammenarbeit in den Wirtschaftswissenschaften', in Busse von Colbe *et al.*, *Betriebswirtschaftslehre*, 3–12.

KRUGMAN, PAUL, 'Technology and Changing Comparative Advantage in the Pacific Region', in Soesastro and Pangestu, *Technological Challenge in the Asia-Pacific Economy*, 25–37.

KUDO, AKIRA, 'A Partnership of Imbalance: Changes in Japan-European Economic Relations', *Annals of the Institute of Social Science*, University of Tokyo, 36 (1994), 57–91.

KUHN, AXEL, and PIELOK, THOMAS, 'Produktivitäts-Management mit Hilfe von Prozessketten', in Wildemann, *Qualität und Produktivität*, 26–42.

KUMAZAWA, MAKOTO, 'Japan's Corporate Society and Democratic Education', *AMPO: Japan-Asia Quarterly Review*, 25:1 (Apr. 1993), 26–9.

KUTTNER, ROBERT, 'Needed: A Two-Way Social Contract in the Workplace', *Business Week* (10 July 1995).

KUWAYAMA, TAKAMI, 'The Reference Other Orientation', in Rosenberger, *Japanese Sense of Self*, 121–51.

LAWRENCE, PETER, 'German Management: At the Interface between Eastern and Western Europe', in Calori and de Woot, *A European Model of Management*, 133–64.

——— '"In Another Country" or the Relativization of Management Learning', *Management Learning*, 25:4 (1994), 543–642.

LAZONICK, WILLIAM, 'Organizational Capabilities in American Industry: The Rise and Decline of Managerial Capitalism', paper, Business History Conference, 23 Mar. 1990, Johns Hopkins University.

———and West, Jonathan, 'Organizational Integration and Competitive Advantage: Explaining Strategy and Performance in American Industry', paper, Fifth International Week on the History of Enterprise, Varese, Italy, 16 Dec. 1993.

LEBRA, TAKIE SUGIYAMA, 'Self in Japanese Culture', in Rosenberger, *Japanese Sense of Self*, 105–20.

LEMINSKY, GERHARD, 'Erfahrungen bei der Verwertung und Umsetzung von Wissenschaft im Arbeitsnehmerinteresse', in Bamberg, Kröger, and Kuhlmann, *Hochschulen und Gewerkschaften*, 367–77.

LESIEUR, G., and PUCKETT, E. S., 'The Scanlon Plan has Proved Itself', *Human Relations*, 9 (1966), 3–19.

Bibliography

LEVINE, DAVID M., 'Business Statistics Curricula Lack Quality', *Quality Progress*, 25:7 (Jul.-Dec. 1992), 77-9.

LEWIN, DAVID, 'Work Organisation, Labour-Management Relations and Participation Practices in United States Enterprises: A Critique and Assessment', in OECD, *New Directions*, 197-221.

LICHTENSTEIN, NELSON, 'Great Expectations: The Promise of Industrial Jurisprudence and its Demise, 1930-1960', in Lichtenstein and Harris, *Industrial Democracy in America*, 113-42.

————'Reutherism on the Shop-Floor: Union Strategy and Shop-Floor Conflict in the USA 1946-70', in Tolliday and Zeitlin, *The Automobile Industry and its Workers*, 121-43.

LIMPRECHT, JAMES A. and HAYES, ROBERT, 'Germany's World Class Manufacturers', *Harvard Business Review* (Nov.-Dec. 1982), 137-45.

LINCOLN, JAMES R., 'Work Organization in Japan and the United States', in Kogut, *Country Competitiveness*, 54-74.

LINK, WERNER, 'Building Coalitions: Non-governmental German-American Linkages', in Maier, *The Marshall Plan*, 282-330.

LITTERER, JOSEPH A., 'Systematic Management: The Search for Order and Integration', *Business History Review*, 35 (Spring 1961), 450-73.

LOCKE, ROBERT R., 'Education and Entrepreneurship: A Historian's View', in Brown and Rose, *Entrepreneurship, Networks and Modern Business*, 55-75.

————'Business Education in Germany: Past Systems and Current Practice', *Business History Review*, 49:2 (Spring 1985), 232-54.

————'Higher Education and Management: Their Relational Changes in the 20th Century', in Kawabe and Daito, *Education and Training*, 26-52.

————'Management Education in West Germany and Great Britain', in Joynt and Warner, *Managing in Different Cultures*, 166-214.

————'Mastering the Lingo', *The Times Higher Educational Supplement* (4 May 1991).

————and MEULEAU, MARC, 'France et Allemagne: Deux approaches de l'enseignement de la gestion', *Revue française de gestion: Les racines de l'entreprise*, 70 (Sept.-Oct. 1988), 186-202.

————————'Gestionnaires: La vogue de l'économie d'entreprise', *Le Monde* (25 May 1989).

LOCKYER, KEITH G., OAKLAND, JOHN S., and DUPREY, CLIVE H., 'Work Study Techniques in UK Manufacturing Industry', *OMEGA: The International Journal of Management*, 11:3 (1983), 293-302.

LODISE, CARMELO, 'Big U.S. Corporations are Giving Up on Economists', *The News* (26 Mar. 1993), 28.

LONGWORTH, R. C., and STEIN, SHARMAN, 'Miseries of the Middle Class: American Dream is Endangered', *San Francisco Chronicle* (16 Sept. 1995).

LORENZ, EDWARD, and WILKINSON, FRANK, 'The Shipbuilding Industry 1880–1965', in Elbaum and Lazonick, *The Decline of the British Economy*, 109–34.

LÜCK, WOLFGANG, 'Das Management-Oktogon. Ein Vegleich: Japanisches und Deutsches Management', in Busse von Colbe *et al.*, *Betriebswirtschaftslehre*, 192–207.

McCLAIN, DAVID, 'Changing Patterns of Managerial Education in Japan and the United States', paper, AUBER 1992 Conference, Honolulu, 13 Oct. 1992.

McCORMACK, GAVAN, and SUGIMOTO, YOSHIO, 'Democracy and Japan', in McCormack and Sugimoto, *Democracy in Contemporary Japan*, 9–18.

McCRAW, THOMAS K., 'From Partners to Competitors: An Overview of the Period since World War II', in McCraw, *America versus Japan*, 1–33.

McMURRAY, ROBERT N., 'The Case for Benevolent Autocracy', *Harvard Business Review* (Jan.-Feb. 1958), 82–95.

MAIER, CHARLES S., 'The Politics of Productivity: Foundation of America's International Economic Policy after World War II', in Peter J. Katzenstein (ed.), *Between Power and Plenty: The Foreign Economic Policies of Advanced Industrial States* (Madison: University of Wisconsin Press, 1978).

——'Society as Factory: Postscript, Ideologies of Industrial Management since the Depression', in id., *In Search of Stability*.

MARROW, A. J., and DAVID, G., 'The Turnover Problem: Why do they Quit', *Personnel Administration*, 1 (1951).

MARTIN, WILLIAM G., 'The World-Systems Perspective in Perspective: Assessing the Attempt to Move Beyond Nineteenth-Century Eurocentric Conceptions', *Review*, 18:2 (Spring 1994), 145–85.

MARUYAMA, MAGOROH, 'Mindscapes, Workers, and Management: Japan and the U.S.A.', in Lee and Schwendiman, *Japanese Management*, 53–71.

MARUYAMA, MASAO, 'From Carnal Literature to Carnal Politics', in Maruyama, *Thought and Behaviour*, 245–68.

——'Theory and Psychology of Ultra-Nationalism', in Maruyama, *Thought and Behaviour*, 1–25.

——'Thoughts and Behaviour Patterns of Japan's Wartime Leaders', in Maruyama, *Thought and Behaviour*, 84–135.

MAURICE, MARC, SORGE, ARNDT, WARNER, MALCOLM, 'Societal Differences in Organizing Manufacturing Units: A Comparison of France, West Germany, and Great Britain', *Organization Studies*, 1:2 (1980), 59–80.

MAYER, MICHAEL, and WHITTINGTON, RICHARD, 'Managing the Large Diversified Firm in Contemporary Europe: Triumphant Multidivisional or Stubborn Holding Company?' paper given at Workshop on Social Constitution of

Economic Actors, in European Science Foundation's EMOT Programme, Berlin, 22–4 Apr. 1994.

MAYO, MARLENE J., 'Psychological Disarmament: American Wartime Planning for the Education and Re-education of Defeated Japan, 1943–45', in *The Occupation of Japan*, 21–127.

Meany, George, 'What Labor Means by "More"', *Fortune* (Mar. 1955), 92–5, 272–9.

MEISSNER, HANS GÜNTHER, 'Sicherung der internationalen Wettbewerbsfähigkeit als Managementfunktion', *ZfbF*, 34 (Jan. 1982), 25–33.

MEULEAU, MARC, 'Les HEC: D'un diplôme marginal à la célébrité scolaire et professionnelle (1881–1980)', paper delivered at the Colloquium on the History of Management, Paris, 11–12 March 1988.

MEYER-DOHM, PROF., 'Einschätzung der VW-Zirkel aus Unternehmenssicht', *Die Mitbestimmung*, 33:11 (1987), 681–2.

MINISTERIUM FÜR WIRTSCHAFT, Technologie und Verkehr des Landes Sachsen-Anhalt (ed.), 'Chemie in Sachsen-Anhalt: Magnet für Folgeinvestitionen', *Invest* (Mar. 1994), no page numbers.

MOGWITZ, GERHARD, 'Qualitätszirkel und Mitbestimmung am Arbeitsplatz', *Die Mitbestimmung*, 33:11 (1987), 683–5.

MONDEN, YASUHIRO, and HAMADA, KAZUKI, 'Target Costing and Kaizen Costing in Japanese Automobile Companies', *Journal of Management Accounting Research*, 3 (Fall 1992), 1–19.

MORI, AKIO, and ALBACH, HORST, 'Das Finanzierungsverhalten japanischer und deutscher Unternehmen', in Busse von Colbe *et al.*, *Betriebswirtschaftslehre*, 103–45.

MORRIS-SUZUKI, TESSA, 'Sources of Conflict in the "Information Society"', in McCormack and Sugimoto, *Democracy in Contemporary Japan*, 76–89.

MÜLLER-JENTSCH, WALTHER, 'The Changing Balance Between Workplace Representation and Industrywide Representation in West Germany', in Tokunaga and Bergmann, *Industrial Relations in Transition*, 197–208.

———REHERMANN, KATHARINA, and SPERLING, HANS JOACHIM, 'Socio-Technical Rationalisation and Negotiated Work Organisation: Recent Trends in Germany', in OECD, *New Directions*, 93–112.

MUTO, ICHIYO, 'Class Struggle in Postwar Japan', in McCormack and Sugimoto, *Democracy in Contemporary Japan*, 114–37.

NAKAGAWA, KEIICHIRO, 'Business Management in Historical Perspective: Lifetime Employment in Japan', unpublished paper, n.d.

———'The "Learning Industrial Revolution" and Business Management', in Yui and Nagagawa, *Japanese Management*, 1–28.

NAGAOKA, KATSUYUKI, 'The Japanese System of Academic Management Education', in Engwall and Gunnarsson, *Management Studies*, 138–54.

NAJITA, TETSUO, 'Presidential Address: Reflections on Modernity and Modernization', *Journal of Asian Studies*, 52:4 (Nov. 1993), 845–53.

NEIPP, GERHARD, 'Forschung und Entwicklung: Qualitätsmanagement', in Wildemann, *Fabrikplanung*, 265–77.

NELSON, RICHARD R., 'National Innovation Systems: A Retrospective on a Study', *Industrial and Corporate Change*, 1:2 (1992), 347–74.

NEUBURGER, HUGH, 'Co-Determination: The West German Experiment at a New State', *Columbia Journal of World Business*, 13:4 (Winter 1978), 104–10.

NEUSS, ANNE, 'Selbstbestimmung statt Mitbestimmung?' *Die Mitbestimmung*, 33:11 (1987), 697–9.

NISHI, TOSHIO, 'Education during the Meiji-Taisho-Showa Periods', in *The Occupation of Japan*, 15–21.

NOMURA, MASAMI, 'Myths of the Toyota System', *AMPO: Japan–Asia Quarterly*, 25:1 (Apr., 1994), 18–25.

NOWOTNY, OTTO H., 'American vs. European Management Philosophy', *Harvard Business Review* (Mar.–Apr. 1964), 101–8.

OBERBECK, HERBERT, and BAETHGE, MARTIN, 'Computer and Pinstripes: Financial Institutions', in Katzenstein, *Industry and Politics*, 275–303.

ODAKA, KUNIO, 'Traditional Democracy in Japanese Industry', *Industrial Relations: A Journal of Economy and Society*, 3:2 (Feb. 1964), 95–103.

OKAMURA, TETSUO, 'I've already Given Up', *AMPO: Japan–Asia Quarterly Review*, 25:1 (Apr. 1994), 30–5.

OKAYAMA, REIKO, 'Industrial Relations in the Japanese Automobile Industry 1945–70: The Case of Toyota', in Tolliday and Zeitlin, *The Automobile Industry and its Workers*, 168–89.

OTAKE, HIDEO, 'The *Zaikai* under the Occupation: The Formation and Transformation of Managerial Councils', in Ward and Sakamoto, *Democratizing Japan*, 366–80.

PARK, SUNG-JO, 'Labour-Management Consultation as a Japanese Type of Participation: An International Comparison', in Tokunaga and Bergmann, *Industrial Relations in Transition*, 153–70.

PARKER, MIKE, 'Industrial Relations Myth and Shop-Floor Reality: The "Team Concept" in the Auto Industry', in Lichtenstein and Harris, *Industrial Democracy in America*, 249–75.

PASCALE, RICHARD, and ROHLEN, THOMAS P., 'The Mazda Turnaround', *Journal of Japanese Studies*, 9:2 (Summer 1983), 219–63.

PERLITZ, MANFRED, 'Die Aufrechterhaltung der internationalen Wettbewerbsfähigkeit als Verpflichtung für Unternehmen und Gesamtwirtschaft', in Dichtl, *Standort Bundesrepublik Deutschland*, 9–49.

PERLITZ, MANFRED, 'Culture and Strategy', *European Business Journal*, 6:2 (1994), 55–62.

———'Why Most Strategies Fail Today: The Need for Strategy Innovations', *European Management Journal*, 11:1 (1993), 114–21.

———and LÖBER, HELGE, 'Brauchen Unternehmen zum Innovieren Krisen?' *Zeitschrift für Betriebswirtschaft*, 55 (1984), 424–50.

PIPER, RÜDIGER, 'Division and Unification of German Business Administration and Management Education', in Engwall and Gunnarsson, *Management Studies*, 116–37.

PÖPPEL, JOACHIM, 'Eine neue Giesserei am Industriestandort Bundesrepublik Deutschland', in Wildemann, *Fabrikplanung*, 136–43.

PORTER, MICHAEL E., 'The Competitive Advantage of Nations', *Harvard Business Review* (Mar.–Apr. 1990), 73–93.

POUSETTE, THOMAS, 'Services in Industry—An International Comparison', in Eliasson *et al.*, *The Knowledge-Based Information Economy*, 135–56.

PREISS, HANS, 'Gewerkschaften und Erziehung', in Bamberg, Kröger, and Kuhlmann, *Hochschulen und Gewerkschaften*, 501–3.

'Problem Lösung—Japan: "Zeit des Gaijin"', *Manager Magazin*, 24:4, 176–93.

PROKESCH, STEVEN E., 'Xerox Halts Japanese March', *New York Times* (6 Nov. 1985).

RAISER, THOMAS, 'The Legal Constitution of Business Enterprises in the Federal Republic of Germany', *Annals of the Institute of Social Science*, University of Tokyo, 34 (Mar. 1993), 27–46.

RAMERTH, EDITH, 'Qualitätszirkel—Stein der Weisen?', *Die Mitbestimmung*, 33:11 (1987), 673–5.

REED, MICHAEL I., 'Organizations and Modernity: Continuity and Discontinuity in Organization Theory', in Hassard and Parker, *Postmodernism and Organizations*, 163–82.

———and ANTHONY, PETER, 'Professionalizing Management and Managing Professionalization: British Management in the 1980s', *Journal of Management Studies*, 29:5 (Sept. 1992), 591–612.

REHDER, ROBERT R., 'The Japanese Lean System vs. Volvo's Uddevalla System', *Columbia Journal of World Business* (Summer 1992), 57–69.

———'Japanese Transplants: In Search of a Balanced and Broader Perspective', *Columbia Journal of World Business* (Winter 1989), 17–28.

———'Sayonara, Uddevalla?', *Business Horizons* (Nov.–Dec. 1992), 8–18.

REITSPERGER, WOLF, 'British Employees: Responding to Japanese Management Philosophies' *Journal of Management Studies* 23:5 (Sept. 1986), 564–86.

————and DANIEL, SHIRLEY, 'A Comparison of Quality Attitudes in the USA and Japan: Empirical Evidence', *Journal of Management Studies* (28 Nov. 1991), 585–99.

——————————'Management Control Systems for J.I.T.: An Empirical Comparison of Japan and the U.S.', *Journal of International Business Studies*, 22:4 (1991), 603–18.

RENNES, PIERRE, 'La Sélection des ouvriers et des employés', *Revue de psychologie appliquée*, 4:1 (Jan. 1953), 23–37.

RHODES, LARRY, 'Legal Bases for Vocational Mediation in Japanese Schools', unpublished paper, University of Hawaii at Manoa, Department of Political science, n.d.

ROACH, STEPHEN S., 'Longer Hours, Harder Lives: Battle Lines are Drawn in U.S. Productivity Clash', *Japan Times* (16 Mar. 1995).

ROKURO, HIDAKA, 'The Crisis of Postwar Democracy', in McCormack and Sugimoto, *Democracy in Contemporary Japan*, 228–46.

ROSENBAUM, HORST-WERNER, 'Marketingstrategien amerikanischer, japanischer und deutscher Unternehmungen der Unterhaltungselektronik—dargestellt an drei repräsentativen Beispielen', *ZfbF*, 34 (Jan. 1982), 67–9.

SAMUELSON, ROBERT J., 'The Death of Management', *Newsweek* (10 May 1993), 55.

————'What Good are B-Schools', *Newsweek* (14 May 1990), 45.

SCHIEB, PIERRE-ALAIN, 'Des modèles nationaux ou un modèle européen?' *La Revue Française de Gestion* (Mar.–Apr.–May 1990), 105–10.

SCHIEFER, FRIEDRICH, 'Faktoren der internationalen Wettbewerbsfähigkeit—aufgezeigt am Vergleich USA, Japan, Deutschland', *ZfbF*, 34 (Jan. 1982), 34–51.

SCHNEIDEWIND, DIETER, 'Zielvorstellungen und Inhalte innerbetrieblicher Information in deutschen und japanischen Betrieben', in Busse von Colbe *et al.*, *Betriebswirtschaftslehre*, 208–16.

SHIMABUKURO, YOSHIAKIU, *Consensus Management in Japanese Industry* (Tokyo: I.S.S., Inc., 1982).

SHIMADA, HARUO, 'Japanese Industrial Relations—A New General Model?—A Survey of the English-Language Literature', in Shirai, *Contemporary Industrial Relations*, 3–27.

SHIMIZU, YASUHARU, 'Japanisches Management: Wandlungen und Internationalisierung', in Busse von Colbe *et al.*, *Betriebswirtschaftslehre*, 173–91.

SHIMOKAWA, KOICHI, 'Product and Labour Strategies in Japan', in Tolliday and Zeitlin, *The Automobile Industry and its Workers*, 224–43.

SHIRAI, TAISHIRO, 'A Supplement: Characteristics of Japanese Managements and their Personnel Policies', in Shirai, *Contemporary Industrial Relations*, 369–82.

Bibliography

SHIRAI, TAISHIRO, 'A Theory of Enterprise Unionism', in Shirai, *Contemporary Industrial Relations*.

SOHINGER, JASMINKA, and RUBINFELD, DANIEL, 'European Labor Markets: The Eastern Dimension', in Ulman, Eichengreen, and Dickens, *Labor and an Integrated Europe*, 271–85.

SORGE, ARNDT, 'Engineers in Management: A Study of the British, German and French Traditions', *Journal of General Management*, 5 (1979), 46–57.

——and Streeck, Wolfgang, 'Industrial Relations and Technical Change: The Case for an Extended Perspective', in Hyman and Streeck, *New Technology and Industrial Relations*, 19–47.

SOSKICE, DAVID, and SCHETTKAT, RONALD, 'West German Labor Market Institutions and East German Transformation', in Ulman, Eichengreen, and Dickens, *Labor and an Integrated Europe*, 102–27.

SOURS, MARTIN, 'The Influence of Japanese Culture on Japanese Management Systems', in Lee and Schwendiman, *Japanese Management*, 27–38.

STARCHER, RONALD, 'Mismatched Management Techniques: Total Quality Management and Management by Objectives are a Counter-Productive Combination', *Quality Progress*, 25:12 (Dec. 1992), 49–51.

STRAUSS-WIECZOREK, GERLIND, 'Taylorismus plus Sozialtechnik statt Mitbestimmung am Arbeitsplatz', *Die Mitbestimmung*, 33:11 (1987), 676–8.

STREECK, WOLFGANG, 'Industrial Relations and Industrial Change: The Restructuring of the World Automobile Industry in the 1970s and 1980s', *Economic and Industrial Democracy*, 8 (1987), 437–62.

——'The Rise and Decline of Neocorporatism', in Ulman, Eichengreen, and Dickens, *Labor and an Integrated Europe*, 80–101.

——'Successful Adjustment to Turbulent Markets: The Automobile Industry', in Katzenstein, *Industry and Politics*, 113–56.

SUGAYAMA, SHINJI, 'Business Education, Training, and the Emergence of the "Japanese Employment System"', in Kawabe and Daito, *Education and Training*, 147–73.

SUGIMOTO, YOSHIO, 'The Manipulative Bases of "Consensus" in Japan', in McCormack and Sugimoto, *Democracy in Contemporary Japan*, 65–75.

SVEJNAR, JAN, 'Codetermination and Productivity: Empirical Evidence from the Federal Republic of Germany', in D. Jones and Svenjnar, *Participatory and Self-Managed Firms*, 199–212.

SWENSON, PETER, 'Union Politics, the Welfare State, and Intraclass Conflict in Sweden and Germany', in Golden and Pontusson, *Bargaining for Change*, 45–76.

TABATA, HIROKUNI, 'Changes in Plant-Level Trade Union Organizations: A Case

Study of the Automobile Industry', *Annals of the Institute of Social Science*, University of Tokyo, 30 (1988), 57–88.

TAKAGI, IKURO, 'Japanese Trade Unions' Responses to Microelectronization', in Tokunaga and Bergmann, *Industrial Relations in Transition*, 235–51.

TALLARD, MICHÈLE, 'Bargaining over New Technology: A Comparison of France and West Germany', in Hyman and Streeck, *New Technology and Industrial Relations*, 284–96.

THELEN, KATHLEEN, 'Codetermination and Industrial Adjustment in the German Steel Industry: A Comparative Interpretation', *California Management Review*, 29:3 (Spring 1987), 134–48.

——'The Politics of Flexibility in the German Metalworking Industries', in Golden and Pontusson, *Bargaining for Change*, 215–46.

THIELBAR, RITA, and LOHNAU, ROLF, 'Qualitätszirkel und TQM—im Mittelpunkt der Mensch? Ein Bericht über den 6. Deutschen Quality Circle Kongress in Hannover', *Die Mitbestimmung*, 33:11 (1987), 721–4.

THIMM, ALFRED L., 'Codetermination and Industrial Adjustment in February 1987: A Few Comments on Ms Thelen's "A Comparative Interpretation"', *California Management Review*, 29:3 (Spring 1987), 149-53.

THOMPSON, PAUL, 'Postmodernism: Fatal Distraction', in Hassard and Parker, *Postmodernism and Organizations*, 183–203.

——and SEDERBLAD, PER, 'The Swedish Model of Work Organization in Transition', in Elger and Smith, *Global Japanization?*, 238–65.

TINNIN, DAVID B., 'Ford is on a Roll in Europe', *Fortune* (18 Oct. 1982), 182–91.

TOBIN, JOSEPH, 'Japanese Preschools and the Pedagogy of Selfhood', in Rosenberger, *Japanese Sense of Self*, 21–39.

TOKUNAGA, SHIGEYOSHI, 'The Structure of the Japanese Labour Market', in Tokunaga and Bergmann, *Industrial Relations in Transition*, 25–56.

TOTSUKA, HIDEO, 'Building Japan's Corporate Society', *AMPO: Japan–Asia Quarterly Review*, 25:1 (Apr. 1994), 11–17.

——'Transformation of Japanese Industrial Relations: A Case Study of the Automobile Industry', *Annals of the Institute of Social Science*, University of Tokyo, 35 (1993), 69–90.

TRIVELLATO, PAOLO, 'Some Notes on Training and Skills Formation in Italy and Japan', *Annals of the Institute of Social Science*, University of Tokyo, 36 (1994), 1–31.

TURCQ, DOMINIQUE, 'Is there a US Company Management Style in Europe?' in Calori and de Woot, *A European Model of Management*, 82–111.

TURNER, LOWELL, 'Prospects for Worker Participation in Management in the

Bibliography

Single Market', in Ulman, Eichengreen, and Dickens, *Labor and an Integrated Europe*, 45–79.

VERDIER, SYLVIA, 'Studenten und Gewerkschaften', in Bamberg, Kröger, and Kuhlmann, *Hochschulen und Gewerkschaften*, 415–22.

VIRCHOW, JÖRG, and FLARUP, JOCHEN, 'Zusammenarbeit zwischen Gewerkschaften und Hochschulen in Berlin', in Bamberg, Kröger, and Kuhlmann, *Hochschulen und Gewerkschaften*, 183–99.

VOLPATO, GIUSEPPE, 'The Automobile Industry in Transition: Product Market Changes and Firm Strategies in the 1970s and 1980s', in Tolliday and Zeitlin, *The Automobile Industry and its Workers*, 193–223.

WÄCHTER, HARTMUT, 'Besprechung und wissenschaftstheoretische Überlegungen zu einem Buch über die Geschichte der Arbeitsforschung in Deutschland von R.-W. Hoffmann', *Arbeitspapier 4*, Universität Trier—FB IV.

——'Praxisbezug des wirtschaftswissenschaftlichen Studiums', *Expertise für die Studienreformkommission: Wirtschaftswissenschaften* (Sept. 1980).

——'Vom Personalwesen zum Strategic Human Resource Management: Ein Zustandsbericht anhand der neueren Literatur', in Staehle and Conrad, *Managementforschung 2*, 313–40.

——and STENGELHOFEN, THEO, 'Human Resource Management in a Unified Germany', *Employee Relations*, 14:4 (1992), 1–37.

WARNECKE, HANS-JÜRGEN, 'Gesetzmässigkeiten in der Produktion', in Wildemann, *Fabrikplanung*, 102–9.

WEIERMAIR, KLAUS, 'Globalization, the Diffusion of Technology and New Forms of Work Organization', unpublished paper, Faculty of Adminstrative Studies, York University, Toronto, Canada.

——'On the Transferability of Management Systems: The Case of Japan', in Buckley and Clegg, *Multinational Enterprises*, 56–76.

WHITLEY, RICHARD, 'Formal Knowledge and Management Education', in Engwall and Gunnarsson, *Management Studies*, 167–90.

——'On the Nature of Managerial Tasks and Skills: Their Distinguishing Characteristics and Organization', *Journal of Management Studies*, 26:3 (May 1989), 209–24.

WHITTAKER, D. HUGH, 'New Technology and the Organization of Work: British and Japanese Factories', in Kogut, *Country Competitiveness*, 124–39.

'Who's Excellent Now?' *Business Week* (5 Nov. 1984), 76–86.

WILDEMANN, HORST, 'Fabrik in der Fabrik durch Fertigungssegmentierung', in Wildemann, *Fabrikplanung*, 15–69.

——'Die "normale" Blindleistung in der Unternehmerorganisation', unpublished, 1–11.

WILL, GEORGE, 'CEOs—Capitalist Heroes?', *Honolulu Advertiser*, 15 May 1994.

WILLIAMS, KARL, MITSUI, ITSUTOMO, and HASLAM, COLIN, 'How far from Japan? A Case Study of Japanese Press Shop Practice and Management Calculation', in Elger and Smith, *Global Japanization?*, 60–90.

WILLIAMSON, OLIVER E., 'Transaction Cost Economics and Organization Theory', *Industrial and Corporate Change*, 2:2 (1993), 107–56.

WOOD, STEPHEN, 'Between Fordism and Flexibility? The US Car Industry', in Hyman and Streeck, *New Technology and Industrial Relations*, 101–27.

YAMAMOTO, KIYOSHI, 'The Beginnings of the Labor Movement in Postwar Japan', *Annals of the Institute of Social Science* (March 1993), 101–40.

——'"Free Flow-Line," Workers, and Robots in Japanese Assembly Industries', *Annals of the Institute of Social Science*, University of Tokyo, 35 (1993), 1–38.

——'The "Japanese-style Industrial Relations" and an "Informal" Employee Organization: A Case Study of the Ohgi-kai at T Electric', *Annals of the Institute of Social Science*, University of Tokyo, 32 (1990), 155–215.

YAMAZUMI, MASAMI, 'Educational Democracy versus State Control', in McCormack and Sugimoto, *Democracy in Contemporary Japan*, 90–113.

YANG, CHARLES Y., 'Demystifying Japanese Management Practices: A Closer Look Reveals the Drawbacks as well as Advantage of Management Japanstyle', *Harvard Business Review*, special report, No. 6 (Nov.–Dec. 1984), 172–82.

YASUMURO, KEN'ICHI, 'Engineers as Functional Alternatives to Entrepreneurs in Japanese Industrialisation', in Brown and Rose, *Entrepreneurship*, 76–101.

YATES, CHARLOTTE, 'North American Autoworkers' Response to Restructuring', in Golden and Pontusson, *Bargaining for Change*, 111–45.

YONEYAMA, ETSUO, 'Japanese Subsidiaries: Strengths and Weaknesses', in Calori and de Woot, *A European Model of Management*, 112–32.

YOSHIDA, KOSAKU, 'The Joy of Work: Optimizing Service Quality through Education and Training', *Quality Progress*, 26:11 (Nov. 1993), 29–33.

——'New Economic Principles in America—Competition and Cooperation: A Comparative Study of the U.S. and Japan', *Columbia Journal of World Business*, 26:4 (Winter 1992), 1–15.

YOSHIYAMA, HIROKICHI, 'The Role of Japanese Businesses in the Establishment of a New Industrial Order', *Columbia Journal of World Business*, 20:4 (Winter 1985), 49–51.

ZALEZNIK, ABRAHAM, 'The Human Dilemmas of Leadership', *Harvard Business Review* (Jul.–Aug. 1963), 51 ff.

ZINK, KLAUS J., 'Qualitätsmanagement als Herausforderung', in Wildemann, *Fabrikplanung*, 278–96.

Bibliography

BOOKS AND THESES

ABEGGLEN, JAMES, and STALK, JR., George, *Kaisha: The Japanese Corporation* (New York: Basic Books, Harper Collins, 1988).

ADAMS, JOSEPH, 'The "British Disease" and the "Japanization" of British Industry: Conjuncture or Continuity in World History', Master's thesis (University of Hawaii at Manoa, 1995).

ALBERT, MICHEL, *Capitalism against Capitalism* (London: FWEW, 1993).

ALLAIS, MAURICE, *A la recherche d'une discipline économique* (Paris: St-Cloud, 1945).

ALLEN, GEORGE C., *The British Disease* (London: Institute of Economic Affairs, 1979).

ALTSHULER, ALAN, et al., *The Future of the Automobile: The Report of the MIT's International Automobile Program* (London: Allen & Unwin, 1984).

American Management Association (eds.), *Operations Research: Mittel moderner Unternehmensführung* (Essen: WKV, 1958).

ANTHONY, PETER D., *The Foundation of Management* (London: Tavistock Publications, 1986)

————*The Ideology of Work* (London: Tavistock, 1977).

AROGYASWAMY, BERNARD, and SIMMONS, RONALD, *Value-Directed Management: Organizations, Customers, and Quality* (Westport, Conn.: Quorum Books, Greenwood, 1993).

Ashridge Management Research Group, *The Quest for the International Manager: A Survey of Global Human Resource Strategies* (Ashridge: School of Management, 1990).

ATKINSON, RICK, *The Long Gray Line: From West Point to Vietnam and After— The Turbulent Odyssey of the Class of 1966* (New York: Simon & Schuster, 1989).

ATSUO, ISHIWARA, *Japanese Management Thinking and Practice and the Internationalisation Pressure* (Singapore: National University of Japanese Studies, 1989).

BAALEN, PETER J. VAN, *Management en Hoger Onderwijs* (Delft: Ebuiron Delft, 1995).

BAKKE, EDWARD W., *Unions, Management, and the Public* (New York: Harcourt, Brace, 1948).

BAMBERG, HANS-DIETER, KRÖGER, HANS-JÜRGEN, and KUHLMANN, REINHARD (eds.), *Hochschulen und Gewerkschaften: Erfahrungen, Analysen und Perspektiven gewerkschaftlicher Kooperationspraxis* (Cologne, 1979)

BARNETT, CORELLI, *The Audit of War: The Illusion and Reality of Britain as a Great Nation* (London: Macmillan, 1986).

BEAUCHAMP, EDWARD R., and VARDAMAN, JAMES M., JR., *Japanese Education since 1945: A Documentary Study* (London: Sharpe, 1994)

BERGER, PETER L., and LUCKMANN, THOMAS, *The Social Construction of Reality* (New York: Doubleday, 1967).

BERGHAHN, VÖLKER R., *Germany and the Approach of War in 1914* (New York: St. Martin's, 1993).

BERLANSTEIN, LENARD R. (ed.), *Rethinking Labor History: Essays on Discourse and Class Analysis* (Urbana: University of Illinois Press, 1993).

BERNSTEIN, MICHAEL A., and ADLER, DAVID E. (eds.), *Understanding American Economic Decline: A Structural and Institutional Approach* (Cambridge: Cambridge University Press, 1994).

BISMARCK, OTTO VON, *Gesammelte Werke*, 12 vols. (Berlin, 1929).

BISSON, T. A., *Zaibatsu Dissolution in Japan* (Berkeley: University of California Press, 1954).

BLOCK, PETER, *The Empowered Manager: Positive Political Skills at Work* (San Francisco: Jossey-Bass, 1991).

BODDEWYN, J. J. (ed.), *European Industrial Managers* (White Plains, NY: International Arts and Science Press, 1976).

BOLLING, G. FREDRIC, *The Art of Achieving Quality* (Aldershot: Gower, Ashgate, 1994).

BOLTANSKI, LUC, *The Making of a Class: Cadres in French Society* (Cambridge: Cambridge University Press, 1987). First published as *Les Cadres: La formation d'un groupe social* (Paris: Editions de minuit, 1982).

BOSSUAT, GÉRARD, *L'Aide américaine, la France, et la construction européenne, 1944–1954*, 2 vols. (Paris: Minister of Finance, 1992).

BOTTERY, MIKE, *The Ethics of Educational Management* (London: Cassell, 1992).

BOYETT, JOSEPH H., *The Quality Journey: How Winning the Baldrige Sparked the Remaking of IBM* (New York: NAL-Dutton, 1993).

BRATTON, JOHN, *Japanization at Work: Managerial Studies for the 1990s* (London: Macmillan, 1992).

BRAVERMAN, HARRY, *Labor and Monopoly Capital: The Degradation of Work in the Twentieth Century* (New York: Monthly Review Press, 1974).

BRODY, DAVID, *Workers in Industrial America: Essay on the Twentieth Century Struggle* (New York: Oxford University Press, 1993).

BROWN, JONATHAN, and ROSE, MARY B. (eds.), *Entrepreneurship, Networks and Modern Business* (Manchester: Manchester University Press, 1993).

BROWN, WILLIAM H., *Management, the Japanese Way* (Tokyo: Sophia University, 1965).

BUCKLEY, PETER J., and CLEGG, JEREMY (eds.), *Multinational Enterprises in Less Developed Countries* (London: St. Martin, 1991).

Bibliography

BUSSE VON COLBE, WALTHER, CHMIELEWICZ, KLAUS, GAUGLER, EDUARD, and LASSMANN, GERT (eds.), *Betriebswirtschaftslehre in Japan und Deutschland* (Stuttgart, 1988).

CALORI, ROLAND, and WOOT, PHILIPPE DE (eds.), *A European Model of Management: Unity in Diversity* (New York: Prentice Hall, 1994).

CAPRA, FRITJOF, *The Turning Point: Science, Society, and the Rising Culture* (New York: Simon & Schuster, 1982).

CAREW, ANTHONY, *Labour under the Marshall Plan: The Politics of Productivity and the Marketing of Management Science* (Manchester: Manchester University Press, 1987).

CHANDLER, ALFRED D., JR., *Scale and Scope: The Dynamics of Industrial Capitalism* (Cambridge, Mass.: The Belknap Press, 1990).

——*Strategy and Structure* (Boston: MIT Press, 1962).

——*The Visible Hand: The Managerial Revolution in American Business* (Cambridge, Mass.: Harvard University Press, 1977).

CHANNON, DEREK, *The Strategy and Structure of British Enterprise* (London: Macmillan, 1973).

CHILD, JOHN, *British Management Thought* (London: Allen & Unwin, 1969).

CHURCHILL, WINSTON S., *The Second World War*, v (London: HM, 1952).

CLARK, RODNEY, *The Japanese Company* (New Haven: Yale University Press, 1979).

COATES, DAVID, *The Question of UK Decline: The Economy, State and Society* (London: Harvester Wheatsheaf, 1994).

COHENDET, PATRICK, HOLLARD, MICHEL, MALSCH, THOMAS, and VELTZ, PIERRE (eds.), *L'Après-Taylorisme* (Paris: Economica, 1988).

COLE, ROBERT E., *Strategies for Learning: Small-Group Activities in American, Japanese, and Swedish Industry* (Berkeley: University of California Press, 1989).

CRAVER, CHARLES B., *Can Unions Survive? The Rejuvenation of the American Labor Movement* (New York: New York University Press, 1993).

CUMMINGS, WILLIAM K., *Education and Equality in Japan* (Princeton: Princeton University Press, 1980).

DAIUTE, ROBERT J., *Scientific Management and Human Relations: Ideas, Topics, Readings* (New York: Holt, Rinehart and Winston, 1964).

DEMING, W. EDWARDS, *Out of the Crisis* (Boston: MIT, CAES, 1986).

——*Quality, Productivity, and Competitive Position* (Boston: MIT, CAES, 1982).

DICKERMAN, ALLEN, *Training Japanese Managers* (London: Praeger, 1974).

DICHTL, ERWIN (ed.), *Standort Bundesrepublik Deutschland* (Frankfurt am Main: *Frankfurter Allgemeine Zeitung* Verlag, 1993).

DORE, RONALD, *British Factory-Japanese Factory: The Origins of National Diversity in Industrial Relations* (Berkeley: University of California Press, 1973).

———and SAKO, MARI, *How the Japanese Learn to Work* (London: Routledge, 1989).

DUKE, BENJAMIN C., *Education and Leadership for the Twenty-First Century: Japan, America, and Britain* (Westport, Conn.: Praeger, 1991).

DUNLOP, JOHN T., *et al.*, *Industrialism and Industrial Man Reconsidered: Some Perspectives on a Study over Two Decades of the Problems of Labor and Management in Economic Growth*, Final report of the Inter-University Study of Labor Problems in Economic Development (Princeton: Princeton University Press, 1975).

DUNNING, JOHN, *Japanese Participation in British Industry* (London: Croon Helm, 1986).

DYAS, GARETH P., and THANHEISER, HEINZ T., *The Emerging European Enterprise: Strategy and Structure in French and German Industry* (Boulder, Colo.: Westview, 1976).

DYER, DAVID, SALTER, MALCOLM S., and WEBBER, ALAN M., *Changing Alliances* (Boston: Harvard Business School Press, 1987).

EBERWEIN, WILHELM and THOLEN, JOCHEN, *Euro-Manager or Splendid Isolation?: International Management—an Anglo-German Comparison* (Berlin: Walter de Gruyter, 1993).

ELBAUM, BERNARD, and LAZONICK, WILLIAM (eds.), *The Decline of the British Economy* (Oxford: Blackwell, 1986).

ELGER, TONY, and SMITH, CHRIS (eds.), *Global Japanization? The Transnational Transformation of the Labour Process* (London: Routledge, 1994).

ELIASSON, GUNNAR, FÖLSTER, STEFAN, LINDBERG, THOMAS, POUSETTE, TOMAS, and TAYMAZ, EROL (eds.), *The Knowledge-Based Information Economy* (Stockholm: Almquist & Wiksell International, 1990).

EMMOTT, BILL, *Japanophobia: The Myth of the Invincible Japanese* (New York: Random House, 1994).

———*The Sun also Sets: Why Japan will not be Number One* (London: Simon & Schuster, 1989).

ENGWALL, LARS, *Mercury Meets Minerva: Business Studies and Higher Education, the Swedish Case* (Oxford: Pergamon, 1992).

———and GUNNARSSON, ELVING (eds.), *Management Studies in an Academic Context* (Uppsala: Motala Grafiska, 1994).

ENTEMAN, WILLARD F., *Managerialism: The Emergence of a New Ideology* (Madison: University of Wisconsin Press, 1993).

ETNER, FRANÇOIS, *Les Ingénieurs-Economistes français (1841–1950)*. Doctoral thesis 'sciences économiques', option: économie appliquée, Doctorat d'Etat, U.E.R. Sciences des Organisations, Université de Paris (Paris IX-Dauphine), 1978.

FORD, HENRY, and CROWTHER, SAMUEL, *Today and Tomorrow* (New York: Doubleday, Page 1926).

FREEDMAN, RICHARD, and MEDOFF, JAMES L., *What Do Unions Do?* (New York: Basic Books, 1984).

FRIEDMANN, GEORGES, *Problèmes humains du machinisme industriel* (Paris: NRF, 1946).

FRUIN, MARK W., *The Japanese Enterprise System: Competitive Strategies and Cooperative Structures* (New York: Oxford University Press, 1992).

——*Kikkoman: Company, Clan, and Community* (Cambridge, Mass.: Harvard University Press, 1983).

FUCINI, JOSEPH J., and FUCINI, SUZY, *Working for the Japanese: Inside Mazda's American Auto Plant* (New York: Free Press, MacMillan, 1990).

FUKUDA, K. JOHN, *Japanese-Style Management Transferred: The Experience of East Asia* (London: Routledge, 1988).

GABOR, ANDREA, *The Man Who Discovered Quality: How W. Edwards Deming Brought the Quality Revolution to America* (New York: Random House, 1990).

GÉLINIER, OCTAVE, *The Enterprise Ethic* (London, 1968), translation of *Morale de l'entreprise et destin de la nation* (Paris: Plon, 1965).

GELLERT, CLAUDIUS, *Vergleich des Studiums an englischen und deutschen Universitäten* (Munich: Thomas-Verlag, 1983).

GIBNEY, FRANK, *Miracle by Design: The Real Reasons Behind Japan's Economic Success* (New York: Times Books, 1982).

GILBRETH, FRANK B., *Motion Study* (New York: Van Norstrand, 1911).

GLOUCHEVITCH, PHILIP, *Juggernaut: The German Way of Business, Why It is Transforming Europe* (New York: Simon & Schuster, 1992).

GOLDEN, MIRIAM, and PONTUSSON, JONAS (eds.), *Bargaining for Change: Union Politics in North America and Europe* (Ithaca, NY: Cornell University Press, 1992).

GOLDFIELD, MICHAEL, *The Decline of Organized Labor in the United States* (Chicago: University of Chicago Press, 1987).

GORDON, ANDREW, *The Evolution of Labor Relations in Japan: Heavy Industry, 1853–1955* (Cambridge, Mass.: Harvard University Press, 1985).

——(ed.), *Postwar Japan as History* (Berkeley: University of California Press, 1993).

GORDON, DONALD D., *Japanese Management in America and Britain: Revelation or Requiem for Western Industrial Democracy?* (Aldershot: Ashgate, 1988).

GOULD, WILLIAM B., *Japan's Reshaping of American Labor Law* (Cambridge, Mass.: MIT Press, 1984).

GRAVES, STEPHEN, *Corporate Flexibility in Japan* (Business series, Bulletin, No. 126; Tokyo: Sophia University, 1989).

HADLEY, ELEANOR M., *Antitrust in Japan* (Princeton: Princeton University Press, 1970).

HAGAN, JACK, *Management of Quality: Strategies to Improve the Bottom Line* (Milwaukee: Irwin, 1994).

HALBERSTAM, DAVID, *The Reckoning* (New York: Morrow, 1986).

HALL, EDWARD T., *The Hidden Dimension* (New York: Doubleday, 1990).

HALL, ROBERT W., *Essentials of Excellence* (Wheeling, Ill.: AME, 1989) (a series of articles by Robert W. Hall, reprinted from *Target*).

——*The Soul of the Enterprise: Creating a Dynamic Vision for American Manufacturing* (New York: Harper Collins, 1993).

HANNAH, LESLIE, *Delusions of Durable Dominance Or The Invisible Hand Strikes Back: A Critique of the New Orthodoxy in Internationally Comparative Business History—1980s*, unpublished book manuscript.

HARBISON, FREDERICK, and MYERS, CHARLES A., *Management in the Industrial World: An International Analysis. A Joint Project of the Industrial Relations Section, Princeton University and The Industrial Relations Section, Massachusetts Institute of Technology* (New York: McGraw-Hill, 1959).

HARRIS, HOWELL JOHN, *The Right to Manage: Industrial Relations Policies of American Business in the 1940s* (Madison: University of Wisconsin Press, 1982).

HART, CHRISTOPHER W. L., and BOGAN, CHRISTOPHER E., *The Baldrige: What it is, How it's Won, How to Use it to Improve Quality in your Company* (New York: McGraw-Hill, 1992).

HART, JEFFREY A., *Rival Capitalists: International Competitiveness in the United States, Japan, and Western Europe* (Ithaca, NY: Cornell University Press, 1992).

HARTMANN, HEINZ, *Amerikanische Firmen in Deutschland: Beobachtungen über Kontakte und Kontraste zwischen Industriegesellschaften* (Cologne and Opladen: Westdeutscher Verlag, 1963).

——*Authority and Organization in German Management* (Princeton: Princeton University Press, 1959).

HASEGAWA, KEITARO, *Japanese-Style Management: An Insider's Analysis of Corporate Success* (Tokyo: Kodansha International, 1986).

HASSARD, JOHN, and PARKER, MARTIN (eds.), *Postmodernism and Organizations* (London: Sage, 1993).

Bibliography

HATAKEYAMA, YOSHIO, *Manager Revolution: A Guide to Survival in Today's Changing Workplace* (Stamford, Conn.: Productivity Press, 1985).

HAYASHI, SHUJI, *Culture and Management in Japan* (Tokyo: University of Tokyo Press, 1988).

HENDRY, JOY, *Understanding Japanese Society* (New York, 1987; 2nd edn., London, 1995).

HENZLER, HERBERT A., and SPÄTH, LOTHAR, *Sind die Deutschen noch zu retten? Von der Krise in den Aufbruch* (Munich: Bertelsmann, 1993).

HIRSCHMEIER, JOHANNES, and YUI, TSUNEHIKO, *The Development of Japanese Business* (London: Allan & Unwin, 1981).

HOFFMANN, STANLEY, and MAIER, CHARLES, *The Marshall Plan: A Retrospective* (Boulder, Colo.: Westview, 1984).

HOFSTEDE, GERT, and KASSEN, M. SAMI (eds.), *European Contributions to Organization Theory* (Amsterdam: Van Gorcum, 1976).

HOGAN, MICHAEL J., *The Marshall Plan: America, Britain, and the Reconstruction of Western Europe, 1947–1952* (Cambridge: Cambridge University Press, 1987).

HOLLAND, MAX, *When the Machine Stopped: A Cautionary Tale from Industrial America* (Boston: Harvard Business School Press, 1989).

HUNTER, JANET F., *The Emergence of Modern Japan* (London: Longman Group, 1989).

HYMAN, RICHARD, and STREECK, WOLFGANG (eds.), *New Technology and Industrial Relations* (Oxford: Blackwell, 1988).

IRIBARNE, PHILIPPE D', *La Logique de l'honneur: Gestion des entreprises et traditions nationales* (Paris: Editions du Seuil, 1989).

ISHIKAWA, KAORU, *What is Total Quality Control? The Japanese Way*, trans. David J. Lu (Englewood Cliffs, NJ: Prentice-Hall, 1985).

IWATA, RYUSHI, *Japanese-Style Management: Its Foundations and Prospects* (Tokyo: Asian Production Organization, 1982).

JACKALL, ROBERT, *Moral Mazes: The World of Corporate Managers* (Oxford: Oxford University Press, 1988).

JANSEN, MARIUS (ed.), *Changing Japanese Attitudes toward Modernization* (Princeton: Princeton University Press, 1969).

JOHNSON, CHALMERS, *MITI and the Japanese Miracle: The Growth of Industrial Policy, 1925–1975* (Stanford, Calif.: Stanford University Press, 1982).

JOHNSON, H. THOMAS, *Relevance Regained: From Top-Down Control to Bottom-Up Empowerment* (New York: Free Press, 1992).

——and Kaplan, Robert S., *Relevance Lost: The Rise and Fall of Management Accounting* (Boston: Harvard Business School Press, 1987).

328

JONES, DEREK C., and SVEJNAR, JAN (eds.), *Participatory and Self-Managed Firms* (Toronto: Lexington Books, 1982).

JONES, STEPHANIE, *Working for the Japanese: Myths and Realities—British Perceptions* (London: Macmillan, 1991).

JOYNT, PAT, and WARNER, MALCOLM (eds.), *Managing in Different Cultures* (Oslo: Universitetsforlaget, 1985).

KAPLAN, ROBERT S., 'Quality in Business School Education and Research', presentation to the Annual Meeting of the American Assembly of Collegiate Schools of Business, St. Louis, MO, 22 Apr. 1991.

KATZ, DANIEL, and KAHN, ROBERT L., *The Social Psychology of Organizations* (New York: Wiley, 1978).

——————and ADAMS, J. STACY (eds.), *The Study of Organizations* (San Francisco: Jossey-Bass, 1980).

KATZENSTEIN, PETER J. (ed.), *Industry and Politics in West Germany: Toward the Third Republic* (Ithaca, NY: Cornell University Press, 1989).

KAUFMAN, GEORGE G. (ed.), *Reforming Financial Institutions and Markets in the United States: Towards Rebuilding a Safe and more Efficient System* (Boston: Kluwer, 1993).

KAWABE, NOBUO and DAITO, EISUKE (eds.), *Education and Training in the Development of Modern Corporations* (Tokyo: University of Tokyo Press, 1993).

KENNEY, MARTIN, and FLORIDA, RICHARD, *Beyond Mass Production: The Japanese System and its Transfer to the U.S.* (New York: Oxford University Press, 1993).

KERR, CLARK, DUNLOP, JOHN T., HARBISON, FREDERICK, and MYERS, CHARLES A., *Industrialism and Industrial Man: The Problems of Labor and Management in Economic Growth* (Cambridge, Mass.: Harvard University Press, 1960).

KLEINDORFER, PAUL R., *The Management of Productivity and Technology in Manufacturing* (New York: Plenum, 1985).

KOCHAN, THOMAS A., KATZ, HARRY C., and McKERSIE, ROBERT B., *The Transformation of American Industrial Relations* (New York: Basic Books, 1986).

KOEHNE, ROBERT J., *Co-determination in Business: Workers' Representatives in the Boardroom* (New York: Praeger Publishers, 1980).

KOGUT, BRUCE (ed.), *Country Competitiveness: Technology and the Organizing of Work* (New York: Oxford University Press, 1993).

KOMAI, HIROSHI, *Japanese Management Overseas: Experiences in the United States and Thailand* (Tokyo: Asian Productivity Organization, 1989).

KOVACIC, BRANISLAV (ed.), *New Approaches to Organizational Communication* (Albany, NY: State University of New York, 1994).

329

Bibliography

KRAUS, ELLIS S., ROHLEN, THOMAS P., and STEINHOFF, PATRICIA G., (eds.), *Conflict in Japan* (Honolulu: University of Hawaii Press, 1984).

KRIEGER, LEONARD, *The German Idea of Freedom: A History of a Political Tradition* (Boston: Beacon, 1957).

KUISEL, RICHARD F., *Capitalism and the State in Modern France: Renovation and Economic Management in the Twentieth Century* (Cambridge: Cambridge University Press, 1981).

KURTZMAN, JOEL, *The Decline and Crash of the American Economy* (New York: Norton, 1988).

LANE, C., *Management and Labour in Europe: The Industrial Enterprise in Germany, Britain and France* (London: Edward Elgar, 1989).

LAWLER, EDWARD E., *High-Involvement Management: Participative Strategies for Improving Organization Performance* (San Francisco: Jossey-Bass, 1986).

LAWRENCE, PETER, *Managers and Management in West Germany* (London: Croom Helm, 1980).

LAZONICK, WILLIAM, *Business Organization and the Myth of the Market Economy* (Cambridge: Cambridge University Press, 1991).

LECLERCQ, JEAN-MICHEL, *Le Japon et son système éducatif* (Paris: La Documentation française, 1984).

LEE, GLORIA L., and SMITH, CHRIS (eds.), *Engineers and Management: International Comparisons* (London: Routledge, 1992).

LEE, KENNETH BOK, 'The Postwar Reforms and Educational Development in Japan, 1945–1970', Ph.D. thesis (University of Southern California, 1974).

LEE, SANG M., and Schwendiman, Gary (eds.), *Japanese Management: Cultural and Environmental Considerations* (New York: Praeger, 1982).

LEESTMA, ROBERT, and WALBERG, HERBERT J., *Japanese Educational Productivity* (Ann Arbor: University of Michigan Press, 1992).

LEVERING, ROBERT, and MOSKOWITZ, MILTON, *The 100 Best Companies to Work for in America* (New York: Doubleday, 1993).

LEVINE, SOLOMON B., *Industrial Relations in Postwar Japan* (Urbana, Ill.: University of Illinois Press, 1958).

LICHTENSTEIN, NELSON, *Labor's War at Home: The CIO in World War II* (Cambridge: Cambridge University Press, 1982).

————and HARRIS, HOWELL JOHN (eds.), *Industrial Democracy in America: The Ambiguous Promise* (New York: Cambridge University Press, 1993).

LILLRANK, PAUL, *Sociological Aspects of Japanese QC Circles*, Discussion Paper, Tokyo, Social Research Institute of Japan, 1984.

————and KANO, NORIAKI, *Continuous Improvement—Quality Control Circles in Japanese Industry* (Ann Arbor: Center for Japanese Studies, 1989).

LIMP, WOLFGANG, *Europäische Management-Institute: Programm und Arbeitsweise der Führungsnachwuchs-Schulung*, RKW (Frankfurt am Main, 1974).

LOCKE, ROBERT R., *The End of the Practical Man: Entrepreneurship and Higher Education in Germany, France, and Great Britain, 1880–1940* (Greenwich, Conn.: JAI, 1984).

————*French Legitimists and the Politics of Moral Order in the Early Third Republic* (Princeton: Princeton University Press, 1974).

————*Management and Higher Education since 1940: The Influence of America and Japan on West Germany, Great Britain and France* (Cambridge: Cambridge University Press, 1989).

LODGE, GEORGE C., *American Disease* (New York: New York University Press, 1986).

LUOSTARINEN, REIJO, and PULKKINEN, TUIJA, *International Business Education in European Universities in 1990* (Helsinki: European International Business Association, 1990).

LUTTWAK, EDWARD N., *The Endangered American Dream: How to Stop the United States from Becoming a Third World Country and How to Win the Geo-Economic Struggle for Industrial Supremacy* (New York: Simon & Schuster, 1993).

McCORMACK, GAVAN, and SUGIMOTO, YOSHIO (eds.), *Democracy in Contemporary Japan* (New York: M. E. Sharpe, Inc., 1986).

McCRAW, THOMAS K. (ed.), *America versus Japan* (Boston: Harvard Business School Press, 1986).

McGUIRE, KENNETH J., *Impressions from our most Worthy Competitor: An Examination of Japanese Approaches to Managing Manufacturing Resources* (Falls Church, Va.: American, 1984).

McKinsey Global Institute, *Manufacturing Productivity* (Washington, DC, Oct. 1993).

————*Service Sector Productivity* (Washington, DC, Oct. 1991).

MAHONEY, FRANCIS X., and THOR, CARL G., *The TQM trilogy: Using ISO 9000, the Deming Prize, and the Baldrige Award to Establish a System for Total Quality Management* (New York: AMACOM, 1994).

MAIER, CHARLES S. (ed.), *The Marshall Plan and Germany: West German Development within the Framework of the European Recovery Program* (New York: Berg, 1991).

————*In Search of Stability: Explorations in Historical Political Economy* (Cambridge, Mass.: Harvard University Press, 1987)

MANT, ALISTAIR, *The Rise and Fall of the British Manager* (London: Macmillan, 1977).

Bibliography

MARSHALL, RAY, *Unheard Voices: Labor and Economic Policy in a Competitive World* (New York: Basic Books, 1987).

MARUYAMA, MASAO, *Thought and Behaviour in Modern Japanese Politics*, ed. Ivan Morris (Oxford: Oxford University Press, 1963).

MÄTTHOFER, HANS, *Humanisierung der Arbeit und Produktivität in der Industriegesellschaft* (3rd edn., Cologne: Bund-Verlag, 1980).

MAURICE, MARC, SELLIER, FRANÇOIS, and SILVESTRE, JEAN-JACQUES, *The Social Foundations of Industrial Power: A Comparison of France and Germany* (Cambridge, Mass.: Harvard University Press, 1986).

MAYER, HERBERT C., *German Recovery and the Marshall Plan, 1948–1952* (Bonn: Edition Atlantic Forum, 1969).

MAYOR, ELTON, *Human Relations in Industrial Society* (Cambridge, Mass.: Harvard University Press, 1933).

The MBA Career Guide (Fall 1994).

MEE, CHARLES L., JR., *The Marshall Plan: The Launching of the Pax Americana* (New York: Simon & Schuster, 1984).

MÉNISSEZ, YVETTE, *L'Enseignement de la gestion en France* (Paris: La Documentation française, 1979).

MILWARD, ALAN S., *The Reconstruction of Western Europe, 1945–1951* (Berkeley: University of California Press, 1984).

MIWA, KEIKO, 'Analysis of the Effect of Major American Ideas upon the Organization of Japanese Higher Education, from 1946 to 1967', Ph.D. thesis (Washington State University, 1969).

MONDEN, YASUHIRO, and SAKURAI, MICHIHARA, *Japanese Management Accounting: A World Class Approach to Profit Management* (Tokyo: Productivity Press, 1989).

MORIKAWA, HIDEMASA, *Zaibatsu: The Rise and Fall of Family Enterprise Groups in Japan* (Tokyo: University of Tokyo Press, 1992).

MORRIS-SUZUKI, TESSA, *A History of Japanese Economic Thought* (New York: Routledge, 1989).

MOUER, ROSS E., and SUGIMOTO, YOSHIO, *Images of Japanese Society: A Study in the Structure of Social Reality* (London: KPI, 1986).

MÜLLER, GLORIA, *Mitbestimmung in der Nachkriegszeit: Britische Besatzungsmacht—Unternehmer—Gewerkschaften* (Düsseldorf: Patrios-Schwann Verlag, 1987).

MURATA, SUZUKO, 'A Study of the Impact of the American Educational System on Higher Education in Japan', Ph.D. thesis (Indiana University, 1969).

MUSGRAVE, PETER W., *Service Sector Productivity* (Washington, DC: McKinsey, 1991).

NAJITA, TETSUO, *Visions of Virtue in Tokugawa Japan* (Chicago: University of Chicago Press, 1987).

NAKANE, CHIE, *Human Relations in Japan* (Tokyo: Ministry of Foreign Affairs, 1972).

——*Japanese Society* (Berkeley: University of California Press, 1972).

NAPHTALI, FRITZ, *Wirtschaftsdemokratie—Ihr Wesen, Weg und Ziel* (Berlin: Verlagsgesellschaft des ADG, 1928).

NEGANDHI, ANANT R., and BALIGA, B. R., *Tables are Turning: German and Japanese Multinational Companies in the United States* (Cambridge, Mass.: Oelgeschlager, Gunn and Hain, 1981).

NELSON, J. R. (ed.), *Marginal Cost Pricing in Practice* (Englewood Cliffs, NJ: Prentice Hall, 1964).

NELSON, RICHARD R. (ed.), *National Innovation Systems: A Comparative Analysis* (New York: Oxford University Press, 1993).

NIND, PHILIP, *A Firm Foundation: The Story of the Foundation for Management Education* (London: Foundation for Management Education, 1985).

NOLAN, MARY, *Visions of Modernity: American Business and the Modernization of Germany* (Oxford: Oxford University Press, 1994).

NONAKA, IKUJIRO, and TAKEUCHI, HIROTAKE, *The Knowledge-Creating Company: How Japanese Companies Create the Dynamics of Innovation* (New York: Oxford University Press, 1995).

NORRIS, CHRISTOFER, *What's Wrong with Postmodernism: Critical Theory and the Ends of Philosophy* (London: Harvester Wheatsheaf, 1990).

The Occupation of Japan: Educational and Social Reform (Proceedings of a Symposium Sponsored by the MacArthur Memorial, Old Dominion University, 16–28 Oct. 1980).

OECD, *New Directions in Work Organisation: The Industrial Relations Response* (Paris: OECD, 1992).

OHNO, TAIICHI, *Toyota Production System: Beyond Large-Scale Production* (Tokyo, 1978; trans. and reprinted by Productivity Press, 1988).

OLIVER, NICK, and WILKINSON, BARRY, *The Japanization of British Industry: New Developments in the 1990s* (Oxford: Blackwell, 1992).

OUCHI, WILLIAM G., *Theory Z* (Reading, Mass.: Addison-Wesley, 1981).

OZAKI, ROBERT, *Human Capitalism: The Japanese Enterprise System as World Model* (New York: Penguin Books, 1991).

PASCALE, RICHARD TANNER, and ATHOS, ANTHONY G., *The Art of Japanese Management: Applications for American Executives* (New York: Simon & Schuster, 1981).

PEGELS, C. CARL, *Japan vs. the West: Implications for Management* (Boston: Kluwer-Nijhoff, 1984).

Bibliography

PETERS, THOMAS J., and WATERMAN, ROBERT H., JR., *In Search of Excellence: Applications for American Executives* (Cambridge, Mass.: Harvard University Press, 1981).

PETRE, F. LORAINE, *Napoleon's Conquest of Prussia—1806* (London: John Lane, The Bodley Head, 1907).

PIORE, MICHAEL, and SABEL, CHARLES, *The Second Industrial Divide* (New York: Basic Books, 1984).

PRASHKER, IVAN (ed.), *Duty, Honor, Vietnam: Twelve Men of West Point* (New York: Arbor House, 1988).

Project Management Team, *Research and Development Programme: Work and Technology*, The Federal Ministry for Research and Technology (Bonn: BMFT, 1990).

QUINN, JAMES B., *Intelligent Enterprise: A Knowledge and Service Based Paradigm for Industry* (New York: Free Press, MacMillan, 1992).

REICH, ROBERT B., *The Next American Frontier* (New York: Times Books, 1983).

——*The Work of Nations: Preparing Ourselves for 21st-Century Capitalism* (New York: Knopf, 1992).

REICH, SIMON, *The Fruits of Fascism: Postwar Prosperity in Historical Perspective* (Ithaca, NY: Cornell University Press, 1990).

The Research Team for Japanese Systems, Masuda Foundation, *Japanese Systems: An Alternative Civilization?* (Yokohoma: Sekotac, 1992).

RICH, P. J., *Elixir of Empire: The English Public Schools, Ritualism, Freemasonry, and Imperialism* (London, 1989).

ROHLEN, THOMAS P., *For Harmony and Strength: Japanese White-Collar Organization in Anthropological Perspective* (Berkeley: University of California Press, 1974).

——*Japan's High Schools* (Berkeley: University of California Press, 1983).

ROSE, MARY, and BROWN, JONATHAN (eds.), *Entrepreneurship, Networks and Modern Business* (Manchester: Manchester University Press, 1993).

ROSENBERGER, NANCY R. (ed.), *Japanese Sense of Self* (Cambridge: Cambridge University Press, 1992).

ROSTOW, WALT W., *The Stages of Economic Growth* (Cambridge: Cambridge University Press, 1968).

SATO, KAZUO, and HOSHINO, YASUO (eds.), *The Anatomy of Japanese Business* (Armonk, NY: Sharpe, 1984).

SCHMIDT, EBERHARD, *Die verhinderte Neuordnung, 1945–1952* (Frankfurt am Main: Europäische Verlagsanstalt, 1970).

SCHONBERGER, RICHARD J., *Japanese Manufacturing Techniques: Nine Hidden Lessons in Simplicity* (New York: Free Press, 1982).

SCHOPPA, LEONARD J., *Education Reform in Japan: A Case of Immobilist Politics* (London: Routledge, 1991).

SCHUCHMAN, ABRAHAM, *Co-determination: Labor's Middle Way in Germany* (New York: Public Affairs Press, 1957).

SENGE, PETER M., *The Fifth Discipline: The Art and Practice of the Learning Organization* (New York: Doubleday, 1990).

SHANNON, THOMAS R., *An Introduction to the World-System Perspective* (Boulder, Colo.: Westview, 1989).

SHIMIZU, RYUEI, *The Japanese Business Success Factors* (Tokyo: Chikura Shobo, 1989).

SHIRAI, TAISHIRO (ed.), *Contemporary Industrial Relations in Japan* (Madison: University of Wisconsin Press, 1983).

SINGLETON, JOHN C., *Nichu, A Japanese School* (New York: Holt, Rinehart & Winston, 1967).

SLIM, FIELD MARSHAL SIR WILLIAM, *Defeat into Victory* (London: Cassell, 1956).

Smith, Bruce L. R., *The Rand Corporation* (Cambridge, Mass.: Harvard University Press, 1966).

SMITH, HUSTON, *The Religions of Man* (New York: Harper & Row, 1986).

SMITH, ROBERT J., *Japanese Society: Tradition, Self, and the Social Order* (Cambridge: Cambridge University Press, 1983).

SOESASTRO, HADI, and PANGESTU, MARI (eds.), *Technological Challenge in the Asia-Pacific Economy* (Sydney: Allen & Unwin, 1990).

STAEHLE, WOLFGANG H., and CONRAD, PETER (eds.), *Managementforschung 2* (Berlin: Gabler, 1992)

STEWART, ROSEMARY, BARSOUX, JEAN-LOUIS, KIESER, ALFRED, GANTER, HANS-DIETER, and WALGENBACH, PETER (eds.), *Managing in Britain* (London: St Martin's, 1994).

STREECK, WOLFGANG, *Industrial Relations in West Germany: A Case Study of the Car Industry* (New York: St. Martin's, 1984).

TANK, ANDREW (ed.), *German Perspectives on Total Quality* (New York: Conference Board, 1993).

TAYLOR, CHARLES R., and HENISZ, WITOLD J., *U.S. Manufacturers in the Global Marketplace* (New York: Conference Board, 1994).

TAYLOR, FREDERICK W., *The Principles and Methods of Scientific Management* (New York: Harper, 1911).

THUM, HORST, *Mitbestimmung in der Montanindustrie: Der Mythos vom Sieg der Gewerkschaften* (Stuttgart: Deutsche Verlag-Anstalt, 1982).

THUROW, LESTER, *Dangerous Currents: The State of Economics* (New York: Random House, 1983).

Bibliography

THUROW, LESTER, *Head to Head: The Coming Economic Battle Among Japan, Europe, and America* (New York: Warner Books, 1993).

——(ed.), *The Management Challenge: Japanese Views* (Cambridge, Mass.: MIT Press, 1985).

TOBIN, JOSEPH J., WU, DAVID Y. H., and DAVIDSON, DANA H., *Preschool in Three Cultures: Japan, China, and the United States* (New Haven: Yale University Press, 1989).

TOKUNAGA, SHIGEYOSHI, and BERGMANN, JOACHIM (eds.), *Industrial Relations in Transition: The Cases of Japan and the Federal Republic of Germany* (Tokyo: University of Tokyo Press, 1984).

TOLLIDAY, STEVEN, and ZEITLIN, JONATHAN (eds.), *The Automobile Industry and its Workers: Between Fordism and Flexibility* (Oxford: Blackwell, 1986).

TREVOR, MALCOLM, *Japanese Industrial Knowledge: Can It Help British Industry?* (London: Gower, 1985).

TSUCHIMOCHI, GARY H., *Education Reform in Postwar Japan: The 1946 U.S. Education Mission* (Tokyo: University of Tokyo Press, 1991).

TYSON, SHAUN, *et al.* (eds.), *Human Resource Management in Europe* (London: Kogan Page, 1993).

TURNBULL, PETER, and CUNNINGHAM, MALCOLM, *International Marketing and Purchasing: A Survey among Marketing and Purchasing Executives in Five European Countries* (London, 1981).

TURCQ, DOMINIQUE, *L'Inévitable Partenaire japonais* (Paris: Fayard, 1992).

TURNER, LOWELL, *Democracy at Work: Changing World Markets and the Future of Labor Unions* (Ithaca, NY: Cornell University Press, 1991).

UEDA, SHUNZO, *Japanese Management in the United States: Flexibility in a Foreign Environment* (Cambridge, Mass.: Program on U.S.–Japan Relations, Harvard Univesity, 1989).

ULMAN, LLOYD, EICHENGREEN, BARRY, and DICKENS, WILLIAM T. (eds.), *Labor and an Integrated Europe* (Washington, DC: The Brookings Institute, 1993).

United States War Department, Military Intelligence Division (eds.), *German Training Methods* (Washington, DC, 1946).

VAGTS, ALFRED, *A History of Militarism: Romance and Realities of a Profession* (New York: Norton, 1937).

VERNON, RAYMOND, *Storm over the Multinationals: The Real Issues* (Cambridge, Mass.: Harvard University Press, 1977).

VOGEL, EZRA F., *Japan as Number One: Lessons for America* (Cambridge, Mass.: Harvard University Press, 1979).

WALLERSTEIN, IMMANUEL, *Historical Capitalism* (London: Verso, 1983).

WALLICH, HENRY CHRISTOPHER, *Mainsprings of the German Revival* (New Haven: Yale University Press, 1955).

WALTON, MARY, *The Deming Management Method* (New York: Dodd, Mead, 1986).

WARD, ROBERT E., and SAKAMOTO, YOSHIKAZU (eds.), *Democratizing Japan: The Allied Occupation* (Honolulu: University of Hawaii Press, 1987).

WEHLER, HANS-ULRICH, *The Second German Empire, 1871–1918* (Leamington Spa: Berg, 1985).

WESTNEY, D. ELEANOR, *Imitation and Innovation: The Transfer of Western Organizational Patterns to Meiji Japan* (Cambridge, Mass.: Harvard University Press, 1987).

WILDEMANN, HORST, *Arbeitszeitmanagement: Einführung und Bewertung flexibler Arbeits- und Betriebszeiten* (Munich: Gesellschaft für Management und Technologie 1992).

———*Das Just-In-Time-Konzept: Produktion und Zulieferung auf Abruf* (3rd edn., Munich: Gesellschaft für Management und Technologie-Verlags KG, 1987).

———*Optimierung von Entwicklungszeiten: Just-In-Time in Forschung und Entwicklung und Konstruktion* (Munich: Transfer-Centrum-Verlag GmbH, 1993).

———*Produktionssynchrone Beschaffung* (Munich: Gesellschaft für Management und Technologie-Verlags KG, 1988).

———*Strategische Investitionsplanung* (Wiesbaden: Gabler, 1987).

———*Unternehmensqualität: Einführung einer kontinuierlichen Qualitätsverbesserung* (Munich: Transfer-Centrum, 1993).

———(ed.), *Fabrikplanung: Neue Wege—aufgezeigt von Experten aus Wissenschaft und Praxis* (Frankfurt am Main: Frankfurter Allgemeine Zeitung, 1989).

———*Qualität und Produktivität: Erfolgsfaktoren im Wettbewerb* (Frankfurt am Main: Frankfurter Allgemeine Zeitung, 1994).

WHITE, MERRY I., *The Japanese Educational Challenge: A Commitment to Children* (New York: Free Press, 1987).

WHITE, MICHAEL, and TREVOR, MALCOLM, *Under Japanese Management: The Experience of British Workers* (London, 1983).

WHITEHILL, ARTHUR M., *Japanese Management: Tradition and Transition* (London: Routledge, 1991).

———and SCHIN-ICHI TAKEZAWA, *Workways: Japan and America* (Tokyo: The Japan Institute of Labor, 1981).

WHITLEY, RICHARD, THOMAS, ALAN, and MARCEAU, JANE, *Masters of Business? Business Schools and Business Graduates in Britain and France* (London: Tavistock, 1981).

WILSON, DICK, *The Sun at Noon* (London: Hamilton, 1986).

Bibliography

WILSON, DONALD, 'The German Soldier: Social Origins of Prowess', Thesis, Master of Arts in History (University of Hawaii at Manoa, 1989).

WOMACK, JAMES P., JONES, DANIEL T., and ROOS, DANIEL, *The Machine that Changed the World* (New York: Rawson Associates, 1990).

WORONOFF, JON, *The Japanese Management Mystique: The Reality Behind the Myth* (Chicago: Probus, 1992).

———*Japan's Wasted Workers* (Tokyo: Lotus, 1981).

WUPPERTALER KREIS (eds.), *Management—Weiterbildung in Deutschland, Ein Handbuch des Wuppertaler Kreises* (2nd edn., Cologne: Hanstein, 1978).

YAMADA, KENJIRO, 'The Japanese Management Style and Higher Education Administration: Concept and Application', Ph.D. thesis (George Peabody College for Teachers, 1979).

YAMAMURA, KOZO (ed.), *Japanese Investment in the United States: Should we be Concerned?* (Seattle: Society for Japanese Studies, 1989).

YAMASHINE, HAJIME, 'Time and Innovation: The View from Japan', Stockton Lecture, London Business School, 1991.

YOSHIDA, MAMORU, *Japanese Direct Manufacturing Investment in the United States* (New York: Praeger, 1987).

YOSHINO, MICHAEL Y., *Japan's Managerial System: Tradition and Innovation* (Cambridge, Mass.: MIT Press, 1968).

YUI, TSUNEHIKO, and NAKAGAWA, KEIICHIRO (eds.), *Japanese Management in Historical Perspective* (Tokyo: University of Tokyo Press, 1989).

INDEX

339

Index

Index

Index

Index

Index

Index